PROSPECTS FOR
POST-HOLOCAUST THEOLOGY

American Academy of Religion Academy Series

edited by
Susan Thistlethwaite

Number 77
PROSPECTS FOR
POST-HOLOCAUST THEOLOGY

by
Stephen R. Haynes

Stephen R. Haynes

PROSPECTS FOR POST-HOLOCAUST THEOLOGY

Scholars Press
Atlanta, Georgia

PROSPECTS FOR
POST-HOLOCAUST THEOLOGY

by
Stephen R. Haynes

© 1991
The American Academy of Religion

Library of Congress Cataloging in Publication Data

Haynes, Stephen.
    Prospects for post-Holocaust theology : "Israel" in the theologies
of Karl Barth, Jürgen Moltmann, and Paul van Buren / Stephen Haynes.
    p.   cm. — (American Academy of Religion academy series ; no.
77)
    Includes bibliographical references.
    ISBN 1-55540-651-3 (alk. paper). —ISBN 1-55540-652-1 (pbk.)
    1. Holocaust (Christian theology) 2. Israel (Christian theology)
3. Theology—20th century. 4. Theology—21st century. 5. Barth,
Karl, 1886-1968. 6. Moltmann, Jürgen. 7. Van Buren, Matthews.
1924- . I. Title. II. Series.
BT93.H39 1991
231.7'6—dc20   91-33004
                                                  CIP

Printed in the United States of America
on acid-free paper

Acknowledgements

I wish to acknowledge the help of all those who made this work possible, especially: Jürgen Moltmann, Paul van Buren, Markus Barth, Bishop David Jenkins, C. E. B. Cranfield, David Jasper, Otto Betz, Robert Hayward, Kerry Robb, Ray Witbeck, and others who discussed this project with me in a variety of settings; the various persons at the University of Durham, England who helped with translation work; The Rotary Foundation, The English Speaking Union of Atlanta and Columbia Theological Seminary, all of which graciously provided funding for a year of travel, research and writing; my doctoral committee at Emory University, and especially its chair Robert Detweiler, from whom I received a great deal in the way of instruction and support; Judith Runyon, James and Nancy Vest, and others at Rhodes College who assisted me with the challenges presented by word processing; and my wife, Natalie, whose patience and love were essential to the completion of this project.

The initial impetus for this dissertation can be traced to a graduate seminar in which I participated at Emory University in the Spring Semester of 1987. It was led by Prof. Jack Boozer, in the semester before his retirement. I feel extremely fortunate to have met and learned from Jack before his untimely death shortly thereafter. This book is dedicated to his memory and in appreciation of his legacy of caring and critical Christian thought, especially as it related to the complex relations between Christians and Jews.

TABLE OF CONTENTS

Part I   Backgrounds

Part II   Israel in Barth, Moltmann and van Buren

Part III   Prospects For Post-Holocaust Theology?

Part I Backgrounds

CHAPTER ONE

INTRODUCTION TO THE STUDY

I. BACKGROUND: THE HOLOCAUST
AND HOLOCAUST THEOLOGY

The events which have come to be referred to as the "Holocaust" have exercised an almost unparalleled influence on the subsequent study of politics, history, literature, philosophy and theology. Although Hitler's "Final Solution" was carried out in virtual secrecy between 1941 and 1945, forty-five years after the end of the war it is difficult to escape the voices of his victims as they are mediated by a host of authors, historians and religious leaders. One reason the Holocaust still commands an arresting voice is the significant hiatus between these unspeakable events and attempts to speak publicly about them.

Reasons for this gap between event and interpretation are manifold. Partly, it is a reaction to the limited amount of sympathetic attention given the "Jewish question" before the 1940s.[1] Also to blame is the fact that accurate information concerning the conception and execution of the Nazi Holocaust was pieced together slowly, and well after it occurred. Even among Germans, it is doubtful that those outside the Nazi leadership and certain segments of the armed forces knew of the "Endlösung" until the Allied liberation. Thus, German church statements from as late as 1943 could speak of the "testimony of the church against the persecution of the Jews," without any indication of awareness that this "persecution" was qualitatively different from that which had occurred in the 1930s.[2]

Psychological interpretations of the "gap" are advanced by A. Roy and Alice Eckardt and by Emil Fackenheim. In addition to the "denial syndrome" which naturally accompanies events of profound evil and/or destruction, these thinkers point to the social and personal factors which they believe have led to the hiatus between the events of the Holocaust and contemporary attempts at understanding. The Eckardts speak of a certain "distancing" from the Nazi era permitted by the passing of a full generation after Auschwitz. This distancing, says the Eckardts, is an important prerequisite for "creative reflection" among scholars, and has led to an important period of grappling with the subject on the part of both Christians and Jews.[3] The Jewish philosopher Emil Fackenheim has suggested other reasons for the delay of scholars in coming to terms with the uniqueness of the Holocaust. First, says Fackenheim, it is difficult to believe that a unique event has occurred in one's own lifetime; second, thought encountering such an event tends to classify it according to established categories (e.g., "radical-evil-in-general"); and third, Fackenheim observes, the question whether a "unique" event can be thought at all is an open one.[4]

Of course the "gap" between the events of the Holocaust and their interpretation has never been an empty space. As early as 1947, Protestant and Catholic churchmen gathered with a group of Jewish leaders to compose a document that came to be called "The Ten Points of Seelisberg."[5] This document is a collection of guidelines for the Christian church, whose responsibility for the perpetuation of anti-Semitism was already becoming clear. Among the "ten points" are admonitions to "avoid distorting or misrepresenting biblical or post-biblical Judaism with the object of extolling Christianity," and to "avoid using the word 'Jew' in the exclusive sense of the enemies of Jesus to designate the whole Jewish people." The fact that such admonitions still occupy a place at the center of the contemporary debate on Christian-Jewish relations[6] is testimony to the incisive nature of this document, and the stubborn persistence of anti-Judaism in Christianity.

Although there were a few early scholarly attempts to understand the Holocaust in its relation to the history of Christian-Jewish relations, their influence was not particularly great when they appeared.[7] In fact, between the end of World War II and the convening of the Second Vatican Council, there are only a few, mostly forgotten, examples of attempts to come to terms with the theological meaning of the Nazi Holocaust.[8] It is possible, then, to begin a survey of theological reactions to the Holocaust which try to redefine the relationship between church and Israel with the "Nostra aetate" declaration, released as a post-conciliar Vatican II document in 1965. "The Declaration on the Relationship of the Church to Non-Christian Religions" represented a conscious change in the way the Roman Catholic Church had traditionally viewed Jews and Judaism. Although it appeared twenty years after the liberation of the Nazi death camps, this document found its impetus in the tragedy of the Holocaust, the church's teaching about and attitudes toward Jews throughout its history, and the Vatican's relationship with the German Reich.[9] One Catholic commentator has distinguished the "Catholic style" in such matters as gradual, but permanent.[10] Indeed, it is difficult to overestimate the lasting influence which "Nostra aetate" has had on Catholic doctrine, liturgy, official policy, religious instruction, and theology.[11]

But "Nostra aetate" has been a beginning and not an endpoint for Christian reflection on the Holocaust and Christianity's attitude toward Jews.Since the late 1960s, many Catholic and Protestant theologians have displayed a deep concern with the Holocaust and its implications which exceeds the precedent set by "Nostra aetate." The movement which is often described as Christian "Holocaust theology" developed during this period, and became a major theological force in the 1970s. Its primary concern was not the amelioration of Jewish-Christian relations through revision of traditional theological doctrines, but criticism of the history and content of Christian theology itself in light of the Holocaust.

A trendsetting work in this theological genre was the American Jewish scholar Richard Rubenstein's *After Auschwitz: Radical Theology and Contemporary Judaism*.[12] Other Jewish scholars such as Eliezer Berkovits,[13] Michael Wyschogrod,[14] Irving Greenberg,[15] and Emil Fackenheim[16] contributed to early Holocaust theology, as did Christian thinkers like A. Roy and Alice Eckardt,[17] Franklin Littell,[18] Rosemary R. Ruether,[19] and Gregory Baum.[20] A focal point for the burgeoning Holocaust theology movement was the "International Symposium on the Holocaust" held in New York City in 1974. The theme of the multidisciplinary symposium was "Auschwitz: Beginning of a New Era?," and it brought together Jews and Christians from a variety of disciplines to share, among other things, insights into new ways of doing theology.[21] Although the term "Holocaust theology" is and was a controversial and tendentious one, we shall adopt it to refer to the movement represented by the works and authors mentioned above, as well as to their shared approaches and conclusions. In the context of this study, we are interested in describing the characteristics of Christian Holocaust theology. These are:

First, Holocaust theology views the Holocaust as a unique or "singular"[22] event, one which represents a turning point, rupture,[23] interruption,[24] crisis,[25] or caesura[26] for theology. This understanding of the Holocaust as *sui generis,* as an event that precipitates a radical hermeneutical shift[27] in history and theology, is often based on testimony (of survivors and historians) which emphasizes the unprecedented cruelty of the Final Solution, and the inadequacy of traditional theodicy to make account of it. Thus the testimony to these events provides "radical counter testimony"[28] to Christian (and Jewish) faith.

Second, Holocaust theology engages in a critical analysis of the Christian tradition vis-a'-vis the Jewish people by focusing on the treatment of Jews by the Christian church (and "Christian" societies),[29] critical exegesis of New Testament texts which have an anti-Judaic effective history and are suspected of being inherently anti-Semitic,[30] and a critique of anti-Jewish tendencies in Christian theology.[31] Typically inherent in such critical analysis of Christian history, literature and theology is a concern to document the relationship between Christian anti-Semitism and the pre-Christian (pagan) and post-Christian (modern) varieties.

Third, Holocaust theology seeks to determine the extent to which Christian theology can be extricated from this historically concomitant anti-Semitism.[32] Christology has come under careful analysis in this context, with anti-Judaism being described, according to Rosemary Ruether's well-known formula, as "the left-hand of Christology."[33]

Fourth, Holocaust theology declares the necessity of terminating the Christian mission to the Jews, traditionally conceived.[34] This necessity is argued for on the basis of the indefensibility of a proselytizing mission in view of Christian complicity in the Holocaust, and the perceived necessity of insuring a tenuous Jewish existence in the post-Holocaust world.

Fifth, Holocaust theology seeks to move Christianity toward a more immanental understanding of the relation between God and history. This is in response to what is viewed as Christian theology's perennial tendency toward triumphalism and spiritualization.[35] In this connection, Holocaust theology argues that the revelatory significance of the Holocaust, and the events of contemporary history in general, be taken more seriously as criteria for theology.[36]

Finally, Holocaust theology attempts to identify the theological and social conditions necessary for a new Jewish-Christian solidarity,[37] occasionally offering constructive suggestions for a Christian or Jewish theology which might enable such a solidarity.

Overall, Holocaust theology has been critical rather than constructive. It has asked difficult questions and arrived at disturbing answers. Rarely, however, has it provided more than a glimpse of how a Christian theology based on these questions and answers might look. In fact, the term "Holocaust *theology*" is something of a misnomer, since some of the thinkers associated with this movement effectively deny that theology in the traditional sense is possible at all "after Auschwitz." In one sense, then, Holocaust theology has as much in common with other types of Holocaust literature as with traditional theology.[38] Like Holocaust memoirs and fiction, it has sought to plumb the depths of evil, history, the divine, and the human psyche in order to apprehend the meaning of the events which haunt those who live in the post-Holocaust world.

It appears that the last decade has witnessed a shift away from the radical and critical mood of early Holocaust theology. In Christian circles, this shift can be seen in growing efforts at making practical changes in the church's doctrine and teaching,[39] as well as in concerns to construct a systematic Christian theologies of Judaism.[40] These developments suggest that despite the fact that Holocaust theology has made its mark on some in the church, the searing indictments of the Holocaust theologians, the majority of Christian churchpeople and theologians do not perceive theology or history to be "ruptured" to the extent that traditional beliefs and forms of expression must be discarded.

But if the Holocaust is not perceived by most Christians as a total rupture for the church and its theology, neither is it seen as a "non-event."[41] The revision of Christian doctrine and praxis currently underway may be gradulalist in orientation, but it has been informed by the arguments of Holocaust theology, and has taken seriously the notion that persistent anti-Semitism is a "Christian problem" which demands the church's house be put in order. As we shall see in the later chapters of this study, a new generation of Christian theologians has begun to take up the challenge of incorporating into systematic theology the revolutionary implications of various doctrinal reformulations vis-a'-vis Judaism.[42] Although these attempts to reformulate systematic theology with Christian-Jewish relations in mind have not been met with overwhelming enthusiasm in the church,[43] they are nevertheless symbolic of a growing desire on the part of a diverse group of Christian thinkers to establish a new basis for Christian reflection--one which takes both the church's past and present into account.

I have chosen to refer to the Christian theologians who have begun to work toward a reformulation of systematic theology in light of the Holocaust as"post-Holocaust" theologians. The work of Jürgen Moltmann and Paul van Buren in particular represents an acknowledgement that the questions posed by Jews and by recent European history call for a reorientation which is at base theological, and which keeps in mind that its primary audience is the Christian church.

II. THE PROTESTANT REFORMED TRADITION

The three theologians under consideration in the following chapters are associated in varying degrees with what may be broadly called the Reformed theological tradition within Protestantism. Before continuing, we shall briefly discuss the characteristics of this tradition, its understanding of "Jews" and "Judaism," and some recent statements on Jewish-Christian relations originating from within this tradition.

The Reformed tradition has its roots in the theology of John Calvin and the Swiss Reformation. Although "Calvinism" assumed Scottish, Dutch, German, English, and American forms as it radiated outward from sixteenth-century Geneva, the connection with Calvin and his theology has remained crucial in the Reformed churches. Along with stressing the various *"solas"* common to the Reformation churches, Reformed theology since Calvin has emphasized the theological concepts of election and covenant, the authority of Scripture, and the continuing importance of (certain aspects of) "law."[44] We shall consider briefly some of these elements of the Reformed tradition as they impinge on our study.

The doctrine of divine election has been a hallmark of Reformed theology since the sixteenth century. Although Calvin tried to maintain a certain tension in his understanding of election, the doctrine emerged from the era of Reformed scholasticism as "double predestination." While Reformed dogmaticians affirmed individual election to salvation or reprobation into the twentieth century, Karl Barth placed the doctrine in a new theological context in his *Church Dogmatics*.[45] By shifting his focus from the election of individuals to the election of Christ, Barth was able to see Christ as representing both "electing God" and "elected man." While Barth's interpretation of election opened him to the charge of "universalism,"[46] it also enabled him to overcome the stumbling block of individual election/damnation by proceeding christocentrically, treating "the election of the individual" only in the context of "the election of Jesus Christ" and "the election of the community."[47]

The notion of covenant is another theological shibboleth of the Reformed tradition. It is prominent in the theology of Calvin, Zwingli and Bullinger,[48] and is a distinguishing theme in the Reformed confessional tradition.[49] Although undeniably an essential tenet of the Reformed faith, the notion of covenant is not sufficiently illuminated either in traditional or contemporary Reformed theology to avoid ambiguity about the number and nature of the covenant(s). This ambiguity can issue in theological confusion when the concept of covenant is employed to make sense of the church's relationship to "Israel."[50]

An emphasis on the authority of Scripture is another distinctive trait of the Reformed theological tradition. Again, this emphasis stems from Calvin,[51] and is given renewed, though nuanced, expression in the theology of Karl Barth.[52] Although Barth's "Neo-Orthodox" understanding of the authority of Scripture has been the target of criticism,[53] Barth's emphasis on the "Word of God" maintains the crucial place of the written and proclaimed "word" in the Reformed tradition.[54]

Recognition of these elements in the Reformed heritage allows an historically-sensitive analysis of the thought of contemporary theologians like Barth, Moltmann and van Buren who work within this tradition. It also serves to illuminate common ground on which Jews and Reformed Christians might meet. The idea of election is, of course, an enormously important one in the Jewish tradition, as is the idea of covenant.[55] The authority of Scripture is also a hallmark of Jewish faith and life, although differing views of what constitutes "Scripture," and the status of critical biblical interpretation represent important distinctions in the way this emphasis on Scripture's authority functions within the two religious communities. The Reformed emphasis on "law" suggests another possible bridge between Christian and Jewish theologies.[56] Indeed, Barth's understanding of the continuity between Christ and the law in his interpretation of Romans 10:4 serves as one contemporary example of such a bridge.[57]

On the other hand, despite the presence of these potential theological links between Reformed Christianity and Judaism, until very recently there have been few attempts to exploit them in the interest of Jewish-Christian relations. The Reformed tradition, in fact, fares little better than others when account is taken of historic Christian attitudes toward Jews.[58] Although Luther's diatribes against "the Jews and their lies" are particularly offensive to the modern conscience, there is little evidence that Calvin's attitude toward Jews and Judaism in his day was fundamentally different.[59] Despite the fact that German Lutheranism is often assumed to lie at the root of much Christian anti-Semitism, careful analysis suggests that personal and social factors may be as important as theological tradition in determining anti-Jewish attitudes,[60] and that anti-Semitism is found among even the most dignified and pious theologians.[61]

Are there obstacles, peculiar to the Reformed tradition, which along with general Christian anti-Judaism impede the quest for a positive post-Holocaust evaluation of Judaism? Perhaps one such obstacle is the theology preserved in the Westminster standards, which until recently were the primary confessions of the the Presbyterian Church in England and America.[62] Westminster "covenant theology," as it is sometimes called, emphasizes the Reformed concepts of covenant and "eternal decree" (election). But the early Reformed notion of continuity between the covenants (which developed from Calvin and Zwingli) is in Westminster theology qualified by the law/gospel dichotomy. Thus the Westminster standards speak of a "covenant of works" and a "covenant of grace."[63] While they do not teach that these covenants are perfectly synonymous with the "Old" and "New" testaments, a "works of the law" stigma is inevitably attached to Israelite religion, and by association, to contemporary Judaism. Here the implicit anti-Jewishness of the law/gospel dichotomy which is usually associated with Lutheranism appears in Reformed theology.[64]

Another problem with which contemporary Reformed theology must deal as it seeks to revise its understanding of "Israel" is its confessional approach to theology. This problem may be illuminated through a consideration of the Presbyterian Church (U.S.A.) and its *Book of Confessions*. The P.C.U.S.A., which is the largest Reformed body in the United States, has as part of its constitution creeds and confessions containing views of Jews and Judaism the denomination has recently disavowed.[65] This means that it is not only the church's past "silence"[66] on the significance of Israel with which new theological formulations must reckon, but confessional statements that reflect the supersessionist assumptions of another era. Since there is no historic Reformed creed or confession which alludes to, let alone explicitly affirms, the continuing election of post-biblical Judaism, post-Holocaust theologians must consider carefully their relationship to this confessional tradition.[67] This situation makes the task of theology both more important and more difficult, as theologians seek creatively to reinterpret a tradition which lives in the church's confessions.

The preceding observations bring to light some of the vicissitudes with which theology written in dialogue with the "church" must live. They also anticipate some areas of tension in the work of Barth, Moltmann, and van Buren.[68] Many contemporary theologians, of course, do not feel themselves constrained to work exclusively within a specific confessional tradition. Even Barth and Moltmann, the two thinkers in our study who are ecclesiastically as well as theologically Reformed, have been influenced in their understandings of "Israel" by currents from outside Reformed theology. Barth, for instance, seems to have been influenced by radical Catholic theologians like Erik Peterson who initiated a pre-Auschwitz reconsideration of "Israel" in Catholic theology,[69] and Moltmann cites the *Heilsgeschichte* Lutheran theologians of the nineteenth century as important sources for a renewed understanding of the significance of "Israel."[70]

Finally, it should be kept in mind that Reformed Christians have attempted several times in recent years to come to terms with their own sins vis-a'-vis the Jewish people, and clarify their church's relationship with "Israel" in a post-Auschwitz world. On the American scene, the Presbyterian Church (U.S.A.) and the United Church of Christ have recently made official statements which affirm for the first time the permanent election of "Israel," and refer to Jews as partners in mission.[71] In Europe, the Dutch Reformed Church has been conscious of its special relationship with "Israel" for some time,[72] and the Church of Scotland and World Alliance of Reformed Churches have also issued recent statements on the relationship of Christianity to Judaism.[73] The problem with which we are concerned, however, is the extent to which these concerns with a renewed understanding of "Israel" have been anticipated by and incorporated into systematic theology. A decade ago, Karl Barth, Hendrikus Berkhof, and Kornelius. H. Miskotte could be described as theological voices crying in the wilderness about the significance of "Israel" for Christian theology.[74] We will explore the work of one former and two newer prophets who sought or are seeking to reform systematic theology and the teaching of the church.

III. TERMINOLOGY AND MODELS

A. Terminology

A major terminological problem confronting our inquiry is resides in the terms "Jew," "Judaism," and, in particular, "Israel." Defining these terms requires historical, political and theological judgments which might be debated at great length. The fact that many use these terms without establishing clear definitions should make us intent to avoid confusion. It is interesting to note that while the terms "Jew" and "Judaism" have held generally negative connotations in Christian theology since the second century, "Israel" has found a more ambiguous function in Christian thought. One reason for this stems from Scripture itself. The formula "the Jews" is used in the New Testament to represent those who oppose Jesus, Paul, or the early church,[75] while

"Israel" is often adopted to refer to those Jews who believe in Jesus as Messiah. The term "Israel" was adopted by Christian theology at a very early stage to refer both to the community which had existed around the Old Testament patriarchs, as well as to the remnant of "Israel" represented by the church. The self-identification of the church as the "true Israel" or "Israel according to the Spirit," derived originally from the New Testament, seems to have been first developed in the theology of Justin Martyr.[76]

While not a New Testament term, "Judaism" has characteristically been used by Christians to refer to the religion of the Jews after the Exile, or in some cases, after the appearance of Jesus or the Fall of Jerusalem in 70 C.E. In fact, one point of continuity between ancient and modern Christian theology is that in the writings of both the Church Fathers and theologians of the twentieth century,[77] "Judaism" is usually afforded no continuing positive role in salvation history. Modern theologians no longer write "tractates" against the Jews like the ones common in the patristic and medieval eras. While assuming the appearance of objective research, however, modern theology and biblical criticism has tended to employ terms like "late Judaism" and "Jewish religious community" in the service of the same ancient *adversus Judaeos* tradition.[78] Much modern scholarship of the last two hundred years has identified the corruption of Jewish (or "Israelite") religion as beginning in the intertestamental period, with this corruption becoming especially evident in the practice of Judaism reflected in the New Testament. One student of Christian anti-Judaism has argued that the historical regression from "Israel" to "Judaism" described by modern scholars is simply a reshaping of ancient Christian anti-Judaism into a form that is academically respectable.[79]

This anti-Jewish tradition in Christian belief and scholarship has only recently begun to be overturned with the help of a renewed emphasis on the permanent election of the people "Israel" (according to another section of the New Testament--Romans 9-11), and an openness to viewing Judaism on its own terms.[80] As models based on the inclusion and "engrafting" of the church into Israel's covenant gradually supplant models of displacement as ways to understand the relationship between the church and Israel, Christian theology is beginning to allow terms that have been part and parcel of the rhetoric of rejection to be redefined. More and more, scholars now argue that the term "Israel" cannot remain an abstract theological concept, but must include Jews and Judaism as they exist today.[81]

Although the question "what constitutes Jewishness?" is generally not belabored by serious Christian theology,[82] the relationship between "Israel" as people and "Israel" as state has received a great deal of attention. While some attempts to deal with this relationship have been convinced by political and religious voices sympathetic to the Palestinian people to defer on the theological status of the Israeli state,[83] others have placed the political dimension of "Israel" in the foreground.[84] Most Christian theologians concerned with Jewish-Christian relations agree that whether or not the state of Israel is afforded theological significance, use of the term "Israel" must not be divorced from the present reality of the Jewish people--that is, it must include an affirmation of "the Jews" as the people "Israel," and Judaism as the form of life and worship given these people by God.

Some theologians argue that the move away from understanding "Israel" as denoting the spiritual identity of the church must lead inevitably to a Christian identity crisis.[85] Since dealing with this crisis is also the task of theology, theologians must consider models for articulating a new understanding of the relationship between church and Israel.

B. Models

Contemporary Christian thinkers concerned with Jewish-Christian relations have suggested various typologies for categorizing the church's understanding of its relationship to Israel. One of the more useful and comprehensive of these typologies was proposed by Bertold Klappert in *Israel und die Kirche* (1980).[86] Klappert claims that he has not constructed these models, but simply described those which are "typical," and which have become "established and historically effective in the history of the relationships between Israel and the church, church and Synagogue, in which the relationship of church and Synagogue has lived, and is still suffering" (11).

The first of Klappert's five "negative" models is the "substitution model," in which, very simply, the church is understood to have replaced Israel in salvation history. Klappert illustrates the persistence of this model with passages from influential Christian thinkers like Paul

Althaus and Adolf Stoecker. The model's theological principles are: 1. that Israel exists on the basis of its rejection of Jesus Christ on the cross; 2. that the history of the people Israel is only a history *post christum crucifixum,* not a history *post christum resuscitatum;* 3. that Israel's rejection of the "gospel" places it under "law," in the sphere of anger and retaliation; 4. that the church is the salvation-historical successor of Israel, insofar as "the church is grounded in Israel, but Israel flows *(müden)* into the church" (Althaus); and 5. that the future of Israel *post christum crucifixum* is conceivable only as the future of individual justified and baptized persons from "Israel" (that is, Jews) existing within the Gentile church. In other words, Israel as a people, according to this model of substitution, has no more future   (14-16). The substitution model Klappert describes has been powerfully effective in Christian history, and, as we shall see in the next chapter, even Barth's Israel-doctrine cannot be understood apart from it.

Next, Klappert describes the "integration model," which is based on the conviction that a remnant of Israel has been integrated into the church. This model is actually a variant of the substitution model, one which utilizes the remnant concept discussed by Paul in Romans 11:1-6. According to the model, "the church as the new people of God replaces Israel insofar as it integrates itself as the elect remnant of Israel" (17). Klappert emphasizes that, according to the integration model, the integration point of church and Israel is always in the church, with the result that Israel's future can be realized only *in* the church.

The "typology model" conceives of Israel as a type (also "first stage" or "fore-portrayal") of the church. "Israel, its history and institutions are, according to this model, types of the church whose final salvation is represented through the church" (18). Klappert stresses that the typology model is "open"--open to interpretation in terms of both substitution and integration. It is also present, he argues, in contemporary church statements, like Vatican II's "Nostra aetate," which describes the salvation of the church as mysteriously exemplified in the Exodus.

The "illustration model" portrays Israel as the exemplary negative-foil of the church. In terms of its historical effectiveness, this model is probably the most important in the history of Christian thought, and (after the substitution model) the one most implicated in Christian anti-Semitism. Klappert attempts to demonstrate that this model is derived from Christian exegesis of Paul's Epistle to the Romans. In this connection, Klappert draws particular attention to Ernst Käsemann, who, as a modern proponent of this model, views the special history of Israel as "an illustration and an example of the failure of human existence in general under the law" (20). Klappert's final negative model is the model of "subsumation." According to this model, Israel retains no special character after the appearance of Christ. This model eliminates the special character of Israel's election and its covenant with God, these being subsumed under the general category of "all mankind" (22). Implied in this model is the "destruction and reestablishment of the people of God" in the church.

Alongside these historic negative models, Klappert adds three which he describes as "positive"--the "complementarity," "representative," and "participation" models. These models stress the continuing election of Israel and the continued co-existence of Israel alongside the church. According to the complementarity model, Israel and the church are understood as "the two complementing, questioning *(Infragestellenden)* or competing, coexisting or pro-existing quantities of the one people of God" (11). This complementarity model, Klappert believes, can generate an atmosphere of mutual dialogue between Christians and Jews. The representation model perceives the church as "representative" for Israel, "insofar as the church steps into the place of the Messiah still not known to Israel, but at the same time keeping open a place for Israel" (12). This model, Klappert emphasizes, can complement and even include the complementarity model. The participation model has two variants, according to Klappert. The "christological-dependence" model understands the church as being "dependent...on the election of Israel confirmed in Jesus Christ and the promised fulfillment of this election with regard to all Israel" (12). The "christological-participation" model speaks of the permanent calling forth *(Hinzuberufung)*...of the peoples of the world into Israel's election history" (12). Both variants are derived from the prophetic image of an eschatological pilgrimage of the Gentile nations to Zion.

Another attempt to categorize the church's theological conceptions of its relationship with Israel is offered by Markus Barth.[87] Barth gives as the possible Christian interpretations of the "gap" between church and synagogue the following: 1. Israel's replacement by the church 2. partial continuity between church and Israel by means of a remnant concept 3. schism in the one people of God which has resulted in a "split people," and 4. complementary existence.[88] This last category, Barth observes, is actually developed in the modern Jewish theologies of Franz Rosenzweig, Leo Baeck, and Martin Buber, where a theory of "two houses" emerges. Barth believes this approach makes the best contemporary sense and should be adopted by Christian theology.[89]

Jürgen Moltmann has developed his own typology for identifying the traditional Christian judgments and prejudices he believes must be condemned if church and Israel are to enter into theological dialogue. These are: 1. the "viewpoint of religious indifference"[90] 2. the "viewpoint of necessary contrast," which is historically related to the Lutheran law/gospel scheme and its application to the Old Testament/New Testament and church/Israel relationships, and 3. the "viewpoint of inheritance," in which the history of Israel is viewed as the prehistory of Christianity, and Israel's place in salvation history is taken over by the church. With these negative views Moltmann contrasts not only his own version of complementarity, but also the relatively positive estimation of Israel's significance in the seventeenth-century "Reformed Federal theology" and nineteenth-century "Lutheran theology of salvation history." In these movements, Moltmann argues, the law/gospel scheme is replaced by a scheme of promise/fulfillment as the key to understanding the relationship between church and Israel.[91] In such Protestant traditions Moltmann locates possible points of continuity between traditional and contemporary understandings of Israel.

American theologian Paul van Buren has been critical of the "positive" models advanced by theologians like Klappert and Moltmann. In particular, he has questioned the promise/fulfillment scheme's appropriateness for contemporary theology, arguing that his own "promise/confirmation" model provides a better safeguard against Christian triumphalism and supersessionism.[92] Other helpful categories for describing the relationship between Israel and the church are the continuity/discontinuity and one covenant/two covenant schemes.

As Michael McGarry has shown in *Christology After Auschwitz*, contemporary models of continuity and discontinuity between Judaism and Christianity tend to be differentiated at the point of Christology.[93] Theologies of discontinuity generally stress the uniqueness and finality of Christ, Jesus as the absolute fulfillment of Jewish faith and Scripture,

Christianity as a successor to Judaism and the new chosen people, and the evangelism of all peoples, including Jews. Theologies of continuity emphasize the relativity of Christ, the proleptic nature of Jesus' messianic stature, Christ as a partial fulfillment of Jewish faith and Scripture, a favorable evaluation of the Jewish "No"to Jesus as a faithful response to their covenant, the continuing validity of Judaism alongside Christianity, and an obligation for Christians to "witness" to, but not convert Jews (98).

It is natural to assume that post-Holocaust theology should assert a "continuity" view of the church's relationship to Israel, replacing a more traditional model of "discontinuity." Historical analysis, however, suggests that the church's task is not so simple. Christian theology has often stressed continuity between "Israel" and the church (the theology of Karl Barth is a striking example), but this continuity was based on a model of integration or typology, and was thus supersessionist and/or triumphalist.[94] For this reason, post-Holocaust theology must consider carefully not only the relationship between (biblical) Israel and the church, but between the post-biblical communities of Judaism and Christianity which exist side by side and are embarked on parallel but separate paths to God's Kingdom.

A view which has dominated many contemporary discussions of the relationship between Israel and the church originated in the thought of the twentieth-century Jewish thinker Franz Rosenzweig. Rosenzweig conceived of the relationship between Judaism and Christianity as analogous to that between "fire" and "rays," both of which have their source in a common "star."[95] Rosenzweig does not minimize the differences between the two "biblical religions." In fact, he elaborates in some depth their distinctive features.[96] But these differences are ultimately overcome, he argues, when the common origin of Judaism and Christianity in the eternity of God is recognized in the light of their common destiny. Many contemporary theological models which understand the relationship of Israel and the church as one of God-willed perpetual tension and coexistence are responses to the overtures of Rosenzweig. Related to the continuity/discontinuity issue is the question whether Judaism and Christianity represent one or two divine covenants. On this issue as well Rosenzweig's work has been seminal. His notion of a "dual covenant," a model based on the conviction that Christianity grew out of Judaism and thus cannot subsume its foundation,[97] has been quite influential. This "dual covenant" model conceives of Christianity as a subsequent manifestation of God's presence to all humanity, originally revealed to the Jews in their covenant.[98]

The complexity of the covenant question is suggested by the fact that interpreters of Rosenzweig have used his "dual covenant" concept to support both one- and two-covenant models of their own. On the Jewish side, Philip Sigal has elaborated elements of "dual covenant theology" in developing a comprehensive theology of reconciliation between Christians and Jews.[99] Paul van Buren has also taken Rosenzweig's work very seriously, and has even been labelled a "Christian Rosenzweigian."[100] Michael McGarry has confirmed the influence of Rosenzweig in contemporary christological reflection by observing that theologies of continuity often utilize what he calls a Rosenzweig-inspired "two-covenant model" to express the continuing validity of Judaism. With the theological foundation laid by Rosenzweig and others, Christian theologians have begun to challenge the traditional understanding of the church-Israel relationship in which the "old" covenant is either superceded (two covenant model) or subsumed (one covenant model) by the "new." This challenge has intensified as scholars try to re-Judaize Christianity through an emphasis on the Jewishness of Jesus and the Christian Scriptures.[101]

Judging from the models outlined by Klappert, M. Barth, Moltmann, van Buren and others, a general consensus seems to be emerging in contemporary post-Holocaust theology which finds it necessary to express the relationship of church and Israel in terms of complementarity or partnership.[102] This overarching *partnership orientation*, which embraces the positive models developed by Klappert, Markus Barth, Moltmann and others, may be founded on a model of continuity between Christianity and Judaism, or one of balanced and respectful discontinuity. It may stress commonality in terms of common humanity, worship,[103] election, or hope. Whatever its emphases, such partnership thinking is based in a vision of God-willed coexistence and common mission to the world. Often implicit in this notion of partnership is the Christian realization that it must affirm an "unfulfilled messianism."[104] This is based on the realization that, although the Messiah has come, redemption is not complete, and will not be so until the arrival of God's kingdom. This awareness is brought to bear, in part, through the witness of the church's partner-in-waiting, Israel.

Of course, the notion of "witness" raises the question whether evangelism or dialogue is the appropriate attitude of the church toward Israel. At this point also, partnership thinking has been employed to overcome many difficulties. The notion of Jews and Christians undertaking missions of mutual witness has been widely influential in contemporary thought. This understanding has gained acceptance as the partnership orientation has made it possible to move beyond the opposition between traditional ideas of conversion through evangelism and the more recent emphasis on non-proselytizing dialogue.[105]

IV. JEWISH-CHRISTIAN RELATIONS
AND THE RETURN TO SCRIPTURE

As might be expected, the contemporary critical analysis of relations between church and Israel has meant a renewed focus on the New Testament; and, in fact, this focus distinguishes recent post-Holocaust reflection from earlier Holocaust theology. Originally, this focus meant demystification or downright rejection of those texts suspected of being "anti-Semitic" or "anti-Jewish." Increasingly, however, Christian scholars have defended the New Testament against such charges by focusing on first-century church/synagogue conflicts, and have even argued that the New Testament contains resources (such as Romans 9-11) for a reconstruction of positive relations between Jews and Christians. Astonishingly, New Testament documents which have traditionally been interpreted by the church as a last word of condemnation upon disobedient Israel are now seen as representing the starting point for reconciliation. This search for truth *ad fontes* is described by Markus Barth, who observes that the present crisis in Jewish-Christian relations has made it "necessary to go back once more to the biblical evidence...and to issue a plea for repentance and courageous action."[106]

While Holocaust theologians argued that renewed Christian-Jewish relations would never be realized as long as Christians dogmatically clung to their Scriptural traditions,[107] many biblical scholars now concern themselves with the the importance of the New Testament for a positive understanding of Israel. While many biblical texts have received attention in this regard,[108] many recent studies have been concerned with the correct interpretation of Romans 9-11.[109] These chapters, traditionally regarded as an addendum to or digression from the main argument of Romans, are now seen by many as the theological climax of the epistle. This new understanding of Romans, and the attempt to "recover the real Paul"[110] which it implies, has been motivated by the pioneering work of many scholars, especially Krister Stendahl and Karl Barth.

Stendahl's approach has been to establish a new center in Pauline interpretation by asking afresh what Romans is "about."[111] Stendahl argues that Romans actually concerns the relationship between Jews and Gentiles, not the (later "Western" and "introspective") question of personal salvation reflected in the doctrine of justification.[112] In fact, according to Stendahl, the theological concept of justification by faith has led in the history of interpretation to a "spiritualization" of Paul's message in which his own concerns in writing the letter are lost.[113] The thematic shift which Stendahl observes is complemented by a corresponding structural shift, in which chapters 9-11 are established as "the real center of gravity" in Romans.[114]

Stendahl's orientation to Paul's epistle is linked to an exegetical methodology rooted in the assumption that recovering original meanings is not only possible, but provides the key to grasping the significance of Romans for contemporary Christianity:

> It is precisely his (Paul's) language and original meanings which in these chapters we are attempting to recapture and revitalize. The problem I am addressing...is what did Paul actually mean? What did Paul actually think?[115]

Despite the fact that the historical methodology underlying Stendahl's approach to Romans has come under theoretical attack in the last two decades,[116] his advice to "seek first the original meanings" continues to motivate scholars seeking a solid New Testament foundation for Jewish-Christian reconciliation. These scholars follow Stendahl in moving confidently from a determination of what the text "meant," to affirmations about what it "means" today--with contemporary ecumenical relations firmly in mind. Specifically, what Romans 9-11 meant in its original context--Paul's affirmation of Israel in his struggle "among Jews and Gentiles"--becomes the basis for what it means in the post-Holocaust world--a theological affirmation of the continuing election of the Jewish people and the permanence of the Jewish covenant(s).

Along with Stendahl's work on Romans, the influence of Karl Barth has served as an impetus for the "recovery of the real Paul" in post-Holocaust biblical scholarship and theology. While Barth's treatment of Romans in *Der Römerbrief* (2nd ed., 1921) has been criticized for its "historical and philological weaknesses,"[117] his discussion of Romans 9-11 in *Church Dogmatics* II:2 stands as a lasting testimony to Barth's exegetical competence. Barth's theological/ exegetical comments on the church/Israel relationship in his section on the "election of the community" has exercised a profound influence on contemporary scholarship. In the words of one commentator, Barth rediscovered Romans 9-11 as a "catalyst" for modern theology.[118] One New Testament scholar who exhibits the influence of Barth's treatment of Romans 9-11 in the *Church Dogmatics* is C. E. B. Cranfield. Cranfield makes his dependence on Barth explicit in the second volume of his widely acclaimed commentary on Romans.[119] He refers to the "decisive amendment of doctrine" signified by Barth's "magnificent section on God's election of grace" in the *Church Dogmatics.*[120] Barth's "suggestive and penetrating exegesis of Romans 9-11," Cranfield continues, "illumines many of the difficulties" inherent in a Christian understanding of Israel.[121]

What is the significance for our study of the "recovery of the real Paul" which has been driven by the work of Barth, Stendahl, and others? Given the growing consensus that Paul argues unequivocally in Romans 9-11 for the permanent election of Israel, the growing tendency to place these chapters at the center of Pauline theology, and the increasing prominence of Romans 9-11 in church proclamations on Jewish-Christian relations, we might conclude that the theological task has been co-opted through a revolution in biblical scholarship. However, while a connection between the theological and biblical disciplines is crucial for any attempt to redefine the church's relationship with Israel,[122] theology cannot uncritically adopt the results of biblical scholarship, as if Paul (or our current interpretation of Paul) were final. Especially in the post-Holocaust era, theology must concern itself with maintaining its integrity as a secondary, but crucial form of reflection against a return to "biblicism," even when this biblicism seems to serve the interests of interreligious dialogue. On this point, Paul van Buren has spoken very saliently:

> I believe that Paul, especially when understood on his own terms as a Jew and a Pharisee, can nourish the church's efforts to turn toward the Jewish people in a spirit of reconciliation and cooperation...Paul, however, cannot be the last word...because God requires of his church its own living response to Paul.[123]

This "living response" of which van Buren speaks must be, at least in part, theological. It must take into account not only the words of Paul, but Christian history and theology in the interim between the first century and our own time, as well as the hermeneutical significance of contemporary events like the Holocaust. This living response must face the challenge of moving the entire church out of the "adversus Judaeos morass"[124] by means of education, dialogue, and theological revision. This living response is guided by the recognition that the real question facing the church is not whether it has a theology of Israel, but whether it can find one appropriate for the post-Holocaust world.[125]

V. FINAL CONSIDERATIONS

A. Method

As a conclusion to this introductory chapter we shall consider aspects of the particular approach that will direct our inquiries in the following chapters. First, we turn to four general observations on method.

1. This essay is hermeneutical. It assumes Holocaust theology's concern with the hermeneutical significance of the *Shoah* in contemporary Protestant thought, but will attempt to determine the broader hermeneutical function of "Israel" (as people, religion, and state). This will include Israel's metaphoric and symbolic functions in Christian theology, as well as its literal description. While our primary intent will not be to trace the metaphoric and hermeneutical function the Holocaust has assumed in recent theology, we will attend to the ways in which the Holocaust has altered and intensified the function of the symbol "Israel." Furthermore, while a critique of the way in which particular theologians understand Israel will be incorporated, no

comprehensive attempt will be made to point out "errors" or distortions vis-a-vis Jewish understandings of Israel.

2. This essay will engage in a history of ideas analysis, attempting to identify similarities and dissimilarities in Barth's understanding of Israel and those developed in the theologies of Jürgen Moltmann and Paul van Buren. Since both Moltmann and van Buren have affirmed Barth's influence on their thought, we shall try to discern the nature and extent of this influence with particular reference to Barth's doctrine of Israel.

3. This essay assumes a cultural-linguistic[126] orientation to the study of religion. This means its author is aware that his perceptions are inextricably tied to a particular religious community. Specifically, this essay is written from the perspective of a white, male Protestant whose tradition can be broadly described as American Neo-Orthodox Presbyterianism. Although he will attempt to adopt a stance that is self-critical and which transcends sectarian bounds, the author cannot hope to view the white male Protestant theologies he is evaluating as if he existed outside a cultural-linguistic community which they have helped to form. While a "Jewish" critique of these theologies will be brought to bear at various points, this critique will come only second-hand, mediated by the author's Protestant interpretation of what Jewish thinkers have said or might say in response to a particular theological formulation. Nevertheless, underlying this engagement with Jewish theology is the assumption that any Christian theology of Israel must also be a theology developed in conversation with Jewish thought, a theology which is done, as it were, "facing the Jews."[127] Attempts to stand above individual "cultural-linguistic" communities and to reflect on Christian-Jewish relations from a general "ecumenical" or "humanist" standpoint will be made far less often, and will necessarily be more tentative.

4. This essay will explore the question of the theological relationship between Israel and church with the aid of contemporary theological models like the ones examined earlier in this chapter. As was discussed above, Christian theologians have advanced a variety of typologies for understanding the church's relationship to Israel, past and present. We will utilize these typologies in trying to determine the kind of theology best suited to a full Christian apprehension of the reality of Israel. Despite this concern with theological models and

typologies, we shall keep in mind that theological models, no matter how well-conceived, do not guarantee good relations between Jews and Christians.[128] Potential for improvement of relations, furthermore, will be assumed to be one of the criteria by which any Christian theology of Israel is judged.

5. In studying Barth, Moltmann and van Buren, we shall try to ascertain what, if any, points of continuity exist between pre-Holocaust and post-Holocaust theology by comparing the discussion of Israel found in Barth with the post-Holocaust treatment of this topic in Moltmann and van Buren. While the degree of continuity present should help in assessing the claims of Holocaust theologians that theology "after Auschwitz" is separated from pre-Holocaust traditions by a yawning chasm, a thoroughgoing critique of Holocaust theology is not the purpose of this study.

B. Why Barth, Moltmann and van Buren?

A few words are in order concerning the choice of Barth, Moltmann and van Buren from among the many theologians in this century who have been concerned with the significance of Israel for Christian theology. First, the present moment is a kind of *kairos* for critically examining the theologies of Moltmann and van Buren, as both thinkers are moving toward retirement and prepare to pass their mantles to a new generation of theologians. Second, the intellectual connections between Barth, Moltmann, and van Buren are significant and interesting. The intellectual ties are evident in the facts that van Buren studied under Barth at Basel, and Moltmann was educated in a Barthian environment at Göttingen. At the same time, however, each of these thinkers inhabit different theological and social worlds, and represent distinct relationships to the Holocaust, as well as to Holocaust theology.

Barth was a Swiss, educated in Germany, who maintained a critical distance from German culture and politics. Although he is generally considered a "pre-Holocaust" theologian, Barth gained in the last two decades of his life a recognition of the plight of the Jews in history, viewed retrospectively through the German Church Struggle and the Holocaust. It is also helpful to remember that while Barth did not argue that theology had been ruptured by the Holocaust, Barth lived and theologized through an earlier cultural break which brought

Western culture and Christian faith into crisis--"the Great War" and its aftermath. The theologies of Moltmann and van Buren are both clearly "post-Holocaust."[129] Moltmann served in the German army during World War II, was a prisoner of war in Great Britian, and has been concerned theologically and politically with the reconstruction of Germany ever since returning there at war's end. Interestingly, however, Moltmann reveals less of an influence by Holocaust theology than Paul van Buren, who did not experience the war directly. Van Buren, an American theologian, trained in Basel, has been influenced by the American tradition of radical theology, and to a lesser extent by Holocaust theology.

Moltmann and van Buren, then, are post-Holocaust thinkers who have been influenced by the Holocaust and Holocaust theology, but have not been led by these influences to break entirely from pre-Holocaust theological traditions. Their decisions to remain Christian, and to remain theologians, implicit in their work, allow Moltmann and van Buren to address the problems of Christian anti-Judaism and Jewish-Christian alienation in the post-Holocaust environment without relinquishing the Scriptural and doctrinal resources of historic Christianity. Both Moltmann and van Buren, in other words, want to maintain Christian identity while pursuing relevance in a post-Holocaust world. Although van Buren's radical approach is more open than Moltmann's "messianic theology" to the charge that identity has been sacrificed in the interest of relevance, neither theologian believes that traditional affirmations must be jettisoned or theology thoroughly secularized.

The hermeneutical principle at work in the theologies of Moltmann and van Buren is a dual one, incorporating what Paul Ricoeur has called a "hermeneutics of suspicion" and a "hermeneutics of retrieval."[130] The hermeneutic of suspicion utilized by these post-Holocaust thinkers is informed by Holocaust theology and its claims, while their hermeneutics of retrieval seek to determine what aspects of the tradition may be salvaged as prospects for post-Holocaust theology. The main result of this dual hermeneutical activity in Moltmann and van Buren is an emphasis on elements of continuity between pre-Holocaust theology and their own work. An immediately apparent point of continuity is that Barth, Moltmann and van Buren each view their own task as systematic theology. At least at this point our study will illuminate an implicit thread of continuity stretching across the "rupture" between the pre- and post-Holocaust eras.

Interestingly, we shall find that while there are strains of Christian theology which each perceive as useful for post-Holocaust theological reflection, both Moltmann and van Buren maintain a critical distance from Barth, and particularly from his theology of Israel. Neither, in fact, engages in a full-blown critique of Barth's Israel-doctrine, and neither is explicitly laudatory of Barth's theology of Israel, even when they adopt Barth's own positions. Our close analysis of the work of Barth, Moltmann and van Buren will illuminate the fact that there have been important advances made over the last two decades in the way Protestant Reformed theology understands and refers to Judaism, the Jewish people, and Israel. Although Barth's reflections on the meaning of Israel set the stage for many of these improvements, his Israel-doctrine continues to serve as a negative foil for many contemporary theological critics. While the "post-Barthians" Moltmann and van Buren develop their theologies of Israel in different directions, they have in common the fact that they find both personal and theological points of contact between the church and Israel which Barth did not recognize.

In the end, one is tempted to try to combine the "radical" approach of van Buren (with its emphasis on the dependence of the church on Israel, its engagement with Jewish thought and the secular world, and its complete rejection of triumphalism) and Moltmann's "messianic" approach (with its retrieval of a positive estimation of Israel in certain strands of Christian theology, its interpretation of Jewish and Christian messianism, and its success in speaking to large segments of the church). Ultimately, however, this proves very difficult, if not impossible. Moltmann and van Buren remain far apart theologically, even in their attempts to create a post-Holocaust theology of Israel in the Barthian tradition. While Moltmann is destined to have more influence on the way the church thinks of Israel, partly because of his work's popularity, van Buren's theology is more indebted to Jewish thought and contains more resources for Christian theological revision which is authentically post-Holocaust.

Finally, while the work of Barth, Moltmann and van Buren represents what the contemporary Protestant Reformed tradition has to offer the church's theological reflection on the meaning of "Israel," there is much work left to be done in determining which of these, if any, might serve as a the basis for the church's post-Holocaust theology. While helping illuminate the present status of post-Holocaust Christian theological reflection, the theologies of Barth, Moltmann and van Buren leave unanswered important questions confronting the church in its relationship to Judaism, the Jewish people and the state of Israel. But because their work represents theology on either side of the "rupture" marked by the Holocaust, comparing the theologies of Barth, Moltmann and van Buren will reveal a great deal about what will ultimately be able to survive it. We come to their work seeking guides for moving beyond Holocaust theology without forgetting its lessons; for filling the vast theological space between Jews and Christians after Auschwitz; and for mending the Christian tradition whose rupture Christian anti-Judaism and its expression in the Holocaust has helped reveal. We seek among them prospects for post-Holocaust theology.

Notes

1. A few exceptions are Jacques Maritain, *A Christian Looks at the Jewish Problem* (1939); James Parkes, *The Conflict Between the Church and the Synagogue* (1934); Erik Peterson, *Die Kirche aus Juden und Heiden* (1933); George Foot Moore, "Christian Writers on Judaism," *Harvard Theological Review* 14 (1921), 197-254; and Kornelius H. Miskotte, *Het Wezen der Joodsche Religie* (1932).

2. See, e.g., the relatively radical anti-Nazi stance outlined in "Extract From a Munich Church Address," in Richard Gutteridge, *Open Thy Mouth For the Dumb: The German Evangelical Church and the Jews 1879-1950* (Oxford: Basil Blackwell, 1976), 350-352.

3. A. Roy and Alice Eckardt, *Long Night's Journey Into Day: Life and Faith After the Holocaust* (Detroit: Wayne State University Press, 1982), 17.

4. Emil Fackenheim, *To Mend the World: Foundations of Future Jewish Thought* (New York: Schocken Books, 1982), 10.

5. Originally published by the International Council of Christians and Jews in 1947, and reprinted in Helga Croner, ed., *More Stepping Stones to Jewish-Christian Relations: An Unabridged Collection of Christian Documents 1975-1983* (New York: Paulist/Stimulus, 1985), 32-33.

6. For a contemporary example of the persistence of these issues, see "Zehn Punkte zur Selbstkontrolle Christlichen Redens mit und über Juden: Eine Einladung zum Umdenken," *Evangelische Theologie* 48:6 (1988), 565-69.

7. See, e.g., A. Roy Eckardt, *Christianity and the Children of Israel* (New York: King's Crown Press, 1948).

8. The most important exception to this generalization is the work of the French scholar Jules Isaac. See especially *Jesus and Israel,* trans. Sally Gran (New York: Holt, Rhinehart and Winston, 1971); and *The Teaching of Contempt: Christian Roots of Anti-Semitism,* trans. Helen Weaver (New York: Holt, Rhinehart and Winston, 1964). See also Raul Hilberg, *The Destruction of European Jewry* (Chicago: Quadrangle, 1961); and Edward H. Flannery, *The Anguish of the Jews: Twenty-three Centuries of Anti-Semitism* [New York: Paulist/Stimulus, 1985 (1965)].

9. See, e.g., the papal statements, "Concordat Between the Holy See and the German Reich" (July 20, 1933) and "Mit Brennender Sorge" (March 14, 1937).

10. Msgr. Jorge Meija, "The Catholic Style," in Croner, ed., *More Stepping Stones,* 5-15.

11. For the influence of "Nostra aetate" on Catholic theology, see Maureena Fritz, "Nostra aetate: A Turning Point in History," *Religious Education* 81 (Winter, 1986) 67-78. See also, Augustin Bea, *The Church and the Jewish People* (London, 1966); and Jacques Danielou, *Dialogue With Israel* (Baltimore, 1966).

12. Indianapolis: Bobbs-Merrill, 1966. With regard to the following discussion, see also, Lewis Feuer, "The Reasoning of Holocaust Theology," *Judaism* 35:2 (Spring, 1986), 198-210.

13. See *Faith After the Holocaust* (New York: Ktav, 1973).

14. See "Faith and the Holocaust," *Judaism* 20:3 (Summer, 1971), 268-94.

15. See "Cloud of smoke, Pillar of Fire: Judaism, Christianity and Modernity After the Holocaust," in Eva Fleischner, ed., *Auschwitz: Beginning of a New Era?: Reflections on the Holocaust* (New York: Ktav, 1977).

16. See *God's Presence in History: Jewish Affirmations and Philosophical Reflections* (New York: Harper and Row, 1972).

17. In addition to other works referred to in this study, see *Your People, My People* (New York: Quadrangle, 1974).

18. See *The Crucifixion of the Jews* (New York: Harper and Row, 1975).

19. See *Faith and Fratricide: The Theological Roots of Anti-Semitism* (Minneapolis: Seabury, 1974).

20. See *Theology After Auschwitz* (London: Council of Christians and Jews, 1976).

21. The proceedings of the symposium are published in Fleischner, ed., *Auschwitz.*

22. See the Eckardts, *Long Night's Journey,* especially ch. 3. See also, A. Roy Eckardt, "Jürgen Moltmann, the Jewish People and the Holocaust," where the author proclaims: "I believe that the historical fate of Christ, considered within the context of the *Endlösung* has destroyed the possibility of traditional Christian affirmations" (690).

23. See Fackenheim, *To Mend the World,* especially ch. 4.

24. See Elizabeth Schüssler Fiorenza and David Tracy, eds., *The Holocaust as Interruption, Concilium* vol. 175 (Edinburgh: T & T Clark, 1984).

25. See R. Rentdorff and E. Stegemann, eds., *Auschwitz--Krise der Christlichen Theologie* (München: Chr. Kaiser, 1980). See also *Long Night's Journey,* where the Eckardts divide history into two eras, "B.F.S." (before Final Solution) and "F.S." (Final Solution); and J. B. Metz ("Facing the Jews: Christian Theology After Auschwitz," in Fiorenza and Tracy, *Holocaust as Interruption,* 30) who stresses the Holocaust's "non transferability," "uniqueness," and "incomparability."

26. See Arthur A. Cohen, *The Tremendum: A Theological Interpretation of the Holocaust* (New York: Crossroad, 1981), ch. 2.

27. See Glenn D. Early, "The Radical Hermeneutical Shift in Post-Holocaust Christian Thought," *Journal of Ecumenical Studies* 18:1 (Winter, 1981), 16-32.

28. Greenberg, "Cloud of Smoke," 9.

29. To some extent, "Holocaust theologians" popularized and radicalized the insights of an earlier generation of scholars which included Parkes, Flannery, and Isaac.

30. The literature on this topic is voluminous. For an introduction to some of the issues, see Alan T. Davies, ed., *Anti-Semitism and the Foundations of Christianity* (New York: Paulist, 1979); Krister Stendahl, *Paul Among Jews and Gentiles and Other Essays* (Philadelphia: Fortress, 1976); J. A. Ziesler, "Some Recent Work on the Letter to the Romans," *Epworth Review* 12:2 (1985), 96-101; Clark M. Williamson, "The New Testament Reconsidered: Recent Post-Holocaust Scholarship," *Quarterly Review* 4:4 (1984), 37-51; and N. A. Beck, *Mature Christianity: The Recognition and Repudiation of the Anti-Jewish Polemic of the New Testament* (Cranbury, NJ: Susquehanna University Press, 1986). For a more in-depth study, see E. P. Sanders, *Paul and Palestinian Judaism* (London: SCM Press, 1977).

31. The most complete contemporary work on this theme is Charlotte Klein, *Anti-Judaism in Christian Theology,* trans. Edward Quinn (Philadelphia: Fortress,

1977). See also G. F. Moore, "Christian Writers on Judaism;" and Eva Fleischner, *Judaism in German Christian Theology Since 1945: Christianity and Israel in Terms of Mission,* ATLA Monograph Series, 8 (Metuchen, NJ: The Scarecrow Press and the American Theological Library Association, 1975); and Rosemary R. Ruether, "Anti-Semitism and Christian Theology," in Fleischner, ed., *Auschwitz,* 79-92.

32. See Ruether, *Faith and Fratricide,* and the foreword by Gregory Baum.

33. In Fleischner, ed., *Auschwitz,* 79.

34. See, e.g., the Eckardts' claim that the continuation of a Christian mission to the Jews constitutes a "spiritual Final Solution" (*Long Night's Journey,* 135).

35. See Gregory Baum, *The Social Imperative: Essays on the Critical Issues That Confront the Christian Churches* (New York: Paulist, 1979), where the author criticizes Alan T. Davies' attempt to distinguish between Christianity and Judaism by appeal to the "trans-historical" nature of the resurrection. See also Elizabeth Schüssler Fiorenza and David Tracy, "The Holocaust as Interruption and the Christian Return to History," in *Holocaust as Interruption,* 83-86, where the authors bemoan the "liberal retreat from concrete history."

36. Baum is concerned, for instance, with the significance of God's word addressing the church through the Holocaust (*The Social Imperative,* 57), while Alice Eckardt believes the Shoah should make us take note of "God's revelation in history" ("A Christian Problem: Review of Protestant Documents," in Croner, ed., *More Stepping Stones,* 18). Irving Greenberg speaks of the Holocaust as "orienting event and revelation" ("Cloud of Smoke," 20ff).

37. Clemens Thoma, *A Christian Theology of Judaism,* trans. and ed. Helga Croner (New York: Paulist/Stimulus, 1980), 153.

38. See, e.g., Lawrence L. Langer, *The Holocaust and the Literary Imagination* (New Haven: Yale University Press, 1975); and Elie Wiesel, "Art and Culture After the Holocaust," in Fleischner, ed., *Auschwitz,* 403-416.

39. In addition to Croner, ed., *More Stepping Stones,* see Croner, ed., *Stepping Stones to Further Jewish-Christian Relations: An Unabridged Collection of Christian Documents* (New York: Paulist/Stimulus, 1977); *A Theological Understanding of the Relationship Between Christians and Jews* (New York and Atlanta: General Assembly of the Presbyterian Church U.S.A., 1987); Markus Barth, *The People of God,* Journal for the Study of the New Testament Supplement Series, 5 (Sheffield: JSOT Press, 1983), 73 n1; and A. Roy Eckardt, "Recent Literature on Christian-Jewish Relations, *JAAR* 49:1 (1981), 99-111.

40. For a discussion of the relation between "Judaism" and "Israel" and its importance for theology, see below, section III.

41. Gerard S. Sloyan, "Some Theological Implications of the Holocaust," *Interpretation* 39:4 (1985), 402.

42. Cf. Allan R. Brockway, "Implications of Interfaith Dialogue for Christian Theology," *International Review of Mission* 74 (October, 1985), 522.

43. John T. Pawlikowski, "Theology to an Urgent Task," (review of Paul van Buren's *Discerning the Way) National Catholic Reporter* (October 17, 1980), 8.

44. See Jack Rogers, *Presbyterian Creeds: A Guide to the Book of Confessions* (Philadelphia: Westminster, 1985), where the author describes these as some of the "essential tenets" of the Reformed faith. See also Ellen Flesseman-van Leer, "Aspects of Historical Reformed Theology Which are Pertinent to the Relations Between the Reformed Churches and the Jewish People," in Alan P. F. Sell, *Reformed Theology and the Jewish People* (Geneva: World Alliance of Reformed Churches, 1986), 3-29. Flesseman-van Leer views the important theological elements in the Jewish-Reformed relationship as covenant, Old Testament, law, good works, and eschatology. She also notes Puritan theology as "one great exception" to the absence of explicit theological references to post-biblical Israel in the literature of Reformed theology.

45. Vol. II. Part 2, chapter 7, "The Election of God" (hereafter II:2).

46. See G.C. Berkouwer, *The Triumph of Grace in Karl Barth's Doctrine of Election* (Grand Rapids: Eerdmans, 1956).

47. Paragraphs 33, 34, and 35, respectively, in *Church Dogmatics* II: 2. For Calvin's discussion of election, see *Institutes of the Christian Religion,* 2 vols., Library of Christian Classics, vol. XX, ed., John T. McNeill, trans. Ford Lewis Battles (London: SCM, 1960), book III, chapter 21 (hereafter III: 21).

48. See Flesseman-van Leer, "Aspects...," 7-8, where she discusses the notion of covenant in Zwingli and Bullinger. For Calvin's view, see Institutes, *passim,* but especially II: 10 and 11 where Calvin outlines the similarities and differences between the "testaments" and the "covenants" they represent. In an important footnote (428, n1) the editor explains that Calvin did not anticipate the "covenant theology" of the seventeenth century (expressed, e.g., in the Westminster Standards and the theology of John Cocceius) which distinguished between a "covenant of works" and a "covenant of grace." Indeed, if the understanding of the covenant(s) in Zwingli, Bullinger, and to a lesser extent, Calvin had remained uncorrupted, then Rogers' statement that "for Reformed Christians, there is just one covenant in the Bible" (*Presbyterian Creeds,* 129) would be more accurate. See also, John Leith, *Assembly at Westminster: Reformed Theology in the Making* (Richmond: John Knox, 1973); and Holmes Rolston III, *John Calvin Vs. the Westminster Confession* (Richmond: John Knox, 1972).

49. In addition to *The Westminster Confession* (1647), especially chapter 7, see *The Second Helvetic Confession* (1566), where the concept of covenant is implicit,

and *The Scots Confession* (1560), in *The Book of Confessions,* Part 1 of *The Constitution of the Presbyterian Church (U.S.A.)* (New York: Office of the General Assembly, 1983). Flesseman-van Leer comments that "in view of the importance of the covenant concept it is surprising that the term itself occurs only marginally in the early confessions and catechisms [of the Reformed tradition] ("Aspects...," 8-9).

50. So Rogers, *Presbyterian Creeds,* 129. It is undeniable that the notion of covenant has served as an "essential tenet" of Reformed faith, despite Rogers attempt to see it given expression in *The Second Helvetic Confession,* where the term "covenant" does not appear. Isaac C. Rottenberg observes that it is "one of the great ironies of Christian history" that Reformed Christians who stress the notions of grace, election, and covenant have found it so difficult to see these ideas as extending to "Israel" ["Witness in Christian-Jewish Relations: Some Observations," *Reformed World* 35:2 (1978), 59]. Flesseman-van Leer concludes that "it [the Reformed concept of covenant] contains thoughts which could have led to a positive evaluation of the Jews, but which were actually worked out in a way that made the Jews invisible, as it were" ("Observations...," 10).

Hendrikus Berkhof is a contemporary Reformed thinker who summarizes "Israel's way" in the Old Testament as a "covenant history." But despite his intention of "letting the Old Testament speak for itself, without bringing in Christ," (249) Berkhof reads Christian categories into his study of "Israel" in a manner similar to traditional Reformed theology [*Christian Faith,* trans. Sierd Woudstra (Grand Rapids: Eerdmans, 1979). For another Reformed attempt to elaborate "the one covenant" in the context of the rediscovery of Israel, see K.H. Miskotte, *When the Gods are Silent* (London: Collins, 1967), 117-119]. This issue is complicated further by the fact that many Jews have rejected the assumptions of covenant theology. See Richard Rubenstein's foreword to Alan T. Davies' *Anti-Semitism and the Christian Mind* (New York: Herder and Herder, 1969).

51. See especially *Institutes,* I: 7.

52. See *Church Dogmatics,* I:1, 110-11, where Barth invokes Calvin (among others) to argue that his "Neo-Orthodox" understanding of the authority of the written Word is implicit in the Christian tradition.

53. See, e.g., Cornelius van Til, *The New Modernism: An Appraisal of the Theology of Barth and Brunner* (London: James Clarke, 1946); and Francis A. Schaefer, *The God Who Is There* (Downer's Grove: Inter-Varsity Press, 1969).

54. It has been observed that "Reformed" culture tends to be aural, rather than visual. This fact may be documented by comparing Reformed churches from the Reformation era with Catholic and Lutheran churches from the same period. Especially significant is the gradual replacement of the altar by the pulpit at the center of places of Reformed worship.

55. In recent Jewish theology, see David Hartman, *A Living Covenant: The Innovative Spirit in Traditional Judaism* (New York and London: Macmillan/Free Press, 1985); David Polish, "Covenant: Jewish Universalism and Particularism,"

Judaism 34 (Summer, 1985), 284-300; Jacob B. Augus, "The Covenant Concept: Particularistic, Pluralistic or Futuristic?," *Christian-Jewish Relations* 14:1(March, 1982), 4-18. See also, Norma H. Thompson, "The Covenant Concept in Judaism and Christianity," *Anglican Theological Review* 64 (October, 1982), 502-24; and P. D. Hanson, *The People Called: The Growth of Community in the Bible*(San Francisco: Harper and Row, 1986). On election, see Jeremy Cott, "The Biblical Problem of Election," *Journal of Ecumenical Studies* 21:2 (1984), 199-228.

56. Cf. the polemic in recent literature against the Lutheran concept of "justification by faith" (and the related law/grace dichotomy) in its relationship to prejudiced views of Judaism, both biblical and post-biblical. See, e.g., Krister Stendahl, *Paul Among Jews and Gentiles and Other Essays;* E.P. Sanders, *Paul and Palestinian Judaism;* W.D. Davies, *Paul and Rabbinic Judaism* (London: SCM Press, 1970); and Charlotte Klein, *Anti-Judaism in Christian Theology.*

57. Barth gives a "teleological" interpretation of Romans 10:4, understanding *telos* as "goal," in *CD* III: 4, 245. This view was largely ignored by contemporary exegetes until C.E.B. Cranfield adopted it in 1979. See Robert Badenas, *Christ the End of the Law: Romans 10:4 in Pauline Perspective,* Journal for the Study of the New Testament Supplement Series, 10 (Sheffield: JSOT Press, 1985), 29-33.

58. There is a tendency to focus on the era of the "church fathers" (the first through sixth centuries) when the history of Christian anti-Judaism is being analyzed. Parkes, e.g., only reaches the period of "Visigoth Spain" in *The Conflict Between the Church and the Synagogue,* and Flannery, although his *The Anguish of the Jews* reaches into the twentieth century, does not give special treatment to the Reformation era or to its major figures (the exception is Luther, to whom three pages are devoted). Ruether's *Faith and Fratricide* follows Flannery in describing the era between the late Middle Ages and the Enlightenment as the "Age of the Ghetto," while curiously skipping over the Reformation era entirely. [This problem is partially overcome in her more recent book, *The Wrath of Jonah: The Crisis of Religious Nationalism in the Israeli-Palestinian Conflict* (San Francisco: Harper and Row, 1989), however, where in chapter three she provides a concise history of early Reformed thought on the "restoration" of the Jews.] These lacunae, and the paucity of studies of anti-Judaism in Calvin and other Reformed thinkers, creates the illusion that this tradition is somehow without the symptoms of this particular disease. One need only study the Reformed confessional and dogmatic traditions to learn that this is not the case, however.

On anti-Judaism in the Reformed confessions, see my "Presbyterians and Jews: A Theological Exploration of the Book of Confessions," *Perspectives in Religious Studies* 15:3 (September, 1988). As examples of the specific forms which "anti-Judaism" takes in Reformed dogmatics, cf. the following statements from the seventeenth and twentieth centuries: "Pagans, Jews, and Mohammedans are open enemies of the church...Jews deny the Holy Trinity and the coming of the Messiah and interpret in a carnal manner the spiritual kingdom of Christ which the prophets foretold." [Johannes Wollebius, *Compendium Theologiae Christianae,* ch. 27, "The False Church," in *Reformed Dogmatics,* ed. and trans., John W. Beardslee, II (New York: Oxford University Press, 1965)]; and "We see already in the Old Testament that the particularity of the election of Israel has nothing to do with particularism, but is precisely and fully directed at the universality of the acts of God in the Messiah for all peoples (G.C. Berkouwer, *Divine Election,*235).

59. It is true that in comparison with the infamous invectives of Luther, especially in works like "Concerning the Jews and their Lies" (1543), Calvin's treatment of things Jewish appears quite moderate. On the other hand, there is evidence of Calvin's personal "exultation at Jewish misfortunes as a fitting reward for their spiritual obstinacy," and for the view that the Calvinist doctrine of predestination provided a "spiritual climate" for anti-Jewish sentiment (See A. Davies, *Anti-Semitism and the Christian Mind,* 109). Furthermore, Calvin's thoroughgoing "supersessionism" (e.g., in *Institutes* IV: 14 and 25) and his description of the ceremonies of the Roman church as a "sort of Judaism" (*Institutes* IV: 10, 13) place him squarely within the Christian anti-Jewish tradition which preceded and followed him. The theological bases of this tradition have been increasingly analyzed in recent theology. In the words of Michael McGarry, "the idea that with the coming of the church the historical mission of the Jewish people is fulfilled, that their role in sacred history has ended at that time and place, is the cornerstone of theological Antisemitism" [*Christology After Auschwitz* (New York: Paulist, 1977), 7]. From the modern perspective, perhaps all we can say of Calvin is that his anti-Jewishness appears to have been primarily theological rather than personal.

60. Robert Erickson, e.g, points out that while Martin Niemöller, Dietrich Bonhoeffer, Emmanuel Hirsch, and Paul Althaus were all German Lutherans, Niemöller and Bonhoeffer opposed Hitler and his anti-Semitic policies, while Hirsch and Althaus became Nazi supporters and were strongly anti-Semitic. Erickson concludes that one must look beyond one's theological tradition for the key to understanding Christian anti-Jewish attitudes [*Theologians Under Hitler* (New Haven: Yale University Press, 1985)].

61. Thus Karl Barth, despite his laudable record in opposing Hitler and incorporating "Israel" into his systematic theology in a new way, can admit to his own "totally irrational aversion" to living Jews. See Michael Wyschogrod, "A Jewish Perspective on Karl Barth," in Donald McKim, ed., *How Karl Barth Changed My Mind* (Grand Rapids: Eerdmans, 1987), 160.

62. This (originally) British creed was the sole doctrinal standard in the British and American Presbyterian churches until very recently, and had a profound influence on American theology in the nineteenth and early twentieth centuries. See Rogers, *Presbyterian Creeds,* 140ff; and Leith, *Assembly at Westminster.*

63. See, e.g., *The Westminster Confession of Faith,* ch. 7; See also Heinrich Heppe, *Reformed Dogmatics,* especially chap. xiii, "The Covenant of Works and the Righteousness of the Law," and ch. xiv, "The Violation of the Covenant of Works."

64. This implicit anti-Judaism may be seen in modern heirs of the Reformed tradition like Hendrikus Berkhof who views Judaism as irredeemably legalistic: "In opposition to Judaistic moralism, Paul speaks liberatingly about justification and (not works, but) faith belonging together" (*Christian Faith,* 444). On the other hand,

Berkhof argues that the Reformed tradition is distinguished by its concern for Israel, arguing that "except for Iranaeus and the Reformed tradition there are, in all these centuries [of Christian history] hardly any examples of a systematic interest in the way of Israel" (224). Ultimately, however, Berkhof confuses a rejection of Marcionism with a positive theological understanding of post-biblical Israel. On their Christian views of the "Old Testament," it is interesting to compare Berkhof's work with that of his predecessor at Leyden, K.H. Miskotte.

65. See *The Confessional Nature of the Church* (Advisory Council on Discipleship and Worship of the Presbyterian Church U.S.A., 1986). Although it does not acknowledge anti-Judaism in the confessional tradition, this document's statement that "the sixteenth and seventeenth century confessions...contain an anti-Roman polemic that would be unfair and inappropriate in contemporary confessions" (section 29.174) sets an encouraging precedent.

66. The authors of the recent Presbyterian study document entitled *A Theological Understanding of the Relationship Between Christians and Jews* lament the fact that "the confessional documents of the Reformed tradition are largely silent on this matter [the relationship of Jews and Christians] (section 24.033). Cf. Eva Fleischner's contention, which in this case must be regarded as overly optimistic and misleading, that the fact that anti-Judaism was never nailed down dogmatically means that there are no dogmatic roadblocks to impede new theological developments (*Auschwitz*, 151).

67. While *The Confession of 1967* leaves open this possibility, it does not affirm it. *A Declaration of Faith*, a confession composed by the Presbyterian Church U.S. (southern branch before the re-union of 1983) does explicitly deny supersessionism (in chs. 3 and 7), but has never been a constitutional document of the Presbyterian church. See Rogers, *Presbyterian Creeds*, 202.

68. Although van Buren is Episcopalian by ecclesiastical affiliation, in many ways his theology is "Reformed." Despite the fact that van Buren understands himself as an "Anglican theologian" ["Discerning the Way to the Incarnation," *Anglican Theological Review* 63:3 (July, 1981), 293], I will refer to van Buren as a Reformed thinker, based on the fact that his work has always revealed a theological affinity for the Swiss Reformation. See below, ch. 5.

69. Alan T. Davies argues for a "cross-fertilization" between Barth and Catholic thinkers like Peterson, Dom Oehmen, Paul Demann, and Karl Thieme, who attempted to revise the traditional Catholic understanding of Israel (*Anti-Semitism and the Christian Mind*, 113-14).

70. Moltmann observes that "a positive estimation of the existence and theological significance of Israel developed first in the Reformed theology of the seventeenth century and later in the nineteenth-century Lutheran theology of salvation history, which was influenced by it." Among these Lutheran thinkers he points to Franz Delitzsch, Chr. Ernst Luthardt, and Chr. von Hoffmann. ["Church and Israel: A

Common Way of Hope?," in *On Human Dignity: Political Theology and Ethics*, trans. M. Douglas Meeks (Philadelphia: Fortress, 1984)].

71. The Presbyterian Church U.S.A. statement is *A Theological Understanding of the Relationship Between Christians and Jews*, adopted by the 199th General Assembly in June 1987. The United Church of Christ statement is actually a series of resolutions adopted as part of the proceedings of the church's annual convention at Cleveland in June, 1987.

72. See, e.g., the General Synod of the Dutch Hervormde Kerk's *Israel und die Kirche*, (Zurich: EVA, 1961); and "Israel, People, Land and State" (1970).

73. See also the German statement "Toward Renovation of the Relationship of Christians and Jews," issued by The Synod of the Protestant Church of the Rhineland in 1980 (English translation in Croner, *More Stepping Stones*, 207-215); and especially Alan P. F. Sell, ed., *Reformed Theology and the Jewish People* (Geneva: World Alliance of Reformed Churches, 1986).

74. Isaac C. Rottenberg, "The Glory of God and the People of Israel," *Reformed World* 34:5 (1977), 215. Hendrikus Berkhof and Kornelius Miskotte are two Reformed thinkers who could well be treated in this essay, as both have been concerned with the significance of "Israel" for systematic theology. See, e.g., Berkhof, *Christian Faith;* and "Israel As A Theological Problem," *Journal of Ecumenical Studies* 6:3 (Summer, 1969); and Miskotte, *When the Gods Are Silent* ; and *Das Judentum als Frage an die Kirche* (Wuppertal: Brockhaus, 1970). See also, below ch. 2.

75. In particular, the gospels of Matthew and John have been attacked as anti-Semitic, partly because of their polemical references to "the Jews." Paul's relationship with his Jewish opponents has also been a subject of recent interest. See A. Davies, *Christianity and the Foundations of Anti-Semitism;* Stendahl, *Paul Among Jews and Gentiles;* and R.W. Klein, "Anti-Semitism as Christian Legacy: The Origin and Nature of Our Estrangement From the Jews," *Currents in Theology and Mission* 11:5 (1984), 285-301.

76. The New Testament text upon which this concept of the church as the "true Israel" has been traditionally based is Galatians 6:16. W. S. Campbell (following Peter Richardson) questions the established interpretation of the church as the "Israel of God" in this verse, and argues that such an idea, when it did first appear around 160 A.D., was based on a misinterpretation of Paul [See, W.S. Campbell, "Christianity and Judaism: Continuity and Discontinuity", *Christian-Jewish Relations* 18:1 (1985), 9-10]. The importance of this verse in the history of theological anti-Semitism is witnessed to by its employment in the work of Paul Althaus (see Moltmann, *On Human Dignity*, 198). See also, Krister Stendahl's foreword to Fleischner, *Judaism in German Theology*, xiv.

77. Barth seems to have been influenced by the choice of this later date for the ending of the history of Israel per se and the beginning of the history of "the Jews," in

Church Dogmatics III: 3. See below, ch. 2. Cf. H. Berkhof, who observes that "Judaism" should not be mistakenly identified with the faith of the Old Testament: "this mode of faith [Judaism] began with the groups who returned from the Babylonian captivity in the fifth and fourth centuries before Christ, but did not get its specific form until after the fall of Jerusalem (A.D. 70)" (*Christian Faith*, 22).

78. See Charlotte Klein, *Anti-Judaism*, ch. 2. Klein describes the scholarly view of "Judaism" which emerged in the nineteenth century and is still very influential, in these terms:

> "What is common to the authors cited here is their view of Jewish religion after the Exile. They see this as a break with the true Yahweh-faith of ancient Israel. Something new emerged, a kind of ethical world-view which can scarcely be called religion any longer. The former religion, founded on trust and love for the God who had rescued the Israelites from bondage and made them his covenant people was forgotten, and a progressive decline set in, leading away from Israel to Judaism" (16).

79. Klein argues that, in fact, once the view of Judaism as a lifeless, legalistic, and self-serving religion was established in modern scholarship, it became accepted by generation after generation of scholars who did not bother to move behind it and objectively examine Jewish sources (Ibid). See A. Davies, "A Response to Irving Greenberg," in Fleischner, ed., *Auschwitz*, where the author refers to "the Neoplatonic distinction between the spiritual Israel (identified with the church) and the carnal Israel (identified with post-biblical Judaism)" (60).

80. See especially, Thoma, *A Christian Theology of Judaism*, 162-167.

81. See, e.g., Peter von der Osten-Sacken's *Christian-Jewish Dialogue: Theological Foundations*, where the author argues that "Judaism" too easily becomes an abstract term which allows us to forget that it describes the lives and observances of actual people [trans. Margaret Kohl, (Philadelphia: Fortress, 1986), 1]. For an example of the persistence of the traditional view, see Berkhof: "what we call Israel here is usually called the Old Testament in the Christian Church" (*Christian Faith*, 221).

82. This question is generally of greater interest to Jews (especially Jews who are religiously conservative), although there are Christian exceptions. See Philip Sigal's (Jewish) theological discussion of what constitutes Jewishness in "Aspects of Dual Covenant Theology: Salvation," *Horizons in Biblical Theology* 5:2 (1980), 28f. See also Fackenheim, *To Mend the World*, 285ff. The question of "Jewishness" has also been taken up by apologists for the "Christian identity" movement in America, though not in a way that merits our consideration.

83. Cf., e.g., the Presbyterian Church (U.S.A.) document *A Theological Understanding of the Relationship of Christians and Jews*, which met serious opposition, led by Middle Eastern Christians, to the affirmation that the covenant with

Israel included the promise of land. In fact, the question of the theological significance of Israel was kept off the World Council of Churches agenda for many years for political reasons (H. Berkhof, "Israel as a Theological Problem," 346).

84. Moltmann, e.g., observes that "with the name Israel, politics come into the discussion" (*On Human Dignity*, 189). In any case, the traditional theological/exegetical view of a contemporary "Jewish religious community" in which nation, religion and country are separated from each other is no longer tenable for Christian theology (cf. C. Klein, *Anti-Judaism*, 21). See also, Klappert, *Israel und die Kirche: Erwagungen zur Israellehre Karl Barths*, Theologische Existenz Heute, 207 (München: Chr. Kaiser, 1980), ch. 5.

85. See, e.g., Peter von der Osten-Sacken, *Christian-Jewish Dialogue*, 175.

86. These descriptions of of Klappert's categories are based on *Israel und die Kirche*.

87. *The People of God*, Journal for the Study of the New Testament Supplement Series, 5 (Sheffield: JSOT Press, 1983).

88. Ibid., 20-27.

89. Ibid., 25. In *The Broken Wall*, M. Barth suggests that the model found in Paul's Letter to the Ephesians is one of "solidarity" between church and Israel (Chicago: The Judson Press, 1959, 123f). Klappert's suggestion that theology adopt a "dependent participatory" model has its parallel here.

90. Moltmann, "Church and Israel: A Common Way of Hope?", 194-202. Here Moltmann is critical, in a way which is reminiscent of Barth (see below, ch. 2) of the (Catholic) tendency to view Judaism under the category "non-Christian religion."

91. Moltmann admits, however, that neither the nature of Israel's "calling to salvation" espoused by these theologies, nor its relationship to the "calling" of the church, were ever sufficiently developed (202). See below, ch. 3.

92. *A Christian Theology of the People Israel*, 13. Franz Mussner suggests that Israel's relationship to the church be seen as "paradigmatic" [*Tractate on the Jews*, trans. by Leonard Swidler (Philadelphia: Fortress, 1984), ch. 2].

93. For a helpful discussion of theologies (and theologians) of "continuity" and "discontinuity," as well as "one" and "two" covenant theologies, see McGarry, *Christology After Auschwitz*, 61-98. An evangelical "discontinuity" view is elaborated by Mark W. Karlsberg in "Legitimate Discontinuities Between the Testaments," *Journal of the Evangelical Theology Society* 28:1 (1985), 9-20. W. S. Campbell stresses both continuity and discontinuity between church and Israel while fully affirming Israel's continuing election in "Christians and Jews: Continuity and Discontinuity." See also M. D. Hooker, *Continuity and Discontinuity: Early Christianity in its Jewish Setting* (London: Epworth, 1986); and T.M. Snider, *The*

Continuity of Salvation: A Study of Paul's Letter to the Romans (London and Jefferson, NC: McFarland and Co., 1984).

94. This is in fact the case in the Reformed tradition, even where there are anticipations of contemporary "continuity" and "one covenant" views (e.g., in Calvin). The same appearance of continuity with an ultimately negative estimation of Jews and Judaism may be found in contemporary theologians like Berkhof, who in his *Christian Faith* adopts Barth's way of speaking of church and Israel as "two forms of the same people of God," and affirms that we see in the Old and New Testaments "one continuous way of God with man" (258), but who concludes that discontinuity between church and Israel exists in fact, because Israel has withdrawn from the "new world community" to which it is called in Christ. Israel, in other words, can only fulfill its central role "in the church" (262). Berkhof believes that discontinuity is also rooted in "different ways of reading the Old Testament (*sic*)." See also, Leonhard Goppelt, "Israel and the Church in Today's Discussion and in Paul," *Lutheran World* 10:4 (October, 1963), 352-72, where the author speaks of a "unique relationship" and close bond between Israel and the church and of the continuing special election of Israel, while concluding that Jews "continue to represent pre-Christian humanity," and still live on the "lower level of promise and law." Ultimately, according to Goppelt, Christians and Jews do not share the same mission or the same hope, despite their "bond."

95. See *The Star of Redemption,* trans. William W. Hallo (London: Routledge and Kegan Paul, 1970), part 3, where Rosenzweig discusses the relationship of "the fire or the eternal life" [Judaism], "the rays, or the eternal way" [Christianity], and "the star or the eternal truth" [God].

96. The tendency in Jewish theology of this century, in fact, has been to carefully distinguish between Judaism and Christianity. In response to this tendency, the Christian theologian Clemens Thoma has been critical of the kind of barriers to reconciliation erected on the Jewish side by works like Martin Buber's *Two Types of Faith (A Christian Theology of Judaism,* 109). On the other hand, the easy continuity which sees Christianity as "Judaism for Gentiles" is also unacceptable to many [cf. Clark Williamson, *Has God Rejected His People?: Anti-Judaism in the Christian Church* (Nashville: Abingdon, 1982), 167].

97. This point was crucial for Rosenzweig in his rejection of the Hegelian notion of "superiority of the universal." See David Novak,"A Jewish Response to a New Christian Theology" (review of Paul van Buren's *Discerning the Way) Judaism* 31 (Winter, 1982), 112-120. Cf. Rosemary Ruether's suggestion of a similar view of Judaism and Christianity at the end of *Faith and Fratricide.* She refers to Jesus' parable of the prodigal son, understanding Judaism as the elder brother who remains in the father's household and Christianity as the younger brother who leaves to chase his vision. The covenants represented by the brothers are "parallel," not supersessionist (*Faith and Fratricide,* 251f.)

98. Ibid., 114. A. Davies sees Rosenzweig as the intellectual progenitor of all "liberal" Christian theologies which link Judaism and Christianity on the basis of a common revelation (*Anti-Semitism and the Christian Mind*, 145).

99. See, e.g., "Aspects of Dual Covenant Theology: Salvation."

100. Novak, "A Jewish Response," 114.

101. This phrase is used by T. M. Snider, *The Continuity of Salvation*, 3. The recent literature on the Jewishness of Jesus, Paul and the origins of Christianity is voluminous, but see: on the Jewishness of Jesus, M. Barth, *The People of God*, 76 n12; on Paul, Clark M. Williamson, "The New Testament Reconsidered;" and J. D. G. Dunn, "The New Perspective on Paul," *Bulletin of the John Rylands Library of Manchester* 65:2 (1980), 95-122.

102. See, e.g., Klappert's elaboration of the models defining the relationship between Israel and the church which result in the perception of the continuing election of Israel: the complementarity model, the representative model, and the christological-eschatological participation model (*Israel und die Kirche*, ch. 2). See also, F. Mussner, *Tractate on the Jews*, ch. 7, "Common Tasks and Goals"; Jürgen Moltmann, "Church and Israel"; Paul van Buren, *A Christian Theology of the People Israel*, ch. 10, "Israel's Mission," and ch. 11, "The Church's Service to Israel"; and *A Theological Understanding of the Relationship of Christians and Jews*,affirmation no. 7.

103. That is,the simple but significant affirmation that (contemporary) Jews and Christians worship the same God. See *A Theological Understanding of the Relationship of Christians and Jews*,affirmation no. 1.

104. "Unfulfilled messianism" is a theological perspective which, as Emil Fackenheim puts it, "hears the Christian Good News as a promise and a beginning rather than an accomplished fact" (*To Mend the World*, 285). It emphasizes that since the world is unredeemed, Christian triumphalism is both premature and dangerous. A shift in emphasis from fulfillment in the past or present to the coming Kingdom is the hallmark of "unfulfilled messianism." See especially Ruether, *Faith and Fratricide;* Gregory Baum, *The Social Imperative;* K.H. Miskotte, *Das Judentum als Frage an die Kirche;* and Isaac C. Rottenberg, "Fulfillment Theology and the Future of Christian-Jewish Relations," *The Christian Century* 97:3 (Jan 23, 1980), 66-9. For a more traditional version of "unfulfillment," see H. Berkhof who argues that although "fulfillment" has come in Christ, there can be no "consummation" as long as the separate ways of Israel and the church exist (*Christian Faith*, 256). A "partnership" model is suggested in Berkhof's affirmation that the church cannot shake off Israel, nor can it do without the awareness it provides that the Kingdom has not arrived. The church's mission to Israel, then, consists in "making her jealous" (263).

105. See *A Theological Understanding of the Relationship Between Christians and Jews*, affirmation no. 3. See also Martin Cohen and Helga Croner, eds., *Christian Mission-Jewish Mission* (New York: Paulist/Stimulus, 1982); and Krister Stendahl, foreword to Fleischner, *Judaism in German Theology*, xv. Even conservative scholars

have espoused a "mutual witness" approach. See James I. Cook, "The Christian Witness to the Jews: A Biblical Perspective," *Scottish Journal of Theology* 36:2 (1983), 145-161. For a dissenting conservative view, see Arthur F. Glasser, "Christian Ministry to the Jews," *The Presbyterian Communique* 11:2 (1988), 6-7.

106. *The People of God*, 7.

107. See, e.g., A. Davies' *Anti-Semitism and the Christian Mind,* where the author writes that anti-Judaism is "inherent in any ideology which regards the New Testament as sacrosanct after the fashion of Protestant biblicism" (112).

108. M. Barth, e.g., has concentrated on Paul's reference to the breaking down of the wall of hostility in Ephesians 2. See *The Broken Wall.*

109. See James H. Charlesworth ed., *Jews and Christians: Exploring the Past, Present and Future* (New York: Crossway, 1990); K. Stendahl, *Paul Among Jews and Gentiles;* Clark M. Williamson, "The New Testament Reconsidered"; Robert Jewett, "Major Impulses in the Theological Interpretation of Romans since Barth," *Interpretation* 34:1 (1980), 17-31; O. Hofius, "Das Evangelium und Israel: Erwagungen zu Römer 9-11," *Zeitschrift für Theologie und Kirche* 83:3 (1986), 297-324; R. Schwarz, "Israel und die Nicht Judische Christen im Römerbrief (Kapitel 9-11)," *Bibel und Liturgie* 59:3 (1986), 161-64; M. Theobald, "Kirche und Israel nach Rom 9-11," *Kairos* 29:1-2 (1987), 1-22; N. Walter, "Zur Interpretation von Römer 9-11," *Zeitschrift für Theologie und Kirche* 81:2 (1984), 172-95.

110. This phrase I have adopted from Paul van Buren, *A Christian Theology of the People Israel,* 283. See also my "'Recovering the Real Paul': Theology and Interpretation in Romans 9-11," *Ex Auditu* 4 (1988); J. D. G. Dunn, "The New Perspective on Paul"; E. P. Sanders, *Paul and Palestinian Judaism;* W. D. Davies, *Paul and Rabbinic Judaism;* and John Fischer, "Paul in His Jewish Context," *Evangelical Quarterly* 57:3 (1985), 211-36.

111. J. A. Ziesler argues that under the influence of Stendahl and others the answer to this question has shifted from "justification by faith" to "entering and being the people of God" ("Some Recent Work on the Letter to the Romans," 98). Stendahl, in turn, claims to have had "his eyes opened" to Paul and his mission by Johannes Munck, the Danish New Testament scholar. See Stendahl's foreword to Munck, *Christ and Israel: An Interpretation of Romans 9-11* (Philadelphia: Fortress, 1967).

112. See especially "The Apostle Paul and the Introspective Conscience of the West," in *Paul Among Jews and Gentiles,* 78-96.

113. Ibid., 5.

114. Ibid., 28.

115. Ibid., 35. Cf. the following statement by Cranfield: "*If we would be true to Paul's teaching,* we must surely repudiate altogether the notion...that the Jewish

people having rejected Jesus Christ has been dispossessed of its election..." [Cranfield and J.A. Emerton, eds., *The International Critical Commentary, Epistle to the Romans,* vol. 2 (Edinburgh: T & T Clark, 1978), 448-9, emphasis mine].

116. Contemporary biblical scholarship has not abandoned the historical-critical method and its "diachronic" approach, but is much more likely than Stendahl to bring "synchronic" methods like literary, structural, semiotic and reader-response criticism to bear on the interpretive task. For helpful guides to these methods and their relationship to traditional criticism, see Edgar A. McKnight, *The Bible and the Reader* (Philadelphia: Fortress, 1985); and Terrence J. Keegan, *Interpreting the Bible: A Popular Guide to Biblical Hermeneutics* (New York: Paulist, 1985).

117. See Paul S. Minear, "Barth's Commentary on Romans, 1922-1972; or Karl Barth vs. the Exegetes," in Martin Rumscheidt, ed., *Footnotes to a Theology: the Karl Barth Colloquium of 1972* (The Corporation for the Publication of Academic Studies in Religion in Canada, 1974).

118. A. Davies, *Anti-Semitism and the Christian Mind,* 114.

119. Cranfield also reveals Barth's influence in his "teleological" interpretation of Romans 10:4. See Badenas, *Christ the End of the Law,* 33.

120. *Epistle to the Romans,* 448.

121. Ibid.

122. Cf., e.g., the prominence of scriptural interpretation in the recent attempts to construct a "Christian theology of Judaism" by Peter von der Osten-Sacken, Clemens Thoma, and Franz Mussner. See also Emil Fackenheim, who confirms the importance of the "backward movement of thought to biblical origin" (*To Mend the World,* 15).

123. *A Christian Theology of the People Israel,* 283.

124. Alice Eckardt, "A Christian Problem: Review of Protestant Documents," in Croner, ed., *More Stepping Stones,* 17-18.

125. Similarly, Glenn D. Early argues that without reform in praxis, hermeneutical shift, theological reconstruction, and recognition of the Holocaust problematic are all ineffectual ("The Radical Hermeneutical Shift in Post-Holocaust Christian Thought," 16).

126. This orientation to the study of religion is elaborated in George A. Lindbeck, *The Nature of Doctrine: Religion and Theology in a Post-Liberal Age* (Philadelphia: Westminster, 1984). Adopting this term to describe my own approach does not mean that I wholly ascribe to, or am attempting to work according to, Lindbeck's program.

127. For the characteristics of a "theology developed in Jewish-Christian dialogue," see P. von der Osten-Sacken, *Jewish-Christian Dialgoue,* ch. 1. Dialogue, as it is described in this essay, is not the ultimate goal of post-Holocaust theology, but one of its important means. Therefore, the necessity of a theology carried out in Jewish-Christian dialogue is not diminished by the objections of authors like Gerard Sloyan, who claims that dialogue is "necessarily assymetrical" ("Some Theological Implications of the Holocaust," 405), or Emil Fackenheim, who describes the different needs which compel Jews and Christians to seek dialogue (*To Mend the World,* 284.)

128. M. Barth, *The People of God,* 26.

129. This term has been used by several recent authors: See, e.g., Glenn D. Early, "The Radical Hermeneutical Shift in Post-Holocaust Christian Thought"; Charles E. Vernoff, "After the Holocaust: History and Being as Sources of Method Within the Emerging Interreligious Hermeneutic," *Journal of Ecumenical Studies* 21:4 (Fall, 1984), 639-663; Irving Greenberg, "Cloud of Smoke, Pillar of Fire"; and Emil Fackenheim, *To Mend the World.*

130. *Freud and Philosophy: An Essay in Interpretation,* trans. Denis Savage (New Haven and London: Yale University Press, 1970), 28.

Part II Israel in Barth, Moltmann and van Buren

CHAPTER TWO

KARL BARTH:
RADICAL TRADITIONALISM

I. INTRODUCTION

Karl Barth (1886-1968) was perhaps the important Protestant theologian of the twentieth century. Regardless of what the next decade brings, Barth's place in the annals of twentieth-century theology is secure. With the possible exception of his contemporary Rudolf Bultmann, no theologian of this century has met with greater praise or vilification than Barth. While it is true that Bultmann's work was influential for both theology and biblical studies (where he revolutionized New Testament study twice in his own lifetime with the methods of "form-criticism" and "demythologizing"), Barth continues to exercise an influence on contemporary thought beyond that of Bultmann.[1] In fact, as important as Barth's influence during his lifetime is the part his work continues to play in current theological discussion. While the impact of Barth's thought was mostly limited to Continental theology until after World War II,[2] the last few decades have witnessed an increasing interest in Barth's work outside the German-speaking world.[3] Areas of contemporary theology which have drawn inspiration from Barth include "narrative theology"[4] and "post-modern" theology,[5] and Barth's name is invoked today in the wake of the modern "church struggle" in South Africa,[6] and in European and American debates on the relationship of theology and socialism.[7] Novel interpretations of Barth's theology continue to appear,[8] and recent celebrations of Barth's birth (centenary in 1986) and of the writing of the "Barmen Declaration" (fiftieth anniversary in 1984) reflect continued interest in Barth's work, and support claims for his contemporary significance.[9]

Not surprisingly, Barth's understanding of "Israel" has been of interest to theologians and biblical scholars as well. Especially in the last two decades, scholars have subjected Barth's Israel-doctrine to extensive analysis and critique. More importantly, the work of many Christian thinkers positively reflects the influence of Barth's discussion of Israel in the *Church Dogmatics*. Among these theologians and biblical scholars are C. E. B. Cranfield, Paul van Buren, Hendrikus Berkhof, Kornelius Miskotte, Jacob Jocz, Helmut Gollwitzer, T.F. Torrance, Clemens Thoma and Markus Barth.[10] As this list suggests, Barth's impact has been felt primarily in Protestant theology, although his Israel-teaching has had some influence on Catholic thinking as well.[11] It is not an exaggeration to say that Barth's understanding of Israel has had the kind of influence on Protestant theology that "Nostra aetate" has had on Catholic thinking about Israel.[12] However, before judging how fortuitous Barth's influence has been, we must examine his Israel-doctrine in more detail. As this is done, we will assess the development of Barth's theology of Israel, while keeping in mind his relationship to the "Jewish question" as it confronted him and his contemporaries.

II. BARTH ON ISRAEL

We begin our study of the development of Barth's Israel-doctrine with a consideration of his *Der Römerbrief* (2nd ed., 1921), which "dropped like a bomb on the playground of the theologians" (Karl Adam), and was the text with which the burgeoning Continental "theology of crisis" was most often identified. Although it remains the one volume most closely associated with Barth's name, few read *Der Römerbrief*. For many, the book provides little insight into Paul's epistle, since it is so intimately related to its historical context in post-World War I Europe. In fact, Barth's *Römerbrief* has long been criticized by biblical exegetes for its "historical and philological weaknesses."[13] Nevertheless, the *Römerbrief* is the proper starting point for any discussion of Barth's theology. This is particularly the case for our analysis of Barth's Israel-doctrine, since some of the themes he develops later in his career are inchoate here. We will focus our attention on Barth's discussion of Romans 9-11, where Paul considers the problem of Israel's unbelief.

A. Romans 9-11 in Barth's *Der Römerbrief*

The most striking aspect of Barth's interpretation of Romans 9-11 in the *Römerbrief* is the claim that the subject of this section of the epistle is the "church." Barth's explication of the ninth chapter of Romans, for instance, is entitled "the tribulation of the church." The tenth chapter Barth introduces with the title "the guilt of the church," and the eleventh "the hope of the church." Barth's titles are problematic for two reasons: first, the word "church" does not appear in these chapters of Romans, and second, Paul's obvious concern in Romans 9-11 is with "Israel." Nor is Barth's proclivity for reading Romans 9-11 with the "church" in view evident only in his section headings. On 9:1 ("...I have great sorrow and unceasing anguish in my heart [for my kinsmen]"), Barth writes, "this is the attitude toward the church engendered by the gospel" (334).[14] In his explication of 9:6-13 (where Paul argues that "not all who are descended from Israel belong to Israel"), Barth introduces the distinction between the "church of Esau" and the "church of Jacob" (341ff.). Barth is discussing here the election and rejection of the church, while Paul introduced the question of election in relation to Israel's patriarchs (9:8-12).

Barth's church-centric reading of Romans is evident again in chapter 10. On 10:1 ("Brethren, my heart's desire and prayer to God for them [unbelieving Israel] is that they may be saved"), Barth writes that "the description of the church which we have just given is often blamed as being typical of those who oppose the church" (371). In chapter 11 this tendency is even more pronounced. Commenting on 11:1 ("I ask, then, has God rejected his people? By no means!"), Barth responds, "can we escape from that essential atheism of the church?" (391). On 11:11 ("So, I ask, have they [Israel] stumbled so as to fall?"), Barth begins, "we now see contrasted with the church, with every church, the 'others'--the Gentiles" (400). On 11:15 ("for if their rejection means the reconciliation of the world..."), Barth speaks of the "casting away of the church" (405). On 11:25 ("a hardening in part has befallen Israel..."), Barth's first words are, "the catastrophe of the church..." (415). And on the second half of the same verse ("all Israel shall be saved"), Barth comments: "the church is concrete mankind, receiving the revelation of God" (415).

What are we to make of Barth's interpretation of Romans 9-11 as a discussion of the tribulation, guilt and hope of "the church"? Clearly, Barth's concern in this early commentary is with the crisis of the church and the crisis of society in post-war Europe. But even keeping this in mind, it is difficult to accept a reading of Romans 9-11 which is in such clear opposition to the sense of the text, especially from a theologian for whom the testimony of Scripture is so crucial. Theologically speaking, there seem to be two options for understanding Barth here. Either he has replaced Paul's "Israel" with the concept of the "church," or "church" and "Israel" are terms he understands as interchangeable because they refer to the same reality. The first option is the one many critics of the *Römerbrief* have settled upon, including some of Barth's earliest reviewers. For instance, Adolf Jülicher commented that the "reading there of 'church' where he [Paul] writes Israel, runs directly counter to the spirit of Paul, as a look at Romans 9:1-5 shows."[15] Adolf Schlatter voiced the same criticism, observing that, "without consideration, the 'church' is spoken of in Romans 9-11. Does the word of Paul remain in tact any longer?"[16] The second option--that for Barth Israel and church are theologically identical--is exercised by a contemporary critic, Dieter Kraft, who speaks of the "synonymousness" of Israel and the church in Barth's *Römerbrief*.[17]

Recalling the models of Bertold Klappert outlined in chapter one, we might say that Barth can be understood here as working either with a substitution/integration[18] model, in which Israel has been completely absorbed into the church, or a participation[19] model, in which the terms "Israel" and "church" are so closely identified that they become synonymous and interchangeable. The important question is "which one is it?" What is behind Barth's equating of Israel and the church in his interpretation of Romans 9-11? Is it the theological tenet, elaborated in Barth's later work, that Israel and the church belong inextricably together in the history of election? If so, the question remains: how should the resulting solidarity be understood--according to the positive model of participation, or the more traditional negative models of integration or typology? In order to arbitrate this dilemma, we return to Barth's text.

Already in his comments on 9:1, Barth uses Israel and church as interchangeable terms: "and now there is thrust upon our attention-- Israel, the church, the world of religion as it appears in history..." (332). On 9:4 Barth says, "Israel--the church--even possesses 'God'" (339). In his comment on 11:11, Barth argues that Israel and the church are both subject to the "tribulation" and "guilt" involved in receiving God's revelation (401). Barth appears once again to view the church and Israel in a synonymous way when he says, commenting on 11:15-18, "the breaking off of the branches of the true olive tree is--the rejection of the Church" (408). Finally, commenting on 11:25, Barth writes that "this salvation concerns all Israel, the whole Church, every Church" (416). Elsewhere in the *Römerbrief*, Barth appears to perceive a close, even synonymous relationship between the Old and New testaments:

> Nothing men can say or know of the gospel is 'new,' for everything they possess is identical to what Israel possessed of old. Historically...the New Testament seems to be no more than a clearly drawn, carefully distilled epitome of the Old Testament (338).

In another place, Barth makes it clear that this continuity between the testaments is grounded in Christ. Commenting on 4:1, Barth quotes Franz Overbeck:

> The Old Testament did not, in the ordinary sense of the word 'precede' Christ. Rather it lived in Him; or, to put the point in another way, it was the concrete image which accompanied and directly reflected His pre-historical life (118).

Barth echoes the words of Overbeck later in the *Römerbrief* when he refers to "the characteristic mark of the Gospel of Christ both in the Old Testament and the New..." (349).

This interpretation of the Old Testament as a fore-portrayal of Christ and of the New Testament rings of supersessionism, and is in fact the hallmark of the model for understanding the relationship of church and Israel which Klappert calls typological.[20] Over a decade before Klappert's book appeared, Friedrich-Wilhelm Marquardt, one of the earliest and most incisive critics of Barth's Israel-doctrine, elaborated Barth's dependence on a typological understanding of the faith and institutions of Israel.[21] If the "identity"[22] of the Old and New

Testaments suggested by Barth in the *Römerbrief* and other early writings is interpreted typologically, then the "synonymousness" of church and Israel would be a function of Barth's integration of Israel into the church. Commenting on 9:3-5, where Paul discusses the various advantages of Israel in salvation history, Barth seems to confirm this interpretation of his theology:

> If it is a matter of being Israelites, of possessing the adoption, the glory, the covenants, the fathers, the giving of the law, the service of God, the promises, and the Christ according to the flesh, does not the Church also possess precisely all this? (339)

Whatever Barth's intention here, his words ring of the traditional integration and typology models that present Israel and its institutions as pre-figurations of the gospel, taken over by the "new people of God."

Other examples in the *Römerbrief* of Barth's dependence on the models of typology and integration are found in his comments on 9:24-29, where Barth affirms that "the process of revelation in Christ is decisive," and speaks of "the eternal moment when the Church of Jacob dawns in Christ" (360), on 10:9-11, where Barth describes "Israel recogniz[ing] the meaning of the name Israel" as a condition of eschatological salvation (381), on 11:12-15, where Barth refers to "the fall and loss of Israel as [it is] manifested in the crucifixion of Christ" (403), and on 11:25, where Barth defines the "coming new man" as made up of the "elect of Israel together with the Gentiles who have been elected in Christ" (415). If we understand this last statement in terms of the others we have considered from *Der Römerbrief*, we must conclude that for Barth the destiny and true identity of Israel lies in the church. This, then, would be his justification for speaking of the two synonymously. Our conclusion allows us to make sense of some of Barth's other statements, like the following, which confuse the two realities:

> If Israel would venture to take its stand upon the election of the Fathers, if the Church would dare to be moved and sustained by the faith of Abraham...how great the Church might be! (419)

This statement is comprehensible only if "Israel venturing to take its stand upon the election of the Fathers" really means Israel entering the church through faith in Christ.

Another element in Barth's interpretation of Romans 9-11 in the *Römerbrief* which tends in the direction of "integration" is his treatment of the "law." Barth's interpretation of Romans 10:4 is "teleological." That is, Barth understands Paul's description of Christ as the "end *(telos)* of the law" to mean that Christ is the law's *goal*--that which gives it "its sense and meaning" (375). Here Barth's interpretation, which emphasizes continuity between the old and new covenants, is an improvement over some traditional interpretations of this verse which stress the law's abolition. At the same time, however, Barth associates "law" with "religion," in a way that infects the former with the same negative connotations as the latter:

> Jesus is the goal to which all law and all religion move. Wherever...men become even dimly conscious of this movement...law and religion make their inevitable appearance (383).

The effect of this coupling of law and religion can only be appreciated when we recall that "religion" is the most frequent target of Barth's attacks in his commentary on Romans 1-8 in *Der Römerbrief.* However, Barth's association of Israel with the frivolous human striving that accompanies "religion" is not entirely implicit:

> Not only does Israel not obtain, but he will never obtain. We know what he is seeking for--his own righteousness, camouflaged as the righteousness of God (x.3). He endeavors to justify and save men by enthroning piety (398).

Given his implicit opposition between law/religion/human righteousness on the one hand, and gospel/revelation/divine righteousness on the other, it is impossible to argue that Barth places the testaments and communities represented by these opposed dynamics on equal footing theologically. Whatever connection exists between the covenants (testaments) is a function of Christ, who is mysteriously present in the Old Testament history of Israel. Ultimately, the same is true of the supposed synonymousness between Israel and the church. For Barth the key to this apparent identity is Jesus Christ:

> There is in the fullness of God no election AND rejection, no Gentile
> AND Jew, no outer AND inner. All are one--in Christ Jesus (404).

From one perspective, Barth's habit of speaking about Israel and the church interchangeably represents a positive departure from the theology of his day. It suggested a kind of Christian solidarity with Israel which the church in Europe certainly needed to be reminded of. It may even be true that since Barth was able to stress in a new way that Israel and church belong together, "both editions of the *Römerbrief* mean a new beginning for reflection on Israel in Protestant theology."[23] Ultimately, however, we doubt whether Barth's approach significantly departs from traditional Christian understandings of Israel as integrated into, or substituted by, the church. At the very least, we must ask whether confusion is not inherent in Barth's use of the terms "Israel" and "church" in the *Römerbrief*, and whether such confusion does not ultimately hinder a Christian theological response to the "Jewish question." For a fuller perspective on these problems, we will consider Barth's activity during the German Church Struggle in the 1930s.

B. Barth and the "Church Struggle"

Whatever one's perspective on *Der Römerbrief*, it cannot be disputed that in this commentary Barth interprets Romans theologically rather than historically. This preference for theological interpretation is especially evident, as we have seen, in Barth's treatment of Israel. For Barth, "Israel" signifies not the Jewish people, past or present, but that theological entity which is the object of God's original revelation--a revelation which is preparatory to, and which is consummated in, Jesus Christ. As we shall see, however, Barth's attempt to treat "Israel" purely theologically was disrupted by the history of Europe and the history of the Jews. About the time of the appearance of the sixth edition of the *Römerbrief* in 1933, the question of "Israel" began to take on a new historical dimension for the church in Germany. Anti-Semitism was certainly not a new problem in Europe, but in the wake of the same cultural apocalypse which made *Der Römerbrief* so salient, anti-Semitism began to flourish, nourished by resentment following Germany's war-time defeat, and the subsequent failures of the Weimar

Republic. In 1928 Barth wrote in defense of a booklet which courageously exhorted the Protestant church to stand firmly against the growing tide of cultural anti-Semitism:

> We are persuaded that the Anti-semitic movement, which in the aftermath of the world war has had so mighty a boom, is irreconcilable with the Christian point of view and is incompatible with our debt of gratitude to the cradle of Christianity.[24]

A more sustained response to European anti-Semitism was required in 1933, when the Nazi "Aryan clause" threatened to become official policy in the German Evangelical Church. In July of that year Barth met the challenge by publishing the first of what became a series of pamphlets under the title *Theologische Existenz Heute*. Here Barth publicly opposed the introduction of Nazi ideology in the church:

> The community of those belonging to the church is defined not through blood and therefore also not through race, but through the Holy Spirit and through baptism. If the German Evangelical Church excludes the Jewish Christians, or if they are treated as second class citizens, they will have stopped being the Christian Church.[25]

With these words Barth declared a *status confessionis* over opposition to the Aryan paragraphs and officially entered the *Kirchenkampf* or "Church Struggle" which threatened to split the German Protestant church. Barth became a leading figure in the "Confessing Church," a movement that tended to oppose Nazi ideology, but which found its *raison d'etre* in resisting attempts to nazify the church. Their struggle was mainly against the *Deutsche Christen* ("German Christians") who saw the church's task as acceptance and support of Hitler and his policies. The threat posed by this group of Nazi-sympathizers in the church became clear in November, 1933 when, at the infamous "Sportpalace Rally," the German Christians showed they were determined to bring together cross and swastika and render Hitler their unquestioning support.

In May of 1934 members of the "Confessing Church" met at the Synod of Barmen for the purpose of registering their opposition to the heresy of the "German Christians."[26] The "Declaration" which emerged from Barmen was composed mainly by Barth, and is still viewed as the example *par excellence* of the heroic stance taken against the Nazis by the Confessing Church. The document has even become established in the confessional tradition of the Reformed church,[27] and remains a landmark symbol of theologically-grounded political opposition. A close look at the Barmen Declaration, however, reveals that it is characterized by opposition to the "false doctrine" and "alien principles" of the German Christians,[28] and not by calls for direct resistance to the totalitarian aims of the Nazi state. More importantly, Barmen's condemnation of the German Christians,

> did not lead on to a theological statement of the promise and tribulation of Israel's election, let alone any expression of solidarity with the Jews in their suffering.[29]

Toward the end of his life Barth admitted that the failure of the Confessing Church to produce such a statement of solidarity with the Jews at Barmen was his own fault:

> I have long since regarded it as a fault on my part that I did not make this question a decisive issue, at least publicly in the church conflict (e.g., in the two Barmen declarations I drafted in 1934). A text in which I might have done so would not, of course, have been acceptable to the mindset of even the "confessors" of that time, whether in the Reformed or the general synod. But this does not excuse the fact that since my interests were elsewhere I did not at least formally put up a fight on the matter.[30]

Regardless of one's reaction to Barth's suggestion that in 1934 he should have gone through the motions *("in aller Form")* of drafting a statement that spoke practically and decisively to the Jewish question, one has to admire his candid admission that he failed on so important a matter.

It is not the case, however, that during this period Barth was unconcerned with the theological significance of the Jewish persecution taking place in Germany. In December of 1933 Barth preached in the Bonn Castle Church on Romans 15:5-13. His words unmistakably reflect the events of the previous year.

> It is not self-evident that we belong to Jesus Christ and he to us. Christ belongs to the people Israel. The blood of this people was in his veins the blood of the Son of God. This people's form he adopted, while he adopted the being of man...Jesus Christ was a Jew, but in taking up

and taking away the sins of the Jews, the sins of the whole world and even our own, the salvation of the Jews has come also to us. How can we, each time we think about this, not be obliged to think above all of the Jews?[31]

Here Barth attacks the Nazis and "German Christians" with their own weapons,[32] as it were, utilizing references to "blood" and race to stress Christ's solidarity with the Jews, as well as the debt of love which Christians owe to Israel. Why, however, did such insightful writing and preaching not translate into the decisive and practical opposition to Nazi policies which Barth later admitted was necessary? The most typical response to this question has been to blame Barth's transcendental, other-worldly theological orientation--the so-called "ethical *Weltresignation*" of dialectical theology.[33] This orientation, some of Barth's critics have reasoned, made him the purveyor of a "belated theology" which prevented him from realizing in time that the battle over the *Judenfrage* had to be fought in the political arena.[34] This explanation does not entirely explain Barth's hesitancy to enter the political arena over the persecution or Jews, however. For despite his alleged failure on the Jewish question, Barth did take up positions in the 30s which could not be justified from a purely theological standpoint.

In 1935, for instance, Barth refused to sign the loyalty oath which was required of him as a professor in a German university,[35] and in 1938, while teaching in Basel, Barth pleaded for Germany's neighbors to actively resist Hitler. In a famous letter to the Czech theologian Hromadka, Barth suggested that every Czech soldier who resisted Hitler would be acting on behalf of the Church of Jesus Christ.[36] Not surprisingly, the Barth who spoke from Basel in 1938 was perceived as contradicting the Barth who had served as a guide at Barmen in 1934. At the time, in fact, Barth was criticized more for taking this "political" stand on Czechoslovakia than he had been for failing to take a political stand at Barmen in support of the Jews. In 1939 Reinhold Niebuhr responded to Barth's apparent reversal with a sharp rebuke:

If Barth had arrived at his present convictions ten years earlier the history of Central Europe might be different, considering how powerful his influence was in accentuating those tendencies of Lutheranism which make it politically neutral.[37]

In the final analysis, it appears that Barth was never able to wed his call for theological solidarity with the Jews to his increasingly vocal, albeit exilic, opposition to Hitler. In addressing a Swiss audience soon after the pogrom of November, 1938, Barth spoke explicitly of Jewish suffering:

> When that takes place which has in Germany now been manifestly determined--the physical extermination of the People of Israel...an attack is being made on the Christian church at its very roots...He who is on principle an enemy of the Jews...is to be recognized as on principle an enemy of Jesus Christ.[38]

Despite the strength of this statement, it shows that Barth continued to understand anti-Semitism and "Israel" in theological terms. Unfortunately, we shall see that Barth never went beyond perceiving them in this way, partly because he had so few contacts with Jews of the kind which could have made Israel and its suffering real for him in a personal way.

In conversations with his few Jewish acquaintances during the 30s, Barth *did* seem quite aware of what was at stake for Jews and for the church under Nazi rule. In 1934 Barth wrote to Rabbi Emil Bernard Cohen:

> You will expect from me nothing other than that thought on the essence, the way, and the mission of your people under the great riddles of our time occupies me with a great depression. We are also in agreement on the fact that the terror which befalls your people today in Germany--I can as a Christian think about it only in shame and horror--is so terrible because in this, known or unknown, the final mysteries of divine grace are touched upon and because with it the Synagogue just as well as the church is called to an entirely new hearing of the divine word and an entirely new responsible decision.[39]

Barth's exchange of letters with rabbi H.-J. Schoeps in 1934 suggests that he desired dialogue with Jews. In this exchange we see Barth's emphasis on the unique solidarity between church and Israel, as well as Barth's preoccupation with Christology. Barth wrote to Schoeps on February 17, 1934:

A systematic theology of Judaism even and precisely "in this time" must of course culminate in the proof that Jesus had to be crucified.[40]

Ironically, in these pieces of correspondence with rabbis in 1934, we encounter more evidence of Barth's tendency to view the "Jewish problem" in purely theological terms, a tendency which contributed to his failure in leading the church in action which might have proven decisive in the political realm during the 30s. Evidence that Barth helped secure safe passage for Jews in Switzerland after 1935, and kept the Jewish question alive there,[41] lead to a final assessment of his role in the church's opposition to Nazi anti-Jewish policies as mixed: although Barth helped keep the church pure from Nazi influence and forcefully argued that ill-treatment of Jews was a denial of Christ, he continued to view the *Judenfrage* through a theological lens which obscured his perception of Jewish suffering and the church's task in responding to it.[42]

As far as the Church Struggle and its relation to the Jewish question is concerned, Barth remains subject to the criticism of Lothar Steiger:

> Whoever argued, so to speak, "purely" theologically, saw only the Jewish-Christians. The Jews fell through the crack between pure and natural theology.[43]

Steiger's statement does apply to Barth, since rather than launching opposition to National Socialism and its Jewish policies in the political arena, Barth became a leader in the "Confessing Church," a movement which focused on opposition to the natural theology of the "German Christians," and sought to preserve the integrity of the church against encroachment by the state. Ironically, the Confessing church ultimately failed to protect even the Jewish-Christians in its own midst, let alone the majority of Jews who were outside the church. Barth is to be commended for eventually assuming a personal stand on the "Jewish question" which many of his contemporaries in the church remained unwilling to assume. But Barth apparently was unable to recognize in time the *political* and *social* implications of his own *theological* understanding of the Jewish people. Yet, in spite of Barth's failure to lead the Confessing Church in decisive and practical support of the Jewish people, the events of 1933 and following had a decisive influence on Barth's theology of Israel. This influence is particularly evident in the *Church Dogmatics*.

C. *Church Dogmatics*

Barth was already at work on his multi-volume systematic theology amid the fateful events of the 1930s. After *Christliche Dogmatik*--a work Barth came to view as a false start--was published in 1927, the first half-volume of the *Kirchliche Dogmatik* appeared in 1932. In the first three half-volumes, Barth gave only limited attention to "Israel." In *CD* I:2 (1938), for example, Barth discusses the relationship of the testaments, concluding that the church of the New Testament is joined inseparably together with the people whose forgiveness is proclaimed in the Old Testament, and that the church and synagogue are thus bound together.[44] As we have seen, this affirmation of solidarity between church and Israel characterized Barth's response to Jewish persecutions during the 30s. Although Barth appears to offer a new understanding of Israel in this discussion of the testaments, he belies a more traditional Christian view of Judaism later in *CD* I:2:

> The Jewish people is a hard and stiff-necked people, because it is a people which resists its God. It is characterized as the people which in its own Messiah finally rejected and crucified the saviour of the world and therefore denied the revelation of God...What has later Anti-Semitism to say, compared with the accusation here levelled against the Jews? And what can it do compared with the judgment under which they have been put at the hand of God himself long ago?[45]

We shall see that these two aspects of Barth's treatment of the church-Israel relationship, one emphasizing solidarity between Israel and the church, the other legitimizing Jewish suffering with references to Jewish history and especially the Jewish response to Jesus, remain in dialectical tension and typify Barth's paradoxical approach to Israel in the *Church Dogmatics*.

CD II:2. Barth's first serious treatment of Israel in the *Church Dogmatics* appears in II:2 (1942). Within his chapter on "the election of God," Barth treats "the election of the community" in the now famous paragraph 34. A great deal has been written on Barth's doctrine of election,[46] and it is not our purpose here to summarize what Barth calls his "reconstruction" (x) of this doctrine. But a brief summary of paragraph 34 will be helpful at this point. After arguing in paragraph 33 that the election of humanity is its election in Jesus Christ--who is at the same time electing God and elected humanity--in paragraph 34 Barth discusses the election of the one community of God,

> by the existence of which Jesus Christ is to be attested to the whole world and the whole world summoned to faith in Jesus Christ. This one community of God in its form as Israel has to serve the representation of the divine judgment, in its form as the Church the representation of the divine mercy....To the one elected community of God is given in the one case its passing, and in the other its coming form.[47]

The preceding statement contains all the principles underlying Barth's understanding of Israel expressed in *CD* II:2, paragraph 34. These are: 1. Election's focus is Jesus Christ. The indissoluble unity of the one community in its two forms (Israel and church) is based in Christ, who is both "crucified Messiah of Israel," and "secret Lord of the church" (198). This community in its entirety can be defined as the "environment" of the man Jesus. 2. This emphasis on the community as the object of election means that we cannot call Jews the "rejected" and the church the "elected" community. Israel, in other words, cannot escape its election, despite its refusal to believe the gospel. However, Israel's continuing election is linked in salvation history with the crucifixion of Jesus and the judgment of God (211). 3. Israel's special service within the elected community is the hearing, reception and acceptance of the divine promise (233). The Church needs this service, which, if Israel is obedient to its election, will lead to its "rising to life in the church." Since Israel hears but does not believe (and, therefore "refuses to hear properly and perfectly"), it places itself in a "vacuum" at the very point where it could and should enter the church. 4. In the election of Jesus Christ, God "appoints for man a gracious end and a new gracious beginning" (259). Israel's specific function is in representing the passing and setting aside of the "old man," of the "man" who resists his election (260).

Before examining more closely these propositions, we must entertain an introductory question: what exactly is the nature of the "Israel" Barth speaks of in *CD* II:2? Barth's answer is that "Israel is the people of the Jews which resists its divine election" (198). This definition, like Barth's Israel-doctrine itself, has a paradoxical character. It is a positive definition inasmuch as it takes into consideration Israel *ante* and *post christum natum.* That is, Barth includes in "Israel" not only biblical ("Old Testament") Israel, but also the Jews who live on as "Israel," even after having rejected Jesus Christ and remaining in the synagogue. On the other hand, of course, Barth's definition comprises a *theologia negativa:* Israel is defined in purely negative terms theologically--as a community which resists its divine election. This resistance is not coincidental, but defines Israel's very essence and determines its relationship to God and the church. We encounter, then, Barth's ambivalent and even contradictory approach to "Israel" in his very definition of the term.

An aspect of the Israel-doctrine elaborated by Barth in *CD* II:2 that is reminiscent of his earlier theology is his emphasis on the unique solidarity between church and synagogue. The church cannot ignore its unity with "the people of the Jews," Barth says, or else it has ceased to be the church (201). In fact, claims Barth, "the church leads no life of its own beside and against Israel. It draws its life from Israel, and Israel lives in it" (205). If this is so, then Barth must explain the *actual* separation between two religious communities which share such a fundamental, though still abstract, unity. This "unity in principle" is undermined, Barth argues, by "unbelief with regard to Jesus Christ." The actual separation in the one community of God originates, then, from the Jewish side. In its disobedience to its election, Israel "creates a schism, a gulf in the midst of the community of God" (208). Israel brings about through its unbelief "a most unnatural severance in God's community" (262), and in disrupting the community, it punishes itself (263).

In *CD* II:2 the abstract, theological unity Barth alluded to in the *Römerbrief* and emphasized in his preaching and writing during the German Church Struggle is elaborated by means of the notion of Israel and church as two forms of the same elect community of God. The destruction of this abstract unity, however, has an objective and historical basis: Israel's rejection of its own Messiah. It is highly significant, therefore, that "the Jews" delivered Jesus up to be crucified (Barth makes this point several times; see 201, 267, and 279). In fact, the form of the community known as Israel is permanently associated with Jesus' crucifixion, just as the form known as the church is defined by Jesus' resurrection:

> The Synagogue cannot and will not take up the message: "He is risen!" But it must still pronounce all the more clearly the words: "He is not here!" It speaks of the darkness that fell upon the world in the hour of Jesus' passing.[48]

One encounters in this passage the compulsion which drives the "Israel" Barth has created in *CD* II:2. Israel's unbelief, its initiation of a schism in the one community of the elect, its loud "No" in resistance to its election, do not release Israel from the role it must play in salvation history. In the era *post christum resuscitatum,* Israel discharges its role "involuntarily," but discharge it it must. Even Israel's unbelief, according to Barth, cannot alter the fact that it remains the "people of its arrived and crucified messiah" (208). Israel cannot escape its "appointed service" any more than it can escape God or its divine election.

And what precisely is this "service" to which unbelieving Israel is appointed? It is to represent the judgment of God, just as the church represents God's mercy. In its representation of this judgment, Israel has been determined as a vessel of dishonor: "Israel in itself and as such is the 'vessel of dishonor.' It is the witness to the divine judgment. It embodies human impotence and unworthiness" (245). We will return later to Barth's troubling doctrine of Israel as a witness to divine judgment. Now we simply point out that, here as elsewhere, it is the cross of Christ that serves as the symbol of Israel's judgment. Barth says that even "the Jews of the ghetto...involuntarily, joylessly, ingloriously...have nothing to attest to the world but the shadow of the cross of Jesus Christ that falls upon them" (209). Is there any hope of redemption in the "wretched testimony" Barth's "Synagogue" is bound to give? Since "God only kills to make alive" (263), Israel is the object of God's "Yes" as well as the "No" manifest in its sufferings. But this "Yes" will rest upon Israel only when it becomes obedient to its election and takes its place within the church. Jesus Christ is "already the secret of Israel's history which has its goal in Him" (227). This means that the end for which Israel is elected is faith in Jesus Christ: "It is in the hope of the Church, therefore, that Israel has its own hope" (301).

In what we have begun to see is typical Barthian fashion, the relationship between church and Israel described here is complementary and symbiotic, but it is also typological and integrationist. As in *Der Römerbrief,* church and Israel in Barth's theological vision are interpenetrating realities which are ultimately inseparable. However, Israel is always seen from the perspective of its proper *telos,* which is life in the church through faith in its Messiah. It is from this perspective that Barth speaks of "the pre-existence of the Church in Israel" (212), declares that Israel's mission is "a preparation for the Church" (233), and states that the church is "in fact the first and final determination of Israel" (266). It is clear from all this that the basis for Barth's vision of complementarity and unity between church and synagogue is Jesus Christ. In the statements cited above the christological focus of Barth's doctrine of election (and doctrine of Israel!) come through clearly. Election is election in and with Jesus Christ; the elected community is "the environment of Jesus Christ"; and Israel will become obedient to its election when it "rises to life" in the church *through faith in Christ.* While Barth denies that the church has become the new Israel, he is clear that Israel must become part of the church.

Barth's focus on Christ in *CD* II:2 paragraph 34 should not be equated with the emphasis on the "Jewishness of Jesus" which characterized Barth's writing and preaching during the Church Struggle. Barth preached that "Jesus was a Jew" in response to specific attempts to ignore the church's Jewish roots. In his systematic theology, however, Barth reveals that the question of Israel is not resolved that simply. Barth's affirmations that the church and synagogue continue to exist "alongside" each other, that the church needs the "contribution" of the synagogue, and that it learns from the synagogue's existence tempt us to conclude that Barth views the two religious communities as "separate but equal" entities. In fact, however, there is only "one community," the unity of which will be complete "when Israel becomes obedient to its election by being awakened through the promise of God being *fulfilled in the resurrection of Jesus Christ"* (260, emphasis mine).

A number of post-Holocaust critics have drawn attention to the anti-Jewish elements in Barth's Israel-doctrine elaborated in *CD* II:2. Barth has been accused of theological anti-Semitism,[49] and one commentator introduces a section of paragraph 34, placed alongside the work of Gerhard Kittell, with the observation that "on this topic the thinking of a Christian anti-nazi [Barth] and that of a Christian nazi [Kittell]...are not very far apart."[50] Indeed, the view of Israel elaborated in *Church Dogmatics* II:2, paragraph 34 does contain material which from our perspective appears anti-Jewish. Barth speaks in traditional Christian terms of the "obduracy" of Israel, and of the Jews as a rebellious and stiff-necked people. He evokes the traditional caricature of a lifeless Judaism when he speaks of the "dead Israel" (205) which has resulted from Jewish unbelief. Barth interprets Israel's movement "into the ghetto" as a confirmation of its election (214), and Barth makes reference to the "refractory Synagogue" (218), the "Synagogue of death" (264), and the "Synagogue 'prepared for destruction'" (227).[51] While Barth is clear that the Church must never become anti-Semitic or even "a-Semitic" (234), the strains of Christian anti-Jewish rhetoric are unmistakable in his theology.

To summarize, there is a peculiar mixture in *CD* II:2 of traditional supersessionist understandings of Israel and affirmations of its "eternal election" (204). This mixture makes Barth's Israel-doctrine, in relation to Christian theology before and since, radical and traditional at the same time. The negative, supersessionist element in Barth's Israel-doctrine is clear in what we can refer to, using Klappert's categories, as his integrationist understanding of the church-Israel relationship. According to Barth, Israel is obedient to its election--it truly becomes "Israel"--only when it has entered the Church. Barth does not explain how Israel is to enter the church and remain Israel, but he is clear that this is how the abstract "indissoluble unity" of the one community he describes is to be realized. The radical, Israel-affirming element in Barth's teaching is evident in his emphases on the continuing and eternal election of Israel, Israel's continuing role in salvation history, and Israel's appointed service within the community of the elect.[52] As we have seen, however, this role and this service, Israel's purpose and its contribution to the community, are all defined by Barth in a way which most Jews and many Christians cannot accept "after Auschwitz." Indeed, one factor that has obscured the positive dimensions of paragraph 34 is that it was published "during the Holocaust,"[53] and thus, some argue, may be read as a theological justification for the *Shoah*. Before discussing further Barth's problematic understanding of Israel as a witness to judgment, we shall examine Barth's treatment of "Israel" in *Church Dogmatics* III:3 (1950).

CD III:3. At the start of the last section we commented that Barth's theology in the *Church Dogmatics* was influenced by his experiences in Germany in the 1930s. This influence can be seen only indirectly in *CD* II:2. It is more apparent, however, in *CD* III:3 where Barth seems to have been awakened to the real history of Jewish existence by the suffering of Jews that culminated in the Holocaust. In fact, the Holocaust seems to have led Barth from a theological consideration of "Israel" to the kind of historical consideration which we argued was notably absent during the German Church Struggle. In paragraph 49 of the *Church Dogmatics,* "God the Father as Lord of His Creature," Barth once again picks up the theme "Israel." Once more Barth emphasizes the continuity between church and Israel, this time by referring to the church's God as the "King of Israel" (176ff.). This King is "continually to be rejected by Israel" (179), however, so that Israel's history is "simply a series of the predicted and inevitable judgments of this King" (179). From this oblique reference to Israel's history with God, Barth moves eventually to a prolonged consideration of "the history of the Jews" (210ff.).

Barth views this history as the most convincing indication (it is almost a "demonstration," he says) of the world-governance of God. Reiterating an earlier claim that the history of the Jews is the only convincing "natural" proof of God's existence (*CD* II:2, 209), Barth argues that this history has a "very special cogency," a cogency which is enlightening (210). Not surprisingly, Barth divides the history of the Jews into two eras--one preceding and one following Israel's visitation by its King, Jesus of Nazareth:

> After the death of Jesus there was a significant interval of some forty years--a kind of final period of grace, a last opportunity for repentance. Then the real history of the Jews began....The definitive destruction of the old form of Israel [in the defeat by the Romans in the year 70] was the negative side of the death of Jesus as a saving event...[54]

Barth does not elaborate further the connection between Jesus' death and the passing of the old form of Israel, but as we saw in our analysis of paragraph 34, the two events stand in a correlative, if not causal, relationship.[55] In pinpointing the end of Israelite and the beginning of Jewish history in the year 70, Barth shares the perspective that has been quite influential in modern Christian thought. He answers the question, "what are the Jews today?" with constant reference to what he believes the Jews became in the year 70 C.E. (or, more accurately, at the death of Jesus). But this leaves him the task of accounting for the fact of the Jews' survival these "1900 years."

Barth begins by pointing out the problematic nature of any talk about a Jewish "race." We cannot say, he argues, that the Jews share a common language, a common culture, a unified religion, or even a single history. Barth concludes from this that we must doubt whether the Jews are really a "people" at all (215). These problems do not keep Barth from seeking to discover reasons for the "mysterious persistence" of the Jews, however. In fact, they only lend more credence to arguments for what he calls the "providential significance" (215) of Jewish history. It is clear that in defining the Jews as "a people which is not a people" Barth desires to distance himself from racial anti-Semitism. Indeed, crucial to Barth's argument here is the contention that "the idea of a specifically Jewish blood is pure imagination" (213). On the other hand, Barth is quick to argue that the history of the Jews is a problem *sui generis*. Since the Jews appear as a people in world history only in a "negative" way (216), they cannot be regarded as simply one people among others.

At this point we notice a clear parallel with the unique place occupied by Israel in Barth's doctrine of election. The special history of the Jews represents "a trace of the divine world-governance" (216), and this is because Jewish identity is based in election, an election which is "still valid" (219). But Barth reminds us, as he did in *CD* II:2, that this election can prove to be a terrible burden for Israel: "It costs something to be the chosen people, and the Jews are paying the price" (220). In an attempt to illuminate the price Jews must pay for their divine favor, Barth engages in a theological/historical analysis of anti-Semitism. How can we explain, Barth asks, this strange disease from which every non-Jew appears to suffer? It is explicable "only if as strangers...the Jews are still the elect of God" (221). Clearly, Barth hopes that in explaining anti-Semitism theologically, he will also be able to offer a theological solution. The thing that annoys us about the Jews, he begins, is not that they are actually better or worse than other peoples (for they are not), but that they are a "mirror" in which we see "who and what we all are, and how bad we all are" (221). Revealing the essence of sinful humanity is part of the "price" the Jew pays for the fact that he is God's elect. For what every person is *coram Deo* is revealed in the Jew in a unique way, at the same time that it is "suppressed and concealed" in all others.

Why is this information not suppressed and concealed in the Jew? Barth does not explain, but only repeats that in the Jew is revealed "the primal revolt, the unbelief, the disobedience in which we are all engaged" (222). Barth argues, in other words, that non-Jews are annoyed with the Jew only to the extent that she serves as a mirror for non-Jewish self-recognition. This identity as a "mirror," of course, is not coincidental to Jewish existence. "Obviously," Barth says, "it is because they are this mirror that the Jews are there" (222). Divine providence has arranged this fact, nor may this "mirror" ever be taken away! Clearly, the "sign and testimony" which is given humanity in the "irritation and annoyance" of the Jew leads to anti-Semitic hatred. Ironically, Barth argues that the anti-Semite actually displays that he has encountered in the Jew a trace of the divine world-governance.

The Jew, according to Barth, is not only a mirror of human sinfulness, he is also a mirror of God's free electing grace, a grace which we all naturally resist. In the existence of the Jew, non-Jews stumble upon the fact that the divine election is a particular election, and that she has been completely overlooked in the particularity of this divine election.[56] The persistence of the Jews, without the historical and cultural supports enjoyed by other peoples, is a constant and irritating symbol of divine grace and mercy, as well as a painful reminder of the relativity of non-Jewish existence (224). It is no wonder, then, Barth concludes, that non-Jews do not appreciate "the message or those who deliver it," that they become anti-Semites, and that they "desire that the mirror should be removed" (225). Barth ends this discussion christologically, declaring that it is the Jew Jesus Christ who appears indirectly in the "desolation and persistence" of Jewish existence. This existence is a sign set up in world history as a manifestation of Christ's Kingdom. It may be misunderstood, but there it remains.

Although it is much briefer, Barth's analysis of the history of the Jews and his theological explanation of anti-Semitism in *CD* III:3 give us nearly as much to consider as his interpretation of Israel's election in

CD II:2. Once again, Barth's attempt to treat "Israel" theologically has a paradoxical character. Barth desires to meet the problem of anti-Semitism head on, as it were, approaching it from a theological perspective in the hope of discovering and undermining its insidious power. Barth sees in the curious persistence of Jewish existence an irrevocable and unique witness to divine providence. While making only oblique reference to the Nazi "Final Solution,"[57] Barth demonstrates an awareness of the destructive effects of anti-Semitism not present in his earlier writings. On the other hand, there are serious dangers inherent in Barth's attempt to make theological sense of anti-Semitism. In fact, Barth's whole project of interpreting "the history of the Jews" in *CD* III:3 has been subjected to stinging criticism. Dieter Kraft, for example, has described this section of the *Church Dogmatics* as a combination of theological reflection and "historico-theological speculation" which is "strikingly untypical" of Barth, and which ends in a diagnosis of anti-Semitism that is "extremely enigmatic."[58] Lothar Steiger accuses Barth of mixing his theology with "phenomenology," and in the process creating precisely the thing he abhored--natural theology.[59]

More disturbing is the fact that Barth's analysis of anti-Semitism in *CD* III:3 may actually provide a justification for the anti-Semitism he is trying to explain. As Alan Davies has observed, with his analysis of what it "costs" to be the chosen people of God, Barth actually incorporates anti-Semitism into salvation history.[60] Another critic has argued that in viewing the Jew as a "mirror of human sinfulness," Barth substitutes the "Jew" for the "law" in the Pauline notion of the recognition of sin in the law,[61] thus perpetuating the Christian tendency to denigrate the Jew. The most serious charge against Barth's discussion of Jewish history and anti-Semitism is articulated by Dieter Kraft: if anti-Semitism is an inevitable corollary of Jewish existence, as Barth appears to argue, then we can only wait for its next outbreak. And if the disease of anti-Semitism is ineradicable because its sources are to be found in Jewish existence itself, then,

> Woe to the Jews who have survived Auschwitz, for at some time this sickness unto death will strike them again--like the plague.Understandably even! For it is only right and fair if man shatters the mirror in which he must perceive his own "original revolt"! Must

not men hate the Jew if he hates in this Jew precisely what he abhors in himself?![62]

It may have been Barth's own recognition of these implications of his theology of Israel which led him increasingly to an appreciation and respect for the state of Israel in the 1960s. If the confrontation of mankind with the Jew whom he hates is inevitable even after the overthrow of fascism, then

> Woe to the Jew who does not then live behind the protective banner of the state of Israel, in the protection of a country which has offered evidence of its existence "today in a way so uncannily similar to the situation testified to in the Old Testament."[63]

It is important to note here an observation we made earlier: that in *CD* III:3 Barth incorporates into his analysis of the Jewish question, presumably in response to the Holocaust, a historical dimension which had been largely absent from his earlier thought. However, the results of this attempt to take Jewish history in the past and present into account are dubious at best, and potentially disastrous. In fact, Barth's discussion of anti-Semitism and Jewish history in *CD* III:3 seems to demonstrate the legitimacy of Richard Rubenstein's post-Holocaust observations about Christian notions of the Jews as a special chosen people. In *After Auschwitz*[64] Rubenstein considers the kind of Christian theology that stresses, on the one hand, an objective relationship between Jewish behavior (what Barth might call "Jewish existence") and anti-Semitism, and on the other, a "special providential relationship" between Jewish history and the will of God. According to Rubenstein, theology based on the notion of Israel as the specially elected people of God and the conviction that this people has not lost its place in salvation history leads to the "inescapable conclusion" that God willed the Nazi slaughter of six million Jews.

The theology about the Jews and the theological necessity of their suffering which Barth constructs "after Auschwitz" (*CD* III:3 appeared in 1950) seems to confirm Rubenstein's accusation that, logically at least, a Christian theology of history which is consistent leads to the conclusion that God willed the Holocaust. Although Rubenstein does not mention Barth in the context of his discussion in *After Auschwitz*, his comments clearly implicate Barth's theology. Barth's emphases on the irrevocable election of Israel, Israel's service as a "witness to judgment" in salvation history, the Jew as a mirror of human sinfulness which irritates and threatens the non-Jew, and Jewish history as a "trace of the divine world-governance" collectively demonstrate Christian theology's tendency to, in Rubenstein's words, regard Jews in "mythical, magic and theological categories." These emphases in Barth's theology of Israel also demonstrate the potential dangers for Jews inherent in a Christian theology of Israel which views Jews as as a perpetually chosen people. We shall return to this matter in the final chapter.

Before moving on, we must point out two more problematical elements in Barth's Israel-doctrine as it has been presented up to this point. First, there is completely absent in Barth's writings, even those that are chronologically post-Holocaust, any discussion of anti-Semitism in its exclusively Christian dimensions.[65] Barth reminds his readers at many points that anti-Semitism is anti-Christian, but Barth does not devote serious attention to the problem of anti-Judaism nourished by the Christian tradition. One can only wonder why Barth, with his intimate personal knowledge of how the Christian church (in the "German Christians," e.g.) and Christian theology (in Emmanuel Hirsch, e.g.)[66] could be infected by anti-Judaism, does not discuss this problem at length in the *Church Dogmatics.*

Second, it is important to realize that in many ways Barth's discussion of the Jew in *CD* III:3 has a highly fictional character. Barth's theology, especially in the *Church Dogmatics,* is often appreciated for its impressive literary qualities. In this case, however, Barth's ability to unfold a theological narrative before the reader obscures some theological problems. Just as Barth's attempt to bring "Israel" into the system of his doctrine of election (*CD* II:2) is abstract and formal, Barth's attempt in *CD* III:3 to explain the history of the Jews and the persistence of anti-Semitism is dependent on a fictionalized "Jewish history" and a mythicized "Jew." Barth's "Jewish history" is the fate of the Jewish people seen from the perspective of their supposed function in salvation history following the rejection of Jesus. Barth's "Jew" is a model of human depravity, of the person who is chosen and called by God, but refuses to respond. Barth's myths of "Jews" and "Jewish history" have little connection with any actual Jewish persons, except that where they are embraced, the myths Barth helps perpetuate can have murderous consequences for Jewish life. As in *CD* II:2, Barth has developed a formal system which appears to be pure theology. But once again the mythical elements in Barth's system enhance the possibility that it will have a fateful relationship with the history in which it is enmeshed.

Paradoxically, while intending to oppose the Nazi myth of "Jewish blood," Barth has created an alternative myth of "Jewish history," a myth determined not by racial theories, but by the salvation-historical event of the Jew's rejection of Jesus. This alternative myth is based on a powerful fiction much older than Barth's theology--that of the "Eternal" or "Wandering" Jew. It is indeed ironic and sad that the theological myths Barth transmits might serve as justifications for a new group of Christians or pseudo-Christians who embrace the Nazi myth and who are bent on the annihilation of the Jewish people.[67]

Why is Barth compelled to recreate this mythic interpretation of Jewish history with its fictionalized "Jew"? In a sense, Barth is only recapitulating elements of the patristic understanding of Israel as a "witness-people"--an understanding to which he was deeply indebted, as we shall see. It is also the case, however, that Barth, like many Christian theologians before and after him, did not enjoy the kind of personal contacts which would have allowed him to gain a knowledge of and sympathy for actual, living Jews. Although Barth's writings and letters reveal a cursory acquaintance with and interest in Jewish theology, Barth lacked the opportunities for personal encounter and dialogue with living Judaism which might have had a positive influence on his doctrine of Israel.[68] Not only was Barth without this important contact with living Judaism, but late in his life he admitted that his personal attitude toward Jews could have had a "retrogressive effect" on his understanding of Israel:

> ...In personal encounters with living Jews (even Jewish Christians) I have always, so long as I can remember, had to suppress a totally irrational aversion, naturally suppressing it at once on the basis of all my presuppositions, and concealing it totally in my statements...[69]

Given what we have observed up to this point about Barth's doctrine of Israel, we might doubt whether in fact this "totally irrational aversion" was really concealed in Barth's statements. In fact, it is tempting to see in this admission an explanation for Barth's discussion of the "original and unconquerable aversion" (222) toward the Jews which he perceives at the root of anti-Semitism. In analyzing this "aversion," is Barth actually working out the sources of his own Jew-hatred, and the aversion of many Christians like him? We are not interested in psychologizing the author of the *Church Dogmatics,* and yet it would be difficult to gainsay Barth's own suggestion that his aversion to living Jews influenced his doctrine of Israel.

CD IV:3, 2. Barth once again takes up the theme "Israel"[70] in *CD* IV:3, second half, this time in the context of paragraph 72, "The Holy Spirit and the Sending of the Christian Community." Barth gives a "separate treatment" (2+ pages of fine print) to the church's missionary activity in relation to Jews. There is a dilemma here which Barth clearly perceives: Given the fact that Israel's appointed end is to enter the church, and the fact that the gospel was originally proclaimed first to Israel, "how can it [the gospel] fail to be addressed to Israel, and indeed to Israel first, in the ages which follow?" (876). On the other hand, the unique relationship between the two communities means that the church's witness to Israel will be "highly singular," that is, different from the witness it gives to non-believing Gentiles and adherents of non-Christian religions. Barth's solution is quite radical, especially for its time:

> In relation to the Synagogue, there can be no real question of "mission" or of bringing the gospel. It is thus unfortunate to speak of Jewish missions. The Jew who is conscious of his Judaism and takes it seriously can only think that he is misunderstood and insulted when he hears this term. And the community has to see that materially he is right. Mission is not the witness which it owes to Israel.[71]

In elaborating on this statement, Barth points out that in relation to the synagogue, Christians do not preach the "true faith" in place of a false one. Jesus was born of Jewish flesh and blood, and "salvation is of the Jews" (Jn. 4:22). The church must assume the election and calling of Israel, since it exists only by being "engrafted" into it. Barth asks the church, then, on what basis it will presume to teach Jews: "What have we to teach him [the Jew] that he does not already know, that we have not rather to learn from him?" (877).

Lest we think, however, that Barth has abandoned his conviction that Israel becomes "Israel" only when it is obedient to its election and reaches its *telos* in the church, Barth brings us back to the "shattering fact" that Israel has denied its election and calling. The synagogue, therefore, "hastens toward a future that is empty," and the Jew represents a picture of existence which is "dreadfully empty of grace and blessing" (877). Since these Jews have repudiated the gospel *a priori* and in principle, there is need neither of "conversations" between Christians and Jews, nor of work for Jewish conversions, which are "highly extraordinary" in any case. What, then, is the church's "witness" to the Jewish people? In a word, the church must follow the advice of Paul who in his epistle to the Romans charges Christians to make the synagogue "jealous." The church has by and large failed to do this in the past, Barth says. It has not lived authentically "before the Jews," and therefore, "it still owes everything to those to whom it is indebted for everything" (878). Barth does not fully explicate his statement that the church has failed to live authentically before the Jews, although surely he is thinking of the Holocaust and the history of Christian anti-Judaism. Barth does tell us, however, how he believes the church should now go about making Israel jealous:

> It must make dear and desirable and illuminating to it Him whom it has rejected...attesting the manifested King of Israel and Saviour of the world...The Church must live with the Synagogue, not, as fools say in their hearts, as with another religion or confession, but as the root from which it has itself sprung.[72]

We see in this section of the *Church Dogmatics* another example of what we shall call Barth's "radical traditionalism." Barth's radicalism is evident in the fact that he is one of the first Christian theologians to call for the abandonment of Jewish missions in the post-Holocaust religious environment.[73] And yet his alternative to Jewish missions-- "making Israel jealous"--is a traditional response based on the New Testament. Although Barth views the problem of mission from the perspective of the unique theological relationship between Israel and the church, he has not relinquished his conviction that Israel must rise to life in the church. In fact, it is because the Jews, who are unaware of their unity with the church, "will not accept what they already are" (*CD*

IV:1, 671), that the church must witness to Israel's "own proper reality and truth" in an attempt to arouse its jealousy.

Barth's treatment of Jewish mission in *CD* IV:3, 2 demonstrates that toward the end of his life, the radical side of Barth's understanding of the church's relationship to Israel found increasing prominence. However, Barth never abandoned or repudiated the fundamental aspects of his doctrine of Israel developed in *Church Dogmatics* II:2 and III:3. We shall turn in the following sections to a consideration of some of Barth's other theological statements on Israel, a survey of Barth's critics. An overall analysis of Barth's "theology of Israel" will be undertaken in chapter five.

D. Other Statements on Israel

"The Jewish Problem and the Christian Answer". A 1949 radio address in which Barth applied his theology of Israel to the recurrent problem of anti-Semitism carried the title "The Jewish Problem and the Christian Answer." This address was given during the period Barth was working on volume III:3 of the *Church Dogmatics*,[74] and many of the themes encountered here are developed in *CD* III:3 as well. In "The Jewish Problem and the Christian Answer" Barth once again condemns anti-Semitism as anti-Christian, adding that it represents a "breakdown of Christian values." He strikes new chords, however, when he speaks of brotherly cooperation between Christians and Jews, and of welcoming the Jewish bid for independence in Palestine (195). Barth also declares that the commandment to "love thy neighbor" must be applied in relationships with Jews. This general admonition to care for and respect Jews is a new theme in Barth's treatment of Israel, which previously tended to stress the particular character of the Jewish people, not their entitlement to universal human respect. Given the connection we have observed between Barth's theology and potential justifications for Jewish suffering, this theme is a welcome one. But, perhaps unfortunately, Barth believes the admonition to love the Jew does not "do justice" to the Jewish problem. Barth is convinced, in fact, that a Christian answer to this problem must take into account several theological considerations.

A "decisive Christian answer" to the Jewish problem must first consider the surprising fact that the Jewish race is still in existence. The

Jews should really no longer have existed after the Fall of Jerusalem in the year 70 C.E., says Barth, and the Christian explanation for the Jews' "surprising position of historical permanence" must be found in salvation history. Jewish persistence is a "mystery of faith...a sign of what the one true God has done once for us all, once and for all in this one Jewish person [Jesus Christ]" (197). The persistence of the Jews in history, in other words, has a christological basis that makes Jewish and Christian existence forever interdependent. Jewish persistence after the crucifixion of Christ and the fall of Jerusalem is a sign of God's continued world-governance and mercy, though to be sure the Jews are "reluctant witnesses." Second, argues Barth, the anti-Semitism which "seems to be just as inexplicable as the very existence and character of the Jews" (198) can only be accounted for if we understand the Jews as "mirrors" which reflect human misery, evil and insecurity. We dislike the Jew and dislike being told that the Jews as a whole are a chosen people, but "in the 'lost-ness' and in the persistence of the Jews that Other One looks down on us" (200). Although our natural response is to turn the "mirror" to the wall, or even to smash it, this does not change what it reveals about us. Yet, ironically according to Barth, this folly of smashing the "mirror" may represent "the only bit of sense in all the nonsense of Antisemitism" (199).

Finally, Barth reaffirms that the Jews are "to this very day the chosen people of God in the same sense as they have been so from the beginning..." (200). Christians, on the other hand, have the promise of God only insofar as they are branches engrafted into the Jewish tree. Not surprisingly, Barth affirms that the solidarity between the Jewish and Christian communities is based in Jesus Christ, who at the same time represents the barrier between them. The Jews, who do not acknowledge the "one Jew," are a "defiant" people, and this defiance is closely related to the anti-Semitism from which they suffer.

Barth actually says very little here that we have not encountered already in our discussion of his Israel doctrine in the *Church Dogmatics*. The address does, however, condense and focus the themes which characterize Barth's theology of Israel after *Der Römerbrief*: 1. Christians are "one with the Jews," but this unity is not realized or accepted by Israel; 2. Jewish existence is a continuing sign of divine election and the sustaining power of divine grace; the Jews, however, still do not accept the very fact which their existence portrays--that they can live only by God's grace; 3. Anti-Semitism requires a theological explanation, which Barth finds in the concept of the Jew as a "mirror" of God's freedom in election, and of the basic sinfulness of human existence. As alluded to above, Barth does not believe that a simple ethical response can constitute an appropriate Christian answer to the "Jewish problem." At the end of "The Jewish Problem and the Christian Answer," Barth reaffirms this conviction:

> We can all admit the truth of the fine words on this subject which we heard at the beginning. It is doubtful, however, whether they are specifically Christian, whether they give to the Jews the honor due to them, and whether they have the power to accomplish anything practical in the matter of the Jewish problem. This problem opens a gulf which is too wide to be bridged by mere human reason and ethics.[75]

We cannot question Barth's intentions in dismissing what he calls "human reason and ethics" as solutions to the Jewish problem. As we have seen, however, Barth's "Christian answer" has its own flaws, and we could easily turn Barth's criticism upon him and ask if his "answer" can really accomplish anything practical in allaying anti-Semitism (or even Christian anti-Judaism). In assessing Barth's Israel-doctrine as a whole, close attention will have to be paid to the implications of his choice of a theological rather than an ethical solution to the "Jewish problem."

Israel and the "Later Barth". The last years of Barth's life saw some important changes, or at least shifts in emphasis, in his theology. Perhaps not surprisingly, there is also evidence of some change in his understanding of "Israel" during this period. Responding to F.-W. Marquardt's critical analysis of his theology of Israel in *Die Entdeckung des Judentums für die Christliche Theologie: Israel im Denkens Karl Barths,* Barth refers proudly to the same "beginnings of improvement" alluded to by Marquardt, and notes some further indications in this direction.[76] In a letter to Marquardt written in 1967, Barth mentions specifically three items which he believes attest to his continuing development: a text he prepared in association with the 1954 meeting of the World Council of Churches, his response to Vatican II's declaration on "Non-Christian Religions" in his book *Ad Limina*

Apostolorum, and his contribution to a panel discussion in Chicago in
1962.[77]

The text Barth refers to in connection with the Evanston meeting
of the World Council of Churches in 1954 was entitled "The Hope of
Israel," a document Barth intended as a supplement to the WCC
document "Christ and the Hope of the World." Desiring to encourage
the authors of the main text to integrate the perspective of Israel's hope,
Barth wrote:

> We have to say first of the people which bases its hope on the same
> object, which is also the ground of our hope, namely in the coming
> Messiah...it [this hope] is based namely in the promises of God, which
> he has given his chosen people. If it can be claimed by a community at
> all that it lives by hope, then this is to be said precisely and first of
> Judaism. Israel is the people of hope.[78]

Barth also refers in his letter to Marquardt to his book *A d
Limina Apostolorum,* which appeared in 1967, the year before Barth's
death.[79] In 1965 Barth had been invited by the Secretariat for Christian
Unity in Rome to attend the last two sessions of the Second Vatican
Council as an "observer." Although illness prevented him from doing
so, Barth arranged to visit Rome after the Council had ended, in
September of 1966. Barth took this visit very seriously, devoting
himself to "serious study" of the sixteen Latin texts produced by
Vatican II, and working out lists of "clarifying" and "critical" questions
for his hosts. Those questions which bear on the Christian
understanding of Israel (and the ones he mentions in his letter to
Marquardt) were directed to the "Declaration on the Relationship of the
Church to Non-Christian Religions" ("Nostra aetate"). Barth asked:

> 6. On what grounds does the Declaration (4, 1ff) speak of the
> past and present history of Israel in the same breath with Hinduism,
> Buddhism and Islam as a "non-Christian religion," while
>   a) the Old Testament does not present a religion at all but the
> original form of the one revelation of God
>   b) and in the existence of later and contemporary Judaism
> (believing or unbelieving) we have the sole natural (i. e., in terms of
> world history) proof of God?
>   7. Would it not be more appropriate, in view of the anti-
> Semitism of the ancient, the medieval, and to a large degree the modern
> church, to set forth an explicit confession of guilt here, rather than in
> respect to the separated brethren?[80]

Barth's questions are illuminating not only for the light they shed on the "Declaration" and Catholic theology in general,[81] but for the picture they provide of Barth's developing understanding of the church-Israel relationship just before he died. In question 7, there is evidence of Barth's awakening awareness of the church's historic (and modern) anti-Semitism, an awareness which is almost completely lacking in his earlier theology. In question 6, we see a concern with the unique significance of Israel for Christianity which is typical of Barth's earlier theology. The fact that Barth can emphasize a point that was fundamental for his own theology as early as the 1930s while taking to task the one document recognized as a turning point for relations between Jews and Roman Catholics is testimony to the progressive side of Barth's Israel-doctrine.[82]

Barth's final reference in his letter to Marquardt is to a panel discussion held in Chicago a few years before his trip to Rome. Barth participated in this discussion with, among others, the American Rabbi Jacob Petuchowski. Their topic was the possibility of Jewish-Christian dialogue. On that occasion, Barth affirmed that

> there is an open way for discussion between Jewish theologians and Christian theologians like me. And indeed we have a real, broad plane for discussion, for we read the same Torah, the same Prophets, and the same Writings.[83]

Again, the content of Barth's statement does not reveal any radical departures from his earlier thought. But the fact that this statement functioned as an overture to dialogue with Jews reveals an attempt on Barth's part to overcome the personal aversion to and isolation from living Jews described earlier.

In some of Barth's published letters from the last years of his life we encounter further indications of development in his understanding of "Israel." In a letter to a Swiss pastor in 1961, for example, Barth concluded by affirming that his "whole concern is...that Israel as Israel should finally be taken seriously as the starting point of every discussion of what Israel should or should not do."[84] It is difficult to determine exactly what Barth means by "Israel" in this context, but this statement *seems* to be evidence that Barth has acquired a new appreciation of the importance of Jewish self-understanding for Christian theology. If this is so, it is a significant transformation, since F.-W. Marquardt in particular has pointed to the insensitivity to "Jewish self-understanding" in Barth's theology. In response to the Israel-doctrine elaborated in the *Church Dogmatics*, Marquardt asks "whether election in Christ must really lead to such a silence in the face of the election-self-understanding of Judaism."[85] Jewish existence and Jewish self-consciousness and theological self-interpretation go together, argues Marquardt, and in Barth's theology Jewish self-understanding is either missing entirely or is treated as a *quantite negligeable*.[86]

Michael Wyschogrod has directed a similar criticism at Barth's theology. Wyschogrod sees in Barth an unwillingness to recognize Israel's faithfulness in the Old Testament, as well as Judaism's obedience in its refusal to discard its biblical commandments. "Reading Barth," Wyschogrod says, "one would gain the impression that there is nothing but faithfulness on God's part and unfaithfulness on Israel's." Wyschogrod stresses that whatever Israel's problems with its God may be, "the quarrel is a family one, between Israel and its God...it is not for gentiles to see the sins of Israel."[87] Alan T. Davies is even more critical of Barth at this point, accusing him of a "religious totalitarianism in which Jews are not permitted to know anything concerning their own identity except what they are taught at the gates of the church."[88] In the letter referred to above, and in his increased interest in dialogue with Jewish theologians toward the end of his life, we see the beginnings of Barth's response to this type of criticism.

Another sign of change may be found in a letter to Louis Glatt written in 1967, in which Barth responds to Glatt's question about the guilt of men (*sic*) in the crucifixion of Jesus. Barth takes this question very seriously, admitting that its answer has often led to problems, "especially in the relationship between Christians and Jews."[89] While Barth argues that human guilt cannot be removed from the event of the crucifixion, he does qualify the notion, prominent in his earlier theology,[90] that the Jews "delivered Jesus up to be crucified":

> As Jesus did his work for men, the guilt of the Jews and also of the Gentiles (in the form of Pilate and his people), to whom the Jews delivered Jesus, is brought to light.[91]

While there is still no recognition here of the murderous effect which the "deicide charge" has had on Jewish life over the last two millennia, Barth's statement appears to soften the charge of Israel's historical guilt in Jesus' crucifixion.

Finally, in the last years of his life, Barth began to recognize in the state of Israel a new sign of God's presence in Jewish history. There is evidence in the later volumes of *Church Dogmatics* and elsewhere[92] that Barth was particularly impressed by the establishment of Israel against great historical odds. In 1949, for example, Barth referred to the "surprising position of historical permanence" achieved by the Jewish nation in Palestine.[93] But Barth became particularly interested in the fate of this nation in the 1960s, especially after the Six Day War in June of 1967. In July, Barth announced that Switzerland was "unequivocally for Israel."[94] Reflecting on Israel's stunning victory, Barth was cautious, but enthusiastic:

> Of course the foundation of the state of Israel [is] not to be seen as an analogy to the conquest under Joshua and thus as a sign that God cannot let his people be defeated. Yet we can read in the newspapers: "God keeps his promise."[95]

Concerning a declaration of the Christian Peace Conference which condemned Israel following the Six-Day War, Barth wrote that it was a "scandal," and considered signing a counter-declaration.[96]

It is difficult to know what effect the events of the last two decades in the Middle East would have had on Barth's willingness to support Israel and its right to secure itself, had he lived. But some have seen in the development of Barth's late theology the logic of Christian Zionism. Dieter Kraft, in particular, believes Barth's support for Israel found its source in a peculiar "theological philosemitism"[97] which arose late in his life as a reaction to the persistent reality of anti-Semitism and its culmination in the Holocaust. All this, Kraft suggests, added to Barth's recognition of the inevitable consequences of his interpretation of the Jew as a mirror of human depravity, led logically to the kind of Christian Zionism which feels compelled to support the state of Israel at all costs. Kraft's argument is somewhat persuasive, since there *is* evidence for Barth's budding Zionism in statements like the following from 1950:

> In the shortest possible time it [Israel] has produced the most striking results, culturally, diplomatically, and against all expectation militarily. It seems to have behind it--and we could not say this of all states--an enthusiastic and self-sacrificing youth. Not from any point of view can we ignore or make light of the existence of this state...the remarkable representative remnant of Israel.[98]

Statements like this, which Kraft describes as "almost euphoric," can be compared to Jewish Zionist claims of the same period, and seem unmistakably to ascribe a religious dimension to the state of Israel.[99] The Zionist interpretation of the late Barth also finds strong support in his enthusiastic responses to the Six-Day War, mentioned above.

We began our discussion of Barth's theology of Israel with evidence of his theological anti-Semitism, and have concluded with what appears to be evidence for a Barthian "philosemitism" and "Zionism." Before attempting to sort out these conflicting interpretations of Barth's Israel-doctrine in chapter five, we shall summarize some of the more prominent critical responses to "Barth on Israel."

III. BARTH AND HIS CRITICS

Only two book-length studies of Barth's Israel-doctrine have been published. Both appeared in Germany, and neither has been translated. In 1967, Friedrich-Wilhelm Marquardt, a former student of Barth, published *Die Entdeckung des Judentums für die Christliche Theologie: Israel im Denken Karl Barths*. From the title it is clear that Marquardt intended to pay tribute to Barth's "discovery" (*Entdeckung*) of Judaism (=Israel?) for Christian theology. Marquardt is quite critical of his teacher, however. In part one, for instance, "The Context of the Barthian Israel-Theology," Marquardt discusses Jewish theological self-representation as a dimension of Christian theologies of Israel and, as we have mentioned, finds Barth wanting. In part two, Marquardt is concerned with Barth's discussion of Israel in the *Church Dogmatics*. Marquardt concludes with an analysis of "the rejection of Israel" in Barth's theology, arguing that Barth's understanding of fulfillment in Jesus Christ ends in the historical removal of important elements of Israel's history, and even the people of Israel itself.[100]

In Bertold Klappert's book *Israel und die Kirche: Erwägungen zur Israellehre Karl Barths* (1980) the author considers Barth's letters and lesser-known texts, as well as his theology of Israel developed in the *Church Dogmatics*. Klappert examines Barth's Israel-doctrine in the context of a typology he uses for describing interpretations of the theological relationship between Israel and the church. He emphasizes that Barth's Israel-doctrine cannot be properly appreciated without a knowledge of traditional Christian models for understanding Israel, especially the negative models of substitution and integration. In fact, Klappert uses aspects of Barth's Israel-doctrine to illuminate each of the five negative models, with the exception of the subsumation model, where Barth's approach serves as a positive point of contrast.[101] While Klappert argues that Barth is dependent on the substitution and illustration models in his interpretation of Romans 9-11 in *Church Dogmatics* II:2,[102] Klappert believes Barth's connection with the Christian tradition lies primarily in his use of the integration model. According to Klappert, Barth sees the relationship of Israel and church in terms of ecclesiological integration, expressed in his conviction that the synagogue must "rise to life" in the church. In Barth's integration model, the integration point of church and synagogue is precisely in the church, and Israel's future is envisioned only in terms of church-existence. An example of Barth's use of the integration model is his interpretation of Paul's statement in Romans that "all Israel" will be saved:

> All Israel is the community which is elected by God in and with Jesus Christ from the Jews and from the Gentiles, the whole church....[103]

Klappert challenges Barth's entire exegesis of Romans 9-11 on the basis of a reevaluation of Paul's original meaning, and argues that the future of Israel in Romans is not describable in terms of integration into the church.[104] What Klappert finds ironic, however, is the fact that Barth's emphasis on ecclesiological integration runs counter to his own "fundamental systematic orientation" in the christological participation or dependence model.[105] According to this model, the church is *dependent* on the election of Israel confirmed in Jesus Christ, and the Gentile "nations" are called forth to *participate* in Israel's election and promissory history. Klappert thinks Barth's dependence on these models is expressed most succinctly in his statement that "Jesus Christ is the crucified Messiah of Israel...Jesus Christ is the risen Lord of the Church...He is, however, precisely as the risen Lord of the church also the revealed Messiah of Israel...."[106] Klappert believes this careful statement reveals Barth's intention of avoiding a traditional supersessionist understanding of the church-Israel relationship.

Klappert, then, observes a serious tension at the heart of Barth's doctrine of Israel. On the one hand, Barth is convinced that the church's calling and election are completely and permanently dependent on the original calling and election of Israel--on the original covenant which was fulfilled in Jesus Christ (christological dependence). On the other hand, at critical points in his doctrine of Israel Barth can see the essence and future of the synagogue only in terms of the church. For Barth, then, even though Israel is permanently elect, it has no positive significance or future outside the church, which is its end and goal (ecclesiological integration). Barth's problematic doctrine of Israel as a "witness to judgment"[107] is related to this dependence on what Klappert calls the integration model. Klappert acknowledges that this notion of Israel as a witness to judgment implicates Barth's theology in the perpetuation of Christian anti-Judaism, and diminishes the prospects for its relevance after Auschwitz. And although Klappert believes Barth's Israel-doctrine should be allowed a voice in the contemporary discussion of Israel's significance for Christian theology, he points out that many of Barth's statements about Israel and its suffering have to be revised in the present situation, laden as it is with consciousness of the Holocaust.

Klappert argues that while it is vexing for the interpreter, this tension at the center of Barth's approach to Israel may help explain other "strange and in themselves contradictory facts," such as Barth's affirmation of and participation in dialogue with Jews, while he publicly expressed skepticism about the efficacy of such dialogue.[108] Ultimately, however, the "tension" in Barth's thought described by Klappert remains a provocative puzzle.

Two recent German responses to Barth's theology of Israel are those of Lothar Steiger and Dieter Kraft. In "Die Theologie vor der 'Judenfrage'--Karl Barth als Beispiel,"[109] Steiger directs his critical focus at Barth's handling of the "Jewish question" as it confronted the church in the 30s. Steiger recognizes that Barth "saw farthest theologically" during this time, but takes Barth's theology of crisis to task for being "belated." Steiger argues that since the theology of crisis (with Barth and Friedrich Gogarten as its main exponents) expressed the crisis of inter-war Europe primarily in theological terms, it was ill-equipped for responding to the "national crisis" and the related Jewish question (89f.). Steiger argues passionately that Barth owed Germans "a discussion with our national destiny" during the Weimar period (91). While Barth's church-political opposition to the German Christians was necessary, it led the Confessing Church to focus on Jewish-Christians, and the Jews were ignored. Steiger notes Barth's difficulties in speaking directly to the "Jewish question" from the pulpit, and stresses that, in the end, the Confessing Church was not even able to protect Jewish Christians. He concludes that post-Holocaust theology must learn from Barth's career, which is a testimony to the disastrous results which a politically "belated theology" may have vis-a-vis "the Jews."

Dieter Kraft, in his article "Israel in der Theologie Karl Barths,"[110] discusses the entire range of Barth's statements on Israel from *Der Römerbrief* to the later volumes of the *Church Dogmatics*. Kraft, an East German at the time the article was written in 1982, comes to this study of Barth's Israel-doctrine in response to recent events in the Middle East, in particular "the genocide of the Palestinian people initiated through the ruling group in Israel and the planned liquidation of the PLO" (59). Kraft is especially concerned with the fact that since 1967 many Christians have affirmed Jewish Zionist political ambitions and displayed an "emphatic philosemitism" which can have the effect of justifying attacks on Palestinians. Kraft argues, however, that this "philosemitism" actually shares the ideological premises of anti-Semitism. In its "enigmatic anthropologizing" and opposition of Jew-love and Jew-hatred as decisive alternatives, it fails to demythologize the Jewish question, but rather keeps it alive (60). For Kraft it is not surprising that Barth, given his association with the church's response to the Jewish question during the Third Reich, is "straightaway made the crown witness of a theological philosemitism" (60). What is surprising, according to Kraft, is that Barth's theology really does supply arguments for such a philosemitism.

Kraft subjects Barth's Israel-doctrine to extensive analysis, and concludes that Barth was pushed into a theological philosemitism by the force of his own analysis of anti-Semitism in the *Church Dogmatics*.

For if it is true, as Barth argues in *CD* III:3, that anti-Semitism is an inevitable reaction to Jewish existence which must break out again and again as the non-Jew encounters the "mirror" of his own concealed sinfulness and rebellion, one who does not desire the destruction of the Jews appears compelled to embrace political Zionism. According to Kraft, the Zionist leanings in Barth's later theology should not be construed as coincidental, but as the result of Barth's own "historico-theologically determined metaphysic" (71). Interestingly, the connection Kraft sees between Zionist ideology and belief in the inevitability of anti-Semitism is explicit in the work of some early Jewish Zionist thinkers.[111] Furthermore, Kraft claims that, ironically, "a certain justification of anti-Semitism develops...from Barth's theological philosemitism" (72). Kraft believes that the uncovering of philosemitism as the "friendly double" of anti-Semitism, and the radical rejection of "Zionism which this philosemitism promotes," are the tasks of contemporary theology which Barth's doctrine of Israel indirectly illuminates. While Kraft tends to obscure the moral distinction between anti-Semitism and philosemitism by stressing some ideological and practical similarities, his discussion of Barth's alleged compensatory Christian Zionism is provocative and will be considered again in the final chapter.

Perhaps surprisingly, Barth's theology of Israel has merited considerable attention in the English-speaking world, with most of this attention coming from the United States. The first response seems to have come in 1952 when Maria F. Sulzbach published an article entitled "Karl Barth and the Jews."[112] Sulzbach was clearly impressed with Barth's teaching on Israel:

> In our time a new Christian doctrine of the Jews has been presented which, if it is eventually accepted by the Christian world to whom it is addressed, should provide a tremendous setback to anti-Semitism at its very roots.[113]

Of Barth's *Church Dogmatics* Sulzbach writes that as far as the Christian concept of the Jew is concerned, it is "one of the most important books of the twentieth century" (586). Barth's distinctive contribution to the modern discussion of the Jew, according to Sulzbach, is his understanding of the continuing relevance of Israel's mission, along with a disavowal of a supersessionistic understanding of the Israel-church relationship. Sulzbach believes Barth's primary significance lies in his teaching that Israel is *still* the chosen people.

Sulzbach's is perhaps the most positive assessment of Barth's teaching on this subject to appear in English. Yet her conclusions are arrived at through a selective and sometimes misleading presentation of Barth's theology.[114] Even more puzzling, however, is Sulzbach's discussion of the traditional Christian view of the Jews as a witness-people. Sulzbach juxtaposes this understanding of the Jewish people with Barth's in order to show how his theology overcomes it. In doing so, however, she ignores the striking parallels between this patristic understanding of Israel and Barth's own.[115] We will elaborate some of these parallels in chapter five.

In 1969 Alan T. Davies came to rather less positive conclusions concerning Barth and Israel in his *Anti-Semitism and the Christian Mind*.[116] Like Sulzbach, Davies affirms that "at a critical moment" Barth's theology stepped into a breach created by traditional theology's understanding of Israel. But Davies' assessment of Barth's contribution to a Christian understanding of the Jews is much different. Davies even questions the originality of Barth's theology of Israel, seeing an important forerunner to Barth in the Catholic theologian Erik Peterson and other "Catholic radicals."[117] Like these Catholic thinkers, Barth rediscovered Romans 9-11 as a "catalyst for modern theology" (114), but unlike them, he works from a christological base which is clearest in his interpretation of election. Davies analyzes Barth's theology of Israel in *CD* II:2, stressing the negative implications of Barth's notion that the Jews are a living witness to divine judgment. Davies points out, however, that Barth succeeds in retaining the Jews in salvation history, and even makes them a part of the Christian kerygma (118). But Davies is especially critical of what he calls Barth's "dogmatic biblicism":

> Barth begins by using Romans 9-11 kerygmatically. This means that his doctrine is subject to the limitation inherent in Paul's treatment of the topic in the context of the first century, notably the exaggerated concern of the apostle with the mystery of Jewish disbelief.[118]

Here, Davies argues, Barth repeats the mistake of his Catholic counterparts who absolutize the Pauline vision of Judaism, and goes even further by transforming the problem of Jewish unbelief into the notion of the Jew as a living mirror of judgment. Barth's Protestant imitators, observes Davies, share this dependence on Romans 9-11.[119]

Davies also accuses Barth of attempting to construct a Christian theology of Israel simply for the sake of systematic "symmetry" (120). Combined with Barth's objectifying of Jews "without any apparent reference to--or knowledge of--real flesh-and-blood Jews or real Jewish faith and religious self-understanding" (190), and the religious totalitarianism" resulting from his christological focus, this places Barth's doctrine of Israel "halfway back in the Middle Ages" (120). Barth "unwittingly misrepresents Judaism," Davies charges, to heighten the contrast with Christianity. The result is that Judaism in Barth's theology is confined to a "theological ghetto" (122). Davies also calls attention to distinct "patristic echoes" in Barth's theology of Israel. Among these are an Augustinian view of the Jews as reluctant witnesses to the truth of Christianity, and a predisposition to argue from history while viewing Jewish survival in terms of divine providence. Davies concludes that although one would like to accept Sulzbach's claim that Barth's theology provides a counter to anti-Semitism, the fact is that Barth only incorporates anti-Semitism into salvation history, making it the other side of Jewish election (124). Davies invokes Hannah Arendt's term "eternal Antisemitism" to describe this process (125). In stark contrast to Sulzbach and others, Davies concludes that Barth's doctrine of the Jews is actually the least satisfactory aspect of his systematic theology.

As Davies and others recognize, Barth's theology of Israel has been terribly influential in Protestant theology.[120] But Barth's Israel-doctrine has also exercised a significant influence on Catholic theology. Philip J. Rosato has identified the "unique and continuing role of the Jews" as one of three Barthian themes which has found a home in contemporary Catholic theology. Rosato himself praises Barth's courageous moral behavior toward Jews, and the "edifying coherence" of his "Judeo-Christian theology."[121]

Barth has also evoked careful response from Jewish theologians. In *Contemporary Christologies: A Jewish Response*,[122] Eugene B. Borowitz treats Barth's theology along with those of several other Christian theologians. Overall, Borowitz considers Barth's thought "absolutistic," traditional, and absent of any common ground on which to engage non-Christians (35). He does not embark on an in-depth analysis of Barth's doctrine of Israel, but on the general question of Christology's relation to anti-Semitism Borowitz treats Barth's theology of the Jews in more depth. According to Borowitz, Barth's understanding of Israel is "dialectical." By affirming that the Jews remain God's chosen people, Barth "consciously negates the theological roots of anti-Semitism" (177). On the other hand, Barth must be called "prejudiced against Jews":

> He does not care what, in fact, is the religious reality of life in the Synagogue or what Jewish practice might say about God's present relations with Jews. Barth's "system" itself assigns Israel a role in history....Here Ruether's association of Christology with anti-Semitism holds true on a theoretical level.[123]

The most positive Jewish response to Barth has come from Michael Wyschogrod, whose interest in Barth's theology has led some to regard him as a "Jewish Barthian."[124] In his writing on Barth, Wyschogrod has echoed Borowitz's reaction to the "dialectical" nature of Barth's theology of Israel. On the positive side, Wyschogrod sees in Barth a generally favorable view of Israel, and is also attracted by the Scriptural orientation which leads Barth toward Israel in a special way: "because he [Barth] is so biblical he is...a member of the family whom Israel cannot ignore."[125] Wyschogrod believes that Barth's theology is founded on an obedient listening to the Word of God and a refusal to supplant this with human theorizing, and these facts provide a point of contact with the Jewish theologian. Wyschogrod recognizes that the Jewish people and Judaism play an important role in Barth's theology, but what is decisive about Barth, he concludes, is his insight into the status of the Jewish people after the decisive event of their rejection of the Messiahship of Jesus of Nazareth."[126] Barth is perfectly clear about the election of the Jewish people and this, Wyschogrod argues, sets him apart from other Christian theologians.

On the other hand, Wyschogrod is quick to add that Barth has a penchant for viewing Israel only in terms of disobedience, and never in terms of faithfulness. While Barth's tendency to ignore Israel's obedience troubles Wyschogrod, he also admits being positively influenced by Barth's keen recognition of Israel's sinfulness.[127] Wyschogrod is aware of an "anti-Semitism in Barth," however. This expresses itself both theologically, as Barth transmits the anti-Semitism which is part and parcel of the Christian tradition, and personally, in the "aversion" to Jews which Barth himself admits.[128] Wyschogrod's conclusion is that Barth's position with regard to the Jews is "ambivalent":

> To see Barth struggling toward the sign that is Israel, to see him fighting against the Gentile nature that demands antipathy to the people of election, to see this nature yield to the Word of God and to Barth's love for that Jew whom he loves above all others is to see the miraculous work of God. The work is incomplete. There remains a dark side....[129]

In the Jewish responses of Borowitz and Wyschogrod we perceive a willingness to appreciate Barth's theological achievement, along with reservations about the negative implications of his Christian theology of Israel. This is not surprising. Nor is it unusual that these Jewish responses to Barth are similar to the responses of Barth's Christian critics. What is interesting is that in some cases Jewish theologians have been even more sympathetic to Barth and his theology of Israel than Christians. Our rehearsal of the views of Barth's critics leads us to wonder whether it is possible to go beyond the ambivalent response to Barth's Israel-doctrine which we find in both his Christian and Jewish interpreters. In chapter five we will offer a detailed analysis of the positive and negative aspects of "Barth on Israel," and a final assessment of the prospects Barth's Israel-doctrine offers for post-Holocaust theology.

Notes

1. Compare, e.g., Barth's leading role in the "Confessing Church" movement in the 1930s with Bultmann's rather ambivalent position toward dissent expressed in "The Task of Theology in the Present Situation," written in 1933 [in *Existence and Faith*, ed., Shubert M. Ogden (London: Hodder and Stoughton, 1961), 158-165].

2. For an account of the peculiar relation between Barth's theology and American "Neo-Orthodoxy" beginning in the 1930s, see Dennis Voskuil, "Neoorthodoxy," in David F. Wells, ed., *Reformed Theology in America: A History of Its Development* (Grand Rapids: Eerdmans, 1985), 250ff.

3. See especially, Richard H. Roberts, "The Reception of the Theology of Karl Barth in the Anglo-Saxon World: History, Typology and Prospect," in C. G. Gunton and D. W. Hardy, eds., *On Being the Church* (Edinburgh: T & T Clark, 1989).

4. See, e.g., David H. Kelsey, *The Uses of Scripture in Recent Theology* (Philadelphia: Fortress, 1975), 39-50; and George M. Stroup, *The Promise of Narrative Theology: Recovering the Gospel in the Church* (Atlanta: John Knox, 1981).

5. See, e.g., Carl A. Raschke, *Theological Thinking* (Atlanta: Scholars Press, 1988); and Hans Küng, "Karl Barth and the Post-Modern Paradigm," *Princeton Seminary Bulletin* 9:1 (1988), 8-31.

6. See, e.g., Charles Villa-Vicencio, ed., *On Reading Karl Barth in South Africa* (Grand Rapids: Eerdmans, 1988); See also the Fall, 1987 issue of *Katallegete.*

7. See especially, George Hunsinger, ed., *Karl Barth and Radical Politics* (Philadelphia: Fortress, 1976), which introduces to English-speaking audiences an originally Continental debate on the relationship of "socialism" to Barth's theology.

8. For example, Eberhard Jüngel, *Karl Barth: A Theological Legacy,* trans. Garrett E. Paul (Philadelphia: Westminster, 1986).

9. See, e.g., Donald McKim, ed., *How Karl Barth Changed My Mind;*Berndt Jaspert, "Karl Barths Theologie am Ende 20 Jahrhunderts," *Theologische Literaturzeitung* 112 (October, 1987), 707-730; and John Thompson, ed., *Theology Beyond Christendom: Essays on the Centenary of the Birth of Karl Barth* (Allison Park, PA: Pickwick Press, 1986).

10. See, e.g., C. E. B. Cranfield, *Epistle to the Romans,* 448-449; Paul van Buren, *A Theology of the Jewish-Christian Reality,* 3 vols. (San Francisco: Harper and Row, 1980-88); Hendrikus Berkhof, *Christian Faith;* Kornelius Miskotte, *When the Gods Are Silent;* Jacob Jocz, *A Theology of Election, Israel and the Church;* Helmut Gollwitzer, *Christen und Juden;* Thomas F. Torrance, *The Mediation of Christ;* Clemens Thoma, *A Christian Theology of Judaism;* and Markus Barth, *The People of God.*

11. See especially, Phlip J. Rosato, "The Influence of Karl Barth on Catholic Theology," *Gregorianum* 67:4 (1986), 659-678.

12. Rosato even claims that a "reverberation of [Barth's influence] is already evident in the documents of Vatican II" (Ibid., 666).

13. Robert Jewett, "Major Impulses in the Interpretation of Romans Since Barth," 18. According to Dieter Kraft, "all the leading exegetes crusaded against Barth's theological interpretation, and showered the systematic theologian with text-critical reproaches." ["Israel in der Theologie Karl Barths, *Communio Viatorum* 27:1 (1984), 61, trans. mine]. See also Paul S. Minear, "Barth's Commentary to the

Romans, 1922-72, or Karl Barth vs. the Exegetes," in Martin Rumscheidt, ed.,
Footnotes to a Theology.

14. All references are to Karl Barth, *Epistle to the Romans,* 6th ed., trans.
Edwyn C. Hoskyns (Oxford: Oxford University Press, 1968). The sixth edition
appeared in German in 1928 and first appeared in English in 1933.

15. Jülicher's review was entitled "Ein Moderner Paulus-Ausleger." The quote
appears in Kraft, 61, trans. mine. Barth's treatment of Jülicher in the *Römerbrief*
certainly did not predispose Jülicher toward a positive review.

16. Schlatter, "Karl Barths Römebrief." In Kraft, 61, trans. mine.

17. Ibid., 61 ff.

18. In describing the "integration" model, Klappert makes reference both to
Romans 11:1-6 ("the church as the new people of God replaces Israel insofar as it
integrates itself as the elected remnant of Israel...," 17), and to Barth's exegesis ("the
eschatological variant of the integration model...will encounter us again in Barth's
exegesis of Romans 11:25, according to which Barth speaks of the rising of the
synagogue into the church," 18). Translations mine.

19. Klappert mentions the "unconditional solidarity between the church and
Israel" expressed in Barth's *Römerbrief,* relating it to the complementarity model (27),
but ultimately understands Barth's Israel-doctrine as existing in the tension between the
"ecclesiological integration" and "christological participation" models.

20. "The typology model is the model of 'fore-portrayal pointing to a superior
counterpart.' Israel, its history and institutions are, according to this model, types of
the church whose final salvation is represented through the church" (Klappert, 18,
trans. mine). Cf. Eduard Thurneysen's comment that Barth was "in full agreement
with Willhelm Vischer's *The Witness of the Old Testament to Christ,* while
recognizing also the differences between the testaments" [Karl Barth and Eduard
Thurneysen, *Revolutionary Theology in the Making: The Barth-Thurneysen
Correspondence 1914-1925,* trans. James D. Smart (Richmond: John Knox, 1964),
18].

21. On Barth's understanding of Israel, Marquardt observes: "It [Barth's
understanding of the offices of prophet, priest and king in relation to Christ] is
exclusively a question of pre-Christian and historically-failed powers, forms and
truths, whose fulfillment can then be seen as Jesus Christ" (in Klappert, 18, trans.
mine).

22. This is the term (*Identität*) used by Kraft: "he [Barth] contradicted also the
view that the OT does not belong in the canon of the church and that the church has
nothing to do with Israel" (61). Kraft also sees this identification in Barth's *Dogmatik
im Entwurf* (1927): "here the making synonymous of Israel and the church follows the
identification of OT and NT" (62). Translations mine.

23. Kraft, 62. Interestingly, Kraft elaborates this statement with the observation that Barth "integrates Israel into the totality of evangelical ecclesiology" (62).

24. In Gutteridge, *Open Thy Mouth For the Dumb*, 58.

25. In Kraft, 63, trans. mine.

26. Gutteridge, 125. See also Klaus Scholder, *The Churches and the Third Reich, Vol. Two, The Year of Disillusionment: 1934: Barmen and Rome* (Philadelphia: Fortress, 1989).

27. See, e.g., *The Book of Confessions of the Presbyterian Church (U.S.A.)*, chap. 8.

28. Ibid., 8.01; 8.07. Barth saw in the "German Christian" movement a primitive, but insidious form of natural theology.

29. Gutteridge, 125. Ironically, Barth had written to a friend just a few months before Barmen that "anyone who believes in Christ...simply cannot be involved in the contempt for Jews and in the ill-treatment of them which is now the order of the day" (Letter to E. Steffens, January 10, 1934, in Rosato, 664). See also Ruether, *Faith and Fratricide*, 224.

30. Jürgen Fangmeier and Hinrich Stoevesandt, eds., *Karl Barth, Letters 1961-68*, trans. Geoffrey W. Bromiley (Edinburgh: T & T Clark, 1981), 250. This letter is even more significant when compared to Barth's statement soon after World War II, that "where the Confessing Church was concerned, during the whole period of the church struggle, as much as was humanly possible was done for the persecuted Jews" (in Gutteridge, 267).

31. Kraft 63-4 (trans. mine). See also Eberhard Busch, *Glaubensheiterkeit Karl Barth: Erfahrungen und Begegnungen* (Vluyn: Neukirchner, 1986). In the fifth issue of *Theologische Existenz Heute* Barth published this sermon, along with a foreword in which he made it quite clear this was a "text-" and not a "theme-" sermon: "The sermon presented here concerns the 'Jewish question,' not because I wanted to touch on it, but because I had to touch on it...in explanation of the text. As a theme neither the 'Jewish question' nor any other question which moves us today belongs in the pulpit" (in Lothar Steiger, "Die Theologie vor der 'Judenfrage'--Karl Barth als Beispiel," in *Auschwitz--Krise der Christliche Theologie*, 93, trans. mine). This passage must be seen as expressing the same principle that led Barth to fight Nazi ideology within the context of the church. In the same foreword, Barth stressed "the fact that one immediately spoils understanding for the church-opposition in Germany if one interprets it as a symptom of an existing resistance against the present state government" (Steiger, 94, trans. mine).

32. See Kraft, 64.

33. Gutteridge, 182, 278. For another view of Barth's involvement in the Church Struggle, see F.-W. Marquardt, "Theologische und Politische Motivationen Karl Barths im Kirchenkampf," *Jungekirche* (May, 1973), 283-303. The influence of the "theology of crisis" in leading Barth away from the kind of political involvement that characterized his pre-war career as a Swiss pastor is revealed by Barth's reflections on his interaction with Emmanuel Hirsch in 1922: "more dangerous than our disagreements is the fact that the political question plays a part in the *foreground* of our discussions which are apparently so remote from the world" (Letter to Eduard Thurneysen, dated February 26, 1922, in *Revolutionary Theology in the Making*, 87). See also, Reinhold Niebuhr, "Karl Barth--Apostle of the Absolute," *The Christian Century* (December 13, 1928); and Paul Tillich, "What Is Wrong With the 'Dialectic Theology'?" *Journal of Religion* 15:2 (April, 1935), 127-135.

34. The idea that Barth's theological response during this period was "belated" (*verspätete*) has been developed by Lothar Steiger. Steiger summarizes the "German" criticism of Barth's handling of the *Judenfrage:* "it is to the reproach of the theology of crisis that it did nothing for the processing of the national crisis. Had they [the theologians of crisis] had a suspicion of the interdependence of the national question and the 'Jewish question,' they might have hurried the great theological renewal which they were to place on the ground and in the service of Weimar. This was the first instance of belatedness (*Retardierung*) which led to delay in each of Barth's next political steps" (90, trans. mine). Even Barth's contemporary, Dietrich Bonhoeffer, can be accused of an ineffective response to Hitler and Jewish persecution in the 30s. In 1933 Bonhoeffer wrote that "The Church of the Reformation has no right to address the State directly in its specifically political actions" ["The Church and the Jewish Question," (1933), in *No Rusty Swords: Letters, Lectures and Notes, 1928-1936*, ed. Edwin H. Robinson and John Bowden (New York: Harper and Row, 1965).

35. Barth agreed to sign the oath of loyalty, but only if he was permitted to add the following disclaimer: "I will be loyal and obedient...so far as I can do so responsibly as an Evangelical Christian...." Barth's offer was declined by the authorities, and he lost his teaching post at Bonn in 1935. [See Berndt Jaspert, ed., *Barth and Bultmann, Letters, 1922-1966*, 78.] For Barth's refusal to sign the oath as an act of political opposition, see Steiger, 94. Steiger also points to the political significance of Barth's lectures in Ethics, given in the summer semesters of 1928 and 1930 at Münster and Bonn: "What Barth had to say here about war, nationalism, customs and race with concrete reference to contemporary circumstances is astonishing and would have been what in public--not only in the academy--should have been discussed and advocated" (91, trans. mine).

36. See Gutteridge, 182; and Martin Röhkramer, "Karl Barth in Herbstkrise 1938," *Evangelische Theologie* 48:6 (1988), 521-45. Between 1938 and 1942 Barth wrote similar "church letters" to France, England and America urging resistance to Hitler.

37. "Karl Barth on Politics," *Radical Religion* (Spring, 1939). See also *The Essential Reinhold Niebuhr: Selected Essays and Addresses,* ed. Robert M. Brown (New Haven: Yale University Press, 1986).

38. In Gutteridge, 298.

39. In Klappert, 11 (trans. mine).

40. In Klappert, 29 (trans. mine).

41. Rosato, 664. See also Fangmeier, ed., 260 n3. In a letter to Ernst Wolf dated August 18, 1967, Barth refers to Swiss guilt with regard to Jewish refugees during the Hitler era.

42. George Hunsinger affirms Barth's failure in his suggestion that one of the things we learn from the history of the Confessing Church in Germany is that "confession without resistance is not enough" ["Barth, Barmen, and the Confessing Church Today: Summary of the Original Text," *Katallegete* (Fall, 1987), 11]. On Barth's resistance to Hitler, see also Richard R. Rubenstein and John K. Roth, eds, *Approaches to Auschwitz: The Holocaust and Its Legacy* (Atlanta: John Knox, 1987), 204-208.

43. Steiger, 92 (trans. mine). Steiger is commenting specifically on Barth's *Theologische Existenz Heute* No. 5 (1933). On this chapter in Barth's career, see also Hans Prolingheuer, *Der Fall Karl Barth: Chronographie Einer Betreibung 1934-1935* (Vluyn: Neukirchner, 1977). For the failure of Barth and the Confessing Church to resist Hitler and his policies during the 30s, see Leif Torjesen, "Resurrection and Ideology: The Theological Origins and Political Setting of Karl Barth's Attack on Natural Theology," (Ph. D. Diss., Claremont Graduate School, 1986); and Paul Leggett, "Against the Swastika: The Challenge of the Anti-Nazi Film to Political Theology," (Ph. D. Diss., Union Theological Seminary in New York, 1982).

44. Kraft, 65. Here Barth goes even further than in his *Christian Dogmatics* of 1927 (where he affirmed that the Old and New Testaments belong together) by affirming that the Synagogue and church belong together as well.

45. *CD* I:2, 510.

46. See, e.g., Berkouwer, *The Triumph of Grace.*

47. *CD* II:2, 195.

48. Ibid., 263.

49. Michael Wyschogrod has declared that "there is in Barth an anti-semitism made up of two parts: the traditional anti-semitism of European Christiandom (*sic*)...and the anti-semitism of Christian theology" ("Why Was and Is the Theology of

Karl Barth of Interest to a Jewish Theologian?" in Rumscheidt, ed., *Footnotes to A Theology,* 95-111).

50. Frank Talmage, *Disputation and Dialogue* (New York: Ktav, 1975), 38.

51. For a more complete catalogue of the terms which Barth uses to describe the Jews and especially "the Synagogue" in paragraph 34 of the *Church Dogmatics,* see F.-W. Marquardt, *Die Entdeckung Des Judentums für Die Christliche Theologie: Israel im Denken Karl Barths* Abhandlung Zum Christlich-Judischen Dialog, Vol. One (München: Chr. Kaiser, 1967), 335.

52. The radical nature of Barth's Israel-doctrine was perceived by Emil Brunner and other members of the "Swiss Society for Aid" when, in 1941, they questioned the orthodoxy of Barth's interpretation of John 4:22 ("salvation is of the Jews") as still binding. See Rosato, 665; and Fangmeier, ed., 263 n5.

53. This is the description of Frank Talmage (*Disputation and Dialogue,* 38). Although *CD* II:2 first appeared in 1942, the ideas presented here probably appeared in lecture form much earlier. Because they were published in 1942, it is tempting to imagine Barth writing these words as the ovens of Auschwitz are blazing. This is probably not fair to Barth, however. In a letter to Oscar Moppert dated February 7, 1965, Barth mentions that information about the persecution of Jews was very limited in the Nazi era, both in Germany and in Switzerland (Fangmeier, ed., 181, see n68).

54. *CD* III:3, 211.

55. For Barth, the moment in salvation history where "Israel" ends and the history of the Jews begins is the moment when Jesus Christ enters history: "At the very moment when salvation comes, and comes of the Jews, Jerusalem and the Temple fall..." (Ibid., 218).

56. Ibid., 225.

57. Barth refers, e.g., to the "worst disaster in all their [the Jews'] history, completely eclipsing all previous disasters" (Ibid., 212).

58. Kraft, 69. Kraft also sees here evidence that Barth's theology has been determined by "speculative anthropological and existential handicaps" (70). In particular, he recognizes a distinct "structural relationship" with existential philosophy. In Barth, Kraft argues, the Jew becomes an "existential experience," through which man perceives his "actuality." The most striking affinity, Kraft argues, is with Sartre's concept of "nausea," since Barth's Jew is certainly "nauseating" in an existential way. Kraft goes on to claim that in the inevitability of this encounter with the Jew in Barth's theology, one is reminded of Camus' "Sisyphos": Barth's non-Jew must "again and again return to this place [outbreaks of anti-Semitism] as a criminal to the scene of his crime."

59. Steiger, 96.

60. Davies, *Anti-semitism and the Christian Mind*, 124. Davies sees here an example of what Hannah Arendt has called "eternal antisemitism."

61. Kraft, 72.

62. Ibid., 70, trans. mine.

63. Ibid., 71, trans. mine. The quote is from *CD* III:3.

64. For what follows, see "The Dean and the Chosen People," in *After Auschwitz*, 46-58.

65. Robert E. Willis makes this point in "Bonhoeffer and Barth on Jewish Suffering: Reflections on the Relationship Between Theology and Moral Sensibility," *Journal of Ecumenical Studies* 24:4 (Fall, 1987), 613.

66. For a discussion of the pro-Nazi and anti-Jewish elements in the thought of Barth's contemporary and one-time teaching colleague Emmanuel Hirsch, see Robert Erickson, *Theologians Under Hitler*.

67. Cf. Alan T. Davies, who suggests that Barth "requires the Jew to play a symbolic role in the Christian revelation" (115); and F.-W. Marquardt, who criticizes Barth for not realizing that he is speaking of actual people when he discusses "the Jew." Davies believes Barth's Jew is as objectified and contrived as "the patristic or medieval Jew of the older theologians" (120), and decries the "absence of real humanity" here (121).

68. In a recent conversation with the author, Markus Barth commented that this contact with Judaism was the main advantage of his own theology of Israel in relation to that of his father (personal interview, Riehen, Switzerland, January, 10, 1989). Paul van Buren relates that Barth once described Martin Buber to him as a "sad, almost pathetic man." A friend of van Buren's who knew Buber, however, described Buber as "jolly." Van Buren sees behind this discrepancy Barth's theological lenses which led him to view Buber as "a Jew" in the manner which his theology portrayed them (personal interview, July 17, 1988, Boston). In response to Marquardt's book on his Israel-doctrine, where Barth is criticized for his lack of understanding for real Jews, Barth wrote: "Biblical Israel as such gave me so much to think about and to cope with that I simply did not have the time or intellectual strength to look more closely at Baeck, Buber, Rosenzweig, etc..." (Fangmeier, ed., 262). As for the "unpublished exchange of letters of Barth with Jews and rabbis" alluded to by Klappert (27), we can only say that those letters that are known do not really qualify the attitude toward Jews expressed in Barth's theology. In general, I believe Klappert tends to overstate Barth's interest in dialogue and Jewish self-understanding (See Klappert, 27-28).

69. Letter to F.-W. Marquardt, September 5, 1967, in Fangmeier, ed., 262.

70. Barth actually mentions the relationship of church and Israel briefly in *CD* IV:1, paragraph 52, "The Holy Spirit and the Gathering of the Christian Community." There Barth recapitulates what he has said about this relationship in *CD* II:2, while emphasizing that there is actually "one covenant," with its center in Jesus Christ, connecting the two forms of the one community. Barth also includes there a brief consideration of "Jewish missions" (670-671).

71. *CD* IV:3, 2, 877. When Barth expressed similar ideas about "Jewish mission" in a meeting with Basel clergy on November 27, 1961 he was taken to task by a zealous pastor who asked if penitence for the Holocaust had to take the form of silence. In a letter dated December 7, Barth affirmed that the concept of Jewish missions was in itself "theologically impossible" (Fangmeier, ed., Letters, 25-6). See also Barth's letter to a Jewish-Christian theological student in America where he stresses "the necessity of not giving up your belonging to the Jewish community" (Ibid., 100).

72. Ibid., 878.

73. A possible source for Barth's stance can be seen in the Dutch Reformed Church's *Fundamenten en Perspektiven van Belijden* (1949), article 8, where the topics of conversation with Israel and missions to non-Christian peoples are treated separately. See Moltmann, *The Church in the Power of the Holy Spirit*, 146.

74. In *Against the Stream: Shorter Post-War Writings, 1946-52,* ed. R. G. Smith (London: SCM, 1954), 195-201.

75. Ibid., 200.

76. Letter to Friedrich-Wilhelm Marquardt, September 5, 1967; in Fangmeier, ed., 261-63.

77. Ibid., 262f. Barth also mentions in this context the introduction he wrote for a book entitled *Stärker als die Angst*. The introduction was not published with the book, but Marquardt included it in an essay in 1968.

78. In Klappert, 44, trans. mine. See also Rosato, 665; and Eberhard Busch, *Karl Barth: His Life From Letters and Autobiographical Texts* (Philadelphia: Fortress, 1976), 402.

79. Trans. Keith R. Crim (Edinburgh: St. Andrews Press, 1969). For what follows, see "Account of the Trip to Rome," 9ff.

80. Ibid., 36-37.

81. See, e.g., Rosato.

82. Lothar Steiger argues, for example, that Barth's statement in *Ad Limina Apostolorum* that the only great ecumenical question is the church's relationship to Judaism, makes him "ahead of us all" (98).

83. In Klappert, 28, trans. mine. See "Fragen von Rabbi Petuchowski, Antworten von Karl Barth," *Criterion: A Publication of the Divinity School of the University of Chicago* 2:1 (1963), 18-24.

84. Letter to H. Poms, December 7, 1961; in Fangmeier, ed., 26.

85. In Klappert, 27, trans. mine.

86. Marquardt, 296, 320; in Klappert, 27.

87. "Why Was and Is...," 109-10.

88. *Anti-Semitism and the Christian Mind,* 120.

89. Letter to Louis Glatt, September 29, 1967; in Fangmeier, ed., 267.

90. See, e.g., *CD* II:2, 263, 279.

91. Fangmeier, ed., 267.

92. Especially *CD* III:3, published in 1950.

93. "The Jewish Problem and the Christian Answer," 196.

94. Letter to Pater Prof. Magnus Löhrer, June 9, 1967; in Fangmeier, ed., 256.

95. From a recording of conversation with friends; in Rosato, 666.

96. Letter to Ernst wolf, August 18, 1967; in Fangmeier, ed., 260, especially n1.

97. Kraft, passim.

98. *CD* III:3, 212.

99. Kraft, 71.

100. See especially 246.

101. Klappert uses Ernst Käsemann as the prime example of the subsumation model in action, and says of Barth in this context: "in contrast, the special character of Barth's position is located in the fact that he connects the exemplary nature of the

existence of Israel or the Synagogue *post Christum resuscitatum* with the special character of the unmitigated and continuing election of Israel..." (22, trans. mine).

102. See, e.g., 20, where Klappert refers to Marquardt's discussion of Barth's *Römerbrief* in terms of "illustration," and 42: "...in Barth's exegesis [of Romans 9-11] the history of Israel turns into a first stage and moment in the framework of the church's history...." On the substitution model in Barth, Klappert again refers to Marquardt (see 18f).

103. In Klappert, 41.

104. Chapter 3, 38-42. Klappert critically discusses the "schismatic theology" inherent in Barth's interpretation of Romans 9, where Barth makes "the church in its opposition to the Synagogue in fact the point of reference of Pauline statements" (39), and refers to Barth's understanding of Romans 10 as "church-criticism."

105. Not surprisingly, Klappert also sees Barth's Israel-doctrine in terms of the complementarity model [in its emphasis on the unconditional solidarity between church and Israel (24) and the double-form of the one community of God (29)], as well as the representation model. In this latter context, Klappert refers to Marquardt's reading of Barth ["Barth thinks about the 'remnant' together with the representative, and has an inclusive understanding of remnant..." (31)], and sees the concept of a Gentile Christian "placeholding for Israel" in Barth's thought. After Auschwitz, however, Klappert believes we must ask "whether the Gentile Christian placeholding for Israel expressed by Barth has reversed itself through suffering and martyrdom into Judaism as Israel placeholding for the church" (32).

106. In Klappert, 34. Cf. Kraft, who says that in Barth, "...the equation is forbidden: Israel = *kata sarka* [according to the flesh] / church = *kata pneuma* [according to the spirit]. Israel and church belong together."

107. See Klappert, ch. 4, "The Problematic of Barth's Thesis of Israel as the Witness to Judgment and Differentiation In the Witness Doctrine."

108. Klappert, 43.

109. In Rendtorff and Stegemann, ed., 83-98.

110. *Communio Viatorum* 27:1 (1984), 59-72.

111. See Regina S. Sharif, *Non-Jewish Zionism: Its Roots in Western History* (London: Zed Press, n. d.), 121, where the author observes that early Zionists like Herzl and Weizmann assumed anti-Semitism to be a natural state of affairs and an almost rational reaction of the non-Jew to the situation of Jews in the Diaspora.

112. *Religion in Life* 21:4 (1952), 585-593. Another early response to Barth's theology of Israel in America can be found in the work of A. Roy Eckardt, who in

1947 classified Barth as a theologian of "discontinuity" between church and Israel in *Christianity and the Children of Israel* (see Davies, 119).

113. Sulzbach, 586. For a more recent expression of this kind of understanding of Barth's theology, see John B. Cobb, Jr., "Barth and the Barthians: A Critical Appraisal," where the author claims that Barth "reduced, if he did not obliterate the theological grounds for Anti-Judaism" (in McKim, ed., *How Karl Barth Changed My Mind*, 172).

114. Sulzbach says, for instance, that "it is the meaning of the resurrection [for Barth] that God is no longer concerned with what the Jews have done," (591) a statement which ignores the importance for Barth of Israel's 'No." Also misleading is the statement that for Barth the Jews are "the symbol of human existence" (593). One can only wish Barths' expression of the matter were so innocuous.

115. See Ibid., 587-589.

116. See especially chap. 6, "Protestantism: A Mind Divided: 1. Karl Barth," 108-130.

117. See Ibid., chap. 5.

118. Ibid., 119.

119. On this point Davies is correct. In the work of Cranfield and others we see an appreciation for Barth's rediscovery of Paul's words on the problem of "Jews and Christians" in Romans 9-11. It is interesting to compare the reaction to Barth's dependence on Romans 9-11 on the part of Davies, who argues that Romans 9-11 is not a proper basis for a contemporary Christian understanding of Jews, and Klappert, who believes that it is, but that Barth has misinterpreted this passage at crucial points. See my "'Recovering the Real Paul': Theology and Interpretation in Romans 9-11," *Ex Auditu* 4 (1988).

120. Davies mentions Helmut Gollwitzer, Jacob Jocz, T. F. Torrance and Hendrikus Berkhof. See also the work of C.E. B. Cranfield, e. g., "Light From St. Paul on Christian-Jewish relations," in David W. Torrance, ed., *The Witness of the Jews to God* (Edinburgh: The Handsel Press, 1982). See also T. F. Torrance, *The Mediation of Christ* (Exeter: Paternoster, 1983) where the author reveals the influence of Barth in 1) arguing that we must understand Christ in terms of "his intimate bond with Israel in its covenantal relationship with God throughout history" (12) and "the inextricable interrelation between God's self-revelation in Jesus and his self-revelation through Israel" (28), and 2) in observing that "the covenant between God and Israel was...established out of pure grace between Israel in its sinful, rebellious and estranged existence" (37), and that ultimately the only answer to the Holocaust is the cross of Jesus (54).

121. "The Influence of Karl Barth on Catholic Theology." Unfortunately, Rosato's appreciation of Barth leads him to an uncritical panegyric of Barth's teaching on and attitude toward "Israel" which does not address their troublesome aspects.

122. New York: Paulist, 1980.

123. Ibid., 178-79.

124. "A Jewish Perspective on Karl Barth," in McKim, ed., *How Karl Barth Changed My Mind,* 156.

125. "Why Was and Is...?", in Rumscheidt, ed., 98.

126. "A Jewish Perspective...," 159.

127. "Why Was and Is...," 105.

128. Ibid., 107.

129. Ibid., 109.

CHAPTER THREE

JÜRGEN MOLTMANN:
TOWARD A COMMON HOPE

I. INTRODUCTION

Jürgen Moltmann is arguably the most influential Protestant theologian in the world today. For twenty-five years his work has been at the forefront of attempts to reinterpret Christian theology in view of the challenges posed by contemporary life. Phrases like "theology of hope," "political theology," and "theology of the cross" have entered or reentered the vocabulary of contemporary theology in large part due to Moltmann's influence. Moltmann has not been alone in his attempts to reorient Protestant theology, but his books and articles have been more accessible to those outside the academy than many of his colleagues', and his work has been routinely translated into English and into other languages. Although Moltmann has not produced a comprehensive "theology of Israel," he has been involved for some time with Jewish-Christian dialogue in Germany, and many of his writings are permeated by his interest in achieving a positive Christian understanding of contemporary Judaism.[1] The purpose of this chapter is to analyze the separate theological strands that comprise Moltmann's theology of Israel, and consider the prospects which this theology represents in the post-Holocaust environment. Before moving directly to a consideration of Moltmann's treatment of Israel, we shall discuss briefly two aspects of Moltmann's background--his personal biography and his relation to Karl Barth--and the implications these have for our study.

A. Biography

Since little is known in America about Moltmann's personal background, we shall begin our study with a brief account of his biography. Moltmann was born in Hamburg in 1926, and by his own account[2] is a member of the "skeptical generation" which lived through the horrors of the Second World War. At the age of seventeen, Moltmann was drafted into the Air Force auxiliary unit manning the anti-aircraft guns protecting Hamburg. Moltmann survived the Allied bombing of Hamburg in July 1943 and the resultant firestorm. In 1944 he was drafted into the German army, only to be captured by the Allies six months later in February 1945. Moltmann spent the next 38 months imprisoned at camps in Belgium, Scotland and England. During this time he underwent a "great change," and eventually discovered a "new power of survival" and a "slow building up of faith." While a prisoner of war, Moltmann relinquished his earlier intentions of studying mathematics and became interested in theology. Moltmann's theological education began informally in 1947 at a prison camp in Sherwood Forest, and formally at the University of Göttingen after his repatriation in April 1948.

Moltmann's thoughts on his return to Germany reflect the ambivalence of an entire generation of Germans:

> We were weighed down by the sombre burden of a guilt which could never be paid off...but really we came back to Germany with the will to create a new, different more humane world.[3]

Moltmann was soon disillusioned, however, by the course of restoration within German society, a course he believed was leading to a "utoptia of the status quo." Moltmann was also disturbed by the incorporation of remnants of the Confessing Church into the Ländeskirchen. While serving his first parish near Bremen between 1952 and 1958, Moltmann was involved in various national protest movements. He began his teaching career in 1958 at Wuppertal, and since then has taught at Bonn and Tübingen, where he has been since 1967.

The 1960s were marked for Moltmann and his contemporaries by the hopeful beginnings of change in post-war Europe such as the Second Vatican Council, the growing humanist wave in European Marxism, and Christian-Marxist dialogue. This was also the period when Moltmann underwent the "epoch-making experience" of discovering Ernst Bloch's *Das Prinzip Hoffnung* (1954-1959). Moltmann's first major book, *Theologie der Hoffnung* (1964) attempted to apply Bloch's methods and themes to theology, and was an instant sensation. After the international disappointments of 1968, however, Moltmann began work on a "political theology" and, later, on a "theology of the cross." In these theological projects Moltmann attempted to take seriously the opposite side of the experience of God in hope, by focusing on the experience of God in "forsakenness and desolation."

Moltmann's biography reflects the experiences of many members of his generation. In his theology's experimental and dialogical character and its ambivalence toward established theological schools[4] there are examples of the general quest for new beginnings in post-war German culture. At the same time, Moltmann's post-war thought reveals a keen sensitivity to what the Nazi experience signified for Jewish-Christian relations in Germany and German existence in general. Moltmann has written a detailed account of the evening in September, 1945 when he and his fellow German prisoners at a camp in Scotland were confronted with photographs from the Nazi death camps:

> the horror at the crimes of Bergen-Belsen and Auschwitz bored its way deeper and deeper into one's soul. I became ill and wanted, more than anything else, to die. How could one have been there and survive it? How could one belong to a nation on which such a burden of guilt lay?[5]

As recently as 1988, Moltmann confirmed the influence of the Holocaust on his early theological development:

> For us young Germans who began the study of theology after the war, "Auschwitz" became a turning point in our thinking and acting. We became painfully aware that we must live, inescapably, in the shadow of the holocaust, which had been committed against the Jewish people in the name of our people. "After Auschwitz" became our concrete context for theology. With the name of the place of the crime we not

only marked a political or moral crisis of our people, but also a theological and church crisis. For us, what was so incomprehensible about Auschwitz was not only the executioners and their assistants, not only the technical perfection of the mass extermination, and not only the experience of the hiddenness of God. For us, it was the silence of the men and women who had looked on or looked away, or closed their eyes only to hand over the victims, so completely abandoned, to mass murder. For us Auschwitz did not turn into a question about the meaning of suffering, as it did for the Jews, but into a question about the strength to live with such a burden of guilt and shame and sorrow.[6]

Eventually, Moltmann came to see the Holocaust and all it meant for Jews and Christians not as an obstacle to theological reflection, but as part of the justification for a new theology which spoke to the post-war world. From his initial indirect experience of the Holocaust in 1945, Moltmann has come to see the crimes of Auschwitz as one expression of a threatened existence to which the contemporary church must respond. This era of threatened existence is characterized by the Holocaust, but also by the era of nuclear terror in which we now live:

> The National Socialist "rule of violence" found its terrible expression in Auschwitz and Bergen-Belsen. Which rule of violence found its expression in Hiroshima and Nagasaki? There is no true Christian community in Germany which can look away from Auschwitz. There is no true Christian community in the world that does not spread awareness of the shadow of Hiroshima and Nagasaki.[7]

B. Moltmann, Barth and the Reformed Tradition

While at Göttingen between 1948 and 1952 Moltmann encountered and imbibed the theology of the Confessing Church, the resistance movement in which Karl Barth was a leader until his exile to Switzerland in 1935. Young German Christians searching the post-war rubble for foundations of a new Germany were attracted to former leaders of the Confessing Church and their record of resistance to Hitler. Men like Otto Weber, Ernst Wolf and Hans-Joachim Iwand, who had been connected with the Confessing Church movement, became Moltmann's mentors at Göttingen. They bequeathed to him both the legacy of Reformation theology, and the desire for critical tension with the contemporary world that has come to characterize Moltmann's theology. Weber in particular encouraged Moltmann to join the

Reformed Church and stimulated his interest in Reformed theology, an interest very evident in Moltmann's early published work.[8] But Wolf and Iwand, both Lutherans, had in common with the Reformed Weber an acquaintance with and appreciation for the theology of Karl Barth. Weber's status as an interpreter of Barth is well-known. Less well-known is the fact that Wolf was a close friend and collaborator of Barth's since the days they were colleagues at Bonn, and that Iwand, the scholar of nineteenth-century theology who introduced Moltmann to the thought of Hegel, was also heavily influenced by Barth.

Moltmann's encounter with Barth's thought was mediated through these men who recognized the importance of Barth's theology, but who were not uncritical Barthians. While Barth's theology of dialectic between church and culture was attractive to those emerging from a period of cultural apocalypse, Moltmann ultimately became even more critical of Barth than his teachers.[9] Moltmann describes the initial attraction of Barth's theology for the first post-war generation in his observation that, although they did not become "Barthians," Barth's theology provided Moltmann and his contemporaries the "first and most enlightening formulation of faith in such experiences."[10] Yet Moltmann was anxious to move beyond Barth theologically. In *Theology of Hope,* his first major work, Moltmann constructed a "missionary" dogmatics (in contrast to Barth's "church" dogmatics),[11] and was critical of Barth's understandings of eschatology and revelation,[12] as well as his complete identification of reconciliation and the Christ event. Moltmann has never repudiated Barth's theology as a whole, and he did not do so in *Theology of Hope.*[13] But he has succeeded in qualifying some of Barth's ideas with an emphasis on the eschatological nature of biblical religion (which he found in the work of Bloch and Ernst Käsemann), and with his discovery of Dutch Apostolate theology. Moltmann has affirmed many times that it was the Dutch theologian Arnold van Ruler who showed him the way beyond Barth by emphasizing Jesus' historical Lordship in contrast to Barth's Christocentrism.[14] Other Dutch thinkers who influenced Moltmann during this early period of his development were Kornelius H. Miskotte and J. C. Hoekendijk, whose "mission theology" convinced Moltmann of the church's relativity and encouraged him to qualify the Barthian notion of theology as a function of the church.[15]

Moltmann's early ambivalence toward Barth's theology was perceived by Barth himself. After reading *Theology of Hope,* an experience which he described to a friend as "stimulating and irritating," Barth wrote to Moltmann from his hospital bed.[16] Barth thanked Moltmann for the "instruction and stimulation" which his book had given, but was forced to conclude that it was not the work of the next generation's "child of peace and promise" who would carry on Barth's theological project. Asking Moltmann to explain how his unilateral subsumption of theology in eschatology avoided the accusation that it was a "baptized *principle* of hope" (that is, baptized Bloch), Barth encouraged Moltmann to outgrow the "inspired onesidedness" of this first attempt at constructive theology and become the aforementioned "child of peace and promise." Moltmann's reply, written almost five months later,[17] reveals that Barth's sharp criticism did not leave him unmoved. After a bit of ceremonious self-denigration, in which Moltmann expresses shame that Barth should have read so thoroughly a "fragmentary theological effort" like *Theology of Hope,* Moltmann affirms that the *"CD"* have been and still are his constant theological companion, and that his work should not be interpreted as a parting of the ways.

Even today commentators on Moltmann's work have emphasized the influence of Barth and "Barthians" like Weber, Wolf and Iwand. Some have even recognized intimate parallels between Barth's dialectical theology of the 20s and Moltmann's theology of hope in the 60s.[18] But there are important differences in the ways Moltmann and Barth do theology. For instance, the vertical transcendence which characterizes Barth's theology becomes in Moltmann a horizontal transcendence,[19] and the Christocentrism found in Barth is exchanged in Moltmann for an emphasis on the Kingdom of God and the unfinished identity of Jesus Christ.[20] Our main concern here, of course, is Moltmann's relationship to Barth's "theology of Israel." Does Moltmann self-consciously journey beyond Barthian territory on this issue as he does on many others? Does he engage Barth's theology of Israel directly, or develop his own apart from it? Before answering these questions we must consider carefully Moltmann's theology of Israel.

C. Conclusion: Moltmann's Education and Early Experiences as Resources for Post-Holocaust Theology

Moltmann's personal experiences as a young auxiliary recruit, an infantry soldier, a prisoner of war and a repatriated German citizen specially qualified him as a foreman in the rebuilding of a post-war German Christianity. Even today, there is a sensitivity to suffering, disappointment and "negativity" in Moltmann's theology which gives it a special relevance to contemporary European life. His experiences have served as important resources for Moltmann's development of an ecumenical theology which engages in critical dialogue with the rival interpretations of contemporary society Moltmann refers to as "conversation partners." Although Moltmann is in agreement with those who stress that theology must not be divorced from the life of the church, he has emphasized that it must also remain in dialogue with institutions that are not and will never become the church. Apart from Marxism, Moltmann's chief conversation partner has been "Israel." At least since his discovery of Ernst Bloch's *Principle of Hope,* Moltmann has been in dialogue with Jewish thought.[21] Moltmann has even suggested that in the case of Bloch it was not so much his neo-Marxism as his "Jewish messianism" which was attracted him.[22] The connection with Jewish thought which began in his application of Bloch's work in *Theology of Hope* has continued to be important for Moltmann, as he has found orientation in the thought of Franz Rosenzweig, Walter Benjamin, Gershom Scholem, Shalom Ben-Chorin, Theodor Adorno, Max Horkheimer, Martin Buber, Abraham Heschel, and Pinchas Lapide. This willingness to learn from and enter into dialogue with secular and religious Jewish thinkers is a factor that has aided Moltmann in developing a post-Holocaust Christian theology of Israel.

A further resource for post-Holocaust theology is inherent in Moltmann's awareness of his place within a theological tradition that has, at its highest points, achieved a positive understanding of Israel and its "special calling." In the Reformed Federal theology of the seventeenth century Moltmann perceives one example of pre-Holocaust reflection on Israel which might provide a basis for contemporary systematic thought. How successfully Moltmann is able to revitalize this tradition we will attempt to judge in chapter five.

II. MOLTMANN ON ISRAEL: EARLY WRITINGS

A. *Theology of Hope*

We shall begin our consideration of Moltmann's theology, as most critical studies have done, with his *Theology of Hope.* In 1974 Rosemary Ruether suggested that a new Christian Christology free from traditional anti-Semitism might be based on the "theology of hope."[23] In 1976 A. Roy Eckardt took Moltmann to task for the "pre-Holocaust" and "triumphalist" character of his work.[24] Yet despite these contradictory assessments of Moltmann's theology, there has been no serious consideration of Moltmann's understanding of Israel in *Theology of Hope.* Although there is no theology of Israel articulated here, the book develops several themes which are constructive for Moltmann's understanding of Israel and the church-Israel and New Testament-Old Testament relationships. While we will not offer a detailed critique of the book,[25] we shall draw attention to several aspects of *Theology of Hope* which bear on Moltmann's approach to understanding Israel.

It is well-known that Moltmann intended *Theology of Hope* as a Christian response to Ernst Bloch's *Principle of Hope,* which had appeared in Germany a few years earlier.[26] As we have noted, it was not only Bloch's revision of Marxism that attracted Moltmann, but what Moltmann refers to as Bloch's Jewish "messianism." It is perhaps odd that Moltmann would make so much of Bloch's Jewishness, since Bloch's version of messianism emerges *within* history as a symbol of hope for the future of an atheistic humanity. Despite his atheism, however, in Moltmann's eyes Bloch's philosophy remains "Jewish." He sees this Jewishness in both the fundamental importance of the messianic element in his work, but also in the central place which the religion of Moses and the prophets maintains for his philosophical reflection.[27]

It is the thought of Bloch and its immersion in the biblical messianic tradition which is Moltmann's strongest link with Jewish thought in *Theology of Hope.* But *Theology of Hope* also reveals Moltmann's acquaintance with contemporary Jewish thought when the author quotes from the work of Martin Buber (14), or when he refers to "modern Jewish theology" in general (124). On another level, *Theology of Hope* reveals the influence of the Hebrew aniconic tradition, particularly as it is transmitted by the Hebrew prophets. Examples of this influence are Moltmann's prophetic interpretation of Bloch's critical atheism as an "atheism for God's sake," and his dismissal of religion in modern society as a "cult of new subjectivity" and a "socially irrelevant *cultus privatus*" which prophetic religion must forsake. Significantly, Moltmann couches his call to the church in vivid prophetic images:

> If the God who called them to life should expect of them something other than what modern industrial society expects and requires of them, then Christians must venture an Exodus and regard their social roles as a new Babylonian exile.[28]

Moltmann also reveals his dependence on the prophetic tradition particularly in his description of the "Old Testament background of the Christian mission" (328). The "eschatological background" of the gospel in prophets like Isaiah and deutero-Isaiah, Moltmann argues, is the basis for the Christian mission of hope, justice, humanization and peace. The Christian community, the community which on the ground of Christ's resurrection waits for the Kingdom of God, must overcome its historical tendency to leave earthly eschatological expectations to "fanatics and sects." It must seek the "historic transformation of life" and the coming Kingdom of God predicated on God's Old Testament promises (329-30). Even critics of Moltmann's *Theology of Hope* have affirmed that it is written "messianically," by which they mean from an Old Testament or Jewish perspective. Hans Urs von Balthasar in particular has classified Moltmann's messianic interpretation of hope as "Jewish," by which he means pre-Christian and partaking of a "Jewish spirit" which animates modern revolutionary and atheistic thought.[29] Balthasar is correct in recognizing this Jewish stamp on Moltmann's theology of hope. He is wrong, Moltmann tries to argue, in distinguishing such a Jewish from a Christian hope.[30]

A further way in which *Theology of Hope* revises Christian theology through adopting a Jewish perspective is in Moltmann's distinction between Hebrew and Greek modes of thinking. Moltmann argues that the idea of an open, future-oriented history is rooted in Hebrew thought and the Jewish and Christian messianism to which it gave rise (259-61), and that Christian theology must preserve its intimate relation to the Hebrew conception of God which is constantly in danger of replacement by the "god of Parmenides."

Along with the various examples of Jewish influence we have discussed, there is a second general feature of *Theology of Hope* which has implications for a Christian understanding of Israel: the general continuity Moltmann perceives between Old Testament Israel and the New Testament church. This continuity between Israel and the church is founded on Jesus' Jewishness and the fact that it was Yahweh who raised Jesus from the dead (141), the fact that the God of the New Testament is the same "God of promise" who is Israel's God, the New Testament writers' affirmation of this fact by using Old Testament categories of expectation (143), and the notion that "the gospel has its inabrogable presupposition in the Old Testament history of promise" (147). In chapter one we noted that Christian claims for continuity with Israel may lead to supersessionism if the promises which the church and Israel are seen to have in common are fulfilled in the coming of Christ. Moltmann does not avoid this difficulty in *Theology of Hope*,[31] but he *intends* to make Christian affirmations without "antiquating the promises of Israel or even putting an end to them" (147). Moltmann expresses the relation of Israel and church in terms of "promise" and "gospel" rather than promise and fulfillment, and thus is able to argue for continuity while avoiding a description of Israel's future in Christian terms. Behind Moltmann's vision of continuity between Israel and church is the work of Gerhard von Rad and his explication of the Old Testament in terms of the "history of promise."[32] Von Rad demonstrates for Moltmann that the reconciling events of cross and resurrection can be understood only in terms of the promissory history of God in the Old Testament.[33] This approach, combined with what Moltmann learned from the "hermeneutics of the apostolate" in Dutch theology, leads him to the conclusion that the Scriptures are not a closed circle with a "heart" or a "center," but are "open towards the future fulfillment of the divine promise whose future they relate" (283).

Moltmann's conception of the "future of Scripture" provides a transition for talking about a third aspect of *Theology of Hope* which has implications for the church-Israel relationship: Moltmann's understanding of the unfinished nature of reconciliation. Moltmann develops his view of the Christ-event in opposition to "fulfillment ecstasy" among the opponents of the apostle Paul and the "presentative eschatology" in the thought of Bultmann, and, finally, over against Barth's theology of reconciliation. As Douglas Meeks has pointed out, Moltmann utilizes Iwand's understanding of the resurrection as pointing beyond itself rather than signifying the eschatological fulfillment of reconciliation to qualify Barth's notion of the eschaton as an unveiling of what has already been realized in the coming of Christ.[34] Moltmann's eschatological Christology reopens the reconciliation which is completed in Barth's theology[35] by incorporating a "not-yet" element absent in Barth. The "dialectic of reconciliation" between cross and resurrection which determines Moltmann's Christology in *Theology of Hope* has an unfinished, hope-oriented character which leaves the future (and thus the future of the church and of Israel) open. Moltmann's claim that the revelation in the appearances of the risen Christ is not only "hidden," but also "unfinished"[36] is a radical statement for a Christian theologian of the early 1960s, and is an anticipation of what contemporary theologians have referred to as "unfulfilled messianism."

Related to this early version of "unfulfilled messianism" in *Theology of Hope* is Moltmann's emphasis on God's identification with negativity in history, an identification which allows him to confront the problem of theodicy and the reality of "negation." This power of negation, according to Moltmann, extends to social relations, political institutions and environmental conditions, and signifies the unredeemed character of the world. The recognition of an unredeemed world does not lead Christians to the same conclusion about the messiahship of Jesus as it does Jews.[37] It should, however, determine the nature of Christian belief about fulfillment in Christ and about the church's *mission* in the world.

Moltmann's discussion of mission is a fourth element of *Theology of Hope* which has implications for Jewish-Christian relations. In a section entitled "The Hermeneutics of Christian Mission" (272-303), Moltmann discusses the missionary practice which is "world-transforming and future-seeking" (288). Although it is not made explicit here, this emphasis on Christian mission which reflects and participates in the immanent aspects of the coming Kingdom can be a bridge to Jewish-Christian solidarity and partnership. The "partnership in mission" theme is developed in Moltmann's later work, but it is inchoate already in *Theology of Hope*.

If promise and mission (*promissio* and *missio*) are the major themes of *Theology of Hope*,[38] then the significance of this book for Jewish-Christian theological relations needs to be considered more carefully. For, as we have seen, in Moltmann's notions of "promise" (implying continuity between the Old and New Testaments and the communities around them, an open future for Israel and the church, and an unfinished component in reconciliation) and "mission" (implying the church's link with the Hebrew prophets and their vision of God's Kingdom), there are significant resources for theological dialogue between Christians and Jews.

B. *The Crucified God*

If *Theology of Hope* reflected the ethos of the 1960s, an era "brimming over with movements of hope and experiences of rebirth and renewal,"[39] then Moltmann's next major work, *The Crucified God*, published in 1972, reflected just as clearly the "reaction and breakdown of hope" that was already apparent in 1968, and which intensified in the 1970s.[40] After first turning his attention to "political theology," Moltmann then applied the experience of God in forsakenness and disappointment to the development of a modern "theology of the cross." Moving away from Bloch and relying on sources as diverse as the critical theory and negative dialectics of the Frankfurt School, Camus' protest atheism, Luther's theology of the cross, and the insights of early dialectical theology,[41] Moltmann engaged in a theological study of the meaning of Christ's cross for Godself. This, in turn, led him to a consideration of God's relationship to suffering and negativity in the world, including the expressions which these assumed in Auschwitz. Although critics have noted the book's failures with respect to post-Holocaust theology, *The Crucified God* does contain some positive resources for a Christian understanding of Israel.

First, Moltmann focuses on the earthly existence of Jesus in a way which is crucial for any Jewish-Christian rapprochement. Moltmann takes seriously Christology done "from below," while attempting to avoid what he calls Protestant Jesuology.[42] Moltmann even suggests that "we can come closer to the history and person of Jesus by doing today what the disciples did, entering into dialogue with Jews and taking their questions seriously" (198). This statement is suggestive of a second positive feature of his second book.

In *The Crucified God* Moltmann reveals a willingness to listen to the Hebrew tradition and to contemporary Jewish theology that surpasses his own standard set in *Theology of Hope*. Moltmann again demonstrates an affinity with the prophetic tradition, with its iconoclasm and radical monotheism. Moltmann's attacks on "theism," the "apathetic" God of Greek (and Christian) philosophy, and the gods of the modern world are based on an essentially Hebrew understanding of God (following the first commandment) and on the aniconic tradition of the prophets (following the second commandment). Even his use of Marx and Freud is determined by their (Jewish) criticism of religion, a criticism Moltmann believes can serve to guide Christian faith away from personal and societal idols.[43]

Other examples of Moltmann's willingness to audit Jewish tradition are evident in his occasional references to modern Jewish theology. Throughout *The Crucified God* Moltmann refers to the work of Jewish thinkers like Franz Rosenzweig, Walter Benjamin, Gershom Scholem and Shalom Ben-Chorin.[44] His greatest attempt at appropriation, however, comes in chapter six where he utilizes and adapts the "pathetic theology" of Abraham Heschel. Moltmann credits Heschel with rediscovering the "situation" of the pathos of God in the writings of the Hebrew prophets, a facet of the prophets' theology which Moltmann claims is lost in the more Hellenized philosophy of religion of Jehuda Halevi, Maimonides and Spinoza.[45] Moltmann believes Christian faith has more in common with the "pathetic" theology described by Heschel than with what he calls Greek "apathetic" theology, and concludes that "Christian theology cannot but learn from this new Jewish exegesis of the history of God in the Old Testament and in the present sufferings of the Jewish people."[46] Moltmann argues that although there can be no Christian "dipolar theology" (Heschel's term for describing God's simultaneous freedom and involvement in history through his covenant relationship with Israel), since no relationship of immediacy between God and humanity can be conceived apart from Christ, Jewish "pathetic theology" can help Christian faith reflect on the new "situation" of God revealed in the experience of the crucified Christ.[47]

There are also signs in *The Crucified God* of a willingness to hear and consider the Jewish "No" to Jesus. In a section entitled "Are you he who is to come?," Moltmann suggests that the "messianic question" not only points to its answer in Jesus, but also hinders this answer. This is because the dispute between Jews and Christians about Jesus is conducted on the basis of their "common question about the future" (100). If, as Moltmann claims, this dispute is between an atonement already believed to be present and a redemption which lies in the future, then Christians can accept the Jewish "No"--as it is expressed in statements by Scholem and Ben-Chorin[48]--as embodying a necessary corrective. In fact, the Jewish emphasis on real redemption in the visible world can accentuate the Christian hope in a fulfilled future redemption, a hope which has been obscured by the succession of one "enthusiastic certainty of fulfillment" after another in Christian history. When Christianity moves beyond its tendency to see the Kingdom of as redemption present in church, state, denomination, or Christianized secular world (101), then Christian triumphalism will be forsaken for a "history of convergence" between the Christian and Jewish hopes.

This history of convergence, Moltmann claims, will allow the hope of the Messiah, which has been made suspect precisely in reaction to Christian Christology, to reemerge in Judaism. It will also allow the Jewish expectation of the Kingdom, generally relegated to the Christian sects, to reemerge in Christianity. Moltmann's attention to the Jewish "No" to Jesus, at least insofar as this "No" arises from the unredeemed condition of the world, creates new possibilities for dialogue with Jewish theology. The Jewish insight that history is unredeemed seems to have found resonance with Moltmann precisely at the point where the hopeful movements of the 60s encountered failure, and seems to have been sharpened by his encounter with protest atheism's emphasis on suffering.[49] Indeed, the incompleteness of redemption becomes a permanent theme in Moltmann's theology after the early 1970s.

Given the degree of Moltmann's openness to Jewish thought in *The Crucified God*, it is difficult to comprehend that this book has been the target of serious criticism aimed precisely at its traditionalism and naïvete' *vis-'a-vis* Jews and Judaism. While this criticism has tended toward exaggeration,[50] it does point up some of the less successful elements in Moltmann's work, especially his treatment of the conflict between Jesus and the institutions of his day, and his attempt at developing a "theology of Auschwitz."

Generally speaking, in his discussion of the historical and eschatological "trials" of Jesus in chapters three and four of *The Crucified God* Moltmann accentuates the discontinuity[51] between Jesus and his contemporaries in order to highlight the novelty of Jesus' message. Moltmann is particularly keen to view the significance of the crucifixion in terms of the conflicts with Romans and Jews which characterized Jesus' life (127ff.). In order to make sense of Jesus' death and view it as the starting point for understanding Jesus' person (and thus for doing Christology), Moltmann moves backward, as it were, from Jesus' death to his life. In doing so, he highlights the inevitability of Jesus' death and the fundamental conflict between Jesus and his message of "prevenient and unconditional grace," on the one hand, and "the devout" who are "guardians of the law" on the other. Part of the explanation for this approach may be found in what Moltmann calls his "dialectical principle of knowledge." This principle leads Moltmann to search for God in that which is "not God," particularly in Christ's abandonment on the cross.[52] The application of this dialectical principle of knowledge in *The Crucified God* compels Moltmann to fasten on the paradox inherent in the story of a righteous God who is condemned by "the law."[53] Also behind Moltmann's emphasis on the conflict between Jesus and his Jewish religious environment in *The Crucified God* are Moltmann's dependence on Pauline theology, his predominantly "Lutheran" understanding of law, and his conviction that first-century Judaism was essentially a religion of works righteousness. This last assumption has been firmly challenged by recent scholarship, both before and since the publication of *The Crucified God*,[54] but is nevertheless central to Moltmann's discussion.

Alice and A. Roy Eckardt have been particularly critical of Moltmann on this issues raised above, taking him to task for his "pre-critical" and "biblicist" approach to Jesus' conflict with first century Judaism, and depicting him as a slave to Paul and Luther. While the Eckardts' penchant for exaggeration obscures their criticism of Moltmann, there is some truth in their critique. The Eckardts are correct, for instance, in observing that "the notion that God's grace is revealed in sinners and his righteousness revealed in the unrighteous hardly originated with Christianity."[55] Furthermore, they are right to argue that Moltmann's description of first-century Judaism as a religion of works righteousness is a distortion.[56] On the other hand, the Eckardts' claim that Moltmann's misinterpretation of Judaism "echoes the prevailing German biblical scholarship before and since 1933" (680), while rhetorically provocative, is also unfair and misleading. Moltmann does not reflect so much German biblical scholarship "before and since 1933" (a reference suggesting there is little if any difference between Moltmann and Nazi apologists like Kittell and Althaus), but the views of Moltmann's "exegetical friends,"[57] in particular Ernst Käsemann.

Käsemann's influence on German biblical scholarship was immense during the 60s and 70s, and the notes in *The Crucified God* suggest the significant extent to which Moltmann has been nurtured by Käsemann's work.[58] As Moltmann explained in a letter to Karl Barth, Käsemann forced him to "think through eschatologically" the origin, course and future of the lordship of Christ.[59] For Moltmann, this meant that the events of Christ's life, death and resurrection had to be understood in light of the enduring "apocalyptic" question--the question of God's righteous lordship on earth.[60] The key to Käsemann's own apocalyptic or eschatological orientation is the placing of "justification" in universal and world-historical perspective.[61] Käsemann follows his teacher Rudolf Bultmann in viewing the Pauline doctrine of justification by faith as the center of Christian theology and the aspect of the biblical message which possesses universal significance. For Käsemann, justification by faith must be eternally contrasted with a *nomos* of cosmic proportions.[62] In contemporary life, this *nomos* is most evident in the community of "good" people which turns God's promises into their own privileges and instruments of self-sanctification.[63]

Not surprisingly, in the New Testament, *nomos* is represented by the "Jewish nomism" against which Paul fought, and against which he developed his doctrine of justification. In opposition to this Jewish "nomism," Käsemann sets up the "law revealed in Christ," a law which revaluates earthly values, casts off the righteous and justifies the unrighteous.[64] Paul's doctrine of justification, which Käsemann claims is the theme of chapters 9-11 of Romans no less than the rest of the epistle, reveals that since creation, God has acted no differently with Jews and Gentiles. His being is the justification of the ungodly and hence the resurrection of the dead and the creation out of nothing. For he acts under the token of the crucified Christ, whom Israel, too, cannot escape.[65]

Käsemann's approach provides Moltmann with a "creation-eschatological" horizon for understanding Jesus' message, and serves as a foundation for Moltmann's universalizing of the significance and future of Christ. But Moltmann appears to have been influenced as well by Käsemann's "anti-nomism," and its application to the struggle between Christianity and first-century Judaism. We see this influence particularly in chapter four of *The Crucified God,* where Moltmann relies on traditional stereotypes of Pharisaism and the supposed "legalism" of first-century Judaism, emphasizing that Jesus' life was characterized by conflict between the God of Jesus and the God of the law and its "guardians." The influence of Käsemann is also evident in Moltmann's emphasis on a "different and new righteousness" in Jesus' message (130), in his statement that the resurrection created a "new righteousness of faith" (175), and in the notion that the conflict between Jesus and the Jews was intensified because promise and Torah had become separated in Judaism (135).[66] Moltmann's perception of a gap between Israel's Torah and the promise with which it was originally connected can probably be traced to Käsemann's notion that in the resurrection of Jesus, God's promises are released from any bond to the law or Israel's election, and become universalized.[67]

Even before the appearance of *The Crucified God,* Käsemann's understanding of justification and its anti-Jewish implications came under scholarly attack.[68] More recently, scholars have described Käsemann's understanding of the relationship between Israel and the church in terms of "illustration" (Klappert) and "opposition" (M. Barth).[69] Regardless of what label his thought is assigned, it is clear that Käsemann stands in the tradition of his teacher Bultmann, for whom the special history of Israel serves to illustrate the failure of human existence in general under law.[70] As Bertold Klappert puts it, with Paul as his crown-witness, Käsemann abolishes the special significance of Israel, and sees in the church a "destruction and reestablishment of the people of God."[71]

In *The Crucified God* Moltmann appears insensitive of the anti-Jewish and supersessionist tendencies in Käsemann's interpretation of the New Testament. Moltmann clearly seeks a theology from which Israel may be viewed in a positive post-Auschwitz light, but the elements of his theology influenced by Käsemann obscure such a view. Although Moltmann has never publicly disavowed Käsemann's influence, the attacks on *The Crucified God* by the Eckardts and others appear to have moved him decisively away from an emphasis on the conflict between law and gospel in Jesus' relationship to Judaism. In fact, despite Moltmann's alliance with the illustration model of Käsemann in *The Crucified God,* he has since condemned this expression of the relationship between Israel and the church, referring to it as the "viewpoint of necessary contrast." Moltmann's later work has even been invoked by Klappert as a witness against the illustration model.[72]

Returning to the Eckardts critique of Moltmann, we should note that while they are useful in reminding us of some of the biblical and historical work which Moltmann *ignores,*[73] the Eckardts are much less helpful in explaining the motivations and sources for what Moltmann *says.* Eckardt does not appear to be aware of or interested in the fact that the conflict between Jesus and the law is necessarily highlighted in Moltmann's attempt to begin theologically with the cross of Christ. Nor are the Eckardts sensitive to the influence of Käsemann's creation-eschatological perspective, a perspective Moltmann has adopted not because he intends to invalidate the promises or election of Israel, but in order to make these universal. The Eckardts are content to describe Moltmann's work in terms of traditional German theological anti-Judaism (using the fateful year 1933 to invoke Nazi images),[74] and leave it at that.

Perhaps even more criticism has been directed at *The Crucified God* for Moltmann's attempt to interpret Auschwitz by means of Christ and his cross.[75] Moltmann's theological concern with Auschwitz reflects both the sensitivities of German theology in the late 1960s,[76] as well as Moltmann's own burgeoning interest in Jewish-Christian dialogue. It is also a function of Moltmann's turn away from Bloch and toward the question of theodicy. After 1968, Moltmann was increasingly attracted to thinkers preoccupied with the questions of evil and suffering, particularly Camus and members of the Frankfurt School.[77] In each case, Moltmann incorporates the testimony of a "protest atheism" which challenges traditional theism on the basis of the world's evil and injustice.

In *The Crucified God* Moltmann does not attempt to develop a "theology of Auschwitz," nor was he particularly influenced at this time or since by Holocaust theology.[78] Rather, "Auschwitz" functions symbolically in *The Crucified God* as one example, albeit a staggering one, of the suffering which is characteristic of the contemporary world and which his theology of the cross must address. Realizing that this theology of the cross has to encompass all the world's misery if it is to overcome the opposition between God and suffering shared by traditional theism and protest atheism, Moltmann adopts Auschwitz as a true test case.

Moltmann claims that the Holocaust actually lends itself to interpretation in light of the cross--via the Jewish notions of God's self-humiliation and suffering with Israel,[79] and specific descriptions of Auschwitz-suffering in terms of a suffering God. Such a description Moltmann finds in a passage from Elie Wiesel's *Night*, a passage Moltmann calls a "shattering expression of the *theologia crucis* suggested in the rabbinic theology of God's humiliation.[80] Wiesel recalls from his death-camp experiences a child hanging helplessly on the gallows, and records that the scene prompted one onlooker to ask, "where is God now?" Wiesel reports hearing a voice within himself answer, "...He is here. He is hanging there on the gallows...." Moltmann comments that this is the only "Christian answer" to the question of God's presence in the Holocaust, and that any other would be blasphemy.

Moltmann's use of this passage from *Night* in support of his theology of the cross has been criticized from several perspectives. First, some have seen in his adoption of Wiesel's story proof that Moltmann understands the Holocaust as a "partial event,"[81] not a unique occurrence which overwhelms all attempts to comprehend it. This criticism is on target, since it is clearly the uniqueness of the *cross*, not the Holocaust, which occupies Moltmann in *The Crucified God*. The conclusion that Moltmann remains a pre-Holocaust thinker, however, is a rhetorical ploy which ignores the fact that Moltmann is *attempting* to make the Holocaust a criterion for Christian theology.[82] Second, some have criticized Moltmann for his apparent blindness to the fact that it is precisely in the wake of the Holocaust that the cross has been stripped of its power as a symbol of redemption.[83] Third, the objection has been made that in his treatment of Auschwitz, Moltmann orchestrates a Christianization and trinitarianization of Jewish suffering which may amount to thinly-veiled triumphalism.[84]

The second and third of these accusations are more difficult to judge than the first. The second is based on a premise ("the cross has lost its symbolic value") which is dubious, and which probably cannot be demonstrated in any case.[85] The third has some merit, although Moltmann's offending statements (that "even Auschwitz is taken up into the grief of the Father," and that Auschwitz is overcome in the "completion of the trinitarian history of God") are more a result of glibness and insensitivity than triumphalist intention. Even within the context of his own argument, in which he is attempting to correlate the sufferings of God represented in the cross and in the Holocaust, Moltmann's conclusions are open to dispute. For it is at least arguable that the godforsakenness of burning *children* in Auschwitz surpasses the suffering of the *adult* Jesus, the latter becoming "non-decisive" in comparison.[86]

Under the collective weight of these criticisms, Moltmann's "theology of Auschwitz" proves unsatisfactory. However, this should not cause us to overlook the fact that Moltmann has attempted to make Christian sense of contemporary Jewish suffering in a novel way. In fact, Moltmann's justification for this attempt is already expressed in *The Crucified God.* He admits that a "theology *of* Auschwitz" would not be acceptable at all had there been no "theology *in* Auschwitz." After all, Moltmann reminds us, the *Shema* of Israel and the Lord's Prayer were prayed there.[87] Furthermore, Moltmann is by no means the only theologian of his generation to interpret Auschwitz and Golgotha in mutual terms.[88] The extensive criticism which Moltmann's effort to do so has received testifies to the importance and influence of his theology.

C. *The Church in the Power of the Spirit*

Moltmann's third major theological work appeared in 1975 under the title *Kirche in der Kraft des Geistes: Ein Beitrag zur Messianischen Ekklesiologie* (E.T., *The Church in the Power of the Spirit.*).[89] *The Church in the Power of the Spirit* is Moltmann's most ecumenical book, and in chapter four he specifically addresses the relationship of the church with its partners in history "who are not the church and will never become the church." These partners include the major world religions, the economic, cultural and political processes of the world, and most important for our study, "Israel." In a section entitled "the church and Israel," Moltmann discusses the significance of Israel and Israel's traditions for the church. Within this section we encounter new emphases in Moltmann's theology, emphases which reflect a move away from his dependence on the law/gospel dynamic which characterized *The Crucified God,* and which represent a response to the Eckardts' triumphalism charge. This "contribution to ecclesiology" includes the closest thing in Moltmann's work to a developed Christian theology of Israel.

Moltmann begins by stressing that a new Christian consideration of the church-Israel relationship has been made necessary by "Auschwitz." This is because "after Auschwitz" the church must reconsider its history of paganization through anti-Judaism, which is actually "abuse of itself" (136), and because the founding of the state of Israel, an event which places Jewish-Christian relations on a new footing was "brought about by Auschwitz" (137). Moltmann goes on to argue that the church's historic anti-Judaism and triumphalism have had the effect of severing the church's links with its enduring origin, partner in history, and brother in hope--Israel (136). Moltmann recognizes in the detachment of the church from Israel and Israel's history a deep-seated self-hatred arising from discomfort with the church's own imperfection and not-yet character. Moltmann sees as the correct theological response to these problems: first, a reassertion of the relevance of the Old Testament *(sic);* second, a rediscovery of Christianity's own provisional nature in relation to the messianic Kingdom (by which Moltmann evidently means the provisional nature of the church, not Christ); and third, a recognition of the church's partnership with Israel (137).

In elaborating the first of these Christian responses to anti-Judaism, Moltmann argues that the negative judgment on Israel inherent in use of the term "Old" Testament obscures the fact that the church has never viewed this section of the Scriptures as superceded. What Moltmann seems to mean is that there has always been a stream within the church's tradition that has maintained the place of Israel in salvation history. As an example (and it is certainly one of the few available) Moltmann refers to the "salvation-historical" theology which arose in the Reformed federal theology of Cocceius in the seventeenth century, continued in Pietism in the eighteenth century and the nineteenth-century Erlangen School, and is evident today (138). This thread of tradition, Moltmann contends, emphasizes that Israel has a "call to salvation" independent of the church, understands the messianic promises of the Old Testament as being fulfilled in Jesus "only in principle," and is characterized by a "millenarian" hope that Christ will reign in history for a thousand years before the "end" (138).

This future millenarian hope in salvation-historical theology is viewed as particularly significant, since Moltmann maintains that when the church has understood itself as the messianic kingdom of Christ, the millenarian hope was rejected as a Jewish dream and a positive view of Judaism was impossible.[90] Moltmann contends that the theology of Cocceius, et. al. recovered millenarianism with its emphases on Israel's conversion in the last days, the subsequent thousand year reign of Christ, and the "second coming" in Jerusalem. This strand of "modern salvation-history apocalyptic," Moltmann concludes, contains the possibility of overcoming anti-Judaism because it vanquishes ecclesiastical absolutism (140). It is not clear, however, that it vanquishes triumphalism, a point to which we will return shortly.

Moltmann argues that rejection of the theology of salvation-history by scholars like Rudolf Bultmann and Paul Althaus has led to a stress on the universality of sin and grace which levels out and annihilates the specifics of Israel's promissory history:

> ...the Old Testament can then be interpreted in terms of human history as a whole, as Judaism can be easily seen as the negative foil to the gospel and Christian existence. The history of the promise recedes behind the antithesis of law and gospel....The justifying gospel is therefore directed towards all men, Jews and Gentiles alike. No special existence in the history of salvation can be ascribed to Israel any longer...(140-41).

This passage is useful not only because it reveals the implications of the work of influential Continental scholars like Bultmann and Althaus, but because it represents a distancing from and self-correction of the illustration model on which Moltmann himself was reliant in *The*

Crucified God. It is important to remember that on this topic the stance of Ernst Käsemann is very similar to that of Bultmann and Althaus which Moltmann now criticizes.

Moltmann goes on to stress, in opposition now to the Catholic scholar Erik Peterson, the continuity between the early church community of Jews and Gentiles and the "Israel" from which this community sprang. In marked contrast to his tendency in *The Crucified God* to paint clear distinctions between Jesus and the "law," Moltmann argues that the community of disciples "remained within the sphere of the law...and in the sphere of the Synagogue" (142). Moltmann even calls this new community a "revival movement within Israel itself." The new mission to the Gentiles did not represent a levelling down of differences between Israel and the nations, only a "reversal in practice of the Jewish order of hope."[91] In Moltmann's Pauline understanding of salvation-history, then the final acceptance of Israel follows the reconciliation of the Gentiles and the "messianic expectation of a remote future turns into a present hope in action" (143). Christianity and Judaism remain bound to each other in the structure of redemption, since the church itself is a "detour to Israel's salvation" (144). Israel's rejection of Christ is only the "external cause" of this detour, not its "inmost reason," and does not change the fact that the church is a "lived hope for Israel" (144).

Moltmann returns to an analysis of Christian theology and its understanding of Israel, this time examining the post-war confessional tradition. In his discussion of "new appraisals of Israel," Moltmann compares the Dutch Reformed Church's *Fundamenten en Perspektiven van Belijden* (1949) with Vatican II's "Declaration on the Relationship of the Church to Non-Christian Religions." Moltmann observes that the Dutch statement recognizes Israel's special significance for the church and speaks of dialogue rather than mission as the church's proper stance toward Jews. The Catholic statement, on the other hand, includes Israel in a discussion of non-Christian religions, an error which Moltmann argues has been perpetuated by other Christian churches and ecumenical organizations. Moltmann observes that while both statements recognize the abiding vocation of Israel, the Catholic document does not avoid portraying Israel as a preliminary stage in the life of the church. Although Moltmann does not make the connection explicit, the Dutch Reformed Church statement appears to be a contemporary example of the type of "salvation-historical" theology Moltmann believes is a resource for a post-Holocaust Christian understanding of Israel.

Moltmann, however, moves beyond both statements in his attempt to describe the precise nature of the fellowship between Israel and the church which these documents envision. Moltmann sees the key to this fellowship in the observation that in the Jews' calling (to hallow the divine name, to hope for the Kingdom, and to do God's will in obedience to Torah)[92] there is a "surprising consensus" with the first three petitions of the Lord's prayer. But Moltmann does not ignore the differences inherent in these two "callings." The church's special vocation, according to Moltmann, is the "service of reconciliation between God and the Gentiles, which heralds the redemption of the world" (148). In order to prepare humankind for the dawn of the messianic era, the church must pursue its unique calling outside the "fence of Israel," and thus can no longer function as a "revival movement within Israel." Its calling (to hallow Gods name, spread hope for the kingdom, and fulfill the will of God) has its foundation in the gospel of Christ. According to Moltmann, the callings of Israel and the church remain distinct, and, in fact, the church and Israel remain thorns in one another's sides. Israel impresses on the church the unredeemed nature of the world, while the church testifies to Israel of the presence of God's reconciliation with the world. In Pauline sense, the two communities make each other "jealous."

Finally in this section on "The Church and Israel" in *The Church in the Power of the Spirit,* Moltmann turns to the issue of Israel as "land." Moltmann affirms that God, people and land must remain inseparable in any Christian understanding of Israel. And yet, he says, the land question is filled with ambiguities that should make Christians cautious. On one hand, the state of Israel is a "sign" of an end to dispersion and a beginning for homecoming. On the other hand, there is the danger that Israel will become like other nations and perhaps be a "curse" to those driven out of Palestine. Furthermore, Moltmann believes that while the founding of the state of Israel is a foretoken of redemption (Rosenzweig), it is an ambiguous one. This state can give support to "Israel" in its special calling, but it cannot signify the end of the church's messianic mission to the world (149). Moltmann argues that Jews should not equate Zionism with messianism, but is quick to add that Christians cannot be expected to give a definitive statement on the meaning of the Israeli state when there is so much variety in Jewish conviction on the matter.[93]

We turn now to a few critical observations and questions on the Christian theology of Israel expressed in *The Church in the Power of the Spirit*. First, it is apparent that Moltmann has reconsidered his implicit use of an illustration model for understanding the relationship of Israel and the church in *The Crucified God*, replacing it with a fairly developed "complementarity" model. There were intimations of this vision of complementarity in *The Crucified God*, but statements there about the church and Israel existing side by side were theological quantum leaps beyond that text's central assertion of a qualitative difference between righteousness as understood by Jesus and his followers and by the Jewish guardians of the law.[94] In response to Moltmann's claim that such a distinction between Jesus' righteousness and that represented by the law does not invalidate but universalizes the promises and election of Israel, Alice and A. Roy Eckardt have accused Moltmann of "triumphalism in the guise of anti-triumphalism."[95] This charge leads us to ask whether Moltmann's attempt to overcome triumphalism in *The Church in the Power of the Spirit* is successful. Despite Moltmann's premise that Israel is one of the church's "partners in history" which cannot be christianized or ecclesiasticized, it is important to ask whether the logic of Moltmann's theology does not lead precisely to a christianization of Israel. It is clear that Moltmann's vision does not include the kind of merging of Israel and church the likes of which we encountered in Barth. But one does recognize in Moltmann's salvation-historical theology an eschatological vindication of the church's claim that Jesus Christ is the messiah of Israel. Even when the church is understood as a "detour for Israel's salvation," and a community which exists "for Israel," it is not possible to detect a bit of selfishness in the church's enthusiasm for the "calling of Israel" at the end of time.

Israel's "call to salvation" (as adapted from Reformed Federal theology) may be independent of the church (which is a provisional entity in Moltmann's theology), but it is not independent of God's action in Christ. Moltmann might respond that it is primarily the messianic *Kingdom* on which both Israel and the church are ultimately dependent, but this is a messianic Kingdom whose Messiah has been revealed as Jesus of Nazareth, and whose nature is universal righteousness, understood in Christian terms. Can we say, then, that Moltmann has succeeded in overcoming Christian triumphalism in its eschatological as well as its historical form? The Eckardts think Moltmann has exchanged a "pure" for a "postponed" triumphalism in *The Church in the Power of the Spirit.*[96] They argue that if the *parousia* of Christ is determined to bring fulfillment to the Christian and Jewish hopes alike (and I do not see how one can avoid this interpretation of Moltmann on the basis of *The Church in the Power of the Spirit*), this necessarily denies that Jews are already in a covenant relationship with God. While I do not believe Eckardt's conclusion is necessary, it is difficult to see how Moltmann's approach can logically escape the label "triumphalist," even though traditional forms of triumphalism have been seriously qualified in his theology. In addition to this problem, Moltmann has opened himself to charges that his concept of a "special calling" for Israel continues to place special demands on Jews--demands which have been deemed unacceptable in the post-Holocaust era.[97]

Finally, we should explore in a preliminary way the relationship of Moltmann's theology of Israel outlined in *The Church in the Power of the Spirit* to Barth's Israel-doctrine. Although Moltmann does not refer directly to Barth in this section of *The Church in the Power of the Spirit,* his discussion of "new appraisals of Israel" has a Barthian tenor. For instance, Moltmann's complaint that the Catholic statement from Vatican II lumps together Judaism with non-Christian religions in general is reminiscent of Barth's comments to this effect in *Ad Limina Apostolorum.*[98] It is also interesting that Moltmann does not criticize the quite Barthian passage from the section of the Dutch declaration he has quoted--a passage which declares that "Israel lives among the nations as the token and mirror of God's judgment."[99] On the other hand, Moltmann offers an implicit criticism of Barth's doctrine that Israel is a witness to judgment when he argues that the "bare fact of the existence and survival of Judaism in dispersion and persecution" (147) is not enough to symbolize the abiding faithfulness of God. Here Moltmann reveals a sensitivity to Jewish life and thought which distinguishes his theology of Israel from Barth's. This sensitivity is also apparent in his observation that Christians must also "recognize how Jews have subjectively remained alive" (147), through their calling to hallow the divine name, etc.

Finally, we must evaluate Moltmann's brief statements on "the land of Israel." Moltmann shares with other post-Holocaust theologians the recognition of the importance of the "land question" for Christian theology. But he also stresses the ambiguity inherent in any statements about the significance of this land and its relationship to the messianic Kingdom.[100] Moltmann, of course, is sensitive enough to recognize the difficulties which Christian support for the state of Israel will inevitably encounter. One wonders, however, whether a Christian theology of Israel can allow these ambiguities to prevent it from developing a clear statement on the religious significance of the Israeli state. Many Christians may share Moltmann's hope that Zionism will not replace messianism in the Jewish mind. But we should like to know from Moltmann more about how he views the relationship between these two forms of hope. We turn now to a consideration of Moltmann's work since *The Church in the Power of the Spirit* as it reflects his developing understanding of Israel.

III. MOLTMANN ON ISRAEL: RECENT WRITINGS

A. Articles

We consider first Moltmann's "Jewish and Christian Messianism," an article that appeared in *The Experiment Hope,* an English collection of Moltmann's essays published in 1975.[101] "Jewish and Christian Messianism" touches on some of the themes developed in *The Church in the Power of the Spirit,* and further elaborates ideas that were set forth for the first time in *The Crucified God.*[102] In this article Moltmann reiterates the "anti-Judaism is rooted in Christian self-hatred" theme which we have encountered in his other work, and expands this Rosenzweigian notion to suggest that Christians' anxiety concerning their own "not yet" should lead them to accept the perpetual "not yet" of the Jewish messianic hope (66). Moltmann once again invokes statements by Scholem and Ben-Chorin[103] in order to accentuate the Jewish understanding of the unredeemed nature of creation and the Jewish belief that redemption must take place within the visible world. Moltmann believes that in these statements Christians are confronted with the essence of the Jewish "No" to the ancient question about Jesus: "are you the one who is to come?" This version of the Jewish "No"

Moltmann then incorporates into the church's theology through a reactivation of Christianity's own original eschatological hope. In this way Moltmann seeks to deny the Jewish claim that Christianity understands redemption as interior and individual, by arguing that this reflects not true Christianity, but Christianity under the "influence of gnosticism." (62) It is not the case, in other words, that "a totally different concept of redemption determines the attitude to Messianism in Judaism and Christianity" (Scholem). With this move, Moltmann appears on his way toward bridging the "wide gulf" between Judaism and Christianity symbolized by Scholem's version of the Jewish "No."

Moltmann's interest in messianism, then, is not academic; it is a function of his vision for Jewish-Christian complementarity. Moltmann elaborates this complementarity with a version of "messianic Christology" that shares what he calls the Jewish messianic vision. In particular, Moltmann believes Christology must learn from "the openness of the Jewish Messiah figure to the greater Kingdom of God" (65). Moltmann responds to Scholem's Jewish rejection of the "personal attributes" in Jesus' messiahship by arguing (in contrast to Christian tendencies toward absolutizing the image or person of Jesus), that Jesus' "person is defined by his destiny" (65). Moltmann is able to make the connection between Jesus and the Jewish messianic hope even more explicit: "He cannot be tied down to an image but rather liberates us from the idols of our present experience as well as of hope in the coming God." (65). In summing up, Moltmann argues that Christian "enthusiasms of fulfillment" must be exchanged for "open eschatological hope."

Another theme developed by Moltmann in "Jewish and Christian Messianism," again in the hope of bridging the messianic gap between Jews and Christians, is the "suffering form of Jesus" (67). Although Moltmann admits that only a few Jewish texts speak of a suffering and dying messiah, he finds correspondences with the idea of a suffering messiah in figures like Job, and in Israel's own suffering. While Moltmann understands the death of Jesus on the cross for those who are suffering as the "deepest realization" of the messianic hope, he does not attempt here to associate this suffering messiah with the suffering of Jews in Auschwitz. For this reason "Jewish and Christian Messianism," which appeared after the publication of *The Crucified God*, reflects a move away from Moltmann's earlier attempt to interpret Auschwitz in relation to the suffering of the Christian messiah. On the other hand, Moltmann continues to see the cross as a foil to Christian triumphalism and an important bridge toward Christian-Jewish solidarity.

Moltmann's quest for a "new convergence of Jewish and Christian hope" (66) leads him to a revision of the christological foundations of Christianity, a project which continues to occupy him fifteen years after "Jewish and Christian Messianism" was written. Moltmann believes that when Christianity, with the help of Judaism, recovers a truly messianic understanding of Jesus, the ambivalence between apocalyptic and utopian expectation will be overcome and Christianity will become a "ferment of dissolution" in the world. Only then will Christians see that a (Jewish) hope in the Kingdom of God and a (Christian) sense of the messianic presence in history can together overcome both expectations of world catastrophe and underestimations of the mystery of evil (63). Moltmann is convinced that only by encountering Jewish messianism can Christianity become aware of its own "eschatological provisionality" before the coming Kingdom--a provisionality suggested by the distinction in I Cor. 15:28 between the Lordship of the Son of Man and the Lordship of God. Encountering and learning from the "Jewish critique" leads the church to a deeper and better understanding of Jesus and his future. The concrete existence of the Jews has the effect of constantly raising the question of Christianity's messianic hope, and reminding the church that, along with Israel, it is on the way to a goal greater than itself.

This little article is important for the way it introduces an eschatological interpretation of Christology, as well as for the way it elaborates a convergence of hope between Jews and Christians based on a genuine hearing of Jewish theology's "No" to Jesus' messiahship. Questions remain, however. For instance, is not triumphalism still implicit in Moltmann's understanding of the messianic Kingdom as the common goal of Judaism and Christianity? And are there not other versions of the Jewish "No" to Jesus which might preclude the covergence Moltmann seeks to achieve. Despite these questions, "Jewish and Christian Messianism" demonstrates that Moltmann has advanced beyond Barth's theology of Israel, both in his willingness to listen to Judaism and his ability to formulate a vision of genuine solidarity between Israel and the church.

In "Christian Hope: Messianic or Transcendent?," (1982)[104] Moltmann responds to critics of his messianic interpretation of Christian hope[105] by reviving a medieval debate between Thomas Aquinas and Joachim of Fiore over whether Christian hope is transcendentally or messianically determined. Moltmann argues that Hans urs von Balthasar, in his critique of Moltmann's work, has repeated the doctrinal decision of Thomas against Joachim. Moltmann observes that Joachim evolved his messianic future hope on the basis of a "recognized correlation between the Old and New Testaments' history of promise" (330). In doing so, Moltmann argues, "Joachim correctly recognized the irrefutably 'forward-looking' character of the biblical promises with their emphasis on historical and eschatological fulfillment...Thomas on the other hand, replaces the biblical history of the promise with a finalistic metaphysic" (332-3).

Moltmann observes that in Thomas' view of salvation history the New Law replaces the Old Law, the church replaces Israel and the Kingdom of God lies beyond history (343). Joachim, on the other hand, recognized the insufficiency of a church without Israel. His presentation of an inner, spiritual and direct knowledge of the truth in the age of the Holy Spirit has Jewish parallels (340), claims Moltmann, and his distinction between the gospel of Christ and the gospel of the Kingdom was intended to "solve the problem of Israel" (345). Moltmann follows Joachim (and Paul) in elaborating the implications of a Christian messianic hope:

> Israel will not be redeemed by the ecclesiastical gospel of Christ itself...[but] by the appearing of the Messiah in glory, the Messiah whom the Christians call 'Jesus' (346).

Israel will be "redeemed," then, at the universal appearance of Christ. This means that the common future of Israel and the church is centered in the *parousia* and Kingdom of their Messiah. This, in turn, leads to a bond of solidarity and dependence between Israel and the church: "the church is incomplete without Israel. Together with Israel, the church places its hopes in the messianic Kingdom which will unify both" (347).

When Christians reaffirm the chiliastic hope which disappears from Christian eschatology whenever the church views itself as a fulfillment of the promised Kingdom, they are able to acknowledge

Israel as an "independent travelling companion on the way to the Kingdom" (348). Thomas and Joachim, then, should be taken together as representatives of two sides of the Christian hope which must accompany each other: "...chiliasm is the immanent side of eschatology. Eschatology is the transcendent side of chiliasm. Thus, there can be no chiliasm without eschatology...and there can be no eschatology without chiliasm" (348).

In this article Moltmann attempts to show that the "openness of the Jewish Messiah figure to the greater Kingdom of God" which he described in "Jewish and Christian Messianism" is inherent in the Christian tradition itself. The messianic theology of Joachim of Fiore, in which the Jewish messianic spirit and the hope in future redemption are preserved, has in common with salvation-historical theology the fact that it "solves the problem of Israel" by maintaining Israel's place in the future of the creation. It is also apparent, however, that both streams of Christian theology understand Israel's penultimate future in Christian terms. By anticipating Israel's redemption in the "universal appearance of Christ" at the end of time, these theologies share in the postponed triumphalism referred to earlier. This fact leads us to ask with the Eckardts whether a Christian theology which envisions Israel's redemption in the messianic future lays enough stress on the covenant between God and the Jewish people.

B. Dialogues

Moltmann's most important recent work devoted to a Christian understanding of Israel is found in his contributions to two dialogues with Pinchas Lapide, an Orthodox Jew. The first of these dialogues took place in 1979 and was published under the title *Jewish Monotheism and Christian Trinitarian Doctrine*.[106] In this dialogue Moltmann attempts to understand Christian doctrine in light of Jewish belief, as his dialogue with Jewish theology enters the dimension of personal encounter with a believing Jew. *Jewish Monotheism and Christian Trinitarian Doctrine* reveals that Moltmann is able to perceive continuity with Judaism in an area traditionally viewed as a theological logjam. But as we shall see, it also reveals the limits of his "messianic" approach for Jewish-Christian understanding.

The statement by Lapide on "Jewish Monotheism" with which he opens the dialogue suggests Lapide's conciliatory position toward Christianity. Lapide accepts a Rosenzweigian view of the church as a "God-willed way of salvation," a *preparatio messianica* of the Gentile world for the reign of God. Lapide is even able to accept the "sonship" of Jesus (although this is understood in a Hebrew rather than in a Greek sense) and the historicity of the resurrection. Lapide displays a broad knowledge of the New Testament and Christian theology, and is perhaps as accommodating of Christian faith as it is possible for a Jewish theologian to be. In fact, both Lapide and Moltmann are deft of searching each other's religion to discover resources for a common rapprochement. At times, one feels they are engaged in competition to display the hidden treasures of the other's tradition.

Lapide elaborates his understanding of the Jewish-Christian relationship by observing that in the first century Christianity was still monotheistic in good Jewish fashion, but was soon corrupted by its confession of a two-in-one and a three-in-one God in the second and third centuries, respectively. Furthermore, Lapide observes, divine ontic relationships began to occupy the church precisely at the point when it began to relinquish its hold on the Old Testament. Moltmann responds to Lapide's overtures in a statement entitled "The Christian Doctrine of the Trinity," where he claims that it is not a "Jewish" versus a "Christian" conception of God which has separated church and synagogue, but a "Jewish-Christian conception" of God versus the "apathetic god of the philosophers." Moltmann appears to accept Lapide's charge that the church's original Jewish monotheism was corrupted by Hellenistic theology in the second and third centuries. But he sees not only monotheism, but trinitarianism as well as fundamental to the early church's faith. In fact, Moltmann traces the doctrine of the Trinity back to its "Hebraic and Jewish roots" (46).

First, Moltmann claims that the doctrine of the Trinity is only a conceptual framework needed to understand the story of Jesus as the story of God. It arose not from Greek philosophy, but from attention to the implications of the crucified Christ for understanding God. Then, Moltmann invokes Abraham Heschel's discovery of "the original Jewish experience of God in the prophets' theology of divine pathos"to show that "the Jewish experience of God cannot be a simple monotheism." In Heschel's "bipolar theology," in which God is free in Godself but committed in the covenant, Moltmann believes he has uncovered a "self-distinction" in the Jewish conception of God. Moltmann adds references to the rabbinic studies of A. M. Goldberg and Peter Kuhn order to confirm the validity of Heschel's notion of a "self-abasement of God" in the *Shekinah*. Drawing on these Jewish witnesses to a self-distinction in the divine, Moltmann concludes that

> systematically...the experience of the co-suffering of God and the recognition of the self-distinction of God in God's co-suffering is the most profound commonality that there can be between Christians and Jews.[107]

As in *The Crucified God*, Moltmann works from the reality of God's suffering to an understanding of God which can take this suffering into account, and so further adapts what he has learned from Heschel concerning the "Jewish possibility" of divine passion (51). As the passion of God is the basis of the Jewish experience of self-distinction in God, so the passion of Christ is the basis of the Christian recognition of the trinitarian self-distinction in God (52). Despite obvious differences and distinctions between Jewish and Christian experience, Moltmann contends that

> The cross on Golgotha reveals the trinitarian difference and the unity of God...this is for the Christian primordial experience the "divine pathos," the "self-abasement" of God, the preparedness-for-Exile Shekinah.[108]

Moltmann concludes that because the giving up "for many" of the *Jew* Jesus is the foundation of the Christian doctrine of the Trinity, it "cannot be viewed as a contradiction to Jewish monotheism" (56).

In response to this remarkable attempt at relating the Christian and Jewish understandings of God, Lapide questions the "separation of God from Himself" which Moltmann adopts from Rosenzweig and Heschel. Lapide believes that despite what other Jews may have suggested in their attempts to affirm God's presence with God's people, there can be no division or self-distinction in the Incomprehensible One. Moltmann counters that, in any case, God's self-distinction is implied by God's self-communication (revelation), although this claim is not developed.

In the informal segment of the dialogue, Lapide takes up the issue of Jewish and Christian messianism and in doing so presents a Jewish response to Moltmann's "messianic" version of Jewish-Christian solidarity (developed particularly in "Jewish and Christian Messianism" and Christian Hope: Messianic or Transcendent?"). Lapide argues that Judaism and Christianity, though both messianic, are actually two distinct *types* of messianic religion: "with you the King stands in the middle, and with us it is the Kingdom" (72). For the Jew, Lapide goes on to say, messianism remains an instrumentality in service of the Kingdom--*who* brings about the reign of God is a secondary matter (73). Messianic speculation in Judaism, therefore, remains "functional," rather than "personal," making Judaism a what- and Christianity a who-religion. In his response, Moltmann finds it difficult to relinquish the unique relationship between God and the Messiah which this view challenges. Moltmann asks if there is not a unique relationship implied between God and Messiah even in the election of a Messiah with only "instrumental" significance (82).

In the end, Lapide and Moltmann find a meeting place in their discussion of messianism. Lapide describes as an "acceptable formula of reconciliation" Moltmann's statement that "through his crucifixion Christ has become saviour of the Gentiles. But in his *parousia* he will also manifest himself as Israel's Messiah."[109] The acceptance of such a statement is surprising given the presence here of what we have called Moltmann's "postponed triumphalism." Lapide's ability to live with this eschatological vindication of Christianity reflects his view that since no Jew knows who the coming Messiah is, Christian certainty can only be countered with a "humble question mark" (79). Lapide even suggests the issue of Jesus' present significance as Christ for the Gentiles can be "bridged over" with the help of Moltmann's affirmation that the reign of heaven has only been initiated, and the suggestion in I Cor. 15:28 that Christ will not sit at the right hand of the Father for all eternity (75). Furthermore, if the Messiah should turn out to be Jesus of Nazareth, Lapide cannot imagine a single believing Jew who would resist this.

While it is doubtful whether Lapide's conciliatory words are representative of Judaism as a whole, it is interesting that Lapide's vision of complementarity between Jews and Christians is similar to Moltmann's own. Both emphasize the recovery of an "originally common hope" as the key to coexistence. According to Lapide, recovering this common hope requires a return *ad fontes* of Israel--a move reflected in the current "Hebrew wave" in Christian theology (75). Lapide's emphasis on the church and Israel as separate "God-willed paths of salvation" is met in Moltmann's own vision of complementarity. As Moltmann expresses it,

> Israel and Christendom are moving on the same path, but with different tasks. Their union into oneness will be brought about only in messianic time in the fullest sense of the word, in the reign of God...Christendom can gain salvation only together with Israel...For the sake of the Jew Jesus there is no ultimate separation between the church and Israel. For the sake of the gospel there is provisionally, before the eschatological future, also no fusion. But there is the communal way of hoping ones.[110]

A second Lapide-Moltmann dialogue was published under the title *Israel und Kirche: Ein Gemeinsamer Weg?: Ein Gespräch*.[111] In this dialogue Moltmann opens the exchange with a statement entitled "Church and Israel: A Common Way of Hope?"[112] Here Moltmann reiterates themes expressed in his other work, as well as elaborating some new perspectives on "Israel." First, Moltmann stresses that Christian faith, especially in Germany, cannot fail to take Auschwitz or its Christian roots seriously. "Authentic" Christian faith resists collective repression, as well as the overwhelming guilt which surfaces when one recognizes Auschwitz as the "endpoint of a long anti-Jewish development in Christianity" (192). This recognition, furthermore, must lead to a rethinking of Christianity's very roots, as well as attention to the political dimension that enters theology whenever the words "Israel"[113] and "Auschwitz" are used.

Moltmann emphasizes that with the remembrance of Auschwitz, politics enters any Christian-Jewish dialogue--partly due to the church's acquiescence to National Socialism, and partly due to a long history that includes the "socialization of the church" and the "nationalization of Christianity" (192). This history has separated Christians from Jews since the time of Constantine, and even since the time of Pilate, Christian-Jewish dialogue has been a theological-political dialogue. Moltmann concludes from this that dialogue cannot be carried on non-politically today. But what does this mean?

First, this means there must be a "critical distancing of Christians from the political and civil religion in which they exist," a distancing that will result in a Christian recognition of the Jews (192). Second, this critical relationship to political and civil religion[114] must be accompanied by a reaffirmation of the chiliastic eschatology which has characterized Christianity whenever it has enjoyed a positive relationship with the Jewish people (204). Chiliasm, Moltmann argues, has too often been labeled a "Jewish dream" or been replaced by some present fulfillment of the chiliastic hope (as in the Constantinian Empire, the chiliastic interpretation of church history following Tyconius and Augustine, or the political messianism of National Socialism). Chiliasm must be revived despite these false interpretations, argues Moltmann, and, more importantly, must remain bound to eschatology.

Moltmann argues that an animated hope for the future of the Jews depends on the kind of messianic restitution of Israel found in the chiliastic theology of the Dutch Federal theologians, Pietists and nineteenth-century Lutherans whom Moltmann has repeatedly referred to in his other work. Moltmann adopts the conviction, central to this "missionary theology," that Israel will be restored after the fullness of the Gentiles has been realized. He then adds that Christians will not come into the salvation of the Kingdom of God without Jews (208). Here Moltmann is clear, in contradistinction to Barth, that it is the Kingdom of God, not the church, which is Israel's future.[115]

Third, "political" dialogue between Christians and Jews means that the "land question" is not ignored. Moltmann affirms that today the very name "Israel" means that issues of land and politics enter the discussion. For Christians this means that "whoever recognizes the covenant of God with Israel must also take the promise of land in earnest" (213). However, since the relationship of this promise and the present state of Israel remains debated among Jews, Moltmann reiterates that Christians may not become champions of the promise's fulfillment in present-day Israel. Any claim for this promise's fulfillment in historical time, says Moltmann, is mitigated by the "ambiguity" of a Jewish existence "darkened" by military, economic, and diplomatic realities.

Two questions arise from Moltmann's discussion of the political dimensions of Jewish-Christian encounter. The first is whether

Moltmann is justified in interpreting seventeenth-century Reformed and nineteenth-century Lutheran theology as if they meant by "Israel" what Moltmann means. Although this question is not easily answered, one suspects these theologies used "Israel" to refer to an eschatological remnant of Jews willing to return to Palestine and usher in the last days, rather than to Jews then living in Europe. If this is the case, Moltmann's contention that in this theology "Christianity waits next to Israel and hopes with Israel for the future redemption of the world" (202) is misleading. Moltmann, after all, is clearly using "Israel" here to refer to the contemporary, often secular, Jews. Moltmann owes us a more thorough description of how salvation-historical theology understood "Israel" and Israel's "calling" before he is justified in looking to it for guidance in contemporary Jewish-Christian relations. Second, we must ask about the implications of Moltmann's statement that Christians cannot become champions of the land promise's alleged fulfillment in the state of Israel. Does this mean that Christians are prohibited from sympathizing with Jewish or Christian religious Zionism? Must they be anti-Zionist? What political loyalties in the Middle East are "authentic" Christians likely to have? Again, we are left wishing Moltmann would say more concerning these questions that are so salient for many Christians.

Besides requiring a commitment to "political" encounter, Moltmann argues in "Church and Israel: A Common Way of Hope?" that preparation for dialogue also requires the overcoming of religious imperialism and the dismantling of theological prejudices. In the first case, Christians must realize that their definitions of Jews, Judaism and Israel are often insufficient because Christians require the "image of the enemy" to strengthen their own identity (190), because dialogue based on these definitions cannot be genuine, and because Christians should not define their Jewish conversation partners or tell them how they must understand themselves. The theological prejudices Moltmann mentions are: the "viewpoint of religious indifference," which denies that Christianity is dependent on Judaism or on the election of Israel (and is roughly synonymous to Klappert's integration model), the "viewpoint of necessary contrast," which understands Christianity as arising from a basic contradiction in Judaism and as bound to Jewish existence only in a negative way (and is very close to Klappert's illustration model),[116] and the "viewpoint of inheritance," which interprets the history of Israel as the pre-history of Christianity and perceives Judaism as an anachronism (and is similar to Klappert's typology model).[117]

Moltmann stresses that each of the "viewpoints" he describes are supersessionist. All three declare the theological death of Israel and dispossess the Jews of their promises. In opposition to these unacceptable viewpoints Moltmann summons Christians to a "two-fold view of Jews," drawn from Romans 11:28. In light of their rejection of the gospel, the Jews are "enemies;" but are enemies "for your sake," since their rejection means salvation for the Gentiles. Moltmann emphasizes that in light of the promises made to the Fathers, the Jews remain "beloved." "Christian universalism," concludes Moltmann, need not abolish the special character of Israel, but can even, following Paul, recognize and respect it.

Moltmann goes on to describe the separate callings of church and Israel which comprise his universalist vision in terms familiar from his earlier writings. Here, however, Moltmann is clear that Judaism's call to do the divine will according to the covenant in no way implies "legalism." It is "false to see only legality and works-holiness in Jewish obedience to the Law" (210). The calling of the church, meanwhile, is to transmit messianic hope to the nations and thus fulfill its role as a *preparatio messianica*--a first step toward the redemption of Israel and the world (212). Moltmann adds that there is more significance in Judaism for Christianity than in Christianity for Judaism, since for Christians there is no history without the Jews. In recognizing the special calling of Israel, the church recognizes better its own calling and its partnership with Israel in the "community on the way through history into the future of God" (211).

C. Moltmann's Christology

At this point we shall consider a final aspect of Moltmann's developing theology of Israel--the theological revision in view of Christian-Jewish relations found in the first chapter of his newest book on Christology.[118] In the early 1970s Moltmann recognized that "without a revision in the christological foundations of Christianity there can scarcely be a new convergence of Christian and Jewish hope."[119] In his newest book Moltmann utilizes the common messianic hopes of Jews and Christians in developing a Christology in Jewish-Christian dialogue. Moltmann claims he is following the path he marked out for himself in *Theology of Hope,* where he stressed that Yahweh raised the Jew Jesus from the dead, and in *The Crucified God,* where he argued for a Christology "from ahead" in opposition to a metaphysical Christology "from above" or an anthropological Christology "from below." Moltmann is consciously transcending his earlier work, however, by emphasizing in a novel way the continuity between the Christian gospel and the Jewish promissory history of the Old Testament.

Moltmann believes that although Christology has almost always torn Jews and Christians apart, it is not necessary that it do so, or that Christology be anti-Jewish. For reasons he has elaborated elsewhere, Moltmann is convinced the expectation of the Messiah actually binds Jews and Christians together. Christology is, after all, only one definite form of the Israelite messianic hope, a form which remains "related to and dependent on" more Jewish forms. Moltmann adapts the work of Jewish thinkers like Martin Buber, Walter Benjamin and Gershom Scholem in an attempt to describe messianism in its quintessential Jewish form, a form he claims transcends any historical fulfillment. While seeking to develop the Jewish categories of the messianic, Moltmann remains fully aware that his perceptions are Christian: "Of course, the concept of the messianic is developed here out of Jesus' own personality and history. What else could a Gentile Christian do?" (9). Yet Moltmann intentionally proceeds in an open manner, attending carefully to Jewish messianic hope and to what Jewish religion and philosophy have to say about it.

Moltmann begins by rejecting every theological claim (including Barth's) that Jesus is the *terminus* of the messianic hope. Moltmann dissociates himself from every "theology of fulfillment of Old Testament prophecy" as well, and seeks a new orientation to Christology that integrates the eschatological history of Jesus and an emphasis on "the Coming One" (*Der Kommende*) into an holistic Christology. Moltmann believes this holistic approach will overcome the historic split between Christology and eschatology--a split which has resulted in Christology losing its true future-horizon in the *parousia* of Christ. Partly as a result of the church's struggle with the synagogue, this whole area of eschatology has often been discredited as a "Jewish dream,"[120] with chiliastic eschatology being excluded from theology altogether. The interrelatedness of Christology and eschatology, Moltmann argues, can only be rediscovered through a return to their common roots in Old Testament messianology. Then the Christian division between faith in Christ and hope for the future will be overcome by an *eschatological Christology*. This in turn will lead to a *christological eschatology* in which Jesus is perceived as the Christ in a "remembered hope" (*errinerte Hoffnung*).

Drawing from biblical texts in Isaiah, Zechariah, Micah and Daniel, Moltmann describes a "two-level" Old Testament messianology that reflects hopes for a *particular* messiah and a *universal* "Son of Man": "The messiah cannot be understood without his special people; the Son of Man comprises all the human beings of all peoples" (21). The two hopes represented here go together, Moltmann argues, since messianism is the historical side of apocalyptic, and apocalyptic is the transcendent side of messianism. This statement reveals that in his interpretation of the Old Testament and of Jewish messianic thought, Moltmann perceives a dialectical relationship between particular and universal hope which corresponds to the dialectic Christianity must maintain in its own future expectation. As Moltmann puts it in "Christian Hope: Messianic or Transcendent?," a (Jewish) chiliastic hope is the immanent side of eschatology, while an eschatological hope is the transcendent side of chiliasm. Moltmann adds that both the Messiah and Son of Man figures are "preliminary and expiring" (22). Reflecting the influence of Lapide, Moltmann argues that there can be no messianic "cult of the person":

> An historically, personally discovered and thus definable Messiah or Son of Man contradicts the intrinsic openness of the messianic and of the apocalyptic hope, an openness which refers to God himself and is thus transcendent....The openness can only be fulfilled if God himself comes together with the Messiah and with the Son of Man.[121]

Both these figures, says Moltmann, are "transparent for the Kingdom of God's divine majesty....In themselves and by their reign, the coming God announces himself" (22). Moltmann desires to keep open and provisional every messianic hope, arguing that messianic claims can be judged only on the basis of their relationship to God's Kingdom. In his survey of Jewish and Old Testament messianism, Moltmann appears to have taken to heart the Jewish conviction that the messianic age must be accompanied by redemption of the world.

Continuing this approach, Moltmann admits that while hope for the Messiah leads the church to Jesus, the same hope is a hindrance to his recognition by Jews. Every Christology, in other words, must face up to the Jewish "No" (29). Moltmann follows Buber's argument that it is not a question of Jews' *refusal* to accept Jesus, but of their *inability* to do so since they perceive no caesura in history. The Jewish "No," then, rooted as it is in Kingdom-faith rather than bad-will or resentment, is a special "No." It is not like the "No" of non-believers, but is a providential "No" which effects a reversal in the order of salvation history. Discovering the will of God in this "No," Moltmann argues, is a key to the repudiation of Christian anti-Judaism. Most significant are the implications this Jewish "No" has for the Christian "Yes." It reminds Christians, for instance, that Jesus is not yet the *parousia* Christ, nor is the resurrected Christ yet the Pantocrator. The Christian "Yes" *based on experienced reconciliation with God* cannot be an exclusive "Yes" as long as it incorporates the Jewish "No" *based on experienced non-redemption of the world.* Moltmann believes a Christian "Yes" that affirms Christ as "becoming" is the key to a "theology on the way"-- a theology which eschews triumphalism:

> The Christian yes to Jesus as the Christ is *not yet* finished and complete, but open instead to a messianic future of Jesus. It is an eschatologically preliminary yes in advance....That is why it cannot be an exclusive and excommunicating yes even if it is spoken with the assurance of a confession of faith. Whoever confesses Jesus as the "Christ" of God recognizes a Christ coming into being, a Christ on his way, a Christ in the motion of an eschatological history of God, and that person steps into the following of Jesus on this Christ-way.[122]

As we observed earlier, Moltmann argues for the necessity of this anticipatory Christian "Yes" by claiming the traditional Jewish understandings of Christianity as a religion of personal and spiritual redemption (by Buber, Ben-Chorin and Scholem, e.g.) are inaccurate. They describe a "certain historical Christianity," but not the message of Jesus or "authentic" Christian faith. Just as Christianity became anti-Judaic when it replaced the "real future eschatology of the New Testament" with chiliastic political theology, Christology which reappropriates the Jewish elements in its tradition can overcome this anti-Judaism. Then, Moltmann says, Gentiles will encounter Israel and the whole of Israel's history through Jesus and his opening up of Israel toward the nations. In a bold move, Moltmann actually turns the Jewish "No" back onto Judaism. Responding to the Jewish claim that there can be no Redeemer in the world before it is redeemed, Moltmann asks if there can be a chosen people in the world before redemption. "Is not even the Torah an impossible possibility in a non-redeemed world," Moltmann continues. Moltmann argues that in "Israel" we are able to perceive an anticipation of redemption in the world which precedes redemption itself. Is it really so difficult, then, he asks, for Jews to understand Christianity as a *preparatio messianica*, as an anticipation of redemption and a way of bringing its own hope for a Messiah to the nations?

Moltmann's Christian overture to Israel also implies a challenge to Christianity, however: it must become a *preparatio messianica* in order to be recognized as such. This will require a radical reformation of the church and a deep revision of its theological tradition.[123] Moltmann concludes that the foundation of a "Christian theology of Judaism" lies

> in a no longer anti-Judaistic, but in a pro-Judaistic Christology. This will only be possible for Christian theology if Jewish theology, because of the Jewish "No," tries to understand "the secret of Christianity" (Buber). After Auschwitz, that might be a quite difficult demand, but it could be a theological question for faithful Jews how God's will is expressed in the mission and extension of Christianity.[124]

In Moltmann's attempt to do Christology in Jewish-Christian dialogue we encounter new dimensions in his vision of complementarity and dependence between the two religious communities. One of these dimensions is the inter-questioning between the Jewish "No" and Christian "Yes" alluded to above. Another is Moltmann's discussion of the Sabbath in relation to the Messiah. Moltmann observes that Jewish messianic hopes can be expressed either in catastrophic-apocalyptic terms--in the statement that the Messiah comes when "all Israel celebrates no Sabbath" (that is, when he is necessary), or in anticipatory terms--in the statement that the Messiah comes when "all Israel celebrates one Sabbath" (that is, when he becomes possible).[125] While the catastrophic-apocalyptic expression of the messianic hope (which Moltmann believes is mirrored in Christianity by popular writers like Hal Lindsey) issues in attempts to force the Messiah's coming by deepening the world catastrophe, the anticipatory expression leads to anticipations of the Messiah's Kingdom in everyday life. The first form of messianic hope spawns apocalypticists, the second revolutionaries. The "revolutionary element" in messianism Moltmann recognizes in the thought of Martin Buber ("all action for God's sake may be called messianic action"), Emil Fackenheim (anticipatory action seeks "to mend to world") and Walter Benjamin ("every second is a little gate through which Messiah can step").

In the relationship of Sabbath and Messiah, Moltmann identifies an important connection. The Sabbath is an "unequivocal anticipation of messianic time in the middle of historical time."[126] It is a sign of creation, liberation and salvation, a symbol of the "life in anticipation" which is messianic hope. In the "quiet, but persistent messianism" of the Sabbath, then, Moltmann recognizes one more point of contact between Jews and Christians and their respective hopes for the world. Christians and Jews can work together to prepare the road for the Messiah and prepare the world for Messiah's coming:

> To prepare the road for the Messiah simply means to live in the light of Advent trying to be open for his coming together with the world. This means that his coming has to be anticipated in perception and action, that "yet already" at least something of the salvation of all things has to be made visible with all our possible effort until the Messiah will complete it in his days.[127]

In this statement the bond between Moltmann's "not yet Christology of hope" and his larger vision of the church-Israel relationship comes into focus. Moltmann stresses that Jews and Christians must work together to prepare the way for the "Coming One." Jews should recognize the possibility of a presence of the future messianic reign in this world, while Christians must recognize that this presence cannot be confused with fulfillment or redemption.

IV. MOLTMANN AND HIS CRITICS

We shall now review the comments of two major critics of Moltmann's theology and its connection to Jewish-Christian relations. First, we shall consider the scathing critique of Moltmann's work published by Alice and A. Roy Eckardt.[128] Although it is exaggerated and misleading at points, the Eckardts' critique is representative of Moltmann's reception by American Holocaust theology. It is worth keeping in mind, however, that the Eckardts' critique of Moltmann emphasizes his major work through *The Church in the Power of the Spirit*, and so does not take into account his recent writings on Israel. The Eckardts' favorite target is *The Crucified God*, which they believe reveals Moltmann's subtle anti-Judaism as well as his identity as a "pre-Holocaust" theologian. These charges must be carefully considered if we are to argue for Moltmann's work as a resource for post-Holocaust theology.

First, it has to be admitted that Moltmann's understanding of Jesus' conflict with the law and its "guardians," which the Eckardts claim is anti-Jewish, is a genuine problem. It is not acceptable to argue, as Richard Bauckham tries to do, that Moltmann's description of the Israel-church relationship elsewhere in *The Crucified God* in terms of "inescapable solidarity" (134-35) protects his Lutheran interpretation of Jesus' relationship to Judaism from being labeled anti-Jewish.[129] The Eckardts are correct in observing that there is something like a quantum leap between Moltmann's discussion of Jesus' righteousness versus the righteousness of the law and his statement that Israel and the church are two communities of hope existing side by side. Moltmann's attempt to make this leap reveals his awareness of the supersessionist perspective which has always accompanied the gospel/law dichotomy in Christian theology. But the leap remains unfounded within the context of *The Crucified God*. Moltmann comes closest to justifying himself when he argues that the conflict between Jesus and Jewish legalism does not invalidate the promises or election of Israel, but makes them universal. In other words, Moltmann believes that the basis of dialogue between Christians and Jews lies prior to "law" in election and promise. This approach is probably destined to offend Jews, however, and confirm Jewish fears that a Christian is interpreting for them the meaning of their traditions.

As we have suggested, Moltmann finds more solid ground for complementarity and solidarity between Christianity and Judaism when he focuses on common messianic hopes for the Kingdom of God. But we must confirm Eckardt's contention that, at least in *The Crucified God,* Moltmann appears closed to a Jewish understanding of the meaning of Judaism and its "law," and add that this problem is related to an enthusiastic acceptance of Käsemann's (Lutheran and Bultmannian) view of the universalizing significance of Jesus' message of righteousness.

The Eckardts are considerably more positive about Moltmann's treatment of Israel in *The Church in the Power of the Spirit,* but they continue to perceive a "pre-Holocaust" triumphalism in Moltmann's thought. They describe as triumphalist Moltmann's implicit claim that the *parousia* of Christ will bring fulfillment of both the Christian and the Jewish hope. Two things must be said about Moltmann's alleged "postponed triumphalism." First, it is not at all clear whether a Christian theology can leave the question of Jesus' messiahship completely open and remain "Christian" in any traditional sense. Second, for reasons that are not clear, Moltmann's "triumphalist" understanding of the relation between the Jewish and Christian messianic hopes is apparently more troubling to Roy Eckardt than to Pinchas Lapide.

The Eckardts' other criticisms of Moltmann are aimed at the special demands he is thought to make upon Israel, his "biblicist" approach to the New Testament, and his tendency to ignore or underestimate the significance of the Holocaust. The Eckardts claim that Moltmann, in developing a Christian understanding of Israel's "special calling," is making unacceptable demands upon Israel. This may be responded to by pointing out that much of this special calling's content is based on the self-understanding of religious Jews. Yet the Eckardts' question whether Christians have the right to assign a special role to Israel in history is a real one, and will be discussed in greater detail in chapters five and six.

The Eckardts' claim that Moltmann's thought qualifies as "pre-Holocaust" is polemical and tendentious, and it reveals as much as anything their perception of Moltmann's ambivalence to Holocaust theology.[130] The Eckardts' more balanced claim that Moltmann perceives the Holocaust as a "partial event" must be taken seriously, however. There is no evidence in Moltmann's work that he views the Holocaust as either quantitatively or qualitatively unique. On the contrary, Moltmann often refers to "Auschwitz" alongside other human-made hells of this century, including the world wars, Hiroshima and Vietnam.[131] While Moltmann does not claim uniqueness for the Holocaust, however, he does view it as an inescapable criterion for Christian theology and "authentic" Christian existence. Auschwitz may not represent for Moltmann the end of Christian faith and theology, but it must lead to a new awareness of how Christian witness which is not authentic can become irrelevant, or worse, murderously anti-Jewish.

Interestingly, Moltmann is caught in a curious dilemma from which the Eckardts will not let him escape. Moltmann is aware that a *Christian* response to the Holocaust and its legacy for Jewish-Christian relations is needed, but when he attempts to interpret Auschwitz using *Christian* symbols (such as the cross) he is taken to task for his insensitivity and naïvete'. Similarly, Moltmann is called a biblicist and a slave to Paul and Luther when he seeks to use the Christian biblical and theological traditions to understand the meaning and nature of Israel. When making these charges, however, the Eckardts do not feel compelled to provide guidance for Christian theologians wishing to reinterpret this tradition. They do offer a reconstruction of the events discussed by Moltmann, one they believe is based on superior historical evidence,[132] but this reconstruction amounts to a rejection of the tradition, not a reinterpretation. While we can accept the Eckardts' observation that Moltmann appears "bound by the dilemmas of Paul" in his understanding of the church and Israel in salvation history, the Eckardts do no demonstrate their claim hat it is impossible to follow Paul's discussion of Israel and avoid the conclusion that Israel has been replaced by the church.[133] Once again, oddly, Moltmann's Paulinism is considerably more disturbing to the Eckardts than to Jews like Lapide.

The only other developed critique of Moltmann's theology as it concerns Jewish-Christian relations is that of Eugene B. Borowitz.[134] Borowitz is less polemical and accusatory than the Eckardts, and in general displays a more balanced understanding of Moltmann's approach and motivations. Like the Eckardts, Borowitz focuses on *The Crucified God* and some of the problems evident there. But ultimately the attention of Borowitz, a Jew, is drawn to different aspects of the book.

First, Borowitz expresses disagreement with Moltmann's interpretation of what crucifixion meant in ancient Judaism and rejects his understanding of Jesus as one "who hung from a tree" (91). Borowitz also argues that the talk of Jesus' "guilt of blasphemy and self-deification" is Moltmann's introjection into the biblical texts about Jesus and his trial. Furthermore, Borowitz takes issue with Moltmann's application of the dialectical principle of knowledge to God:

> Moltmann, conceding the unredeemed quality of the world, wants to create a dialectical Christology in which God reveals the truth through the opposite of God, the forsaken and despised Jesus. This causes him, to my mind, to exaggerate greatly.[135]

According to Borowitz, if Jesus' situation as the crucified one makes him utterly opposed to our expectations of a Messiah, this leads to a Devil-as-Messiah, and does not do justice to an understanding of God as Holy One (93). Even if we accept Moltmann's principle that God is revealed in God's dialectical opposite, Jews can think of others, Borowitz argues, more qualified to open the way dialectically for God: "Jesus suffered a day--Jews at Auschwitz lingered for months before being sent to a gas chamber."[136] While his words are reminiscent of the Eckardts' response to Moltmann's "theology of Auschwitz" in *The Crucified God*, Borowitz is not claiming that Jesus' cross has no redemptive significance after the Holocaust, only that Moltmann's argument is self-defeating.

An aspect of *The Crucified God* highlighted by Borowittz (but on which Alice and Roy Eckardt are silent) is Moltmann's engagement with Jewish thought. Borowitz comments that Moltmann has learned from contemporary Jewish thought in a way "unparalleled" by the other Christian theologians whom Borowitz considers. He points to Moltmann's familiarity with the work of Jewish religious thinkers like Heschel, Buber, Ben-Chorin, Scholem and Rosenzweig, but also adds members of the Frankfurt School like Adorno and Horkheimer to the list of Moltmann's Jewish teachers. But while Borowitz believes Moltmann has been significantly influenced by his personal dialogue with Jewish thought, he also perceives a major gap between Jewish understandings of Christianity and Moltmann's interpretation: while Jews may find Moltmann's interpretation of Christianity as a religion of corporate and historical rather than personal and spiritual redemption close to their own doctrine, they would not find his interpretation typical of the Christianity they have experienced for centuries (89). Such a criticism might be overcome if Moltmann, rather than arguing that the Jewish "No" based on an unredeemed world does not touch Christianity "as it really is," stressed that this "No" is actually a needed corrective and should be allowed to effect a reformation at the roots of Christian theology.

In any case, Borowitz' Jewish criticism of Moltmann is fairer to Moltmann than the Christian critique brought by the Eckardts, since it takes seriously Moltmann's intentions, and recognizes the resources for Jewish-Christian *rapprochement* which his thought represents. Neither the Eckardts nor Borowitz discuss Moltmann's more recent work, however, and this fact qualifies their conclusions, since Moltmann's theology of Israel is still in development. Nor does either critic assess Moltmann's relationship to Barth and his theology of Israel. This is a topic we shall consider in chapter five, when we offer a final analysis of Moltmann's theology of Israel.

Notes

1. Disappointingly, significant criticism of Moltmann's theology of Israel has not appeared. The only full-length study of this topic in any language is a Tilburg (Netherlands) dissertation by J. Jansen entitled, "Partners op Weg naar het ene Rijk van God? Kerk en Israel in de Theologie van Jürgen Moltmann" (1984).

2. For what follows, see especially Moltmann's *Experiences of God*, trans. Margaret Kohl (Philadelphia: Fortress, 1980), 6-16; and *Following Jesus Christ in the World Today: Responsibility for the World and Christian Discipleship* (Elkhart, IN/Winnipeg: Institute of Mennonite Studies, CMBC Publications, 1983).

3. *Experiences of God*, 6.

4. See Richard J. Bauckham, *Moltmann: Messianic Theology in the Making* (Basingstoke: Marshall Pickering, 1987), viii.

5. Moltmann, "Forgiveness and Politics: Forty Years After the Stuttgart Confession," in *Case Study 2* (New World Publications, 1987), 40-52.

6. "Political Theology and the Ethics of Peace," in *Theology, Politics and Peace*, ed. Theodore Runyon (Maryknoll, NY: Orbis, 1989), 31-42; 34. See also Moltmann's "God Is Unselfish Love" [in *The Emptying God: A Buddhist-Jewish-*

Christian Conversation, ed. John B. Cobb and Christopher Ives (Maryknoll, NY: Orbis Books, 1990), 116-124] where he responds to Masao Abe's Buddhist interpretation of the Holocaust as a problem of *karma* in this way: "...according to this karma interpretation, Auschwitz loses its horrible uniqueness and becomes relative...As a German and as a Christian I can not speak about Auschwitz in this way. I belong to the people who committed these crimes; I belong to the generation from which the murderers came even if I personally had nothing to do with them. I therefore live in the shadow of Auschwitz and exist in the presence of those who were gassed and murdered" (122-23).

In light of such clear and powerful statements as these, it is difficult to make sense of claims by the Eckardts and those they have influenced that Moltmann's theology is "pre-Holocaust."

7. Ibid., 51.

8. See, e.g., Moltmann's first published work, *Prädestination und Heilsgeschichte bei Moyse Amyraut. Ein Beitrag zur Geschichte der Reformierten Theologie zwischen Orthodoxie und Aufklärung,* a revision of his 1952 Göttingen dissertation; and *Christoph Pezel (1539-1604) und der Calvinismus in Bremen,* the published form of his 1956/7 Göttingen Habilitationsschrift. Moltmann was also editor of *Calvin-Studien* during this early part of his theological career when many of his publications dealt with Reformed theology and history. See Dieter Ising, et. al., eds., *Bibliographie Jürgen Moltmann* (München: Chr. Kaiser, 1987).

9. The best discussion in English of Barth's relation to Moltmann and Moltmann's teachers is still M. Douglas Meeks, *Origins of the Theology of Hope* (Philadelphia: Fortress, 1974). To the author's knowledge there is no work devoted exclusively to the theological relationship between Moltmann and Barth.

10. Ibid., 12. It is also significant that one of Moltmann's first major publications was *Anfänge der Dialektischen Theologie* (1962-3), a collection of documents representing the work of Barth and other leaders in the "dialectical theology" movement which Moltmann edited. See also "Theology in Germany Today," in Jürgen Habermas, ed., *Observations on the "Spiritual Situation of the Age": Contemporary German Perspectives,* trans. Andrew Buchwalter (London and Cambridge, MA: MIT Press, 1984), where Moltmann describes the witness of the Confessing Church captured by the Barmen Declaration of 1934 as expressing a "decisive and truly epochal change in the recent history of Protestant theology and the Protestant church" (198).

11. Meeks, *Origins,* 29.

12. See Moltmann, *Theology of Hope: On the Ground and Implications of A Christian Eschatology,* trans. James W. Leitch (New York; Harper and Row, 1967), ch. 1; and *The Future of Creation,* trans. Margaret Kohl (London: SCM Press, 1979), 23ff.

13. One can still see in *Theology of Hope* a dependence on Barth's covenant view of reality, a siding with Barth over against Bultmann's theology of existence, and a Barthian emphasis on the importance of Israel's history for Christian theology (see Meeks, *Origins*, 43, 67, et passim).

14. The work of van Ruler which influenced Moltmann is *Die Christliche Kirche und das Alte Testament* (München: Chr. Kaiser, 1955); See *Experiences of God*, 11; and Meeks, *Origins*, 99.

15. See especially, Meeks, *Origins*, 25.

16. In Fangmeier, ed., *Letters*, 174-76.

17. Ibid., 348-49.

18. See, e.g., Bauckham, *Messianic Theology*, 145 n15. For an example of a lingering "dialectical" element in Moltmann's criticism of "religion," see his "The Challenge of Religion in the 80s" [*The Christian Century* (April 23, 1980), 405-408] where Moltmann strikes a Barthian chord with his statement that "religious experience is as much a challenge to the Christian faith as is secularization" (465).

19. I have adopted this term from John Cobb, "Barth and the Post-Barthians," in Mckim, ed., *How Karl Barth Changed My Mind*.

20. See Kelsey, *The Use of Scripture in Recent Theology*, 54-5.

21. According to Moltmann, his relationship in Hamburg with a Jewish uncle named Fritz Valentine was important for him before and after the war. Valentine, who emigrated to England in 1938 but returned to Germany in 1946, helped Moltmann find the courage to return and attempt to rebuild (personal interview, Tübingen, January 9, 1989).

22. See Bauckham, *Messianic Theology*, 148 n28.

23. In Flieschner, *Auschwitz*, 76.

24. "Jürgen Moltmann, the Jewish People and the Holocaust," *JAAR* 44:4 (December, 1976), 675-91.

25. The best introduction to Moltmann's thought in English is Meeks, *Origins*. There is, however, a small but growing body of work introducing Moltmann's work and interpreting various aspects of it. See C. Morse, *The Logic of Promise in Moltmann's Theology* (Philadelphia: Fortress, 1979); F. Herzog, ed., *The Future of Hope: Theology as Eschatology* (New York: Herder and Herder, 1970); W.-D. Marsch, ed., *Diskussion über die 'Theologie der Hoffnung' von Jürgen Moltmann* (München: Chr. Kaiser, 1967); and R. Gibellini, *La Teologia di Jürgen Moltmann* (Brescia: Queriniana, 1975). For a fuller bibliography, see Richard Bauckham, "Bibliography: Jürgen Moltmann," *The Modern Churchman* 28:2 (1986), 55-60.

26. In addition to Bauckham, *Messianic Theology,* ch. 1 and Meeks, *Origins,* ch. 1, see Moltmann, *Im Gespräch mit Ernst Bloch: Eine Theologische Wegbegleitung* (München: Chr. Kaiser, 1976). Moltmann has described *Theology of Hope* as a "parallel theological treatment of the philosophy of hope on the basis of the Christian faith's own presuppositions and perspectives" (*Experiences of God,* 11).

27. See especially, Bauckham, *Messianic Theology,* 14-22.

28. *Theology of Hope,* 324.

29. See Moltmann, "Christian Hope: Messianic or Transcendent?: A Theological Discussion With Joachim of Fiore and Thomas Aquinas," *Horizons* 12:2 (1985), 328-9.

30. Ibid.

31. As will become clear later in our analysis of Moltmann's theology, there is a universalizing tendency in his thought which tends to christianize the supposed openness of Israel's future: "In the gospel the Old Testament history of promise finds more than a fulfillment which does away with it; it finds its future. 'All the promises of God in him are yea, and in him Amen' (II Co. 1:20). They have become an eschatological certainty in Christ, by being liberated and validated, made unconditional and universal" (147). This tendency reveals the influence of Ernst Käsemann and is never overcome in Moltmann's theology.

32. See especially Meeks, *Origins,* 70. Von Rad was, in turn, influenced by the theology of Barth.

33. Ibid., 71.

34. See Ibid., 97-8.

35. See *Theology of Hope,* 50-58; 84ff.

36. See *Theology of Hope,* 228-9: "According to Karl Barth the future of Christ is mainly only a matter of unveiling...[but] the expression of 'unveiling' for revelation must be dropped, and in its stead revelation must be conceived as an event that takes place in promise and fulfillment....'In Christ all the promises of God are yea and Amen' (II Co. 1:20)...but not yet fulfilled. Therefore the Christian hope expects from the future of Christ not only unveiling, but also final fulfillment...Not a mere repetition of his history, and not only an unveiling of it, but something which has so far not yet happened through Christ."

37. Ibid., 229.

38. See Bauckham, *Messianic Theology,* 39.

39. *Experiences of God,* 12.

40. *Der Gekreuztigte Gott* appeared in 1972 and has been translated into at least eight languages. For a discussion of this "breakdown" and its influence on the "theology of hope," see Walter H. Capps, *Hope Against Hope: Moltmann to Merton in One Decade* (Philadelphia: Fortress, 1976).

41. See Bauckham, *Messianic Theology,* 54; and *The Crucified God,* 5, 225.

42. *The Crucified God,* 89ff.

43. See especially, Ibid., 296, 306ff.

44. See especially, Ibid., 100, 164ff.

45. Ibid., 270-1.

46. Ibid., 267.

47. Ibid., 274.

48. See Ibid., 100.

49. Bauckham, *Messianic Theology,* 57; Borowitz, *Contemporary Christologies,* 93.

50. Bauckham, *Messianic Theology,* 154 n16.

51. Ironically, this discontinuity is drawn out in the midst of attempts to affirm continuity between Judaism and Christianity, as the following passage suggests: "...it is no longer a matter of indifference or chance that Jesus was a Jew, appeared in Israel, came into conflict with the guardians of his peoples' law, and was condemned and handed over to the Romans to be crucified..." (99).

52. See Bauckham, *Messianic Theology,* 67ff.

53. Ibid., 69.

54. See, e.g., E. P. Sanders, *Paul and Palestinian Judaism.*

55. Eckardt, "Jürgen Moltmann...," 680.

56. Ibid.

57. See Moltmann's letter to Karl Barth dated April 4, 1965 in Fangmeier, ed., *Letters,* 348.

58. In the section "Jesus and the law: the blasphemer," for example, three of five footnotes in the first two pages refer to Käsemann's work.

59. In Fangmeier, ed., *Letters*, 348.

60. Meeks, *Origins*, 76.

61. See Klappert, 23.

62. Käsemann, "Justification and Salvation History in the Epistle to the Romans," in *Perspectives on Paul* (London: SCM Press, 1971), 60-78; 72.

63. Ibid.

64. Ibid., 75.

65. Ibid.

66. See also, *The Crucified God*, 175ff: "At the deepest level the question of world history is the question of righteousness...Even the Christian Easter faith in the last resort stands in the context of the question of the divine righteousness in history: does inhuman legalism triumph over the crucified Christ, or does God's law of grace triumph over the works of the law and of power?" (175); "...the resurrection of the crucified Christ reveals the righteousness of God in a different way, namely as grace..." (176); "...Jesus broke through legalistic apocalyptic because he proclaimed *justitia justificans* rather than *justitia distributiva* as the righteousness of the Kingdom of God." (177); "The dispute over the resurrection of Jesus is concerned with the question of righteousness in history. Does it belong to the *nomos* which finally gives each man his deserts, or does it belong to the law of grace as it was manifest by Jesus and in the resurrection of the crucified Christ?" (178).

67. Bauckham, *Messianic Theology*, 32.

68. See Krister Stendahl, *Paul Among Jews and Gentiles and Other Essays* (Philadelphia: Fortress, 1976).

69. See Klappert, 20 and 22, where Käsemann's work is used to document the subsumation model in action, based as it is on the "destruction and elimination of the special character of Israel's election and the covenant of God with Israel and...as a consequence of this destruction, the subsumation and classification of Israel's special character under the prevailing general category of all mankind" (trans. mine).

70. Klappert, 20.

71. Ibid., 23.

72. See "Church and Israel: A Common Way of Hope," 196-7; and Klappert, 21.

73. Eckardt, "Jürgen Moltmann...," 677. Eckardt takes up radical historical criticism of New Testament texts (guided by Haim Cohn, who is not a biblical scholar) to argue that the "trial" Moltmann describes is not compatible with the facts of history. However, it is Eckardt who is "out of balance" when he makes statements like the following: "it is incorrect to say that Jesus stood in opposition to contemporary Judaism and its representatives. He did not come into conflict with the law or with his people" (677).

74. Eckardt makes the connection with 1933 even more explicit when he argues that "Christian negativism about the Jewish law offers...a negative form of alliance with National Socialist Ideology" (679).

75. There may also be philosophical problems inherent in Moltmann's understanding of God's suffering on the cross. See D. G. Attfield, "Can God Be Crucified? A Discussion with J. Moltmann," *Scottish Journal of Theology* 30:1 (1977), 47-57.

76. Bauckham, *Messianic Theology*, 56.

77. Ibid.

78. See Ibid., 153 n5 where Bauckham points out rare references in Moltmann's work to the work of Richard Rubenstein and Emil Fackenheim.

79. See *The Crucified God*, 272-3.

80. Ibid., 273.

81. See Eckardts, *Long Night's Journey Into Day*, 87ff., where Moltmann is discussed as an exponent of the Holocaust as a "partial event."

82. For another view, see John T. Pawlikowski, "The Holocaust and Contemporary Christology," in Fiorenza and Tracy, *The Holocaust as Interruption*, 43-49, where the author describes *The Crucified God* as "the first comprehensive attempt at christological statement that takes the Holocaust experience with utmost seriousness" (44).

83. See Eckardt, "Jürgen Moltmann...," 685.

84. Ibid., 675; J. B. Metz, "Facing the Jews," 29; See also Markus Barth, *The People of God*, 24, where Moltmann's theology is associated with triumphalism. James F. Moore makes a quite similar charge against the work of another German theologian, Dorothee Sölle, who he believes "universalizes the suffering of Christ," and "ultimately subsumes Judaism under the wing of Christianity." [See "A Spectrum of Views: Traditional Christian Responses to the Holocaust," *Journal of Ecumenical Studies* 25:2 (Spring, 1988), 212-24].

85. Arguing that the cross *should* have no symbolic redemptive significance, or that it does not have this significance for *some* people would be more reasonable than arguing that this significance has been lost altogether. In any case, a symbol's power exists or does not exist independently of our arguments about it.

86. Eckardt, "Jürgen Moltmann...," 687.

87. In 1968, while participating in a conference entitled "Hope--After Auschwitz and Hiroshima?," Moltmann repeated his observation that since there were prayers in Auschwitz, perhaps God was in Auschwitz. However, Moltmann is much less willing here than in *The Crucified God* to elaborate a "theology of Auschwitz": "for my part, I would like to enter into the community of those who have no answers, but questions, and who have no explanations, but only a cry" [in Walter Capps, ed., *The Future of Hope* (Philadelphia: Fortress Press, 1970), 96]. I am grateful to Professor Moltmann for bringing his participation in this conference to my attention. On this point, cf. Metz, "Facing the Jews," 29: "We [Christians] can pray after Auschwitz, because there were prayers in Auschwitz."

88. See, e.g., Ulrich Simon, *A Theology of Auschwitz* (London: SPCK, 1978); Franz Mussner, *Tractate on the Jews*, 130; Clemens Thoma, *A Christian Theology of Judaism* (#160); T. F. Torrance, *The Mediation of Christ;* Franklin Sherman, "Speaking of God After Auschwitz," *Worldview* 17:9 (September, 1974), 26-30; and Douglas J. Hall, "Rethinking Christ," in Davies, ed., *Antisemitism and the Foundations of Christianity,* 167-187. Even Jewish theology can at times make a connection between the cross and the Holocaust. See Moltmann and Lapide, *Jewish Monotheism and Christian Trinitarian Doctrine,* trans. by Leonard Swidler (Philadelphia: Fortress, 1981), 66.

89. *The Church in the Power of the Spirit: A Contribution to Messianic Ecclesiology,* trans. Margaret Kohl (London: SCM, 1977).

90. See, e.g., the Reformed confessions included in *The Book of Confessions* of the Presbyterian Church (U.S.A.) for examples of this tendency.

91. This concept is also important in Käsemann's work. See "Justification and Salvation History."

92. In contrast to Moltmann's description of Jewish legalism in *The Crucified God,* obedience to Torah is described here as a "living commitment to the service of righteousness" (147). Cf. Eckardt, "Jürgen Moltmann...," 688.

93. Moltmann stressed this point in a personal interview (Tübingen, January 9, 1989).

94. As Eckardt puts it, "within the bounds of *The Crucified God,* what is the possible ground for asserting that Israel 'rightfully exists alongside the church' and in consequence 'cannot be abolished'?" ("Jürgen Moltmann...," 682).

95. Ibid., 683.

96. Ibid., 689. For another perspective on this problem, see Bauckham, *Messianic Theology*, 138-39.

97. Eckardt, "Jürgen Moltmann...," 688.

98. See chapter two. Even Moltmann's format in this chapter of *The Church in the Power of the Spirit*, in which he considers Israel and the world religions separately, is a testimony to the influence of Barth's theology of Israel.

99. *Church in the Power of the Holy Spirit*, 145. The fact that Moltmann does not critique this statement does not, of course, mean that he concurs with it, but his silence is curious. See also, "Church and Israel: A Common Way of Hope?," 209.

100. See also "Jewish and Christian Messianism," where Moltmann says that "the founding of the state of Israel also has a double effect: simultaneously fulfilling and negating" (67).

101. In *The Experiment Hope*, trans. M. Douglas Meeks (Philadelphia: Fortress, 1975), 60-68. See also "Messianic Hope In Christianity," in *Christians and Jews*, Concilium 98 (New York: Seabury, 1974), 61-68.
    See Gregory Baum, *Christian Theology after Auschwitz* (London: The Council of Christians and Jews, 1976), for a single paragraph of criticism on Moltmann's theology of Israel in *The Experiment Hope*. Baum observes: "Moltmann says very beautiful things about Jewish existence before God and unites Jews and Christians in a common waiting for the promised fulfilment. Yet in the same book, he turns to such a definitive ad unqualified affirmation of Christ's unique mediatorship that the positive things said about the Jews in earlier paragraphs are quickly forgotten...." (11).

102. See especially, *The Crucified God*, 98ff.

103. See, e.g., *The Crucified God*, 100; and *Jewish Monotheism and Christian Trinitarian Doctrine*, 81.

104. *Horizons* 12:2 (1985), 328-48; originally appeared in *Münchener Theologische Zeitschrift* 33:4 (1982), 241-60.

105. Especially Hans Urs von Balthasar, "Towards a Christian Theology of Hope," *Münchener Theologische Zeitschrift* 32:2 (1981), 81-102.

106. English translation, Fortress Press, 1981.

107. Ibid., 50;

108. Ibid., 54.

109. Ibid., 79; the statement is from *The Church in the Power of the Spirit*.

110. Ibid., 74, 90.

111. *Israel und Kirche: Ein Gemeinsamer Weg?: Ein Gespräch* (München: Chr. Kaiser, 1980). This book has not been translated.

112. This essay is translated and appears in *On Human Dignity: Political Theology and Ethics*, 189-217.

113. Moltmann defines "Israel" here in this way: "it embraces the biblical Israel, post-biblical Judaism, the various forms of historical Judaism, and finally the present state of Israel" (193).

114. See *Theology of Hope*, ch. 5.

115. See 89-90. Here the notion of the provisionality of the church, which Moltmann apparently adopted from Dutch Apostolate theology, is very important.

116. Moltmann seems to be distancing himself from his own reliance on this "viewpoint" in *The Crucified God*.

117. See also *Theology Today: Two Contributions Towards Making Theology Present*, trans. John Bowden (London: SCM Press, 1988), 30-34.

118. *The Way of Jesus Christ: Christology in Messianic Dimensions*, trans. Margaret Kohl (San Francisco: Harper and Row, 1990). This work will be referred to here as "Christology," with the page references corresponding to those in the proofs for the German edition, gratefully received from Prof. Moltmann in early 1989. Moltmann's discussion in chapter one of *The Way of Jesus Christ* ("The Messianic Perspective") utilizes material from previous books and articles, including "Messianic Hope In Christianity." Supplemental material for this discussion is taken from the first of the Samuel Ferguson Lectures, given by Prof. Moltmann at Manchester University, February 20, 1989. The title of this lecture was "Who Is Jesus Christ For Us Today?: Christology Between Christians and Jews."

119. "Jewish and Christian Messianism, " 66.

120. Here Moltmann cites "The Helvetic Confession," Article 11.

121. *Christology*, 22.

122. Ibid., 32-3.

123. Ibid., 36; also "Who Is Jesus Christ For Us Today?"

124. Ibid., 36.

125. Ibid., 26-28.

126. "Who Is Jesus Christ For Us Today?"

127. *Christology*, 27.

128. "Jürgen Moltmann..."; and *Long Night's Journey Into Day*, 87-110.

129. *Messianic Theology*, 73.

130. Cf. Eckardt's argument that he can "not see a way totally to dissociate the title *The Crucified God* from the ancient and infamous charge of deicide..." ("Jürgen Moltmann...," 677), with Moltmann's statement that "for a Christian there can be no question of any guilt on the part of the Jews for the crucifixion of Jesus" (*The Crucified God*, 135). The conclusion that Moltmann's theology is "pre-Holocaust" is shared by British scholar Isabel Wollaston in an unpublished dissertation manuscript graciously shared with the author.

131. See, e.g., *The Crucified God*, 220.

132. The Eckardts argue, not persuasively, that "the conflicts and happenings he [Moltmann] replicates do not reflect historical truth" ("Jürgen Moltmann...," 677).

133. *Long Night's Journey*, 107.

134. *Contemporary Christologies: A Jewish Response*, chap. 5, 83-98. For criticism of Moltmann's work which indirectly concerns his theology of Israel, see Rebecca Chopp, *The Praxis of Suffering*, 115-16; and Carl Braaten, "A Trinitarian Theology of the Cross," *Journal of Religion* 56 (1976), 113-121.

135. Ibid., 92.

136. Ibid.

CHAPTER FOUR

PAUL VAN BUREN: RADICAL THEOLOGY ENCOUNTERS THE JEWISH-CHRISTIAN REALITY

I. INTRODUCTION: VAN BUREN IN CONTEXT

We turn now to a consideration of American theologian Paul van Buren, who has been intimately concerned with Jewish-Christian theological relations since the mid-1970s. In the 1980s van Buren sought to move beyond the limitations of American Holocaust theology, and began to view himself as a constructive theologian in the service of the church. As we consider van Buren's background and the intellectual sources for his work on the Jewish-Christian reality, we will attempt to understand what makes van Buren's work unique.

A. Background

Paul Matthews van Buren was born in 1924 and grew up in Glendale, Ohio in an upper middle class "Christian" home. In 1942 van Buren joined the Coast Guard and received two years of training as a navy pilot, only to be commissioned just as the Second World War was ending. In 1945 van Buren entered Harvard University to study government. It was during his undergraduate years at Harvard that van

Buren felt "called" to pursue the study of theology. At a funeral service for a relative van Buren was moved by a reading from I Corinthians 15. The Apostle's witness to the resurrection became a challenge for van Buren, and he sought to discover whether this witness might be true, and what the implications of this truth might be.

Although uninterested in parish ministry, after graduating from Harvard van Buren enrolled at The Episcopal Theological School to study theology. His main interests were biblical interpretation and the theology of Karl Barth, but van Buren was forced to pursue the latter on his own. In 1951 van Buren traveled to Basel to continue his education under Barth, the man he considered theology's leading light. Van Buren wrote his doctoral dissertation on Calvin's Christology under Barth's supervision, and returned to the United States in 1954. After serving the Episcopal church in a downtown Detroit mission, van Buren left the parish ministry in 1957 for a teaching position at Episcopal Seminary of the Southwest in Austin, Texas.

Van Buren's seven years at Austin were productive, but not without controversy. In addition to his vocal involvement in local civil rights issues during the early 60s, the seminary establishment was disturbed by van Buren's first book, *The Secular Meaning of the Gospel,* which appeared in 1963. Under the influence of Wittgenstein (whose work van Buren discovered through William Poteat, his colleague in Austin) and Dietrich Bonhoeffer, van Buren sought to reconceive Christian theology by means of a radical critique of theological language and an embrace of the "secular" outlook. The book was very influential and was soon associated with the work of radical theologians like Thomas J. J. Altizer and William Hamilton, who were coming to be seen as spokesmen for the "death-of-God" movement in theology. Although van Buren claims his connection with the work of other radical theologians of the 60s was superficial, and that the so-called "death-of-God" movement was a journalistic invention, *The Secular Meaning of the Gospel* largely created van Buren's theological reputation. Even today, in fact, van Buren's name is most often associated with the issues and problems that concerned him in his early work.

Throughout the 60s and into the 70s van Buren viewed himself as an analytic philosopher of religion at work on the problems associated with the meaning of religious language. Despite his early reputation as a theologian of secularity, van Buren eventually became critical of "secular" theologies as irrelevant to the crises of the early 70s. Feeling unable to speak about the *matter* of theology, van Buren turned more and more to considerations of its *method*.[1] Soon, however, van Buren realized that philosophers of religion were writing only for each other, and he was not even satisfied with the results of his own investigations.[2]

In 1974 van Buren assumed administrative responsibilities at Temple University, where he had been teaching since 1964. Ironically, his experience as department chair would signal the major theological turning point in van Buren's career. While interviewing and reading the works of candidates for faculty positions in Judaic Studies, van Buren discovered a "living" Judaism which eventually led him to the conclusion that everything he had learned about Judaism from the Christian tradition was in error. It was at this point that van Buren's interest in systematic theology was rekindled and the philosophical questions on which he had been working began to seem trivial alongside the theological issues involved in a reconsideration of Judaism and its witness to God. The linguistic problems which occupied van Buren in *Theological Investigations* and *The Edges of Language* suddenly receded into the background in his next book, *The Burden of Freedom*, as van Buren's participation in a Christian religious community became his new theological starting point.[3] Despite the radical break described above, van Buren has been able to perceive a thin line of continuity between his earlier work and his new interest in what he called "the Jewish-Christian reality":

> In *Theological Investigations* (1968) and *The Edges of Language* (1972), a path from that earlier book [*The Secular Meaning of the Gospel*] to this little one [*The Burden of Freedom*] may be discerned, which may clarify how the two could come from the same person.[4]

Van Buren spent the last third of the 1970s formulating the change of mind he had experienced during the middle third, and in 1980 published *Discerning the Way,* the first volume of his *A Theology of the Jewish-Christian Reality.* Van Buren no longer described himself as an analytic philosopher of religion, but as an Anglican theologian doing systematic theology on behalf of the Christian church.[5] Volume two of van Buren's project, *A Christian Theology of the People Israel*

(1983) and volume three, *Christ in Context* (1988) are to be supplemented at some point by a fourth volume that will treat the relationship of the Jewish-Christian reality and other religions. Before looking at the first three volumes of his theology of Israel in more detail, we shall consider some of the sources behind van Buren's work, including the theology of Karl Barth, radical theology, Holocaust Theology and and the thought of Franz Rosenzweig.

B. Sources

The question of van Buren's relationship to Karl Barth is a complex one. What is clear is that the personal relationship between the two men ended in 1962 when Barth realized his former student had left the Barthian fold. While spending a sabbatic leave in Geneva during the 1961-62 academic year, van Buren forwarded to Basel a draft of what would become *The Secular Meaning of the Gospel*, asking Barth for his comments. The manuscript apparently caused Barth several sleepless nights and led him back to his former student's dissertation in an attempt to discover where the "disease" had begun. Eventually van Buren was summoned to Basel by Barth's assistant, Fräulein von Kirchbaum. Over coffee Barth conveyed his disappointment concerning the fact that van Buren had apparently gone back into the hands of the "enemy" (by which he meant Bultmann and the theology of the nineteenth century). At the train station, Barth warned van Buren not to tell anyone he had been Barth's student. There was no correspondence of any kind between the two men after this parting.[6]

Despite their personal break, however, van Buren has continued to affirm his indebtedness to Barth and his belief that Barth's theological accomplishment is the most significant of the twentieth century. For instance, in a reminiscence entitled "Karl Barth as Teacher" (1985) van Buren remembers with pride that he missed not one of Barth's lectures during his three years at Basel, and describes them as "one endless and endlessly exciting sermon."[7] As a mature theologian, van Buren has been most indebted to Barth's understanding of theology as a function of the church, for his discovery of the "strange new world of the Bible," and for his "representative" Christology. In addition, van Buren credits Barth with the discovery that election must be considered in a community, rather than individual context, and applauds Barth for placing the doctrine of election within his discussion of the doctrine of God.[8] Surprisingly, although critics of the radical theology of the 60s have identified Barth as an important influence for this movement,[9] van Buren denies that Barth's theology was behind *The Secular Meaning of the Gospel*.

On the other hand, van Buren does name Barth as an important source for his theological approach to Israel. Van Buren admits that the usefulness of Barth's work for his own "theology of Israel" is diminished by Barth's failure to recognize the continuing relevance of the Sinai covenant, and that Barth's insight into the church and Israel as two parts of a single people of God is an exception that "only highlights the general pattern" of Christian theology.[10] Yet according to van Buren, Barth continues to serve him as a good teacher, and one finds evidence in *A Theology of the Jewish-Christian Reality* that both the method and content of Barth's theology of Israel have had a fundamental influence on van Buren. Strong methodological links between the two thinkers are evident in van Buren's conviction that a theology of Israel must be written as a function of, and on behalf of, the church, and his understanding of Israel's election as the foundation of all Christian talk about the Jewish people. Specific similarities in content are more difficult to establish due to Barth's generally negative view of post-biblical Israel. Even so, at certain points in van Buren's work one encounters distinct echoes of Barth's Israel-doctrine. In the following passage, for instance, there are strains of Barth's characterization of Israel in *Church Dogmatics* II: 2:

> Whether Israel likes it or not, and it has usually not liked it, it has just turned out to be the case that Israel is a witness to the world...there is, as it were, almost an inevitability to it...they [the Jews] stand, regardless of what they do or say, whether they want to or not, as God's signposts, his witnesses.[11]

Overall, Van Buren describes Barth's theology of Israel in *Church Dogmatics* II:2 as "fascinating and awful."[12] But van Buren continues to struggle with Barth's theology, and this is evident in his decision to explore this section of the *Church Dogmatics* with a new generation of theological students at Heidelberg University.[13]

Another source for van Buren's theology of Israel is what we will call "radical theology." Van Buren's first book, *The Secular*

Meaning of the Gospel, is generally recognized as a paradigm for the
theological genre known as "radical," "secular," "secularizing" or
"death-of-God" theology.[14] The "radical" theologian, according to
David Tracy, argues that "the Christian God cannot but alienate human
beings from one another, from the world, and from their authentic
selves."[15] This definition does not appear to capture the essence of van
Buren's current theological project. By substituting "Christian anti-
Jewish tradition" for "Christian God" in Tracy's description of the
radical theologian, however, we arrive at a fairly accurate description
of van Buren's strategy in *A Theology of the Jewish-Christian Reality.*

It might appear that in this project van Buren has assumed the
posture of a "revisionist" theologian, that is, one who attempts to *revise*
the Christian tradition in light of contemporary experience. In the
words of Tracy, the revisionist theologian believes that "contemporary
Christian theology is best understood as philosophical reflection upon
the meanings present in common human experience and the meanings
present in the Christian tradition.[16] This description does not do justice,
however, to van Buren's project of reinterpreting the "Jewish-Christian
reality," and in fact van Buren is quite clear that he rejects Tracy's
description of the task of theology.[17] Nor would van Buren accept
Tracy's understanding of Neo-Orthodoxy as a "self-critical moment in
the history of liberalism."[18]

Critics who classify van Buren as a radical or secular theologian
generally do so on the basis of his work before 1975. Nonetheless, there
are real elements of continuity (as van Buren's comment cited above
confirms), between *The Secular Meaning of the Gospel* and *A Theology
of the Jewish-Christian Reality.* On one level, many of van Buren's
preoccupations in the 60s--his emphasis on the Jesus of history, his
questions about the nature of religious language and his emphasis on
contemporary human experience--are still evident in his newer work.
At a deeper level, however, both *The Secular Meaning of the Gospel*
and *A Theology of the Jewish-Christian Reality* are "reconstructions"[19]
of Christian faith--the first a reduction of Christianity within ethical
and historical dimensions, and the second a purification of Christianity
vis-'a-vis its understanding of the Jewish people. The project of
purification which we are presently considering in this chapter is a
"radical" reconstruction of Christian faith in the literal sense of that
word--it seeks, that is, to rediscover the *roots* of Christian faith in the

Hebrew people's experience of God. This requires a careful consideration of the significance of Israel's election and Torah, and a "listening in a new way to that central proclamation of the Apostles from which the church began."[20]

Van Buren's theology of Israel, therefore, is "radical" in at least two ways. First, it shares some of the preoccupations of radical theology as it developed in the 1960s, including the influence of the late Bonhoeffer, a this-worldly, historical perspective, and a dialectical relationship to the legacy of Neo-Orthodoxy.[21] But it also is "radical" in responding to the dilemma facing modern Christianity after the Holocaust with a return to the roots of the church--most notably Israel's Law and Covenant, and their interpretation by Jesus and Paul.

To what extent is Holocaust theology a source for van Buren's theology of Israel? It would be impossible to understand van Buren's work on the Jewish-Christian reality completely outside the wider context of American Holocaust theology. But van Buren has never been one for theological bandwagons, and so it is not surprising that he has attempted to dissociate himself from this "movement." While he does acknowledge some of his colleagues at Temple have been part of it, van Buren sees "Holocaust theology" as a sloppy term and its practitioners as men and women who are for some reason unable to remove the Holocaust from their minds. In contrast, van Buren believes it is primarily living and not dead Jews with which Christian theology must come to terms, and that the continuing covenant is a more suitable and "positive" subject for theology than the Holocaust.[22] Van Buren has even written that the hard and fresh theological thinking required of the church has little to do with "Holocaust Theology, whatever that may be."[23]

On the other hand, van Buren's work does share some of the characteristics of Holocaust theology. Like many Holocaust theologians, van Buren is impatient with a reformist approach to theological change, preferring, as we have maintained, a radical orientation. There are also strains of "Holocaust theology" in van Buren's "Comments on Tillich,"[24] a short essay which in its scathing denunciation of Tillich's "Lutheran" anti-Judaism is reminiscent of the Eckardts' attacks on Moltmann. The International Symposium on the Holocaust, held in New York in June 1974, provides one example of the way in which Holocaust Theology provided an important stimulus for van Buren's theological reorientation. Although van Buren did not attend the symposium, he was asked to review a collection of papers from the conference edited by Eva Fleischner and appearing in 1977.[25] Van Buren's review of Fleischner's *Auschwitz: Beginning of a New Era?* appears to mark the point at which he began to entertain the notion of the Holocaust as a revelatory and reorienting event for theology. Irving Greenberg's essay "Cloud of Smoke, Pillar of Fire," which van Buren calls "one of the more thought-provoking essays produced in some decades,"[26] receives van Buren's careful attention in his review. Van Buren appears especially drawn to Greenberg's argument that the Holocaust must either signal the end of faith in God, or become a "reorienting event, that is, revelation."[27] As we shall see, van Buren has established as a systematic principle in *A Theology of the Jewish-Christian Reality* the notion that the Holocaust is in fact a reorienting event and "revelation."

Van Buren's ambivalent relationship to Holocaust theology may be elaborated with respect to three well-known books: Franklin Littell's *The Crucifixion of the Jews,* Rosemary Ruether's *Faith and Fratricide* and Richard Rubenstein's *After Auschwitz.* The work of Ruether and Littell is described by van Buren as seminal in its illumination of the radical theological consequences of a Christian awareness of Judaism.[28] Rubenstein's book, furthermore, van Buren believes to be the most important work of the Holocaust theology genre.[29] And yet each of these books represents for van Buren one of Holocaust theology's crucial flaws. Littell's *Crucifixion of the Jews* van Buren sees as the result of a Christian thinker attempting to mount a theological bandwagon. Rubenstein's *After Auschwitz,* in abandoning the "myth" of an omnipotent God of history, must relinquish the election of Israel as well. (Van Buren's rejection of this move is implicit, since Israel's election is precisely the point where he begins his theology of Israel). Finally, Ruether's *Faith and Fratricide* is subject to the criticism that her assessment of the inherent anti-Judaism of Christianity is exaggerated, since it does not explain the survival of the Jews in "Christian" lands.[30]

More influential for van Buren's theology of Israel than so-called Holocaust theologians are biblical scholars like Krister Stendahl and Lloyd Gaston, both of whom have aided him in reading the "Apostolic Writings" (van Buren's term for the New Testament) in a way that presupposes continuity between Judaism and early Christianity, and therefore provides a biblical starting point for contemporary reformulation of Jewish-Christian relations. It is in part this willingness to cull the Apostolic Writings (and especially the letters of Paul) for resources leading to a positive understanding of Judaism that sets van Buren apart from Holocaust theology and allows him to view the theological glass of the church's relationship to Israel as half full rather than half empty.[31] In summary, despite his view that the Holocaust is a reorienting event for Christian faith, van Buren insists his eyes have been opened to the Jewish-Christian reality not by the Holocaust, but by the Jewish people living after and in spite of it.[32]

Finally, we shall consider the thought of Franz Rosenzweig as a source for van Buren's theology of Israel. Alan Davies has observed that the work of the twentieth-century German Jewish thinker Franz Rosenzweig is behind all liberal Christian theologies of Judaism.[33] Whether one classifies van Buren's approach to Israel as "liberal," or as "radical" as we have done, it is clear that Rosenzweig is a fundamental influence on his thought. In fact, several of van Buren's reviewers have identified evidence of Rosenzweig's impact on *A Theology of the Jewish-Christian Reality*.[34] There is some confusion, however, about how best to describe van Buren's debt to Rosenzweig. Alan Davies and David Novak, for instance, refer to *Discerning the Way* as a revision of Rosenzweig's "two covenant theory."[35] While these critics are correct in perceiving Rosenzweig's footprints in van Buren's understanding of the relationship of Israel and church, van Buren maintains that there is "no [two covenant] theory in any of Rosenzweig's writings."[36] Van Buren's own view is that there exists "one eternal covenant," and that Jesus is portrayed by the early church as standing within that covenant. If this view is Rosenzweigian, as van Buren seems to think, then it is probably best to describe van Buren's Rosenzweig as a "one-covenant" or "dual covenant"[37] thinker.

Rosenzweig's most crucial contribution to van Buren lies in his being a Jewish thinker who was able to appreciate and incorporate into his system the Christian church. Throughout *A Theology of the Jewish-Christian Reality* van Buren highlights Jewish traditions (including Rosenzweig's philosophy) that are predisposed to understanding the church as a new stage in the history of Israel's covenant. Rosenzweig's own approach might be called a "special exception" theology, since it views the church as a unique expression of the God of Israel's relationship to the Gentile world, and therefore a special case within the non-Jewish religious universe. There are theologies in the Christian tradition of theologies in which the Jews come to God as the result of a special exception to the normal path of evangelization and entrance into the church (in a mass conversion at Christ's *parousia,* for example). But van Buren responds directly to Rosenzweig's overtures by stressing that the *church comes to the God of Israel* in an exceptional way--through inclusion in Israel's eternal covenant through the Jew Jesus.[38] In van Buren's view, Jesus is such an integral part of Israel's covenant that "the church should be amazed that there was and is also a word of God in Jesus for the church..." (II: 259).

There is still another aspect of Rosenzweig's work which has been an important impetus for van Buren's thinking. In a 1984 article entitled "Theological Education for the Church's Relationship to the Jewish People,"[39] van Buren refers to a letter in which Rosenzweig confirmed the Fourth Gospel's claim that Jesus is the only way to "come to the Father," so long as one keeps in mind that since Israel is already with the Father, it is not in need of a way of "coming" to God. Van Buren refers to this interpretive move as "Rosenzweig's *tour de force,"* and sees it as affirming his conviction that Jesus represents and renews the intimacy existing between the Jewish people and God.

Throughout the three volumes of *A Theology of the Jewish-Christian Reality* the Apostolic Writings (van Buren's term for the New Testament) are often interpreted according to this Rosenzweig-inspired model which views Jesus as one who came to save Gentiles and to confirm God's original covenant with the Jewish people. In *A Christian Theology of the People Israel,* for instance, van Buren claims that Jesus' statements about "the lost sheep of the house of Israel" (e.g., Mt. 10:6) communicate Jesus' concern with lost Jews and leading them to be good Jews (254). The word which Jesus spoke to his people, in other words, was the same word which they had heard from Moses and the Prophets: "be Israel!" Van Buren interprets Jesus' saying that he was sent to the "sick" (Mk 2: 17, Mt. 9: 12-13; Lk. 5: 31-32) to mean that "healthy, righteous Israel" had no need of him precisely because they already knew and served God (*Christ in Context,* 88). Referring to the story of Jesus' healing of a paralytic in Mark 2, van Buren claims "it is a misunderstanding of the covenant to think that only God can forgive sins" (*Christ in Context,* 134). Finally, van Buren observes that the "yoke" Jesus urges his disciples to take upon themselves (Mt. 11: 29-30) is a reference to the Torah, "for the Torah was the yoke that God had given to Israel" (*Christ in Context,* 141). Because van Buren does not always make this fact clear, it should be pointed out that his readings of these New Testament passages are in conflict with the way they have been and generally still are read in the church. These novel and bold interpretations are testimony to van Buren's exegetical courage, and to the spirit of Rosenzweig at work in *A Theology of the Jewish-Christian Reality.* In fact, it could be argued that van Buren's whole approach in *A Theology of the Jewish-Christian Reality* is a direct response to Rosenzweig's overtures to the church made earlier in this century.

Finally, it should be noted that van Buren is also indebted to what Davies calls the "liberal Protestant" understanding of the relationship between Christianity and Judaism--a view whose classic proponent is James Parkes. For this approach, Judaism and Christianity represent the same religious reality, but Israel and the church result from a "division of vocations."[40] As we have seen, van Buren is also influenced by the "Barthian" understanding of the relationship of Israel and the church, based on Israel's election, which Davies distinguishes from the "liberal" view. In the final analysis, it may be impossible to discriminate between the various sources behind a particular aspect of van Buren's theology. For example, even in van Buren's emphasis on Israel's election, one of his fundamental systematic principles, it is very difficult to distinguish the influences of Barth and Rosenzweig.

II. VAN BUREN ON ISRAEL

We now turn our attention to the text of van Buren's *A Theology of the Jewish-Christian Reality.* We shall survey the arguments and examples that make up the three volumes of this work before attempting to distill the systematic principles which animate van Buren's theology of Israel.

A. *Discerning the Way*

Van Buren begins the first volume of *A Theology of the Jewish-Christian Reality* by introducing his metaphor of "the Way." Van Buren observes that we begin on "the path that has been shown to us, with the

Way provided for us by the One," although for the moment the meanings of "us," "Way," and "One" remain unclear. Van Buren suggests his project might be called "systematic theology," but is really only a conversation which takes place among all those who walk together along the Way. Van Buren's intended audience is the "full range of thoughtful Christians," and in this sense he is writing a "church theology" (I:35). The occasion for van Buren's addressing of the church is the important change of mind it has experienced under the influence of contemporary history. This change of mind finds its most important expression, van Buren maintains, in the "Nostra aetate" pronouncement of Vatican II. Van Buren's framework for reflection on this change is to be "historical" and "particular," terms that will take on meaning as he proceeds.

In "The Context of Theology" (Step One on "the Way"), van Buren stresses that theology does not exhaust the conversation of those walking in the Way, but that talking (theology) and walking (living by faith) go together. Faith, after all, is not a matter of thinking, but of walking in a certain manner. In fact, van Buren argues that the logical difficulties presented by the Way are far less a problem than the actual difficulties of walking it. While Christians can never forget their triumphalist past and must learn from the mistakes of those who talked and walked before them, these others cannot be more than "helpers" and do not relieve Christians of their "living responsibility" to God here and now. Even the authors of the Apostolic Writings cannot dominate Christian talk or always have the last word (I:47). In fact, the documents of the New Testament provide minimal aid for our walking, since the contemporary church, not being Jewish, is really not the "church" that produced these documents. On the other hand, van Buren claims the Apostolic Writings are anti-Judaic only because they have been read and interpreted as such. Whether they will be so in the future remains an open question (I:62).

In "The Subject of Theology" (Step Two), van Buren begins with the recognition that Christians cannot speak about their Way without speaking of God. This statement may appear self-evident, but it should not surprise us if van Buren proceeds carefully at this point, considering his long-standing interest in the meaning of religious language. In this context van Buren introduces, but does not dwell on, the cultural, logical, and moral difficulties associated with God-talk. His new orientation can be described as "cultural-linguistic": "we come to speak of God because we learned from our parents and others of the linguistic community to pray and so to speak of God" (I:30). This means that "our way" and "our conversation" should be considered things that "only make sense within...our walking" (I:54).

The one point of necessary agreement in Christian walking and talking is that "the One whom we speak about is always and only the God of Israel" (I:32), the God whom faithful Jews (including Jesus) have always called upon. Christians cannot ask, "Israel apart, what do we mean by God?" When speaking of God, the church means only "this God." Here van Buren gives expression to a systematic principle that governs his entire theology of Israel: "the assertion that the church adores Israel's LORD is fundamental for all its conversation and all its theology" (I:33). According to van Buren, only four Jewish voices-- Jehuda Halevi, Maimonides, Menachem HaMe'iri and Franz Rosenzweig--have allowed the possibility that the church worshipped Israel's LORD. One of van Buren's tasks in *A Theology of the Jewish-Christian Reality* is to explore and respond to this strand of Jewish thought and tradition.

Van Buren also begins to deal in this chapter of *Discerning the Way* with the doctrine of revelation. Barth's view of revelation as God's self-disclosure is taken seriously, but is dismissed for ignoring the role of the knower which van Buren argues is inherent in all personal knowledge. As he will make clear in Step Eight, van Buren defines revelation as an acknowledged reinterpretation of tradition in response to Jewish history. The revelational pattern emerges when historical events *reorient* an individual, and then a community. Following Irving Greenberg and Norman Perrin,[41] van Buren opens the way for perceiving revelation in the midst of contemporary history by understanding Scripture itself as a reinterpretation of Jewish tradition in response to reorienting events.

In his discussion of "theological responsibility" in Step Three, van Buren describes incoherence, not irrelevance or illogicality, as the worst form of wandering from the Way (I:51; 102). This claim arises from van Buren's philosophical orientation to theology as well as his use of the cultural-linguistic model for the study of religion.[42] As a second aspect of theological responsibility, van Buren discusses the necessity to avoid "secularization" and "spiritualization," both of which history has shown can lead to the slaughter of Jews. Two further elements of this chapter that are worthy of comment are van Buren's development of a complementarity model for viewing the relationship between Israel and the church, and his concern with practical matters having to do with contemporary Jewish-Christian relations. Van Buren envisions Israel and the church walking along in "close proximity," but without fusion, and, like Moltmann, invokes I Corinthians 15:28 (where Christ hands over the Kingdom to the Father who becomes "all in all") as proof that final reconciliation between Israel and the church will take place when Christ steps into the background. Van Buren's vision of what Klappert calls "complementarity" is also similar to Moltmann's. Van Buren's concern with Jews becoming Christians, with groups like "Jews for Jesus" and with modern forms of Christian Judaizing (I:63-65) should also be noted in passing, since van Buren's familiarity with these practical features of contemporary Jewish-Christian relations is something which distinguishes his theology of Israel from that of Barth and Moltmann.[43]

In Step Four van Buren considers the significance of the Christian belief in "the triune God." Although van Buren will devote all of volume three of *A Theology of the Jewish-Christian Reality* to a consideration of the church's Christology, he attempts here to break ground in understanding the meaning of the church's trinitarian confession. Van Buren begins with a consideration of the work of the Spirit: the church confesses its belief in the Spirit as a result of the historical fact of the Gentiles coming to worship the God of the Jews (I:73). The Gentiles, in fact, actually learn from this strange new step in the history of Israel's covenant who the triune God is. In general, the doctrine of the Trinity is only a formulation of the duality of continuity and novelty in God's overture to the Gentiles (III:194). The doctrine teaches that although the inclusion of the Gentiles through Jesus was a genuine *novum* in Israel's covenant history, it cannot in any way annul or detract from that history.

This means that the church must understand Jesus in a way that adds glory to God's people and God's covenant. Jesus has to be interpreted not as a divine *hypostasis,* but as a Jewish rabbi whose teaching, ministry and followers were all Jewish. Since Israel must be the foundation of the church's claim to Jesus' Sonship, the equality of the Son with the Father can only be an equality born of obedience

(I:76). Jesus is not the LORD, but *the church's* Lord. The church confesses God as triune because that is how God is *for the church.* "We confess this same One as triune because that is how He is our God and how He has made us Gentiles to be walkers in the Way, alongside of His people" (I:87).[44]

The "historical rootedness of the doctrine of the Trinity" (I:92) van Buren elaborates is in some ways similar to Moltmann's claim that this doctrine is simply the Christian way of saying that the story of Jesus is also the story of God. Also reminiscent of Moltmann's approach to understanding the doctrine of the Trinity is van Buren's survey of Jewish teachings which suggest distinctions in God (e.g., the Kabbalist concept of *Sefiroth* or "emanations"). There are significant differences, however, in the way the two theologians approach their subject. While Moltmann finds that the trinitarian confession arises from the historical suffering of Jesus on the cross, the historical "event" in which van Buren believes the doctrine of the Trinity is rooted is the "gathering of a Gentile church into the worship of Israel's God." Furthermore, while Moltmann elaborates connections between the ways Jews and Christians understand God, van Buren assumes the fact that Christians worship Israel's God, and attempts to show that the doctrine of the Trinity is compatible with this view. Finally, the conclusion reached by van Buren in his survey of Jewish teaching on the nature of God is not (as in Moltmann) an attempt to defuse the whole concept of monotheism and view it as "Greek," but the statement that "we do indeed worship the LORD, the God whom they worship" (I:92).

In Step Five, "Speaking of God: The Nature and Attributes of God," van Buren steps aside from the Way, as it were, and observes that in the last quarter of the twentieth century the validity of God-talk has been called into question by the rise of secularity. Van Buren observes that while those who walk in the Way are responsible to God rather than to the "secular age," secularity's claim that God no longer works in history must be taken seriously. In van Buren's view, Dietrich Bonhoeffer and Richard Rubenstein are theologians who have faced up to the fact of secularity. A theology which understands the challenge of secularity will lead Christians to speak of God's activity differently than did many of their predecessors. But even Calvin's thesis that knowledge of God and knowledge of ourselves are intimately related leads in the direction van Buren wants to go: "if we find that we must change our views of ourselves, then with that will come changes in our understanding of God" (I:98). Van Buren's conclusion, though not explicit here, is that at the present moment in history God wants God's creatures to assume greater responsibility for the covenant and for the completion of creation.

Two other matters of interest are dealt with in this chapter. First, van Buren takes up the discussion of God's personal nature, arguing that God is actually the "normative person" (1:102ff.).[45] Second, van Buren explores the connection between the crucifixion of Jesus and the Holocaust, noting that the two are bound by God's apparent absence. The two events tell us something about God's presence-in-absence, van Buren argues: if Jesus is "the truth about God," then God must have been present in the deathcamps--the God of Golgotha would have to have been there.

In the next two chapters ("steps" six and seven) van Buren considers the nature and authority of the Bible. Van Buren maintains, following the lead of canonical critics like James A. Sanders,[46] that Christians have the Bible not from its "original authors," but from those who have preceded them in the Way. Van Buren calls on the church to recognize that

> to speak of the Scriptures of Judaism apart from the Talmud, and to speak of the Bible of Christians apart from the patristic interpretation, will hardly help us to see the role that these carried books have played (I:125).

In both the Jewish and Christian traditions we notice a formative period stretching from the first through the fourth centuries C.E., and each must be considered a "creative undertaking which shaped their understandings of Torah and Gospel" (I: 125). When we add van Buren's conviction that the Bible comes to us as a multilevel collection of interpretations and reinterpretations, we are well on our way to seeing Judaism and Christianity as the products of two different interpretations of Israel's Scriptures.

Van Buren contends that throughout the Bible, from the story of Abraham to the Apostolic Writings, "flesh and blood Israel holds the center of the stage" (I:131). In making this statement van Buren is arguing, first of all, that the Bible and its action are to be anchored in the reality of this world. This means that the events concerning Jesus of Nazareth should be interpreted *historically* (as a "radically new beginning of a further stage in God's dealings with His creation"), and never *ahistorically* (as the making explicit of what was said previously in signs and figures). Secondly, by focusing on "flesh and blood Israel," van Buren intends to combat the theology of displacement which portrays Christ as the "message of the Bible."

In Step Six van Buren begins to explain in sociological terms the anti-Jewish polemics found in some parts of the Apostolic Writings. He does so by recalling the environment of mutual rejection between Torah-faithful Jews and "Christians" in the first century. Even when interpreted sociologically, however, van Buren believes that hostility toward Jews is a greater problem for interpreting the Apostolic Writings than that posed by so-called mythological language. It is partly for this reason that the Bible cannot be the last word in the church's theological "conversation." In Step Seven van Buren discusses the function of the Bible. The Bible's function, or service, is primarily that of reminding the church who God is and is not, and who Christians are and are not. First, it reminds the church that God is not some philosophical "Absolute," but a God who is both temporal and historical. The Bible also reminds the church that God is not alone in sustaining God's Creation. God is not a God who does it all for God's creatures, but one who has chosen them as cooperators.

At this point van Buren develops the human responsibility theme he introduced in Step Five. Van Buren makes use here of the Bonhoefferian notion that in our time God has decided it is time God's creatures assumed the obligations of adulthood. Contemporary events like the Holocaust and birth of the state of Israel show us that God is not the all-Doer that the ancients believed God to be, and they powerfully underscore the importance of human responsibility. The Holocaust does so in a negative way (as an example of the failure of human responsibility in protecting Jews) and the state of Israel, founded by "Jewish guns and Jewish effort," does so in a positive way (as an example of the fruits of human responsibility). Both events, van Buren argues, are a challenge to the traditional Christian notion of "grace alone."[47]

The Bible also has the function of reminding Christians who *they* are and who *they* are not. In particular, it reminds Christians they are not Jews, but Gentiles: there were others called before the church was called, which has now been called to join Israel in its great commission to prepare for God's Kingdom. The Bible, then, reminds the church of the historical continuum in which it exists. Finally, the Bible reminds Christians of what has and has not happened. While something dramatically new has occurred in the history of God's covenant--a codicil has been written which includes the Gentiles--the *parousia* or advent of God's Kingdom has not come. Van Buren picks up at a later point the implications of this fact for Christian faith.

In Step Eight, "The Course of the Way: History as Revelation," van Buren elaborates his innovative understanding of "revelation." Specifically, van Buren tries to identify revelation's "pattern." In doing so he is dependent on the insights of others,[48] but he puts these insights to use in developing an interpretation of revelation that is distinctly his own. Van Buren's starting point is the statement that "in the event called revelation, something happens to certain human beings" (I:167). The judgment that there has been revelation, however, is made by the community which comes after these persons. In every case except that of Abraham, revelation comes to persons who are bearers of a tradition. In other words, "revelation begins against the background of a tradition of revelation" (I:169). The pattern of revelation begins with tradition, but continues in reorientation[49] of a person (typically a prophet), and eventually leads to the reorientation of a whole people and their tradition. Such reorientation is always rooted in historical events:

> The more firmly tradition became established, the more clearly the impact of historical events in Israel's social and political history emerged as the occasion of revelation. Revelation has to do with what is going on in Israel's history...in the sense that the history itself is seen to be revelatory (I:170).

Under the impact of historical events the traditions of Israel were from time to time reinterpreted. Van Buren perceives examples of this "pattern" in three moments of renewal in the history of biblical Israel: in the stories of Joshua at Schechem, Josiah and the discovery of the Temple scroll, and the post-Exilic restoration under Ezra. In each case, the people of Israel accept a reinterpretation of tradition that reflects changed historical circumstances.

A crucial implication of these observations is that the Scriptures can be seen as the result of successive reinterpretations of Israel's tradition that develop under the pressure of the "latest event." The Apostolic Writings and even the "gospel" follow the same pattern--they represent a reorientation of Israel's tradition in the wake of an historical "event" (the inclusion of the Gentiles in Israel's covenant viewed from the post-Easter perspective). What is truly significant about van Buren's discussion of the pattern of revelation is his claim to have rediscovered that pattern in contemporary history after eighteen centuries of dormancy. Van Buren believes that the pattern of revelation--a pattern of reinterpretation under the pressure of reorienting events in Israel's history--is once again asserting itself within the church. He is referring, of course, to the "radical reversal" of Christian teaching on the Jews since 1965,[50] a reversal clearly prompted by events in Jewish history (the Holocaust and the founding of Israel). Van Buren stresses that he is concerned only with reinterpretations of tradition that *have already occurred,* at least implicitly, in the statements of responsible ecclesiastical authorities. He observes that a variety of bishop councils and church synods have clearly and unequivocally affirmed the continuing existence of God's people Israel and God's covenant with them. If the reorientation represented by the statements of these church authorities leads to a reorientation of the entire Christian community, then, van Buren believes, we will be able to speak of these events in Israel's history as "revelatory." This entire discussion is an excellent example of why van Buren is a "radical" (and why he is not a "Holocaust") theologian. Van Buren builds his understanding of "history as revelation" not on the Holocaust and its implications, but on the pattern of revelation evident in Israel's history. He then applies this pattern to the church's evolving understanding of the events of the Holocaust and the founding of the state of Israel.

In Step Nine, "The Goal of the Way: The Redemption of Creation," van Buren emphasizes the implications of the theological principle that "the Redeemer is the Creator." He follows the tack of Moltmann and others who stress that Israel's hope for the redemption of creation was and is this-worldly, and that Israel's hope has been subtly corrupted by the church. In words reminiscent of Scholem and Ben-Chorin, van Buren argues that "the open, national hope of Judaism was transformed into the inner personal and spiritual hope of the church" (I:190). Van Buren points to Iranaeus as one Christian voice who spoke of redemption in "this created order," but his voice is a lonely one and needs to be supplemented by the voices of contemporary Jews. Christians who listen will hear that "our hope is really theirs." Although apprehended in a Gentile way, the Christian hope for this world is the same as Jewish hope: "we do not have a different hope any more than we serve a different God" (I:196). Since the church has lost its connection with Israel's hope by emphasizing the "first act of the drama [of redemption] as decisive," van Buren argues that attention to Israel's voice will entail that it cease speaking of Easter as the "end of history."

B. *A Christian Theology of the People Israel*

In the second volume of *A Theology of the Jewish-Christian Reality* van Buren drops the Way metaphor and assumes a more direct approach to his subject matter. If there is a metaphor to replace *walking in the Way* in volume two, it is Van Buren's emphasis on the church's duty to *ask* about and to *hear* Israel's testimony. Van Buren argues that Israel's God cannot be heard apart from God's witness Israel, and this becomes a systematic principle for his theology.

In the introduction to this volume van Buren classifies a "Christian theology of the people Israel" as an integral part of the church's self-critical reflection--a part which concerns the church's duty and ability to hear the testimony of the Jewish people to God (II:1). Also in the introduction to this volume we find the longest engagement with the theology of Karl Barth anywhere in *A Theology of the Jewish-Christian Reality*. In a section entitled "the task and criterion of theology," van Buren suggests revisions of Barth's understandings of certain methodological issues in light of the Jewish-Christian reality. He asks: is the "proximate criterion" for theology the Bible, or the Bible interpreted by the church and the Jewish people? Is proclamation really the single primary commission of God's people, or is this commission to love God? Is revelation essentially God's self-revelation, or does revelation also take the forms of Torah and/or Jesus? If van Buren believes Barth's theology provides a useful starting point for reflection on the task and criterion of theology, he does not see Barth as providing a foundation for speaking positively of Israel. Van Buren admits that on this point he "feels acutely the lack of teachers" (II:xv).[51] Moreover, van Buren stresses that the church has always had a "theology of Israel,"--although it has been a negative one-- and that this fact accounts for the resistance to a contemporary Christian theology that takes seriously the Jewish "No."

But if the church is to hear Israel's "No," according to van Buren, there is reason for the church to expect Israel to make sense of its "Yes." In response to the claim of Clemens Thoma that Christianity has little meaning for Judaism (a statement one finds in the writings of Moltmann as well), van Buren writes that "if the existence of the Gentile church is due to the intention of the God of Israel, this can hardly be a matter of indifference to Israel" (II:16). In fact, throughout *A Theology of the Jewish-Christian Reality* van Buren accentuates Jewish traditions that are sympathetic to viewing the church as a God-willed reality.

Van Buren makes clear once again in this introduction that it is neither the Holocaust nor the state of Israel which have made a theology of Israel necessary for the church. These events only bring to light what should have been recognized long ago: that an explicit theology of Israel is no less important for the church than its Christology. Van Buren is equally clear that a Christian theology of Israel must begin with the fact of Israel's election, and in this aspect of van Buren's thought we notice his most important connection with Barth's theology of Israel. Van Buren follows Barth in finding Israel's continuing election in the testimony of the Apostle Paul, but he also believes it is the presupposition of the history and mission of Jesus as well (II:24). As in Barth, the church is wholly "dependent" on the election of Israel. Unlike Barth, however, van Buren maintains that the church has no independent story to tell of its own, but offers only a "confirmation" of Israel's story (II:111).

Following Paul, van Buren argues that Israel's "No" was for the sake of the Gentiles, according to the will of God. But Israel's "No" was only negative in a secondary sense. What the church perceives as Israel's "No" was primarily a "Yes" to God and God's covenant. Van Buren goes so far as to claim that "the church is absolutely dependent on Israel's Yes...to God at Sinai, reaffirmed each generation through Torah faithfulness" (II: 35). The task of a Christian theology of Israel, then, is to help the church hear and learn from Israel's primary "Yes" and secondary "No,"[52] both of which it is built upon.

In chapter one of *A Christian Theology of the People Israel,* van Buren clarifies his use of the term "Israel?" Israel is

> the one people of God, from Abraham through Moses, including all of the Israel of which we read in the Scriptures, but also and explicitly Israel since biblical times, throughout its history up to our own day. I mean primarily present, living Israel, both in the Land and in the Diaspora. I mean, in short, the Jews (II:17).

A Christian theology of Israel will seek to understand Israel in its own terms--as people, not as a religion or another church. Furthermore, according to van Buren, it will cultivate a nonidealized view of the Jewish people, one affirming their election by God's grace alone (II:33).

In chapter two, "Israel's Testimony to Creation," van Buren observes that the confession of God as Creator comes for Israel only on this side of the Exodus, and for the church only on this side of Pentecost. The relationship between Creator and creation is discovered by Israel "in the Exodus by way of Sinai" (II:52). Van Buren's contextual understanding of creation (for which he is indebted to Gerhard von Rad, Karl Barth, and the rabbinic teaching of a pre-existent Torah) issues in the conclusion that "creation is for the sake of Torah-shaped life, for the sake of Israel in the covenant..." (II:59). Like Israel, the church knows God as Creator through knowledge of God as Redeemer. Israel was created in the Exodus, an event van Buren refers to as "protoredemptive." The Exodus event was an "actual if qualified redemption" which leads Israel to hope for a full redemption. Since the event in which the church was born (Jesus' resurrection) was protoredemptive as well, the church must look for its full redemption in the future, just as does Israel.

In chapter three, "The Reality and Risk of Creation," van Buren elaborates the nature and meaning of Israel's future hope. Israel hopes for God's future in *this* world, and is itself a sign of hope for a threatened creation (II:114). Israel also is a sign for an "Augustinian" church of the goodness of creation and the reality of sin and evil. Israel's witness is that all creation is good, but incomplete, that serving the Creator means taking responsibility for creation, and that what is real is possible (II:88). Israel sees the human "image of God" in the ability to respond to God, an ability that has not been lost in Adam's disobedience. "Sin" is not a central theme in Israel's story, according to van Buren, and "evil" points precisely to creation's unfinished character. Furthermore, since creation was for the sake of the covenant (chapter two), "it depends for its completion on the free response of God's dialogical partner" Israel (II:99). Here we see another example of the human responsibility theme which pervades *A Theology of the Jewish-Christian Reality:* Israel is a sign for the world that God requires cooperation in overcoming threats to creation. Van Buren believes this sign has important implications for the church. God desires that all God's covenant partners assume far more responsibility than in the past for moving creation toward its completion (II:174-75). It is in this context that van Buren intimates his understanding of the Holocaust's uniqueness. Together, he says, the Holocaust and the founding of the state of Israel comprise a watershed in *Jewish history* (II:170). But the Holocaust "stands alone" as an attack on God's covenant which was nearly successful. It is open to discussion, van Buren thinks, what effect Hitler's success in eliminating the Jews would have had on the God of Israel and on this God's Creation.

In chapter four van Buren considers more carefully Israel's election and especially the significance which this election has for Israel's relationship to "the nations." Van Buren reiterates here that God's election of Israel is the foundation for everything Israel has to say, and credits Franz Rosenzweig with the rediscovery (several years before Barth began working on the *Church Dogmatics)* of the centrality of election for biblical faith.[53] Jewish peculiarity, van Buren reminds us, is always rooted in election, and the state of Israel, considered without respect to divine election, can only exist as one nation among others (II:124). Since there are particular and universal aspects of Israel and Israel's God, why is it, van Buren asks, that the particular elements have appeared so prominent to non-Jews? As a corrective to this tendency, van Buren considers several examples of Israel's "universal witness," including the teachings of Rav Kook (Chief Rabbi of Jerusalem from 1919-1935) and the tradition of the Noachide covenant and its seven commandments. Although the Noachide covenant has generally not provided for the inclusion of the Christian church in Jewish thought, van Buren sees here an untapped resource for understanding in Jewish terms the relationship between Israel and "the nations." Interestingly, van Buren locates another resource in the biblical story of Ishmael, which he believes teaches that "election is for the sake of God's purposes for all those who are not the elect" (II:140).

In chapter five, "The People of Israel," van Buren identifies the concrete form of Israel's election as its life in Torah. Throughout the centuries the church has failed to see the importance of Israel's acceptance of Torah for its election. Even today this distortion remains:

> The Gentile church has heard clearly Israel's testimony to its deliverance from Egypt. It has not heard Israel's testimony that Israel became free not at the Red Sea, but at Sinai....the logic of a Gentile theology that moves directly from the Exodus to the general statement that God is a god of the liberation of the oppressed, is too simplistic for Israel (II:156-7).[54]

As we have seen, however, the Exodus event is not without significance. In fact, van Buren claims that the Jewish people can serve as a model for peoples of the third world who are increasingly challenged to take their destinies into their own hands. Israel's "witness" (which van Buren believes has been hindered by the "absurdity" of the notion that Zionism is racism) may be especially effective, van Buren believes, for American Blacks.[55] Van Buren notes the irony of escalating Black-Jewish antagonisms in American social and political life, and challenges Blacks to learn from Israel's history a way in which to see their own history--to "hear God's invitation expressed in the enduring peoplehood of the Jews" (II:179). Furthermore, van Buren maintains, Zionism and the Black Power movement are "correlative."

Even if we overlook van Buren's anachronistic application of the term Black Power to the contemporary situation of African-Americans, his attempt at "correlation" is problematic. It is no doubt motivated by van Buren's genuine concern for both "peoples," but it is doubtful whether any white Protestant theologian may legitimately ask Blacks to be more like Jews, or encourage Black theologians to use Zionism as a model for "winning self-determination under the banner of black power" (II:182). One would not be surprised, in fact, if contemporary African-Americans seeking self-determination for their people perceived themselves to have more in common with Palestinian Arabs than either Israeli or American Jews.

Toward the end of chapter five van Buren admits that by
claiming election makes Israel different, he is actually siding with some
Jews and in opposition to others. Yet he defends this stance by arguing
that Jews who claim there is nothing unique about the state of Israel or
the Jewish people, though correct from a "secular perspective," are in
conflict with the weight of Jewish tradition (II:164). Echoing Jewish
thinkers like Eliezer Berkovits and Emil Fackenheim, van Buren
reiterates that "a secular Jewish self-understanding ...provides no solid
base for understanding the Jewish people as unique." (II:180). As we
shall argue in the final chapter, however, the uniqueness of the Jewish
people is an idea which a Christian theology of Israel must handle with
great caution.

In chapter six van Buren confronts more directly the problem of
"the land." God has elected Israel to "landed life," but, as can be seen
from the clash between kings and prophets in Israel's history, landed
life is inherently ambiguous. The land, van Buren argues, is God's gift
as well as God's challenge to Israel (II:190). And what of the
relationship between "the land" and the state of Israel? Israel's "return
to its land," symbolized by the founding of the modern state of Israel is
"surely a step in the direction of the fulfillment of the promise of
Israel's election" (II:193). Van Buren wonders, though, why such a
statement is so difficult for many Christians to make or accept. While
Christian theology has been fond of stressing God's "mighty acts" in
biblical times, it is not so sure that God acts the same way today. The
result is that many Christians[56] will accept the legitimacy of the religion
known as Judaism, but not of Zionism. This reluctance is tied, van
Buren argues, to the church's difficulty in accepting the reality of
landed life in general. The church does not share Israel's sense of place,
nor does it readily understand that this land is different from all other
lands because its people is different from all other peoples (II:195).
While Christian theology can not be expected to settle disputes over the
meaning of this land, "the church has no choice but to affirm this
promise." In short, van Buren follows Walter Brueggemann and others
in arguing that "the land" should have more of a place in Christian
reflection on the ways of God, not least since Israel's witness to land is
another reminder of the church's future dependence on the people
Israel (cf. Zechariah 8: 22ff.).

It is evident from chapter six of *A Christian Theology of the People Israel* that van Buren has adopted a Christian Zionist outlook,[57] and one which is primarily messianic as opposed to nationalist in focus. Van Buren charges that Christians who claim to be pro-Jewish but anti-Zionist reveal that they take exile to be normal for the Jewish people. These Christians, he says, have accepted Jews only on Gentile terms without allowing the Jewish people to define themselves. For van Buren, anti-Zionism is anti-Jewish: "Anti-Zionism is in fact an anti-Jewish position. To be against Zion is to be against Israel. It was so in biblical times and it is so now" (II:200).

While van Buren's position is clear and coherent, it appears to ignore the fact that many Jews choose to deny just what he affirms--that anti-Zionism is necessarily anti-Jewish. And beyond this, one wonders how van Buren understands the many anti-Zionist Jews, some of whom are devoutly religious, who by his definition are "anti-Jewish." Also troublesome is the fact that van Buren does not seem to have considered versions of Zionism which stress at the same time the promises of Jews and the rights of Palestinians.[58] While van Buren admits there have been serious hindrances to Israel's witness in its land, he argues that some of these have been beyond its control. The continuing drain of war on the material and spiritual resources of the country and what van Buren calls the "burden of occupation" have certainly taken their toll. But van Buren does not believe that Israel's light to the nations has been extinguished by the Israeli state's shortcomings. In fact, for van Buren "there seems no likelihood at all" that the state of Israel could become a nation like all others (II:201). What van Buren considers an impossibility, however, is self-evident for many Jews[59] (Zionist and otherwise) who view the state of Israel differently than he.

In chapter seven van Buren focuses on Israel's Torah and its significance for Christian theology. As he has stated earlier, van Buren believes Israel's fidelity to Torah represents a simultaneous "Yes" to God and "No" to the church. It is crucial, van Buren adds here, that Christian theology cease viewing this "No" according to the traditional scheme of law and gospel. Augustine and Luther, van Buren argues, misunderstood Judaism in their assignment of Judaism to the category of "law." Judaism is not about "law," van Buren says, but about Torah, and Torah is good news, even "gospel," for the Jew. Israel's Torah-life is joyful, as is evident, for instance, in the "halakhic joy" of the rabbis.

But the church has falsely depicted the Jewish people as sad and sorrowful. Van Buren maintains that the church can no longer see in Torah a burden for Israel. It must overcome its Augustinian "introspective conscience" (Krister Stendahl's term), and listen to Israel's witness that Torah is God's gift, that grace is for the sake of works, and that the primary form of revelation is commandment (II:210ff).

Israel contradicts the church by remaining faithful to Torah, but it also raises the question whether the church, with its spiritualizing and moralizing of God's commandments, really knows the God who gave Torah to Israel. Van Buren perceives Israel's antidote for these tendencies in the church in Jesus himself, who held a "liberal" view of Torah but whose interpretations were in some cases more strict than those of his Jewish interlocutors. Van Buren's conclusion is that Jesus, who taught a righteousness of God apart from but not contrary to Torah, "called his people to greater not less fidelity to the Torah of God" (II:231).

Perhaps not surprisingly, van Buren discovers in the writings of Paul an attitude to Torah not dissimilar to Jesus' own. For van Buren, Paul's teaching on the matter is summarized in Romans 3:21 ("in Christ the righteousness of God has appeared apart from Torah") and 10:4 ("Christ is the *telos*--the goal--of the law"). Most importantly, Paul denies that the new enactment of God's righteousness for the Gentiles in Christ can be contrary to Torah, since it was announced in Torah as a promise to Abraham. Van Buren's conclusion is bold and consistent, if controversial: "...for Paul the value of the Torah as God's gift to Israel had not been changed by the coming, death and resurrection of Christ" (II:234). But while the church should be attentive to Torah, it is not subject to it, since it is Christ-shaped, not Torah-shaped life that God wills for the church. But

> as Israel has God very near to it by having God's Torah very near, so
> the church draws near to God by drawing near to the Torah-faithful Jew
> Jesus....the Gentile church has its relationship to Torah by means of
> holding onto Jesus Christ in his obedience to God and as the church's
> authoritative teacher (rabbi) who interprets God's commandments to
> them (II:236, 238).

In chapter eight, "Israel and Jesus," van Buren elaborates these ideas in discussing Israel as Jesus' "essential context." It is not enough to recognize that Jesus was born a Jew; we must be as specific as God was: "Jesus was born a Jew in *eretz Yisrael* in the first century of the Common Era, a Jew of that time and of that Judaism which was taking shape under the guidance of Israel's Sages and Pharisees" (II:241). According to Matthew, van Buren argues, Jesus stood on the stricter (Pharisaic) side of the broad movement of reform which Ezra initiated and which came to flower in rabbinic Judaism. In fact, the "spirit of Javneh" matches closely Jesus' call to renewal, since "both challenged the Jewish people to discover new ways in which to be Israel" (II:266). If God chose as the context for the life of God's incarnate Word the Judaism being shaped by the Pharisees, then overcoming the "unreliable portrait" of the Pharisees offered by the gospels must become the urgent task of the church. Van Buren admits, however, that since this task requires the application of biblical criticism, it will be a long and difficult one, and may never alter the attitudes of many Christians.

While van Buren concedes that Jesus came into conflict with at least some Jews of some standing in Jerusalem,[60] he stresses that the concern of Jesus for his people is not a debatable point. Van Buren marshalls biblical evidence to show that "Jesus spoke in the language of Israel, to Israel and about Israel" (II:244). While the church has traditionally understood the "Israel first" orientation in the ministry of Jesus and the apostles as proof that the Jews who rejected Jesus were without excuse, van Buren believes the priority of Israel in Jesus' ministry was based in his positive view of Israel and a relatively negative view of the Gentiles. The turning point for the "wholly intra-Jewish affair" which surrounded Jesus was God's revelation to the Pharisee Saul, who believed he was called to preach among the Gentiles. Paul's interpretation of Jesus' significance according to the Hebrew Scriptures, however, reveals that his call was the unfolding of a purpose as old as the covenant with Abraham: "Jesus was for the Gentiles because God had always planned to bring them into his covenant purpose" (II:248). Van Buren's conclusion is that the contradiction many scholars perceive between Jesus and Paul is one only in appearance.

Van Buren emphasizes in this chapter that the church "depends" on the unqualified Jewishness of Jesus. Jesus is "Israel-for-the-church,"

"Israel effectively enlightening the Gentiles," and his "re-presentational identity" makes the humility and generosity of God in God's covenant with Israel present to Gentiles. As van Buren puts it, "Jesus Christ recapitulates and embodies Israel's reality, its relationship to God, and its calling to be a light for the Gentiles" (II:253). But, if this is Jesus' meaning for the church, what does "Jesus as Israel" mean for Israel?

Van Buren argues that the word of God in Jesus intended for Israel was "be Israel." In particular, this meant accepting the humbling fact of God's election, being inwardly directed toward God, and maintaining Torah-fidelity.[61] Being Israel, then, is primarily a process of Torah renewal. God's word in Jesus, which was in "fundamental accord" with both the written and oral Torah, was a renewal of the covenant such as Jeremiah had proclaimed (Jer. 31:31). Van Buren emphasizes this was not a *new,* but a *renewed* covenant. In other words, the covenant partners are the same, and Torah is still at the covenant's center.

In his identity as a message to Israel and "Israel-for-the-church," Jesus should be understood in both universal and particular terms:

> God set Jesus in the world to be there for all the others by making him to be Israel in exemplary fashion. Jesus could be for all the others because Israel was and had always been for all the others. Abraham had been called for the sake of the world. Now in Jesus this calling of Israel had been put into effect for all the Gentiles (II:260).

This accentuation of Israel's universal calling is crucial to van Buren's understanding of Jesus and the relationship of church and synagogue. Since Jesus cannot be interpreted apart from his context in Israel, it is difficult for van Buren to sustain the argument that Jesus has significance for the church if he has no significance for Israel. This is why van Buren must conclude that both Christians and Jews have "resisted the reality" of that which the God of Israel has done through Jesus Christ (II:262). It seems not to have crossed Christian minds, van Buren observes, that Jewish "stubbornness" is actually fidelity to Torah; nor does it seems to have occurred to Jews that "Torah's Author might do a new thing outside Torah" (II:276).

Ironically, in order to maintain Jesus' significance for Israel, van Buren must deny that Jesus is the "Messiah of Israel." The problem here is two-fold. Not only is Israel too conscious of what God has not yet accomplished with creation to accept Jesus as its Messiah; but van Buren believes that as long as the church affirms that its relationship with Israel is determined by the identity of Jesus as the Messiah of Israel (as in post-Holocaust statements like that of the German Rhineland Synod in 1980), there is really no hope of complementarity and coexistence between Jews and Christians. Van Buren argues that the church has made an "anti-Jewish symbol" out of the sign of the messiah, and on this point at least, he appears to have the witness of history on his side.[62]

In chapter nine, "The Witness of Israel's Rejection of Christianity," van Buren refines his argument concerning the importance of Israel's "No" to the church. He maintains that Israel does *not* reject Jesus (even the "historical" rejection of Jesus by his people lacks evidence), but rather traditional Christianity and the traditional understanding of Paul's gospel. Nor can the Jewish "No" to Christianity be traced to the origins of the church, which was essentially a "Jewish movement within the range of Jewish sects or tendencies possible in this period" (II:271). Israel's rejection of Christianity was and is motivated by fidelity to Torah, and is in part a response to the church's historic weakening of the Jewishness of its Jewish members. Van Buren's argument that Jewish faithfulness to Torah necessitated rejection of "traditional" Christianity is a version of the "what else could they have done?" argument utilized by Buber and Moltmann, who explain Israel's rejection of Christianity in terms of Jewish inability to put faith in a "redemption" for which there appears no evidence.

Van Buren elaborates his claim that the church has misinterpreted Paul's gospel by emphasizing that this gospel can only be heard if Paul is allowed to be a Jew to the core. With no insight into the Jewishness of Paul and Paul's writing, "Paul's gospel of the reconciliation of the Jewish people and the Gentiles...was thereby transformed into the grounds for centuries of hostility, persecution, and suffering" (II:281).[63] The "other gospel" of this other Paul, van Buren maintains, had to be rejected by Israel. Unfortunately, however, this original rejection has led most Jews to adopt this same (mis)reading of Paul.

Finally in chapter nine, van Buren examines Jewish claims (made by Rosenzweig and others) that spiritualization is the fundamental illness of the church. Van Buren considers and critiques the Christian principles of "law versus gospel" (which ignores the "covenantal nomism" of Judaism and the concept of Torah as good news for Israel), of "works versus faith" (which ignores the fact that Israel does not need the church to learn the necessity of divine mercy), of "justification by faith" (which is too "interior" and asks too little of God's covenant partners), and of "redemption in principle" (which places the world as it appears in second place to the world of invisible reality and does not take seriously Israel's claim that the Redeemer is the Creator). This witness of Israel against the church's spiritualization of God and God's creation van Buren juxtaposes with the "Jewish prayer" Jesus taught his disciples. In direct contradiction to the church's spiritualizing tendencies as outlined above, in "the Lord's Prayer" Jesus prays for the coming of God's Kingdom, for God's will to be done on earth, for daily bread, and for creaturely deliverance from evil. What Christians know as "The Lord's Prayer" is actually Israel's prayer, van Buren claims, and one which the church needs desperately to hear anew if it is to overcome its traditional tendencies toward spiritualization.

In chapter ten van Buren considers Israel's "mission." In simplest terms, this mission is to bear witness to the incompleteness of creation and the possibility of creaturely cooperation in working for its completeness. Here van Buren sounds once again the call to responsibility to which we referred earlier. Van Buren argues that this change in understanding of the covenant in the direction of partnership and responsibility is linked to the Lurianic kabbalistic response to the horrors of expulsion from Spain in 1492. Jewish involvement in socialism and the Zionist movement are seen as modern results of this crisis. Israel, in practicing "holy worldliness" and "worldly holiness," witnesses to the possibility of creaturely cooperation with God. It witnesses by the fact that no area of its life falls outside the covenant relationship--it knows, in other words, no religious/secular distinction. Finally, van Buren observes, there is in Israel's witness to the possibility of cooperation with others and with God a "reality corresponding to the vision of the last days of Dietrich Bonhoeffer," an expression of what Bonhoeffer called "religionless Christianity."

In this chapter van Buren also considers the conflict with "the nations" inherent in Israel's mission. Van Buren notes that Israel is placed in a state of tension with other nations by its call to holiness in an unredeemed world. This tension has led to formulation of the so-called "Jewish question," which van Buren believes is more accurately called the "Gentile question." The more recent "Palestinian question"--the supposed obligation of Israel to do something about the Arabs of Palestine--van Buren argues is actually a question to the Arab states as to when they will make peace with Israel. But the true nature of this "Palestinian question" is obscured because the world holds a double standard in relation to Israel's behavior, asking of it what it asks of no other state.[64]

In the final chapter of *A Christian Theology of the Jewish People* van Buren discusses "the church's service to Israel." Essentially, this service consists in aiding Israel in its task of being a light for the nations. Van Buren explores the history of Christian mission to the Jewish people, observing that the missionary church of the nineteenth century could make no sense of Israel's present existence precisely because it saw itself as the reason for Israel having existence. Van Buren strikes a Barthian chord in his contention that the Christian mission to Jews is a "strange modern idea," an incoherent notion, and a "striking sign...that the church had forgotten where it came from..." (II:324). Although van Buren occasionally lapses into polemical overstatement (he claims, for example, that "every [missionary] effort is in effect an attempt to rid the world of Jews"), his discussion of the proper mission of the church toward the Jewish people is compelling. He argues that since the church's relationship with Jews depends on the covenant, Christians may only relate to individual Jews as one of the Jewish people. He also insists that the mission which the church has to the Jews can only be "special." Again echoing the words of Barth, van Buren affirms that the church's relationship with, and thus its mission to Israel is *sui generis*. Furthermore, van Buren reiterates that what makes Israel special for the church is its election, and therefore the church's service to Israel should consist in "helping Israel to be Israel, to be itself as it is defined by its election" (II:333).

According to van Buren, the church's demeanor should be that of a servant who renders both an "external" and "internal" service to Israel. In its external service, the church should function as Israel's Anti-Defamation League. Part of this "ADL" service is to help protect the Jewish state, and this means that "facts" have to be taken seriously: "The church is called to fight the defamation of the Jewish state that is based on distortion of the facts" (II:336). In uncharacteristic fashion, van Buren makes a contention that is not only biased (this is really no surprise given his openly pro-Israel orientation), but naïve. What serious historian or political scientist argues that the key to solving the puzzle of hostility and conflicting claims in the Middle East is a simple collection of "the facts"? Even on the religious plane, one can see the great difficulty the church has in ascertaining the "facts" of the situation in the Middle East each time it assembles to make an official statement on its relationship with the Jewish people.

The church's internal service, according to van Buren, consists in taking Israel's election more seriously than it has done, and this service may allow Jews to take it more seriously as well. In seeking to draw the lost sheep of Israel back into covenant with God (and into Torah-fidelity), the church is only "re-presenting Jesus in his primary work" (II:343). If Christians believe that Christ became a servant of the Jewish people (Ro. 15:8-9), they must ask in what way he continues to be so and seek to follow him in this service. The eventual result of this service, van Buren hopes, will be the church and Israel living together as "supportive partners."

C. *Christ in Context*

Volume three of *A Theology of the Jewish-Christian Reality* is devoted to an examination of the church's Christology.[65] In the foreword to this volume van Buren presents the principles which must guide a Christology for the Jewish-Christian reality. Every proper christological statement will make clear, first, that it gives glory to God the Father and, second, that it is an affirmation of the covenant between God and Israel. In chapter one, "The Place of Christology," van Buren argues that although Israel, the church and the world are all essential to the context of Christ, the church is the starting point and the place for christological reflection. But this priority of the church means that Christology must take into account the church's calling, as well as the negative aspects of its subsequent history. The church must also understand that it tells a story which is unfinished, and that every one of its claims is put forth in hope.

The church's reflection on the things concerning Jesus of Nazareth involves it in a dilemma. The church may no longer be able to accept the writings in its canon as definitive for its understanding of Christ, "having seen in the Holocaust the ultimate fruit of the way the passion narratives were written" (III:16). But van Buren believes the "anti-Judaic Jesus" of the Apostolic Writings is not a direct and necessary result of christological reflection (as Rosemary Ruether argues), but arises from traditional interpretations of certain sections of the Apostolic Writings. If van Buren is right, this presents a challenge to the church:

> since this anti-Judaic Jesus was unknown to Paul and is not the Jesus of important strata of the gospels, the church today is responsible for deciding how it will understand the relationship between Jesus and his people (III:22).

Reading the canon selectively is something the church has always done. Van Buren argues, therefore, that in allowing a present concern (the repudiation of the church's anti-Judaic past) to shape the way this canon is read, the church is doing precisely what it has done from the beginning. In other words, theology has always been practically concerned with the correction of the church's *behavior,* and must remain so today.

Van Buren turns next to a discussion of the "function" of Christology. As confessional statements, he says, christological assertions are human responses which supply important information about those who utter them. For this reason, analysis of christological statements in the Apostolic Writings must focus on the human context in which they were uttered. While all talk about Jesus' "self-understanding" or "inner experience" remains speculative, van Buren is convinced we can be "quite certain" of what went on between Jesus and his disciples: "that Jesus awakened in them a trust in God as a Father who loved the most unlovable is a matter that may be established historically" (III:43). Thus, the experiences his disciples claim to have had in Jesus' presence provide a "firm basis" for christological reflection, and are "all the church needs to know" (III:43).[66]

Van Buren's believes a functional interpretation of Easter (as expressed in the confession, "Jesus is alive!") is preferable to talk of physical resurrection, and more faithful to the church's early witness. After all, the first witnesses to Jesus were concerned only with his relationship to the God of Israel's story. This story, which is the original context of the church's talk about and reflection on Jesus, remains its most essential context. Van Buren observes that for centuries, however, the church has been led by its standard christological formulations (arising from patristic concerns with Christ's "divinity") to ignore this "actual context" of the things concerning Jesus found in Israel's story.

In the following chapter van Buren elaborates his notion of Israel as the context of Jesus Christ. Since the fundamental context of the story of Jesus is the covenant between God and Israel, speaking of the "divinity of Jesus" apart from this covenant can give rise to a Jesus who is out of context and thus incomprehensible. It is "the whole history of the whole covenant" (III:68) which is the context for Christ. Or, to put it another way, one "sequence" of the story of biblical Israel is the story of Jesus of Nazareth, Israel's gift to the Gentile church. Thus, the continuing unfolding story of Israel remains the context of Jesus. This fact makes necessary a critical analysis of the Christian notion of Jesus' appearance as a once-for-all event. It also leads the church to reevaluate classical Christology's assignment of the "universal context of all humanity" as the background for understanding Jesus (III: 108). Placing Christology back into the context of Israel's story means, first, following Israel's lead back into history, and second, translating Christology into the present tense.

These moves "into history" and "into the present tense" make an "ahistorical" Christology impossible. But they have deeper implications. With the church coming to see Israel's covenant as a living reality, and with the Jewish people having reemerged on the plane of history, the state of Israel becomes part of the context for the church's Christology as well:

> Christology today has to take the State of Israel into account, in all its secularity, as part of the Jewish history and reality, and if it fails to do so, it will fail as a Christology for a church that has acknowledged the Jewish people as the Israel of God (III:65).

Next, van Buren describes what he calls the "proximate context" of Jesus Christ--the church. Since one "meets" Jesus Christ primarily in the Christian community, through preaching and the sacraments, van Buren argues that the Rahnerian concept of "anonymous Christian" (Christians outside the community) is incoherent. But those who *have* already met Christ in word and sacrament may also meet him in Israel, that is, in the Jewish people who are Jesus' brothers and sisters. The church does not know how else God may be met apart from Jesus Christ and Israel, but in this special case of Israel it will have to insist that "God *can* be met apart from Jesus Christ" (III:86).

Returning to one of the principles set forth at the beginning of this volume, van Buren stresses that the church's Christology must affirm that it worships only God. A "high" Christology does not reaffirm the "God-man" of the church's anti-Judaic past, but stresses that it is God whom the church meets in Jesus of Nazareth. Van Buren maintains that the early apostolic witnesses did not claim Jesus was God but that where Jesus was, God was, and that "Jesus is the effective means to God's end" (III:96). This early witness, in fact, preserved the important fact that Jesus "made absolutely no claims for himself," but proclaimed God's coming reign. While a "latter, more developed witness" to Jesus found in the New Testament qualifies this perspective,[67] we may be confident, van Buren assures us, that Jesus had no cause of his own, since his whole cause was God's cause. Likewise, the church can have no cause of its own, but only the cause of worshipping and serving the Father of Jesus Christ.

Because the church's Christology is and will remain unfinished, the church remains unfinished as well. Christology must be a "thoroughly diachronic" enterprise, and therefore every title or function ascribed to Jesus should have a date assigned to it (III:102). Christology remains at the center of what the church has to say, and a church which is not christocentric (that does not affirm Christ as the church's way to the Father) is inconceivable. At the same time, however, Christology must be informed by the church's witness preserved in texts like I Cor. 15:28 where it is clear that this christocentrism is temporal, that it has its limit in God, as it were.

In chapter five van Buren elaborates his understanding of Easter. For van Buren, the raising of Jesus was essentially God's self-confirmation, and, in particular, a confirmation of his covenant with Israel. Likewise, the witness of Easter is primarily a witness to God--it invites us to trust that "God is persistent, not that he is victorious, and this applies to Jesus as well" (III:121). Easter should not tempt the church to regard itself as triumphant. It demonstrates, rather, how God has drawn the church into the "strange story" that began with Abraham.

In response to Roy Eckardt's claim that Christian belief in the resurrection implies triumphalism, van Buren emphasizes that Easter faith is not at the root of Christian anti-Judaism. Rather, Christian anti-Judaism has grown from the fateful transformation of the original witness to Jesus into the church's witness to an anti-Judaic Jesus in conflict with his people. Van Buren even claims that belief in the resurrection stands in the way of anti-Judaism, insofar as the resurrection is understood as demonstrating the continuity of the risen one with Jesus of Nazareth (III:109-110).

The inherent ambiguity of and diversity in the church's Scriptural witness to Easter suggests for van Buren that we are safer in calling this event an "act of God" than an "historical fact." Thus, Easter faith can be described as "a response to the confrontation with God that Jesus effected after his death" (III:118). But van Buren emphasizes that the resurrection was an act not only of God, but also of those who bore witness to it. Van Buren sees this human element in the resurrection event as confirming the covenantal character of Easter and serving as a further invitation to covenantal cooperation with God.

In "Jesus of Nazareth: the Presence of God" van Buren elaborates the problem stemming from the fact that the early Christian eschatological hope for world transformation, the "essential context of the message and work of Jesus as the Gospels present them," has not been realized. The church's typical response to this failure of eschatological hope has been to spiritualize this hope or view it as having been fulfilled in the church. On the other hand, a serious shortcoming of early Christian eschatology was that it led the church to ignore Israel's historical continuity. The perception of a radical break with the "old era" in the appearance of Jesus has contributed significantly to the church's tradition of anti-Judaism, as has the idea that Jesus inaugurated a "new covenant."[68] In rethinking the eschatology of early Christianity and that of Jesus himself, the church must realize, first of all, that the future of the world does not lie in God's hands alone, but also with Israel and the church; and second, that Paul's last comment about "the end" (in I Cor. 15:28) warns us against "dividing honors" between God and Jesus in the eschatological future. Ultimately, God alone will be "all in all." Van Buren's conclusion is that the church should attend less to early Christian eschatology and take with more seriousness the present in which it lives.

In the next chapter van Buren considers the significance of "the crucified one." Here he is more specific than elsewhere in his work about the proper influence of the Holocaust on Christian thinking. The church today, he argues, is compelled to reconsider all past reflections on the passion of Christ in light of the passion of six million Jews. "Auschwitz" problematizes the claim that the cross represents victory over death, and it challenges Christians to reconsider the "once for all" character of the Christian message. Van Buren formulates the principle that the death of the one Jew Jesus cannot be interpreted so as to lessen the significance of the death of six million Jews. In fact, he argues, the Holocaust should actually assist in providing parameters for christological reflection: "we shall learn to speak of Auschwitz from the perspective of the cross...by first learning to speak of the cross from the perspective of Auschwitz" (III:165).[69]

In order for the Holocaust to inform our understanding of the cross, however, the orthodox hesitation at perceiving God in Jesus' suffering on the cross must be overcome. The Christian tradition has tended to maintain a distinction between the impassible Absolute and the Jew who died at Roman hands. Van Buren observes that if the church believes that the death of the Son hurt God, then it should also admit that the death of six million Jews hurt God even more. There is a moral as well as theological necessity in this realization: "If God was not there, suffering with his people, if God did not suffer a loss there at least as painful as that suffered on Golgotha, then that God is not worthy of respect by moral persons" (III: 165).

In the same chapter van Buren attempts an "historically reasonable reconstruction" of the reasons for the death of Jesus. He follows E. P. Sanders in viewing Jesus as a "divinely called prophet of Jewish restoration," but rejects Sanders' conclusion that Jewish opposition led to Jesus' death. Van Buren concludes that Jewish complicity in the arrest and trial of Jesus is an unnecessary assumption, since Jesus' "demonstration" in the Temple area could easily have been punished as a challenge to Roman law and order. Van Buren argues that death was not Jesus' intention, nor is there any theological necessity for thinking that God knew in advance the role which the cross would play in "God's future." Proceeding "covenantally," van Buren suggests that God accepted the cross and the disciples reaction to it as an opportunity for a contribution toward the renewal of God's creation (III:172).

From whence does such a radical interpretation of Jesus' death and its significance for the church come? Van Buren's answer is not surprising: this God who makes a new beginning of God's work on the basis of the disciples' response to the cross is the "covenantal God we have come to understand from the witness of Jewish, and especially rabbinic and Lurianic thought" (III:173). This "Jewish" interpretation of Jesus' cross does not deny the importance of the cross for the church, for it is still a "turning point in the story that began with Abraham" (III: 180). But it is in keeping with van Buren's principle of understanding Jesus in solidarity with his people and in continuity with their divine covenant.

Van Buren devotes chapter eight to considering the "novelty of Jesus Christ." Partly in response to critics who claim that he has interpreted Christianity as "Judaism for Gentiles." Van Buren attempts to describe the "novelty in continuity" represented by Jesus, by declaring that Jesus Christ produced an "utter novelty within the continuing history of God's covenant." On one side of van Buren's complex formulation of Jesus' relation to Israel's covenant history is a "discontinuity of radical novelty," and on the other is the "fundamental continuity apart from which Christology would lose its bearings" (III:183). Despite this essential continuity with the covenant, van Buren believes that for Jews the Christian movement must have seemed a betrayal of the covenant. In fact, it is an open question whether Israel could have survived as Israel had they accepted this "new stage of the covenant." A remnant of Jews experimented with this new possibility and took the risky step of apostasy in welcoming the Gentiles into God's covenant. But since the distinction between Jew and Gentile had no place in the Christian movement, van Buren believes it was necessary for most of Israel to remain in the path of Torah. According to van Buren's interpretation of the Apostolic Writings, this option seems to have appealed to Paul, and "may even have been God's choice" (III:193).

Van Buren claims that the blindness of Israel to the novelty in the stage of its covenant with God represented by Jesus is directly related to the church's blindness. Christian theologians like John Calvin who van Buren believes perceive the continuity of the covenant and the novelty of its renewal in Christ, also ignore the continuity of Israel alongside the church. And even "Nostra aetate," according to van Buren, fails to recognize the "novelty in continuity" which Israel needs to see. The "radical continuity" between Israel and the church, then, must be treated carefully. While the church's use of the term "Messiah" suggests its radical continuity with biblical Israel, van Buren claims it is unacceptable because it does so at the price of redefining the Jewish understanding of the role of the Messiah, Israel's hope, and God's promises (III:202). Paul expressed this continuity by emphasizing that Christ became a servant to the Jewish people to *confirm* the promises to the patriarchs (Ro. 15:8-9). Van Buren is convinced that this way of looking at the matter is preferable to the emphasis on *fulfillment* which one encounters in the gospels.

In chapter nine, "The Eternal Son," van Buren tries to make sense of the church's confession that Jesus is the only and eternal Son of God. He begins by observing that in the story of Jesus we encounter two distinct biblical ways in which God is active: God *in* the events ("God himself is present in this man") and God *behind* the events (God is noticeably absent in the story of the passive Jesus being betrayed and executed). Van Buren comments that if we understand God as directing events from *behind* the scenes in the story of Jesus, "the Son of God comes closer to mediating God's presence as Israel does" (III:209).

Van Buren then considers the fourth-century Arian controversy and the Nicaean christological formulation to which it led. Following the recent work of Robert C. Gregg, van Buren suggests that while contemporary theology may be more open to the Arian belief that the Son of God actually died on the cross, neither Arians nor the orthodox in the fourth century could entertain the notion of God's suffering. What is more problematic for van Buren is that the creedal decision at Nicaea essentially ignored the story of God's covenant with Israel, and thus "ignored almost completely the context of Christ" (III:216). This fact makes Nicaean formulation inadequate for a church seeking to live within the Jewish-Christian reality. Van Buren maintains that the church requires a more radical notion of Incarnation than either the Arians or the orthodox were able to entertain in the fourth century, one based on the covenantal context of Jesus Christ and able to preserve the Jew Jesus when speaking of the eternal Son of God. For van Buren this notion--based on a "concept of God drawn from Israel's story of its life with God"--is that of a God who is "compromised"[70] through covenantal self-determination, through commitment to "utterly particular historical peoples" (III:219-20). In order to function properly, van Buren believes the symbol of the incarnation cannot be applied to general categories like "God" and "man," but only to God's real involvement with Israel and the church.

From this perspective, what the church has called the "Incarnation" is fully coherent with the covenant between God and Israel. Van Buren even believes that "trinitarian" passages like John 1:14 can be read covenantally ("the covenantal Word of the God of the covenant *became* flesh and dwelt among, being one of, the covenanted people" is van Buren's translation of this verse). Van Buren claims it is misleading to speak of the divinity of Jesus in the Fourth Gospel, since it demands an infinitely more daring move than calling Jesus a divine man:

> The move that the Fourth Gospel dares the Church to make is that of risking and trusting the judgment that this man is precisely the way in which the suffering Father of Israel and all creation has chosen to open a radically new chapter in the continuing history of his involvement in human affairs which he began with Abraham (III:224).

Such an approach, while it perceives continuity between Israel and the church even in the church's highest christological statements, assigns a functional nature[71] to much of the church's confession about Jesus. The problem here is that arguing Jesus is God's only begotten Son "for the church" appears to undermine not only the absoluteness, but also the uniqueness of Christ. But what van Buren evacuates from Christian confession in one place, he replaces in a larger context: the church, while not unique in its apprehension of God, is now viewed as part of the unique covenantal history of God and Israel.

In the next chapter van Buren elaborates his notion that the doctrine of the Incarnation must be understood in a covenantal context. In framing the Incarnation in the language of Israel's covenant, the church can make it "unavoidably clear" that its confession of the Incarnation affirms the continuing covenant between God and Israel. This covenant connection helps ensure that the church can not say "incarnation" without saying "Jew" at the same time (III:250).

Understanding the "word of God" in covenantal context requires that the church overcome its tendency to privilege the Word which came to the prophets, and thus assign priority to the prophetic books over Torah. In "putting the Torah first" the church can come to understand the Writings and Prophets as commentary on the "Word of God" received by Moses at Sinai. Van Buren believes that the term "Word of God" is best understood not as the word given to a prophet, but as "God's outgoingness that let the world be and bound Israel to himself, and himself to Israel for the world's good" (III: 248). Even the prologue of the Fourth Gospel affirms this idea that God is this one who goes out from Godself to the other (van Buren understands the "became" in Jn. 1:14 as referring back to Israel's creation story). Van Buren concludes that the incarnation of the Word in Jesus Christ is "grounded in and added to" the incarnate word of God which Israel has in the Torah, so that Jesus can be regarded as embodying for the church what the Torah represents for Israel.

When the strengths and weakness of the patristic doctrine of the Incarnation are weighed (III:236ff.), the church is left with the problem that Jesus can no longer be properly understood in terms of the unworkable concept of divine *hypostasis*. Thinking in such metaphysical categories causes the church to lose sight of the eternal covenantal story linking God and Israel, and so hinders the church from making its confession "to the glory of the Father." Van Buren applies his covenantal approach to Christology to an understanding of the lordship of Christ. Extending his habit of explaining Christ's functions as the functions of the God of Israel applied to the church, van Buren argues that the "rule" of Christ is actually the covenant rule of God extended to the church. The Spirit's role is to tie the church to the people of God by leading the church to Christ, who in turn leads it to the God of Israel.

In the final chapter of *Christ in Context* van Buren invokes once again Paul's words in I Corinthians 15:28: "When all things are subjected to him [i.e., the Son], then the Son himself will be subjected to him [i.e., the Father] who put all things under him, that God may be all in all." Van Buren stresses that in this passage, and also in Paul's doxological conclusion to his discussion of Israel in Romans 11:33-36, Paul's vision of the future is "unqualifiedly theocentric" (III:284). Van Buren observes that Paul uses the words "all in all" to refer to the final realization of God the Father's original creative purpose. For the devoted Jews Paul and Jesus, the end of God's story could only be God the Father. Van Buren believes this vision of Christ's ultimate submission to the Father can help lead the church to confess a hope that rises above dominion. In making "Son of God," a Jewish term of service, a title of power and dominion, the church has obscured the fact that the glory of this Son is revealed precisely in his service to the God of Israel. The church must learn to speak in Jewish terms of a new kind of glory--the glory of humility--and substitute it for traditional talk of of dominion.

III. VAN BUREN'S SYSTEMATIC PRINCIPLES

With our survey of van Buren's *A Theology of the Jewish-Christian Reality* complete, we shall outline and elaborate some of the systematic principles which appear to guide his theology of Israel.

1. *In the post-Holocaust era, the church must recapture an Hebraic emphasis on particularity and historical concreteness.*

Van Buren elaborated a similar principle in *The Secular Meaning of the Gospel* with his understanding of Christian faith as the expression of an "historical perspective." In *A Theology of the Jewish-Christian Reality* this principle is given expression in van Buren's claim that the Apostolic Writings must be exegeted historically and in the context of the internal conflicts of first-century Judaism,[72] in his desire to recover a "Western historical consciousness,"[73] in his conviction that since the Redeemer is the Creator redemption must consist in an historical and material completion of Creation, and in his repudiation of a Christian universalism which tempts the church to ignore its historical connection with Israel and speak in general human categories.

2. *The church learns from Israel and from contemporary history the importance of human responsibility in guaranteeing the future of the covenant.*

In the 1970s van Buren denied there was anything in present movements of human "hope" which merited our trust.[74] Throughout *A Theology of the Jewish-Christian Reality,* however, van Buren stresses that covenantal thinking means assuming human responsibility for the covenant and for God's creation. Van Buren's theological voluntarism is perhaps most evident in his view that the foundation of the state of Israel is a paradigm of human courage and human responsibility--an assuming of responsibility for the future of the covenant.

3. *A functional understanding of many Christian doctrines is necessary for maintaining their significance for a Christian theology of Israel.*

Especially in volume three of *A Theology of the Jewish-Christian Reality,* van Buren stresses that confessions of Christ are confessions about who Christ is "for the church." Perhaps the most important example of this principle is van Buren's interpretation of Christian trinitarian doctrine as expressing the continuity of the church's story with that of Israel, and as a description of the means whereby the God of Israel has reached out to Gentiles.

4. *Revelation is a continuing process encompassing the reinterpretation of traditions in response to new events in Jewish history.*

Van Buren rejects the orthodox understanding of revelation as the communication of propositional truth, as well as the Neo-Orthodox conception of revelation as God's self-communication in particular events (culminating in the Christ-event). He argues instead for a view of revelation as a process of reinterpretation in response to reorienting events--a process which has reappeared in the wake of contemporary historical events like the Holocaust and the founding of the modern state of Israel.

5. *The continuing existence of the Jewish people, not the Holocaust, is the proper focus of post-Holocaust Christian theology.*

While the Holocaust has implications which are critical for the church's understanding of Israel, the Holocaust cannot cause the church to lose its focus on the Jewish people, their covenant, and their God. Van Buren does not argue that the Holocaust is "unique" in any philosophical sense, or even that the Holocaust has changed the way theology is to be done. He does believe, however, that since the Holocaust has helped many parts of the church affirm the perpetual nature of God's covenant with Israel, it may indeed have revelational significance for the church's understanding of God.

6. *The church adores Israel's LORD.*

This assertion that the church worships and serves the same God which Israel worships and serves is "fundamental for all its [the church's] conversation and all its theology" (I:33). For van Buren, it can be no other way, since "noetically and ontologically God and Israel are indivisible and inseparable" (III:255).

7. *Jesus must be understood in a manner which adds glory to Israel.*

Christological statements which do not glorify Israel and Israel's God do not place Jesus in his proper context, and therefore can only distort the meaning of Jesus and the church's understanding of the Jewish-Christian reality.

8. *It is the church's duty to hear the testimony of the Jewish people to God.*

This testimony is found not only in Israel's interpretation of its Scriptures, but also in the rabbinic tradition, and in the very existence of the Jewish people.

9. *The Jewish "No" to Christianity arises from a decision to remain faithful to Torah.*

The Jewish "No" is a unique response to Christianity: it is primarily a "Yes" to Torah-faithfulness, and a "No" to the church only secondarily. The presence of the Jewish "No" helps remind the church of its dependent and unfinished character. To see this "No" as originating in a Jewish rejection of Jesus' message leads to distortion, as does the view that Jesus was rejected as "Israel's Messiah."

10. *The existence of the church cannot be unimportant for Judaism.*

The new chapter in the covenant represented by God's overture toward the Gentiles has to do with Israel only indirectly. But because Christianity "effects the hidden goal of God's Torah to bring the nations into the plan that began to develop with the calling of Abraham" (III: 183), Jews can and should recognize the church as a step toward the fulfillment of God's redemptive plan for creation.[75]

11. *The church is included in the hope of Israel through its connection with Jesus Christ.*

Jesus is for the church what Sinai is for the Jews--he is the point at which the church's inclusion in God's covenant grace begins. Here we encounter an "inclusion" model that is almost the inverse of the integration model described by Klappert. Rather than Israel being integrated at some point in the future into the church, the church is "included" once for all in Israel through Jesus.

12. *The church cannot speak about "Israel" without speaking about the land and state of Israel.*

Israel's promise of land cannot be spiritualized or otherwise dismissed. The church has a special service to Israel and its people, and this service includes making known the "facts" of Israel's situation in the Middle East *vis-'a-vis* its Arab neighbors.

13. *The church's story of redemption is unfinished, and all its affirmations are set forth in hope.*

The church's Easter faith is built on a "protoredemptive" event, and so it confesses an unfulfilled messianism until the final redemption of creation. Even the glorification of Christ will be a step toward God the Father becoming "all in all."

14. *The relationship between Israel and the church is one of continuity as well as discontinuity.*

Continuity between the church and Israel is a major thrust of van Buren's theology, seen most clearly in his "one covenant" thinking. The discontinuity element in van Buren's theology is expressed in the fact that the church and Israel have been given different "ways" to walk in the "Way."While the church is called to cooperate with Israel, grow alongside Israel and come ever closer to Israel in a relationship of mutual support, there is to be no fusion or even unity between Israel and the church until God becomes "all in all." Even the "common goal" which Jews and Christians have for the future is actually not common: "Israel's vision centers in Israel's restoration, the church's eye is on the figure of Christ (III:199).

15. *The church is dependent on Israel.*

In the past, present and future, the Gentile church is "absolutely dependent, ontologically and teleologically on the continuing existence of God's Israel" (II:162). Van Buren observes that the dependent[76] church is supported by the life of the Jewish people in the same way the Diaspora is supported by the Jewish state (II:319).

16. *The necessity and foundation of the church's theology of the Jewish people is Israel's election.*

Election, and nothing else, makes the Jewish people unique and gives Israel its unique significance for the church.

17. *A Christian theology of Israel should be based in covenantal thinking.*

Jesus represents a *novum* in the covenant history of God and Israel, but he also represents a *codicil* which does not annul the covenant. Christianity is best understood as a special extension and renewal of Israel's covenant which makes Gentile service to God possible.

18. *The Apostolic Writings must be read from a perspective which highlights Jewish-Christian continuity and solidarity.*

With the help of historical-critical methods[77] like redaction criticism and canon criticism, van Buren's Christian theology of Israel returns *ad fontes* of the Jewish movement we know as the church and searches the Apostolic Writings for evidence of solidarity between the church and Israel. Disregarding calls to attend only to the final form of biblical texts, van Buren seeks diachronically to isolate the "early apostolic witness" from the anti-Judaic testimony of later biblical witnesses.

19. *A Christian theology of Israel must take seriously the Jewish identity of Jesus and Paul.*

It is the anti-Jewish Jesus of parts of the Apostolic Writings, and not the historical Jesus, who is at the source of the church's anti-Judaism. Jesus was at home in a Pharisaic context and issued a call to Jewish renewal that corresponds to the "spirit of Javneh." The Augustine-Luther-Käsemann line of interpretation that has made Paul a Gentile must be discarded in favor of a view of Paul as a Pharisee and a Jew to the core.

In the next chapter we offer a final analysis of van Buren's theology of Israel by suggesting the strengths and weaknesses of his theological project in *A Theology of the Jewish-Christian Reality,* and the prospects his work presents for Christian post-Holocaust theology.

Notes

1. Van Buren, "Theology Now," *The Christian Century* 91 (May 29, 1974), 585.

2. Van Buren, "Probing the Jewish-Christian Reality: How My Mind Has Changed," (Twenty-First in a Series) *The Christian Century* 98 (June 17-24, 1981), 665. See also Lonnie D. Kliever, *The Shattered Spectrum: A Survey of Contemporary Theology* (Atlanta: John Knox, 1981), 36. Van Burens' major works during this period were *Theological Investigations* (1968) and *The Edges of Language* (1972).

3. See, Van Buren, "Probing...," 665-6; and "Theological Education for the Church's Relationship With the Jewish People," *Journal of Ecumenical Studies* 21

(Summer, 1984), 501, where van Buren argues that we experience God only by way of our respective linguistic communities.

4. Van Buren, *The Burden of Freedom: Americans and the God of Israel* (New York: Crossroad/Seabury, 1976), vii. Van Buren provides another example of the continuity he perceives between *The Secular Meaning of the Gospel* and *A Theology of the Jewish-Christian Reality* when he quotes a passage from his earlier work in chapter six of *Christ in Context* (142).

5. See, van Buren, "Probing...," 668; and "Discerning the Way to the Incarnation," *Anglican Theological Review* 63 (July, 1981), 293.

6. Personal interview with Paul van Buren, Boston, July 16-17, 1988. See also Busch, *Karl Barth,* 403 for Barth's statement that van Buren "rushed so wildly out of my school."

7. Van Buren, "Karl Barth as Teacher," *Religion and Intellectual Life* 2: 2 (Winter, 1985), 85.

8. Personal interview.

9. See, e.g., Kliever, *The Shattered Spectrum,* 33; Cobb, "Barth and the Post-Barthians," in McKim, 173; Langdon Gilkey, *Naming the Whirlwind: The Renewal of God-Language* (Indianapolis: Bobbs-Merrill, 1969), especially 113-116; and John Macquarrie, *New Directions in Theology, Volume 3: God and Secularity* (Philadelphia: Westminster, 1976), 40.

10. *A Theology of the Jewish Christian Reality,* vol. 3, *Christ in Context* (San Francisco: Harper and Row, 1988), 195 (hereafter III:195).

11. *The Burden of Freedom,* 74.

12. Personal interview.

13. The importance of Barth's influence on van Buren has not been lost on his critics. One critic of van Buren's theology of Israel has accused him of betraying "a Neo-Orthodox confidence in the traditional biblical words" [Gregory Baum, review of *Discerning the Way, Commonweal,* October 24, 1980, 599], and another has described his project as a "thoroughgoing revision of orthodox Christology along neo-Barthian lines" [Mark W. Karlberg, "Israel as Light to the Nations: A Review Article," *Journal of the Evangelical Theology Society* 28:2 (June, 1985), 210].

14. See David Tracy, *Blessed Rage For Order: The New Pluralism in Theology* (Minneapolis: Seabury, 1975), 31, where van Buren is cited as a leading example of the "linguistic analysis of radical secularism," and Macquarrie, *New Directions,* 22, where van Buren's *The Secular Meaning of the Gospel* is called the "most lucid and philosophical expression that this position [the "death-of-God" theology] has so far received."

15. Ibid., 31.

16. Tracy, *Blessed Rage,* 34.

17. See, *A Theology of the Jewish Christian Reality,* vol. 1, *Discerning the Way* (San Francisco: Harper and Row, 1980), 52 (hereafter 1:52).

18. Tracy, *Blessed Rage,* 32. The claim by James F. Moore ["A Spectrum of Views: Traditional Christian Responses to the Holocaust," *Journal of Ecumenical Studies* 25:2 (Spring, 1988), 212-224] that van Buren is essentially a conservative theologian because he resorts to a two-covenant view which predates the Holocaust is superficial and misguided. It is also contradicted by Moore's own assertion that van Buren is "not strictly orthodox" in his view of revelation (217).

19. See, e.g., *The Secular Meaning of the Gospel,* chap. 4; and *The Burden of Freedom,* 6.

20. *Burden of Freedom,* 101.

21. See Gilkey, *Naming the Whirlwind,* 109ff. In a personal interview, van Buren reported that while he does not reject the label "radical theologian," he prefers to see his work as a response to personal questions guided by the assumption that others are asking questions that are similar.

22. Personal interview. For van Buren's theology of Israel as a response to the Holocaust, see Richard L. Rubenstein and John K. Roth, *Approaches to Auschwitz: The Holocaust and Its Legacy* (Atlanta: John Knox, 1987), 296-300.

23. "Theological Education...," 497. See also *A Theology of the Jewish-Christian Reality, Volume 2: A Christian Theology of the People Israel* (San Francisco: Harper and Row, 1983), 18 (hereafter II: 18): "what is needed is therefore not a 'Holocaust Theology,' whatever that may be, but, I shall argue, a Christian theology of the people Israel."

24. *NICM Journal* 7 (Spring, 1982), 15-20.

25. "Christian Theology and Jewish Reality: An Essay-Review," *JAAR* 45: 4 (1977), 491-495.

26. Ibid., 493.

27. Ibid.

28. Personal interview; *Burden of Freedom,* 6.

29. Personal interview.

30. See "Christian Theology and Jewish Reality...," 492-3, where van Buren follows Yosef Yerushalmi's argument that if Ruether is correct, then the existence of the Jews throughout the Middle Ages is inexplicable. See also *Christ in Context*, 22, where van Buren explicitly repudiates Ruether's claim that anti-Judaism is the "left-hand" of Christology. A further example of van Buren's ambivalent relationship to the conclusions of Holocaust theologians is his treatment in *Christ in Context* of A. Roy Eckardt's position that the Christian teaching on the resurrection is essentially triumphalist and anti-Jewish (109-10).

31. See, *Burden of Freedom*, 88.

32. "Probing...," 688.

33. *Anti-Semitism and the Christian Mind*, 134.

34. In their reviews of *Discerning the Way*, David Novak calls Rosenzweig van Buren's most important contact with Judaism ["A Jewish Response to a New Christian Theology," *Judaism* 31 (Winter, 1982), 114], while Gregory Baum describes Rosenzweig as van Buren's "principle inspiration" (598), and A. Roy Eckardt notes that the (Rosenzweigian) idea of Jesus leading Gentiles into Israel's covenant was introduced into American Christian theology around 1960, and that van Buren shows a "rather odd inattention" to this fact ["Burned Children," *The Christian Century* (October 1, 1980), 923]. In personal conversation, van Buren demurs at the label "Christian Rosenzweigian."

35. See Novak, "A Jewish Response...," 114; and Alan Davies, review of *Discerning the Way, New Catholic World* (November/December, 1981), 281.

36. *A Theology of the Jewish-Christian Reality*, III: 147. Van Buren claims that the term "covenant" appears only five times in *The Star of Redemption*, and never in the sense in which the word is used by the early Protestant covenant theologians or modern biblical theologians.

37. The notion of a "dual covenant," that is, one covenant in two different aspects, seems to be in line with van Buren's thought at this point, although he does not employ this term.

38. See also Clemens Thoma, who in a very similar way speaks of "one Israel in its two-fold form" (*A Christian Theology of Judaism*, 175).

39. *Journal of Ecumenical Studies* 21:3 (Summer, 1984), 489-505.

40. Davies, *Anti-Semitism and the Christian Mind*, 151.

41. See *Discerning the Way*, 5-6, where van Buren adopts Perrin's notion that in the apostolic authors' use of the Scriptures, "the text is reinterpreted in the light of immediate experience and immanent expectation," resulting in "a long and constant process of interpretation and reinterpretation," to argue that the Bible cannot be

removed from the historical process. Redaction criticism and canon criticism, argues van Buren, help us to view the Bible as consisting of "layered reinterpretations of a sacred tradition occasioned by successive events in Israel's history.""That structure," says van Buren, "invites further reinterpretation in response to further events, even up to our own times."

42. It is tempting to see here a connection with the writings of George Lindbeck, and suspicions of this connection are intensified by van Buren's attack on David Tracy and the "Chicago School's" approach to theological method (I:52ff). It is probably the case, however, that van Buren's affinity for the cultural-linguistic religious model that is developed in Lindbeck's work is related to their common background in the philosophy of Ludwig Wittgenstein. While Lindbeck's *The Nature of Doctrine* appears in the bibliography at the end of *Christ in Context*, van Buren claims not to have read the book until he was nearly finished with this third volume.

43. Concern with the phenomenon of Jews who convert to Christianity is typical in evangelical considerations of church-Israel relations. But van Buren considers not only the case of so-called Jewish-Christians, but also Christian-Jews (Christians who convert to Judaism), a phenomenon which, as he rightly observes, is generally ignored. Furthermore, for van Buren the existence of Jewish-Christians only represents the "utter dependence" of the church on Israel (II:35).

44. Van Buren is careful in all this to avoid the distortions known to the early church as the heresies of Sabellianism and Modalism. Van Buren takes the concept of *hypostasis* seriously, although he prefers Barth's translation, "way of being [Himself]" to the more common English term "person."

45. The lengthy discussion God's personhood in which van Buren engages here is one of the weak points of this volume. It is of little value to his theological project, and its conclusion--that since God is a person, God must have a body--has been severely criticized by David Novak. See Novak's review of *Discerning the Way* (118ff.).

46. Although Sanders' name appears a total of only three times in the indexes to the three volumes of *A Theology of the Jewish-Christian Reality*, his influence on van Buren's understanding of the relationship between canon, community, and tradition appears to be significant.

47. Because van Buren returns again and again to the responsibility theme, I have conflated here what he says on this point in step seven (153ff.) and step eight (180ff.).

48. One can detect the influence of H. Richard Niebuhr's *The Meaning of Revelation* in these pages, as well as the work of Norman Perrin, James A. Sanders and Irving Greenberg mentioned previously.

49. As we have suggested, van Buren's use of the word "reorientation" in connection with revelation is dependent on Irving Greenberg's "Cloud of Smoke,

Pillar of Fire." The term reorientation occurs at least eight times in the space of five pages (169-173).

50. See 174-75. Van Buren refers to statements by the Pastoral Council of the Catholic Church in the Netherlands (1970), the French Bishops' Committee (1973), the Faith and Order Commission of the World Council of Churches (1967), the United States National Council of Bishops (1975), and the Synod of the Reformed Church in the Netherlands (1970).

51. Van Buren is even critical of contemporary theologians' attempts to construct a "Christian theology of Judaism" (Clemens Thoma's, for example) and to systematically critique the Christian tradition (Bertold Klappert's, for example). Van Buren sees the only solid background for his reconstruction of Christian theology in George Foot Moore's *Judaism in the First Centuries of the Christian Era* (first published in 1927) and E. P. Sanders' *Paul and Palestinian Judaism* (1977).

52. In comparing this understanding of Israel's rejection of Christianity to that of Moltmann, it is important to note that both theologians see Israel's as a special "No" which is incomparable with all others. On the other hand, while Moltmann believes that Jews reject the church's Jesus on the basis of the world's unredeemed state (a problem of which "authentic" Christianity is fully aware), van Buren's vision of the disagreement between church and synagogue is not as open to eschatological reconciliation. For van Buren, Israel "rejects the church's faith in the name of the church's God" (II:33). Israel's "No," according to van Buren, is not based in the Jewish response to the historical Jesus, but in Jewish fidelity to Torah (and Jewish survival). Moltmann's argument that Jesus is the "Messiah on the way" answers his own version of Israel's "No," but does not respond to van Buren's, since for van Buren Jesus cannot be considered the Messiah of Israel at all.

53. Just as important to van Buren's understanding of election's significance in interpreting the Jewish-Christian reality, however, is Irving Greenberg's suggestion that there has been a change in the terms of God's covenant with Israel. Israel is now in the midst of a "third stage" in which people must take the lead in the covenant, and God is the silent partner. This stage was inaugurated by the foundation of the state of Israel. Its similarity with Bonhoeffer's notion of the "world come of age" is unmistakable (II:121). See "The Third Great Cycle of Jewish History" (New York: CLAL, 1981).

54. This implicit reference to "liberation theology" should be read together with van Buren's explicit charge that this theology often has an anti-Jewish tenor (I:60).

55. Van Buren argues, referring to a well-known United nations resolution, that Zionism cannot be racism, since the Jews are a people, not a race. Whether or not one accepts this argument, there can be no denying that there are forces in the world community staunchly opposed to the existence and peace of the state of Israel. Zionism is necessary to resist these forces, but van Buren's statement that "the ideal of Zionism...may be seen as an invitation to the nations of the world to set for themselves

a goal of justice" (II:177) is problematical. While it may be clear to van Buren that Zionism is synonymous with the goal of justice (he argues, for instance, that Torah demands one law for Israel and for its resident aliens), this fact is less evident to others, and perhaps is less evident for van Buren in 1991 than in 1983 when this volume was published.

For alterative views of Jewish-Black relations, see Roberta Strauss Feuerlicht, *The Fate of the Jews* (New York: Times Books, 1983), ch. 6, "Jews and Blacks;" and A. Roy Eckardt, *Black-Woman-Jew: Three Wars for Human Liberation* (Bloomington: Indiana University Press, 1989).

56. Van Buren refers in particular to the response by the Middle East Council of Churches to the World Council of Churches Consultation on the Church and the Jewish People (II:187).

57. Van Buren describes the cornerstone of Zionism as "the conviction that Israel has been called by God to life in the land of Israel" (II: 192), and adds that landed life means "self-rule under God" (II:199).

58. For the charge of insensitivity to Palestinians in van Buren's "Christian Zionism," see Naim Stifan Ateek, *Justice, and Only Justice, A Palestinian Theology of Liberation* (Maryknoll, NY: Orbis, 1989), 63-65. Ateek assails the "one-sidedness and naïvete' with which the political situation is treated [in van Buren's work], and claims that van Buren "writes without a hint of the complexities of the political dilemma and the possibility of injustice" (63). Ateek refers explicitly to *Discerning the Way*, but his criticisms apply as well to *A Christian Theology of the People Israel*. For a contemporary discussion of the Zionist "tradition of dissent" which stresses coexistence with Arabs rather than the establishment of a Jewish nation, see Marc Ellis, *Beyond Innocence and Redemption: Confronting the Holocaust and Israeli Power* (New York: Harper and Row, 1990).

59. See especially, Roberta Strauss Feuerlicht, *The Fate of the Jews*, and Marc Ellis, *Toward a Jewish Theology of Liberation* (Maryknoll, NY: Orbis, 1987).

60. In this statement van Buren is more cautious than the Eckardts (in his criticism of Moltmann). As we saw in the last chapter, the Eckardts deny that Jesus conflicted with first century Judaism at all.

61. Barth also argued that Jesus calls Israel to "become Israel," and that this was synonymous with an acceptance of its election. But van Buren does not mean here what Barth meant: that Israel should become Israel by entering the church. Given the similarity in expression, however, it is interesting that van Buren is not more careful to dissociate himself from Barth at this point.

62. In *Christ in Context* van Buren argues that referring to Jesus as "Israel's Messiah" is "exceedingly misguided and dangerous." In the first place, there is no unified "Jewish idea" of the Messiah; second, the claim that Jesus is the Messiah of the Jews is refuted by the anti-Judaic behavior of the church; and third "it is a task of a Christology after Auschwitz and Vatican II to point out that none of the possible uses

of the term 'Messiah' is sufficient to catch even a modest part of what the Church wants to say of the things concerning Jesus of Nazareth" (III:9-10). On page 137 of the same volume van Buren writes that he prefers to speak of Jesus as "God's anointed," adding that calling Jesus "Israel's Messiah" implies that Jesus fulfilled an essential expectation of Israel: the rescue of the Jewish people from oppression by Gentiles.

63. See the same page (281) where van Buren credits "this reading of Paul" as being behind what we referred to in chapter three as the doctrine of the Jews as a "witness people."

64. While van Buren's discussion of this issue reveals his grasp of the various elements in the Middle East situation, it also shows how quickly statements on the matter can become out of date. As these pages are being written, it is Arabs who appear interested in "making peace with Israel," and Israel's leadership which is resisting.

65. *Christ in Context* has received a quicker critical response than the first two volumes of *A Theology of the Jewish-Christian Reality*.. See, e.g., the following reviews: William Barr, *Encounter* 50 (Spring, 1989), 192-94; Mary Byles, *Cross Currents* 38 (Winter, 1988-89), 496-99; James Carpenter, *Anglican Theological Review* 71 (Spring, 1989), 216-18; Arthur Cochrane, *Princeton Seminary Bulletin* 10: 3 (1989), 281-82; Daniel Harrington, *Theological Studies* 50 (March, 1989), 174-75; Glenn Hinson, *Review and Expositor* 85 (Summer, 1988), 570-72; Clark Williamson, *Theology Today* 45 (January, 1989), 478+; John Koenig, *Horizons* 16 (Fall, 1989), 379-80; Daniel Lasker, *Journal of Ecumenical Studies* 26 (Spring, 1989), 362; John Pawlikowski, *Christian Century* 105 (November 16, 1988), 1049-50.

66. One is reminded by this discussion of van Buren's treatment of the meaning of Jesus for his disciples in *The Secular Meaning of the Gospel*. Although the metaphor of "contagion" used there to describe Jesus' effect on the first believers is absent, the point that what is important is not Jesus' identity but his effect on persons is present.

67. In the category of "later" witnesses van Buren places some of the gospel accounts (particularly *John)* and some of the epistles (especially *Hebrews)*. Van Buren's historical confidence in the "early" apostolic testimony is particularly evident on page 76, where he concludes that "the author of the prologue [of John] is wrong," since he is flatly contradicted by what van Buren takes to be an earlier witness.

68. Van Buren recognizes that there is Scriptural evidence for talking of a "new covenant" (for instance in the Epistle to the Hebrews), but is unable to accept it since it is contrary to the witness of the Gospels and Paul, and so must "set it aside" (III:145).

69. This formulation of the matter is precisely the reverse of Moltmann's who in *The Crucified God* wants to understand Auschwitz from the perspective of the cross of Jesus.

70. Van Buren uses the term "compromised" in *The Burden of Freedom* (57) to describe God's choice to be in relationship with Israel.

71. See, for example, 210: "Jesus' authorization by God to perform this function [leading the church to become fellow citizens with Israel] for the Church is what the Church acknowledges when it confesses him Son of God"; 228: "the Church confessed Jesus to be God's only child because he proved to be the sole origin and foundation of its life"; and 294: "Jesus is the Son of God precisely because he leads the Gentile Church to the God of Israel."

72. See also, "How Shall We Now Exegete the Apostolic Writings?," *American Journal of Theology and Philosophy* 3 (1981), 97-109.

73. See Charles E. Vernoff, "After the Holocaust: History and Being As Sources of Method Within the Emerging Interreligious Hermeneutic," *Journal of Ecumenical Studies* 21 (Fall, 1984), 641.

74. See "Theology Now," 586.

75. In a recent conversation, when asked what Jews might learn from Christians, van Buren responded that Jews might learn from Christianity about the nature of forgiveness and about the vicissitudes of wielding political power.

76. Van Buren uses the word "dependent" to describe the church-Israel relationship on I:83; II:152, 162, 319, 331, and 352; and III:77 and 125.

77. At this point it is helpful to recall what we observed in chapter one about the usefulness for Jewish-Christian dialogue of historical-critical methods for reading the New Testament. Charles Vernoff has observed that van Buren's approach to the Jewish-Christian reality is an example of the way contemporary events may lend moral reinforcement to the historicizing perspective ("After the Holocaust...," 646).

Part III Prospects for Post-Holocaust Theology?

CHAPTER FIVE

PROSPECTS

I. BARTH'S THEOLOGY OF ISRAEL

We begin with a consideration of Barth's theology of Israel: its positive and negative dimensions and the resources it offers for contemporary post-Holocaust theological reflection.

A. Positive Dimensions

As the aspects of Barth's doctrine of Israel which are "positive," that is, which qualify traditional Christian anti-Judaism and provide a basis for constructive Christian thought about Israel, the following must be emphasized:

1. Barth makes the problem of "Israel" central to his theology by placing it at the center of his doctrine of election. Barth's emphasis on the continuing election of Israel has influenced Protestant theology in a way that rivals the effect of "Nostra aetate" on Catholic thinking.[1] Barth attempts to take biblical Israel and the problem of unbelieving Israel *post christum crucifixum* with equal seriousness and therein lies one of his chief contributions to Protestant dogmatics.

2. In making Israel a central feature in his dogmatic "system," rather than an afterthought or addendum, Barth gives systematic expression to the seemingly self-evident fact that without God's

covenantal history in Israel, there would be no church. Barth makes Israel's elective and promissory history, therefore, part of the foundation upon which his theology of the church is built.

Significant is the fact that Barth's major treatment of Israel in the *Church Dogmatics* falls within the context of his discussion of divine election. Barth's placement of Israel and the church under the heading of "the election of the community" allows him to define Israel in the same terms in which he defines the church: election and calling.

3. Barth perceived, from the time of *Der Römerbrief* onward, an intimate relationship between the church and Israel, the two forms of the "one community of God." Barth recognized an "ontological unity" (*CD* IV:1, 671) between Israel and the church which has been described by commentators as "synonymousness," "dependence" and "participation." However one interprets this relationship, it is clear that Barth maintained his conviction of a unique bond between Israel and the church until the end of his life. We see it expressed with a new force in 1967 when he rebuked the Roman Catholic Church for classifying Judaism as a "non-Christian religion."

4. In addition to rediscovering "Israel" for Protestant theology, Barth also rediscovered Romans 9-11. Barth's justification for retaining Israel in salvation history is found in his "minute exegesis" of this biblical passage in *CD* II:2. While Romans 9-11 had generally been interpreted in the Christian tradition as a treatise on the doctrine of predestination,[2] Barth finds in Paul's epistle an affirmation of the continuing election of Israel. Barth does not see here, as have Augustine and others, a ringing denunciation of the Jews in which the fate of unbelieving Israel is settled,[3] but a proof of the mercifulness of God in God's schismatic action in salvation history.[4]

5. Barth focuses on the witness of Scripture. While this quality has led critics like Alan Davies to accuse him of a dangerous biblicism, Michael Wyschogrod sees in Barth's attention to the word of Scripture a point of contact with Jewish theology. Indeed, it seems that in the case of two religious communities who share, in part, the same sacred texts, any attempt at theological communication must consider the interpretation of common Scriptures. In the spirit of the church of the Reformation, Barth seeks to let God speak through the Bible.[5] Critics who interpret this desire as necessarily opposed to the cause of Jewish-

Christian co-existence and partnership reveal above all their own prejudices.

6. Barth considered himself a theologian of the church, first and foremost. Barth was surely an academic theologian, but his primary point of reference was the Christian "church," however abstractly this church was conceived in his theology. While this fact qualifies Barth's theology to be used in theological dialogue with Israel, Barth's part in real dialogue was and is diminished because his understanding of Israel remained even more abstract than his understanding of the church.

7. Barth's contention that Christians should no longer speak of a mission to Jews reveals a sensitivity to Christian-Jewish history, Jewish self-understanding, and the solidarity between the two religious communities. Furthermore, Barth's statement that proper Christian "witness" to Jews must take the form of making the synagogue jealous is successful in maintaining an emphasis on Christian identity and a sensitivity to contemporary interreligious relationships.

8. Barth continually stressed that the "Jewish question" was in fact a "Christian question." He saw in anti-Semitism an attack on Christ, and believed the church could not be a-Semitic, let alone anti-Semitic. From the beginning Barth opposed Hitler's "Aryan" policies, and fought their introduction into the church. He preached boldly on the Jewishness of Jesus in 1933, and after.

B. Negative Dimensions

To these positive aspects of Barth's Israel-doctrine, we now add some observations on its negative dimensions--those which perpetuate traditional Christian anti-Jewish biases and therefore serve as obstacles to improved Jewish-Christian relations.

1. Despite the radical nature of Barth's theology of election--its affirmation of the continuing election of Israel and of solidarity between the church and Israel, for Barth this solidarity is based in the "one Jew" Jesus Christ, whose "environment" is Israel. As a result, election is always related to Christology for Barth. Barth's doctrine of election is focused in Jesus Christ as "electing God and elected man," and this christological focus leads to unfortunate consequences for Barth's understanding of Israel.

Israel must be defined as the form of the elected community which resists its election, which is disobedient, which hears but does not believe. This consistently negative determination of Israel is made necessary by 1) Barth's inability to see beyond Israel's "No" to Jesus Christ and 2) Barth's "fulfilled messianism. For Barth, the coming of Christ means that God's promises, election and covenant have been fulfilled, and that all things have been made new.[6] Under these conditions an Israel which does not recognize its Messiah and enter the church in obedience to its election can only be described negatively. Terms like "witness to judgment" and "Synagogue of death," therefore, proliferate Barth's theology.

2. Barth's negative determination of Israel as disobedient, obdurate, and legalistic participates in the creation of an "Israel" *post Christum crucifixum* which is a theological abstraction. Barth's Judaism ("the Synagogue") is a lifeless and graceless religion of self-righteousness, while Barth's Jew is a mythicized "mirror" of human sin and insecurity. Jewish history is a fiction in which an eternal anti-Semitism finds increasingly destructive ways to reveal its contempt for the "Eternal Jew." The abstract, fictionalized, and mythical character of Barth's theology of Israel is a result of his personal isolation from Judaism and aversion toward living Jews, and the necessity he apparently felt to incorporate "Israel" within his theological system. Most troubling is that the formal system of Barth's doctrine of Israel, though it is recognizable as pure theology, cannot function in isolation from history. It existed and continues to exist in the context of the ongoing real history of Jewish suffering and Christian-Jewish conflict. Barth's system, then, cannot be dismissed as an irrelevant formalism, but must be judged, like every other ideology, according to its history of effects.

3. Barth's theology of Israel opens him to charges of anti-Judaism and anti-Semitism. Barth's anti-Judaism is revealed in his dependence on the traditional characterizations of Judaism common to Christian theology, mentioned above,[7] and his recapitulations of supersessionist theology in *Der Römerbrief* and the *Church Dogmatics*.[8] Barth's anti-Semitism may be seen in his own admission of a "totally irrational aversion" to living Jews. On the other hand, toward the end of his life Barth attempted to compensate for both personal and theological manifestations of anti-Jewishness with a renewed interest in dialogue

with living Jews, and a keen interest in and support for the state of Israel.

4. Barth transmits pre-Holocaust Christian habits of referring to Israel *post Christum crucifixum* derogatorily as "the Synagogue,"[9] of utilizing the scheme of promise and fulfillment to describe the relationship of Israel/Old Testament and church/New Testament, of referring to the pre-existence of the gospel and the church in Israel, and of using the law/gospel dynamic to elaborate the relationship of church and synagogue.[10] Barth's theology also evinces parallels with the patristic understanding of the Jews as a "witness people." Although commentators have recognized and have been critical of the patristic elements in Barth's theology of Israel,[11] Barth's connection with the "witness people" doctrine has not been sufficiently illuminated.

The theory of the Jews as a witness people[12] arose during the fourth century and is commonly associated with the theology of Augustine.[13] Augustine used the theory as a theological explanation for the survival of the Jews after the time of Christ, as well as for their increasing misfortunes. According to this theory, while the role of the Jews is still providential,

> they [the Jews] are at once witnesses of evil and Christian truth...they subsist "for the salvation of the nation but not for their own." They witness by their Scriptures...and by their dispersion and their woes. Like Cain they carry a sign but are not to be killed.[14]

It is precisely its two-sided perception of the problem of Jewish existence that distinguishes this theory of the witness people. The Jews are to be preserved (since they are a sign of God's providence in history) and even preached to "in a spirit of love"[15] (since the salvation of Israel predicted by Paul is dependent on their coming to Christ at his *parousia*), but meanwhile their dispersion and suffering witness to God's judgment on their superceded religion, and God's desire that all people find life in Christ.

In Barth's theology of Israel, we encounter a contemporary manifestation of the patristic theory of the Jews as a witness people. Barth's emphases on solidarity with the Jews, on a Christian condemnation of anti-Semitism, and on the Jews' calling to enter the church correspond to the "positive" side of the witness people theory, i.e., the Christian responsibility to protect Jews and to preach Christ to them in order that their eschatological salvation may be realized. Barth also strongly affirms the providential work of God in the history of the Jews, a "positive" element of witness people thinking. Barth directly confirms the history of the Jews as a sign of divine world-governance in *CD* III:3, and confirms it indirectly in the recurring statement that the existence of the Jews is the only legitimate natural proof for the existence of God.[16]

On the "negative" side, Barth's description of the synagogue as lifeless, of the unbelieving Jew as the "passing man," of the Jews as rejecting and crucifying Christ,[17] and of Israel *post christum crucifixum* as a witness to divine judgment correspond to the side of the patristic witness people theory which emphasizes that the Jews without Christ are cursed and therefore remain dispersed, persecuted, and miserable. The following collection of excerpts from "The Jewish Problem and the Christian Answer" brilliantly illuminates Barth's connection with the witness people doctrine:

> They [the Jews] could and can disappear just as little as God's faithfulness can come to an end...This continued existence of the Jews which is so puzzling is a sign which cannot be ignored....Yet they are no more than the shadow of a nation, the reluctant witnesses of the Son of God and Son of Man...whom they rejected, yet who has not ceased to call them....[18]

What is significant about Barth's connection with the patristic understanding of the Jews and their history is its dual effect on Christian attitudes toward Jewish worth and Jewish survival. The witness people theory began as a theological construct to explain and justify Jewish existence and suffering after Christianity became a state-sponsored religion, but also to protect Jews, since it was assumed that their role in salvation history was not terminated with their rejection of Christ. The mood of theological ambivalence surrounding the anachronism of Jewish existence in which the witness people theory arose is reflected in the ambivalence toward Israel in Barth's theology of Israel. Although Barth affirms a special solidarity with and debt of love toward Jews, their rejection of Jesus determines their history as one characterized by divine judgment.

Scholars have observed that in spite of its anti-Jewish orientation, the adoption of the witness people doctrine by Christendom after the fourth century actually saved many Jewish lives.[19] It did not eliminate Jewish persecution, but in its call for Jews to be preserved as witnesses to human faithlessness and divine judgment, it actually enabled the Jewish community to persist for centuries in Christian lands, albeit often in the ghetto. In this sense, Hitler's comment to church officials in 1933 that he merely wanted to do more effectively to the Jews what the church had been trying to do for centuries represents a tragic misunderstanding of the historic Christian attitude toward Jewish survival.[20] Sadly, however, the kind of modern, racial anti-Semitism which triumphed in the Nazi era was not mitigated at all by the Christian beliefs in the sacredness of Jewish existence and the importance of Jews in salvation history which animated the theory of the witness people. This alone is sufficient to call into question in the era after Auschwitz any Christian theology of Israel that is allied with the notion of the Jews as a witness people. If anything, the Holocaust has shown it is no longer possible to rely on Christian good will or notions of solidarity between Christianity and Judaism to safeguard Jewish existence.

5. Barth's personal record *vis-'a-vis* the Jews is actually a mixed one. While the "Jewish problem" was at the forefront of his theologizing and preaching at various times during his career, Barth did not use his influence in the German church to oppose effectively Nazi persecution of the Jews in Europe. In fact, one of the ironies of Barth's career is that while "the Jew" was a major focus for his theology of Israel, most living Jews were virtually ignored during the period of the Church Struggle because the attention of Barth and others was on Jewish-Christians and their relatives within the church. Even in relation to other Protestant churchmen like Dietrich Bonhoeffer, Barth's response to the persecution and ultimate destruction of Jews has to be found wanting. Furthermore, Barth's stance on political opposition does not seem to have been significantly altered by the events of the 30s and 40s. After the war he wrote that "the church today, contrary to its action between 1933 and 1945 ought to stand quietly aloof from the present conflict, and not let off all its guns before it is necessary."[21]

C. Summary

How, finally, shall we classify Barth's understanding of Israel, and what prospects for post-Holocaust theology, if any, does his thought represent?

First, it is undeniable that Barth's Israel teaching has been very influential in Protestant and Catholic theology for several decades, and continues to be so. Barth's statement, made late in his life, that the church's relationship to Judaism was the only great ecumenical question of the age, has provided inspiration for many of the theologians influenced by him. Even those who find Barth's theology of Israel ultimately unsatisfactory, however, have been unable to dismiss it easily. As a result, Barth's understanding of Israel has won him both high praise (Sulzbach and Rosato, e.g.) and harsh censure (Davies, e.g.). Although it has been called both, Barth's Israel-doctrine is neither the source of contemporary Christian anti-Judaism nor the solution for ending it.

Nevertheless, Barth's view of Israel remains an important starting point for contemporary theological discussion of Jewish-Christian relations because Barth was critically engaged with the pre- and post-Reformation theological tradition as deeply as any modern theologian. This means there is in Barth's thought a certain *continuity* with the past--a past which the church cannot relinquish without losing its identity, and which Christians who wish to overcome anti-Judaism must meet head-on. Similarly, Barth continued to take the testimony of Scripture seriously when much of theology had abandoned Scripture as a primary source for theological reflection. In fact, it is Barth's Reformation habit of assigning great import to the words of Scripture which leads him to an encounter with Israel, and this encounter has left a permanent impression on his theology. But while Barth's thought represents *continuity* with patristic, medieval and Reformation theological traditions which are in danger of being forgotten in much of the church, it is also true that Barth's is a theology of *discontinuity*. As is well-known, Barth's theology was first forged in the era of cultural crisis and historical rupture which followed World War I. This fact remained evident throughout Barth's work. Although he did not feel the force of the break represented by the Holocaust in the way many contemporary theologians have, Barth's is a theology informed by the historical ruptures of twentieth-century Europe. This is significant since it suggests that Barth took history and the modern world with great seriousness, even if Barth's theology is not addressed specifically to the era "after Auschwitz."

Second, Barth's theology of Israel demonstrates the usefulness and also the limitations of relying on theological models to classify Christian views of Israel. Klappert's work reveals in an illuminating way Barth's dependence on a traditional integration model, as well as the more radical christological dependence model. Klappert also demonstrates, however, that Barth's theology can be linked in some way to nearly every model, both positive and negative, in the taxonomy he introduces. This may mean that in the end we can only say that Barth has one foot in a world of traditional Christian thought about Israel, and one foot in a more radical world of thought characterized by an emphasis on Israel's continuing significance for Christianity.

Third, Barth's theology illuminates the tendency of Christians to pontificate on the meaning of "Israel" and the significance of Judaism without taking Jewish self-understanding into account. Several commentators have criticized Barth for this fault, and with good reason. But Barth is certainly not alone in his susceptibility to this error. In fact, Barth's failure is only one prominent example of a fault that has characterized Christian theology at least since the time of the second-century apologists, and which to a large extent still does. A contributing problem, of course, is the *actual* separation of the Jewish and Christian religious communities. This separation has characterized Western history in the common era and may still be observed in many segments of contemporary society, including our theological institutions. Barth's ignorance of Jewish theology and his nearly complete lack of contact with living Jews only serves as one glaring and tragic example of this separation.

Oddly, Christianity's history of co-opting Jewish existence and Jewish religion to serve its own purposes appears to be a peculiarly Christian failure. It is difficult to think of examples of Jewish theologians who provide detailed descriptions of what contemporary Christianity means, without the slightest reference to Christian theology or Christian self-consciousness. Yet we find this, until very recently, everywhere in the Christian tradition. This tendency to impose a Christian understanding of "Israel" on Jews and Judaism leads to the kind of abstract and fictionalized portraits of Jewish life and faith we encounter in Barth's theology. Such a glib and superficial Christian understanding of "Israel" also obscures the need for interaction and dialogue between Christians and Jews, a need which must be recognized if Christians are to exposed to Jewish self-understanding in the first place. Although Barth is not to blame for this legacy of theological imperialism, his work represents the extent to which it can affect even a theologian of great influence and integrity. Post-Holocaust Christian theology must overcome this proclivity for defining the nature of Jewish life, history and religion for Jews. If the mutual isolation of the two communities is to be overcome, and the solidarity which Barth has expressed theologically is to be realized, Christian theology will have to encounter living Judaism in new and profound ways.

Fourth, Barth's theology of Israel reveals some of the obstacles to Jewish-Christian relations inherent in traditional Christology, based as it is on a fulfilled messianism. Christian theology which incorporates an unfulfilled messianism has the advantage *vis-'a-vis* Judaism that it allows for a positive interpretation of the Jewish "No" to Jesus. That is, theology which operates under the conviction that the messianic kingdom was initiated, but not fulfilled, in Jesus can take seriously the Jewish insistence that, whatever the identity of Jesus, the world remains unredeemed. Any messianic claims with regard to this Jesus must be qualified, therefore, with Jesus' identity as Messiah to be fully confirmed only in the eschatological future.

It is precisely this Jewish "No" to Jesus which Barth is unable to interpret in a positive manner. Although this "No" does not retroactively define the character of biblical Israel in Barth's work to the extent it does in some Christian theologies, it certainly determines the history and essence of Judaism *post christum crucifixum*. While the logic of Barth's theology often seems to lead in the direction of a positive determination of post-biblical Israel apart from the church, Barth is theologically traumatized by the stark fact of Israel's rejection of its Messiah. Commenting on Barth's description of the close connection of Israel and the church in *CD* II:2, Bertold Klappert asks:

> Is not the crucified messiah of Israel at the same time the resurrected messiah of Israel and only from there also the crucified redeemer of the world and the resurrected Lord of the church?[22]

Klappert's question reveals how easy it might be to begin from Barth's original presupposition of solidarity between Israel and the church as two forms of the same elect community and arrive at a more positive systematic determination of Israel after the Christ-event. The problem, which even Klappert seems to ignore, is that Israel's "No" to Jesus is an even more fundamental presupposition for Barth, and as such determines his Israel theology even more than the motif of solidarity. This basic presupposition is largely implicit in Barth's theology, but Israel's "No" is clearly at the center of his system--it is not a foil to the system which originates outside it.

It remains to be seen whether post-Holocaust Christian theology as a whole will find a way to take this "No" as seriously as Barth does (lest real differences between Christians and Jews be obscured), while viewing it sympathetically and perceiving in it a word which the church needs to hear. In the future, post-Holocaust Christian theology must help the church perceive the need to adopt some version of unfulfilled messianism (perhaps that of Moltmann or van Buren) which is faithful to the Christian gospel and motivated by the vision of Christians and Jews living alongside each other as partners waiting for the consummation of God's Kingdom.

Fifth, Barth's emphasis on Jewish election, its continuing validity, and its character as a witness to God's existence and world governance leads to pressing questions about the relationship of the doctrine of election and Jewish suffering. In Barth, Richard Rubenstein's observations on the connection between Christian views of the Jews as a chosen people and the divine willing of Jewish persecution and destruction seem to be confirmed. The centrality of election in Barth's doctrine of Israel, as well as his conviction that "a Christian answer to the Jewish problem" must take into account the miraculous persistence of Jews and must explain anti-Semitism in its historico-theological dimensions, lead us to be skeptical of the prospects in Barth's thinking for post-Holocaust theology. If it is possible that these elements in his theology (which might well lead Rubenstein to categorize Barth's understanding Jews as "mythical") could contribute to anti-Semitism by suggesting that opposition to Jewish persecution is resistance of God's will, then such a theological approach simply cannot be embraced in the wake of the Holocaust. In this case it appears that after Auschwitz the ethical-humanitarian approach to Jewish suffering and anti-Semitism which Barth dismisses will have to take precedence over a theological approach.

Sixth, Barth's overall theological relationship to Israel reveals the temptation for Christian theology to resort to an unprophetic Christian Zionism[23] in an attempt to ease its its bad conscience *vis-'a-vis* Jewish suffering in Western history and in the Holocaust. Dieter Kraft has argued that Barth's own response to this suffering was a compensatory "philosemitism"--a pro-Jewish bias activated by his conviction that anti-Semitism was inevitable in the contact of "mankind" with the "Jew"-- and that this philosemitism issued logically in Barth's inchoate theological and political support for the state of Israel. Kraft's analysis of Barth illumines the fact that modern Zionism has always been motivated to some extent by the persistence of anti-Semitism.[24] The sort of Christian Zionism we see in the later Barth has been brought to crisis in the 1980s, Kraft argues, as it has found itself allied with an aggressive Israeli state that oppresses Palestinians in order to insure its security and expand its borders. "Compensatory" Christian philosemitism, according to Kraft, leads to a simplistic Christian Zionism which is increasingly indefensible. While we will not attempt to establish or discredit Kraft's claims, his analysis of Barth should be qualified with two observations.

First, anti-Semitism and philosemitism can and must be distinguished according to their moral status and historical effects. Second, Kraft's own political preference for Middle Eastern Arab States clearly prejudices his critique of Barth. One point of Kraft's analysis should be taken seriously, however. He is surely correct that the kind of unprophetic Christian Zionism stimulated solely by guilt for the Holocaust can hinder both peace and justice in the Middle East and result ultimately in a failure of Christian duty toward non-Christians.

Finally, Barth's theology reveals that an emphasis on the unique relationship between Israel and the church need not necessarily yield a Christian understanding of Judaism that is genuinely post-Holocaust.[25] Barth never tired of pointing out the unique bond that makes Christianity unable to conceive of Judaism as another "religion," and yet his theology of Israel is deeply implicated in historic Christian anti-Judaism, as we have seen. This fact encourages us to seek a theology which combines a Barthian sense of solidarity between the church and

Israel with an unequivocal affirmation of the equal partnership of Israel alongside Christianity.

With this in mind, we now turn to a final consideration of Israel in the theology of Jürgen Moltmann.

II. MOLTMANN'S THEOLOGY OF ISRAEL

A. Moltmann and Barth

The relationship between the understanding of Israel in the theologies of Moltmann and Barth is a topic deserving of further study. Given the general influence of Barth on Moltmann (an influence that is confirmed both by Moltmann and Moltmann's critics), we would expect Moltmann's theology of Israel to include at least an implicit response to Barth's thought on the subject. Moltmann has alluded to Barth's theology of Israel only infrequently, however. It may be that Moltmann is anxious to distance himself from a view of Israel which, as we saw in chapter two, presents major obstacles for Jewish-Christian relations. Whatever the case, we may observe a few significant commonalities and differences.

First, Moltmann stresses in good Barthian fashion that there is one people or community of God consisting of both Jews and Christians.[26] Moltmann goes beyond Barth, however, in his conviction that Jewish and Christian exegesis belong together in interpretation of the Scriptural witness of the one people of God.[27] Second, Moltmann's "messianic" theology is indebted to Barth's opposition to the existentialism of Bultmann. Moltmann contrasts his messianic interpretation of Christian faith, which is anti-existentialist,[28] with Bultmann's spiritualizing and individualizing notion of salvation. We also saw in chapter three other Barthian moves in Moltmann's theology of Israel: Moltmann stresses that anti-Semitism is unacceptable in Christianity, calling it the church's abuse of itself; Moltmann criticizes "Nostra aetate" for speaking of Israel in the context of "non-Christian religions"; and Moltmann affirms that the state of Israel is a "sign," albeit an ambiguous one. Perhaps the greatest commonality between Moltmann and Barth is their focus on Paul's discussion of Israel in Romans 9-11 and their reliance on a Pauline understanding of the church-Israel relationship--one which stresses irrevocable election, a temporary reversal in the order of salvation history, and a charge to the church to make the cast off synagogue jealous.

This commonality points up a major difference, however, since Barth sees n Paul the unbelief of Israel, its casting off, and its ultimate integration into the church, while Moltmann sees an emphasis on God's action in "hardening" Israel, an action over which Israel has no control. For Moltmann, the Jewish "No" to Jesus becomes the "external occasion" for the God-willed extension of Israel's promises to the Gentiles. While Barth stresses that the grace of God toward unbelieving Israel expressed in Romans 9-11 is *in spite of* Israel's "No," Moltmann perceives the grace of God toward the Gentiles as being through and even *because of* Israel's "No." For Moltmann, finally, church and synagogue make *each other* jealous--another example of how Moltmann's reading of Paul differs from Barth's. These differing interpretations of Paul's message reveal that what a theologian brings to a particular biblical text is of great importance in determining what he or she finds there. While Barth brings to Romans 9-11 a traditional certainty that Christ has fulfilled Israel's hope and has thus initiated God's redemption of the world, Moltmann brings to this same text a belief in the functional and provisional nature of the church and an unfulfilled messianism rooted in Paul's words in I Corinthians 15:28 and their interpretation by Dutch Apostolate Theology.[29]

The importance of Moltmann's roots in Barth's theology and the Confessing Church movement cannot be overlooked, and Moltmann describes these roots as "epochal and seminal for contemporary theology."[30] Yet, clearly, Moltmann desires to go beyond the doctrine of Israel and the approach to the "Jewish problem" represented in Barth and the Confessing Church. For example, Moltmann takes Christian anti-Judaism and its historical effects more seriously,[31] and denies that Israel is a witness to God's judgment,[32] or that Jesus is an Israel-transforming fulfillment of the messianic hope.[33] Moltmann learns more from Jews--and presumes to teach Jews less--than Barth. He perceives continuity and complementarity between Jews and Christians in terms of Israel's past election (stressed by Barth), but also in terms of their present callings and future messianic hopes as well. Thus there is a more genuine and respectful complementarity between the church and Israel in Moltmann's theology, one that is greatly superior to the abstract continuity claimed by Barth.

B. Positive Dimensions

The positive aspects of Moltmann's theology of Israel, especially as they represent improvements over the theology of Israel found in Barth and the Christian tradition, are:

1. Moltmann displays an exemplary openness to Judaism as a conversation partner and as a guide for rethinking Christian theology.[34] One encounters in Moltmann's work not only a familiarity with the writings of Heschel, Buber, Benjamin, Scholem, Ben-Chorin, Bloch, Rosenzweig, Adorno, Horkheimer and Lapide, but a willingness to let Christian faith be informed and, to some extent, transformed by these Jewish voices. Moltmann has described "seeing and reading with the eyes of Jews"[35] as a Christian starting-point for the improvement of Jewish-Christian relations, and one encounters attempts at this kind of seeing and reading throughout Moltmann's work. Two examples are his emphasis on the unredeemed character of the world (mediated primarily through Ben-Chorin), and his functional understanding of the church's Christology (mediated primarily by Lapide and Scholem).

2. A related positive dimension of Moltmann's thought is his willingness to take seriously and interpret positively the Jewish "No" to claims for the messiahship of Jesus. In this Moltmann distinguishes himself from Barth and most other Christian theologians who have preceded him. Moltmann has listened to the Jewish "No" based on non-redemption of the world long enough to let it qualify the Christian "yes," and closely enough to hear in it a providential "No" from God. In considering the Jewish "No" to Jesus, Moltmann has constructed a theology which reveals the systematic penetration of "unfulfilled messianism." This unfulfilled messianism is evident in Moltmann's view of the church as a provisional structure, and his subordination of ecclesiology and Christology to the coming messianic Kingdom.

3. Moltmann's ability to identify the foundations of complementarity between Judaism and Christianity, even in areas which are traditional battlegrounds, is remarkable. This ability stems from Moltmann's knowledge of and willingness to listen to the Jewish tradition, discussed above, and his talent for relating seemingly opposing beliefs in dialectical and even dependent terms. In Moltmann's interpretations of Christian trinitarian doctrine, of Jewish and Christian

messianism, of the callings of Israel and the church, and of their common future hope, we have important examples of his vision of complementarity.

4. The political orientation of Moltmann's theology lends an important dimension to his analysis of Jewish-Christian relations. Although Moltmann's observation that Christian anti-Judaism stems from Christian self-hatred is not original, his association of this theme with political chiliasm is. Moltmann sees in the implicit failure of Christian attempts to equate Kingdom and state the roots of resentment toward Jews whose future hope for this world is belittled as a "Jewish dream." Although it is difficult to judge Moltmann's claim that Christians and Jews have had good relations when Christian chiliasm has been a live hope, it does suggest a source of Christian anti-Judaism that has been largely overlooked, and illuminates a new foundation for complementarity.

5. Moltmann brings into the discussion with "Israel" aspects of the church's tradition which are too often forgotten or dismissed in post-Holocaust theology. In addition to his respect for the Scriptural tradition, (something he shares with Barth), Moltmann displays a thorough knowledge of the doctrinal and creedal traditions of the church. This knowledge assists him in his analysis of Christian theological prejudices and his culling of resources for better relations. In his allusions to the theology of Israel developed by Joachim of Fiore and the Reformed Federalist, the Pietist, and the Lutheran salvation-historical schools, Moltmann reveals a "conservative" stance vis-'a-vis the Christian theological tradition unusual among theologians who seek to affirm "Israel" in a radical way.

C. Negative Dimensions

The following negative aspects of Moltmann's theology of Israel must be mentioned as well:

1. Moltmann has offered no developed critique of Barth's theology of Israel, despite the facts that he is considered one of his generation's most important interpreters of Barth and that Barth's theology of Israel is entangled in some of the Christian prejudices Moltmann has tried so hard to extricate and replace. Are we not justified in expecting from Moltmann a serious engagement with

Barth's theology of Israel? At least it may be said of Barth that he developed a fully conceived Israel-doctrine, "pre-Holocaust" though it may have been. While Moltmann has provided us with glimpses of a theology done in the shadow of Auschwitz, he is yet to match Barth's achievement of creating a systematic theology of Israel able to stand on its own. On the other hand, perhaps we misunderstand Moltmann's work if we expect from more than a "contribution" to systematic thought on Israel.

2. There are remnants of traditional Christian anti-Jewish biases in Moltmann's early work, especially in *The Crucified God*. These mainly reflect a Lutheran tendency to contrast the gospel with "Jewish legalism." Moltmann's first attempt at developing a model of partnership in which Israel and the church exist side by side, coming as it does in the context of his discussion of God's vindication of Jesus' message of righteousness apart from the law, shows that Moltmann did not immediately come to terms with the negative implications of the gospel/law dichotomy for Jewish-Christian relations. Moltmann has largely overcome this particular error in his subsequent work, however.

3. There is a primitivism in Moltmann's theology which leads him to underestimate the recalcitrance and intractability of the Christian anti-Jewish tradition, as well as overestimate the possibilities of activating a relatively obscure stream of Christian theology in the contemporary milieu. Moltmann is overly enthusiastic and insufficiently critical in his call for the church to rediscover the "special calling" of Israel developed in early Reformed and Lutheran theology. He has not established that this theology is capable of providing a basis for the vision of complementarity he describes, nor does he supply any evidence that this theology overcame Christian anti-Judaism in its own time.[36] Moltmann embraces traditions that he says "solve the problem of Israel." But this way of describing their function leads us to wonder if he has not given sufficient care to Jewish self-definition. Another example of Moltmann's primitivism is found in his response to criticisms of Christian faith using the argument that they do not implicate the message of Jesus or the "authentic" faith of the church. While this *may* be true, it does not speak to those who recognize the faith of the church precisely in such criticisms.

4. Moltmann is open to the criticism that his desire to affirm Christian identity in our era has led him to sacrifice relevance to the radical events of suffering that have punctuated the twentieth century. Despite Moltmann's careful attention to the relevance-identity dilemma,[37] there is some truth in the charge that Moltmann moves too quickly toward an affirmation of Christian identity in the face of epochal events like the suffering of Jews in Auschwitz.[38]

5. The triumphalism Alice and A. Roy Eckardt have argued is implicit in Moltmann's universalizing of Christian hope in "christological eschatology" calls into question the efficacy of Moltmann's unfulfilled messianism as a foundation for Jewish-Christian relations. What viable alternatives there are to Moltmann's "postponed triumphalism," and how Jews might respond to them are questions which for now remain unanswered.

D. Summary

Finally, what are the prospects for post-Holocaust theology inherent in Moltmann's work?

1. As in the case of Barth, we notice side by side in Moltmann the operation of traditional and more radical models for understanding Israel. On the one hand is *The Crucified God,* where we encounter Moltmann's implicit use of the *illustration* model. It might even be argued on the basis of Moltmann's earlier work that *subsumation* thinking is at work behind his postponed triumphalism.[39] On the other hand is Moltmann's later work which reveals the *dependence* function Judaism and Christianity serve for each other, as well as the extensive *complementarity* Moltmann envisions between Judaism and Christianity. Moltmann has clearly repudiated the illustration model in his later work, but its presence in his most important and influential book reveals how difficult it is to do Christian theology without traditional anti-Jewish biases.

2. Moltmann's emphasis on the political nature of the dialogue between Jews and Christians makes his theology applicable to this dialogue in new ways. Moltmann's political orientation leads him to qualify the traditional versions of Jesus' trial by stressing that he was crucified by Roman occupying forces largely for political reasons. It also allows him to recognize that Christian anti-Judaism finds its source

in the political chiliasm which has been characteristic of Christianity from time to time since the Constantinian revolution. Perhaps most importantly, Moltmann's political orientation to theology means he approaches Middle Eastern politics with respect for the theological significance of Israel, but determined to avoid naïve' support for power which may be used to violate the rights of the powerless. Both "political theology" and "liberation theology" have been recognized by Jews as Christian movements with important roots in the Hebrew tradition.[40] This fact alone seems to confirm the importance of Moltmann's political orientation for Christian-Jewish *rapprochement*.

3. The charges of triumphalism and absolutism made against Moltmann are important to consider. But these bogey-words should not obscure Moltmann's intentions--which are to universalize the Jewish/Christian hope without demeaning or subsuming Jewish faith or threatening Jewish existence. Whether he succeeds is unclear (especially in view of Paul van Buren's thoroughgoing anti-triumphalist approach) and is for Jews to determine. If Jews can follow Pinchas Lapide in responding to his overtures, Moltmann's project could allow Christians to confess the essence of what they have always believed about Jesus, while leaving theological space for Jewish covenant existence, for Jewish hope, and even for the Jewish "No" to Jesus' messiahship. Moltmann's significance, then, is located in his ability to develop a Christian theology of Israel which is *both* Christian *and* affirming of Israel.

4. We have argued that Moltmann's theology is significant for its ability to make constructive use of the Jewish "No." One wonders, however, if Moltmann can incorporate as successfully as he has the "No" based on the Jewish hoped-for redemption of the world other versions of the Jewish "No" (for instance, the version based on Jesus' and his followers' apparently non-Jewish attitude toward Torah).

5. Jürgen Moltmann's optimism about overcoming Jewish-Christian antagonism and correcting the anti-Jewish biases that have nearly always characterized Christianity engenders hope that these goals are within the range of theological possibility. Moltmann's optimism is in stark contrast to the mood of Holocaust theology which has tended to be much more cautious, and at times deeply pessimistic, about the prospects for reforming Christianity. But are not Moltmann's optimism and hope desperately needed by Christians and Jews seeking to justify

the tedious and daunting project of constructing post-Holocaust theology?

III. VAN BUREN'S THEOLOGY OF ISRAEL

A. Positive Dimensions

Some distinctly positive features of van Buren's theology of Israel as outlined in chapter four are:

1. Van Buren does not begin his theology of the Jewish-Christian reality with speculation about the philosophical or theological significance of the Holocaust, or with an account of the historical results of the church's anti-Judaism, but with recent statements by the church suggesting it wishes to affirm the continuing existence of the Jewish people and their covenant.

2. Van Buren's theology of Israel includes and, in fact, is based upon a thoroughgoing rejection of Christian triumphalism past, present and future. This rejection of triumphalism is based in his understanding of the church as a de-absolutized extension of God's original covenant with the Jewish people.

3. With the help of "exegetical friends" like Krister Stendahl and Lloyd Gaston, van Buren has adopted an approach to Scripture which is radical in the sense of identifying the roots of Christian anti-Judaism and sources for its elimination. Yet his approach is also conservative in relation to Holocaust Theology and its skepticism toward the possibility of the New Testament serving as a source for post-Holocaust Christian theology. Van Buren argues that, interpreted correctly, the Apostolic Writings (and especially the letters of Paul) can actually serve as a foundation for the church's post-Holocaust understanding of Israel.

4. Despite the resources for Christian-Jewish rapprochement inherent in the Apostolic Writings, van Buren insists that the church's theology of Israel must be built upon a fresh theological "living response."

5. By charging the church to take seriously Israel's witness to Torah-life, and emphasizing that Torah cannot be subsumed under the Christian category of "law," van Buren challenges the application of gospel/law thinking to Christian-Jewish relations and undercuts the charge of Jewish "legalism."

6. In opposition to Christian tendencies toward quietism, van Buren stresses the mutual nature of covenant, at one point defining the covenant as a game in which God's moves depend on those of humankind. In Van Buren's view of covenant, "...God has committed God's own future into human hands, [so] that the course of history is determined in part by human action" (III:187).

7. Van Buren emphasizes the uniqueness of the Jewish people, though not in isolation from divine election, the unique relationship Israel has with the church, or the church's unique responsibility to the Jewish people.

8. Van Buren understands the Jewish "No" to Jesus as based in Torah-faithfulness, denying that Jesus was or is Israel's "Messiah" as understood by Christians. This interpretation of the Jewish "No" reveals greater respect for Jewish faith than versions which portray it as a provisional "No" that will be overcome by Jesus' future vindication as Messiah of Israel.

9. While Jewish existence remains a kind of "sign" in van Buren's theology, it is a sign not of God's judgment, but of God's election and God's continued involvement in an unfinished creation.

10. Unlike many systematic theologians, van Buren explores practical issues in his discussion of church-Israel relations, such as the significance and special problems of Jewish-Christians and Gentile-Jews.

B. Negative Dimensions

Some problems inherent in van Buren's theology of Israel are:

1. Van Buren views human experience as a source for theology to an extent bound to make orthodox Christians uncomfortable.[41] Van Buren claims as inspiration Calvin's thesis that knowledge of God is related to knowledge of self, but there is also in van Buren's theology a "secular" orientation rooted more in the radical theology of the late Bonhoeffer than in the Protestant Reformation. While this does not make van Buren's orientation unique, it does stand to diminish his ability to communicate among mainline Christians.

2. Whether Jesus has real significance for the Jewish people, and whether Christianity is more than an appendix to Judaism[42] are questions van Buren does not satisfactorily address in *A Theology of*

the Jewish-Christian Reality. If it is the case that Jews need nothing which Christians have, then on what legitimate basis can van Buren legitimately ask Jews to affirm a positive significance in the church?[43]

3. Van Buren's belief that God's creation of human freedom keeps God from decisively intervening in human affairs would appear to have the undesirably effect of absolving God of responsibility for evil and suffering in events like the Holocaust. If the message conveyed in the Holocaust is the importance of human responsibility, is there not a morally superior way for God to get this message across?[44]

4. Some aspects of van Buren's *A Theology of the Jewish-Christian Reality*, especially the linguistic concerns of his prolegomena in volume one, and some of his more involved discussions of rabbinic and medieval Jewish thought, are sure to be of little interest to many in the church, which after all is van Buren's intended audience.

5. In his unwavering respect and support for the state of Israel and the Zionist spirit which founded and continues to sustain it amid great opposition, van Buren reveals a lack of sensitivity to the situation and suffering of Palestinian Arabs. Van Buren argues, for instance, that "if it is well with Israel, it will be well with the world." In such statements we see van Buren's genuine concern for Israel's security, but also his myopia in failing to recognize the interests of groups in the Middle East whose "wellness" often appears to be inversely proportionate to Israel's.[45]

6. Despite his admonition that the church hear and learn from Israel's testimony, van Buren takes liberties in defining "Israel" that many of his Christian predecessors and contemporaries have been criticized for.[46] Van Buren claims to define Israel on Israel's terms. But does van Buren's "Israel," which tends to be Orthodox, "rabbinic," Zionist and to stress Torah-life over messianic hope represent the essence of Jewish life and faith? If so, are there not other forms of Jewish faith and practice which merit van Buren's attention? Perhaps only Jews are qualified to respond to these questions, but it is the case that many Jews do not recognize themselves in van Buren's "Israel."[47]

7. Van Buren's belief that most Jews of Jesus' time reacted to Jesus' message in just the way they had to in order to remain faithful to God attenuates, if it does not completely eliminate, the tragic dimension from the church's story of Jesus. Is there not some way to affirm the tragedy inherent in the story of Jewish rejection of a Jewish prophet

and his message from God (all of this van Buren affirms) without lending support to Christian anti-Judaism? The only tragedy van Buren associates with the gospel story is the ultimate failure of the synagogue to recognize the significance of the new thing God had done *among the Gentiles.*

8. There is a problematic primitivism in van Buren's theology, exemplified by his confidence in his ability to isolate the "early Christian witness" on which his statements about Jesus and the early church are based. Furthermore, van Buren's primitivism appears to be inconsistent, for he claims that "early Christian eschatology" can no longer serve as a guide for the church's hope.

9. Van Buren continues to use exclusively male language to refer to God, even as most seminaries and graduate schools of Religion in America emphasize the importance of "gender inclusive language."

10. Van Buren's fundamental conviction that the church and Israel worship the same Lord needs to be defended, since it is not shared by many in the church. This fact may be a barrier to the assimilation of his theology where it is needed most--among grassroots Christian communities.

11. While van Buren argues that his understanding of the covenant is "Jewish," it is debatable whether it qualifies as "biblical," since it does not deal adequately with the various biblical ways of speaking about God's covenant(s). One scholar has argued that van Buren's view of "covenant" bears little if any resemblance to the view of classical Reformed Protestantism.[48] If this is the case, van Buren needs to defend his novel interpretation of this biblical notion.

12. Van Buren's affirmation of the Jewish people at times borders on a sort of racial philosemitism. Rosemary Ruether has argued that van Buren believes Jews are "impeccable," while he assumes Arabs are "a people filled with baseless hatred." Although Ruether's characterization is not completely fair, her observation that van Buren is an "anti-Semite turned inside out" may contain an element of truth.[49] If it does, it is because van Buren adopts a philosemitic outlook intended to "compensate" (to use Dieter Kraft's term) not for his own anti-Jewishness presumably, but for that of the entire Christian tradition.

13. There seems an inherent contradiction between van Buren's cultural-linguistic approach to the study of religion and his innate confidence in an historical method for sorting out what did and did not

happen in the first century. Specifically, the epistemological relativism and coherence theory of truth which are linked to the cultural linguistic model operative in parts of *A Theology of the Jewish-Christian Reality* gives way at other times to a more optimistic epistemology linked to van Buren's confidence in the historical interpretation of ancient texts.

14. It seems contradictory for van Buren to attempt to highlight and encourage Israel's universalist traditions (in order for Israel to make theological sense of the church) at the same time he is arguing that "noetically and ontologically God and Israel are indivisible and inseparable" (III:265).

C. Summary

Paul van Buren's *A Theology of the Jewish-Christian Reality* has been praised by Christians and Jews alike as a milestone in the theology of Jewish-Christian relations. One scholar has even referred to van Buren's work as laying the groundwork for all of post-Holocaust scholarship.[50] We shall try now to identify the specific aspects of van Buren's work which make it useful for the church's task of developing a post-Holocaust theology of Israel.

First, van Buren has cited as his motivation for writing *A Theology of the Jewish-Christian Reality* a desire to help the church walk through the door opened by Vatican II and other Christian statements affirming Israel's continuing significance in salvation history. It cannot be claimed, therefore, that van Buren is answering questions no one is asking. Van Buren's many references to the ecclesiastical statements to have appeared in recent years make it clear that he is addressing the issues which the church and the churches have set before him. While it is not clear the extent to which van Buren's work has influenced recent church statements on Jewish-Christian relations,[51] *A Theology of the Jewish-Christian Reality* provides an important resource for Christian theologians commissioned to reformulate the church's understanding of Israel.

In 1976 John Macquarrie made much of the fact that van Buren no longer appeared to value the act of prayer or the exercise of his Christian ministry. Macquarrie concluded that "such consequences seem to follow inevitably from his book [*The Secular Meaning of the Gospel*]."[52] Readers of van Buren's new project can only be impressed by the seriousness with which he now accepts his calling as a Christian theologian in the service of the church. Van Buren is aware that a Christian theologian writing about Judaism performs his work "on a tightrope," but he has bravely and conscientiously faced the demands of this task.

Second, van Buren's is the first theology of Israel written in the Barthian tradition which merits comparison with Barth's theological project. Van Buren has obviously qualified Barth's vision of the church-Israel relationship in important ways, yet he begins where Barth begins--with God's freedom expressed in Israel's election. Nonetheless, we can direct at van Buren the same question we asked of Moltmann's: doesn't this interpreter of Barth owe us a careful critique of Barth's theology of Israel, its strengths and weaknesses? Such a critique is only implicit in *A Theology of the Jewish-Christian Reality.*

Third, van Buren expresses the relationship of church and Israel in novel terms, terms which do not easily fit the categories of Bertold Klappert which have guided our explorations.[53] While we do recognize in van Buren what Klappert calls the "dependence" model (in which the church is dependent on Israel for its life, election and relationship to God), van Buren elaborates what can more accurately be called an "inclusion" model--a model which envisions the church as included in the story of Israel's covenant with God through its faith in the Jew Jesus. In one sense, this inclusion model is an inversion of what Klappert calls the "integration" model (where God intends Israel's integration into the church). When we recall the dependence of Barth's Israel-doctrine on the integration model, it becomes easier to recognize the extent to which van Buren's inclusionary approach has modified Barth's "radical traditionalism."

Fourth, it is important to observe that van Buren's premises, as useful as they are for bringing the church back into contact with Israel, do not necessarily lead all Christians to the conclusions which he has reached. Many evangelical Christians, for instance, are discovering the Jewishness of Jesus and the early church, coming to terms with the anti-Jewish traditions of Christianity, and even wishing to re-Judaize Christian faith. All the while, however, they retain their conviction that Jewish evangelism is acceptable and necessary. One example is John Fischer's *The Olive Tree Connection,* where the author suggests ways in which Christians can share with Jews their faith in "Yeshua of Nazareth" using the "Jewish Bible."[54]

Fifth, van Buren gives the distinct impression he believes that to be a post-Holocaust Christian means to be Zionist. For instance, the *mission* of the church as van Buren conceives it includes not only service to the Jewish people, but service to the state of Israel. This fact will diminish the reception of van Buren's theology among many Christians whose political loyalties in the Middle East are with Arabs or are divided, and among those who flatly reject van Buren's argument that anti-Zionism is necessarily anti-Jewish. Furthermore, van Buren's strong political preference for the state of Israel is destined to make many Jews of the left uncomfortable. Part of this discomfort will result from the weight van Buren assigns to the fact and implications of Israel's election. But also important is that van Buren's Christian Zionism cannot recognize what some Israeli and non-Israeli Jews believe: that Israel must compromise with Palestinians and its Arab neighbors in order to achieve peace.

It is impossible to read van Buren's *A Theology of the Jewish-Christian Reality* in 1991 without asking of it questions that have been brought to the world's attention by the uprising that began in December, 1987 and the recent rightward swing in Israeli politics. Van Buren calls on Christians to take the "facts" of the Middle East situation seriously. But we can only wonder what van Buren make of the "facts" that Palestinian children under ten and Palestinian men over seventy have died in the uprising,[55] that Israeli forces appear to have committed a variety of abuses and atrocities, or that the Israeli government is resisting steps which even Israel's friends view as necessary for peace in the Middle East. Does van Buren believe that Christians are bound to support the Likud Party over Labor because it more explicitly affirms the land promise which van Buren argues is part of God's continuing covenant? Should the Gush Emunim be the object of Christian sympathy and support, since its members affirm the election and land promises absolutely? These are issues that a serious consideration of van Buren's work cannot ignore, and which will make its future utilization by the church problematic.

Sixth, despite the resources represented by van Buren's contribution to the church's task of developing a living response to its new recognition of Israel, a Christian reader of *A Theology of the*

Jewish-Christian Reality wonders whether the battle for a positive theology of Israel is destined to end in Pyrrhic victory. We have mentioned the loss of confidence in a large part of the Apostolic Writings and the loss of the tragic dimension in the story of Jesus' life and death which seem to be implied by van Buren's theology of Israel. Much more disturbing for many in the church, however, will be the restriction to a functional significance of the church's christological claims, and the denial that Jesus can be considered in any sense the Messiah of Israel. Van Buren argues that it is the problem of internal coherence with which theology should be most concerned. But van Buren's use of a cultural-linguistic model of religious truth to establish coherence challenges Christian uniqueness in a way many in the church will find foreign and unacceptable.

Seventh, the prospects of van Buren's theology of Israel for post-Holocaust theology must be measured against what we shall say in the next chapter about the problems associated with basing a Christian understanding of Israel on the doctrine of election. Yet, despite the drawbacks just mentioned, those who agree with van Buren that the church's theology is in need of revision *vis-'a-vis* Israel cannot escape the challenge he issues at the end of *Christ in Context:*"if not this," van Buren asks, "then what?"

IV. BARTH, MOLTMANN AND VAN BUREN

A. Post-Holocaust Theology and the Legacy of Basel

At this point we shall attempt to integrate the results of our analysis in previous sections and earlier chapters and offer some overall conclusions. We argued in the second chapter of this study that Barth's influence on contemporary Protestant theological understandings of Israel has been significant and lasting. We saw in chapter three that Jürgen Moltmann has adopted to a great extent Barth's "covenant view of reality," that Moltmann's "messianic theology" has been influenced by Barth's opposition to existentialist and spiritualizing interpretations of the gospel, and that Moltmann has embraced the *Church Dogmatics* as his constant theological companion. We also observed that Moltmann displays a Barthian understanding of the unique status of Judaism which precludes its labelling as a "non-Christian religion," and a Barthian apprehension of the "one people of God" consisting of Israel and the church, and, finally, that Moltmann shares Barth's dependence on the Pauline view of "Israel" expressed in Romans 9-11.

In chapter four we discovered that Moltmann's Barthian emphasis on Romans 9-11 as a source for the church's understanding of Israel and Israel's future *post christum crucifixum* is shared by Paul van Buren. Van Buren even follows Barth's exegesis of Romans 9-11 in specific details, such as his "teleological" reading of Romans 10:4 ["Christ is the goal *(telos)* of the law"]. Furthermore, van Buren echoes Barth in his insistence that christological reflection begin "from above."[56] A commonality that is less specific but more important, is the fact that Barth, Moltmann and van Buren share an emphasis on the importance of Scripture in theological reflection. Despite their differing readings of Paul (Barth sees in Romans 9-11 an explanation of Israel's elect but judged present status; Moltmann an emphasis on the reversal of the original order of salvation history, van Buren an emphasis on the church's inclusion in the covenant of a still vibrant Israel) should not obscure the fact that each theologian proceeds on the assumption that Scripture remains an important criterion for a theology of Israel. As we noted in chapter one, the "return to Scripture" is an aspect of post-Holocaust theological reflection that is not valued by all scholars.

At many points, van Buren develops his theology apart from or in opposition to Barth and Moltmann. For instance, van Buren rejects an affirmation fundamental for both Moltmann and Barth--that Jesus is Israel's Messiah.[57] Van Buren remains "Barthian," however, in his emphasis on Jesus Christ, and his views of Israel as the true environment of Jesus and of Christ as the point where Israel and the church intersect. But for van Buren it is not the messiahship of Jesus that is the basis for the unity of Israel and the church, but the fact that Jesus, Israel and the church worship and serve the same God.

In some cases van Buren simply adapts Barth's theology of Israel in ways that fit his own vision. For instance, van Buren reverses Barth's integration model in his inclusion paradigm (so that instead of Israel being integrated into the church, the church is included in Israel). Also interesting is van Buren's transformation of Barth's talk of the church's need for the "special service" and "appointed service" performed by Israel within the elect community, into his notion of the *church's service to Israel.* Overall, we can say that van Buren is more in tune with the radical side of Barth's theology of Israel than with the traditional side. This means, of course, that he is also more in tune with the potentially Zionist and philosemitic side of Barth than with the potentially anti-Jewish side. Evidence for this fact can be found in van Buren's application of messianic language to the state of Israel, despite his refusal to use it in reference to Jesus.

We have indicated points where both Moltmann and van Buren appear to have been influenced by Barth's Israel-doctrine. This connection is easier to establish in the case of van Buren, however, since he has been explicit concerning his debt to Barth. Once this debt is recognized, there are places in *A Theology of the Jewish-Christian Reality* where the reader distinctly senses Barth's presence behind van Buren's text. One example is van Buren's discussion of mission to the Jews in volume one, where the text brings to mind Barth's treatment of the issue in *Church Dogmatics* IV:3, 2:

> It would be a total denial of our own Way if we even pretended to try to show it to Jews, for they already have their way of being in the Way....The only "call to faith" that is proper for us to give to a Jew would be the call to a fully secularized Jew asking him or her to be faithful to the walking of his or her own people.[58]

For another example of a formal connection between van Buren and Barth on Israel, we look to a passage from volume two of *A Theology of the Jewish-Christian Reality,* one that has clear parallels with Barth's analysis of Jewish existence in *Church Dogmatics* III:3:

> Jews are different. They are called by God to be different....The result is that the Jews never totally fit into their environment. This has nearly always given rise to more or less resentment on the part of non-Jews, Gentiles. Israel's self-understanding raises questions, sometimes uncomfortable questions, about the self-understanding of other peoples, and this contributes to the phenomenon of Gentile anti-Jewism. It has always been so and there seems to be no reason that it will not continue.[59]

Also interesting is a comparison of van Buren's emphasis on the church's dependence on Israel with Barth's declaration in *Church Dogmatics* II: 2 that "the church lives no life of its own beside and against Israel. It draws its life from Israel and Israel lives in it" (205), and comparison of Barth's argument that there is one covenant (*C D* IV:1) with van Buren's developed one-covenant theology.

Moltmann and van Buren were each profoundly influenced by Barth during their formative periods, with each maintaining a critical relationship to Barth and his legacy in their attempts to do constructive theology. When they reveal Barth's influence, Moltmann and van Buren differ in the way they express it. Both build on the Barthian conception of a continuity between Israel and the church centered in Jesus Christ, just as both agree with Barth that the church's special calling is the service of reconciliation between God and Gentiles. But while Moltmann emphasizes a common messianic hope as the bridge toward a complementary relationship between Christians and Jews, van Buren focuses on the history of Jesus of Nazareth and his "covenant context" as the keys for understanding the organic relationship between Jews and Christians. In addition, while Moltmann adopts Barth's christocentrism almost without reservation (in the argument, e.g., that no immediacy between God and humanity can be conceived apart from Christ), van Buren transforms Barth's christological monism into a monism of God's covenant with the Jewish people.[60]

One example of a common departure from Barth can be seen in their strategies in developing a theology of Israel. We have discussed Barth's isolation from Jewish life and Jewish self-definition. Moltmann and van Buren, on the other hand, are paradigmatic in the way they enter dialogue with Jewish thought. First, Moltmann and van Buren audit carefully Jewish witnesses. For example, both listen to and utilize Jewish apprehensions of God to interpret Christian doctrine. Moltmann uses Heschel to understand and explain the Trinity and van Buren takes up the notion of God's compromise through covenantal self-determination to interpret the Incarnation. But, having listened, Moltmann and van Buren are not reluctant to speak. And when they do speak, they are clear that they have not silently accepted all they hear from Jews. Van Buren, for instance, does not accept the Jewish tendency to ignore the significance of the church for Jewish thought. Moltmann is disturbed by Jewish claims that the essence of Christianity is belief in an interior and individual redemption, and he wonders why Jews cannot perceive the church as a preparation for the messianic Kingdom. Moltmann is willing to affirm that Judaism is more important to Christianity than vice versa, but both Moltmann and van Buren both argue that Jews who wish to dialogue with Christians should seriously consider the church's role in God's plan to redeem the world.

Perhaps the point at which Moltmann and van Buren together move furthest from Barth is in developing of their versions of what we referred to in chapter one as "unfulfilled messianism." Both insist, in opposition to what they view as Christianity's perennial tendency to misunderstand its own identity, that the church is not and never will be identical with the Kingdom of God. The idea that the world was redeemed "in principle" at the coming of Christ is considered by both Moltmann and van Buren to be meaningless and dangerous. Both attend carefully to Jewish voices who stress that redemption is a this-worldly and historical process and insist that there can be no Redeemer unaccompanied by such a redemption.

Here there are differences as well, however. Moltmann amends the Barthian view of Christ's revelation as an "unveiling" by emphasizing an inaugurated reconciliation and a still-to-come redemption. Van Buren is more uneasy with traditional descriptions of Christ's work, and does not believe it is accurate or helpful to refer to Jesus as Messiah. More importantly, the version of the Jewish "No" to Christianity heard by van Buren is not open to reconciliation, since it is based on Torah-faithfulness. Moltmann's version of the Jewish "No" is open to eschatological reconciliation. Barth's version, it will be recalled, which is based on the blindness of Israel, demands immediate reconciliation.

Both Moltmann and van Buren believe the preferred route to an "unfulfilled messianism" involves reflection on the provisional and/or functional nature of Christ in his relation to God and the completion of God's creation. More interestingly, both demonstrate a fascination with the Pauline idea (expressed in I Cor. 15:28) that the reign of Christ is an interim on the way to some future point at which God will become "all in all." Relying on this Pauline vision of the future, Moltmann stresses the provisionality of the church relative to the messianic Kingdom, while van Buren emphasizes the fact that neither Israel nor the church are ends in themselves, but exist for the renewal of God's creation. Van Buren is more consistent in avoiding any suggestion that one religion will find its fulfillment in the other. For van Buren, there will be no fusion of Judaism and Christianity until God becomes "all in all." For Moltmann fusion is accomplished with the arrival of the messianic Kingdom. (For Barth, of course, fusion was to take place as soon as Israel came to its senses and recognized its calling in the church). One result of van Buren's consistency on this point is that there can be no genuinely common messianic hope between Israel and the church. There can be no hope, that is, which resolves the church's unfulfilled messianism and Israel's hope for redemption at the same time.

Van Buren goes well beyond Moltmann in his willingness to speak of Christ in relative and functional terms. It is doubtful whether either thinker, and especially van Buren, has correctly gauged the resistance in the church which serious suggestions of Christ's relativity and provisionality are likely to provoke. On the other hand, their common emphasis on a New Testament passage as the basis for this view of Christ's ultimate submission to the Father will encourage many Christians to reflect carefully on the extent to which Christ has fulfilled the hopes of the church, of Israel, and of all creation. Ultimately, Moltmann's unfulfilled messianism is more successful in relating to the traditions of the church, since he has kept alive the notion of Jesus as the church's "Messiah" (and the eschatologically revealed Messiah of Israel), and since he has not followed van Buren in the problematic path of sublimating Christian messianic hope in the modern state of Israel. For Moltmann there can be no historical fulfillment of the messianic hope that does not mean the arrival of God's Kingdom. Van Buren, influenced by a version of religious Zionism transmitted to him through Abraham Kook, entertains a more dialectical view of the relationship between history and fulfillment.

There are other non-Barthian aspects of Moltmann and van Buren's theologies of Israel which are parallel. Both Moltmann and van Buren bring to the theological task an "historical" emphasis which challenges the Christian tendency toward spiritualization in all its manifestations. This historical element can be described in two ways. First, while Barth saw the continuity between Israel and church in essentialist and abstract terms, both Moltmann and van Buren construe this continuity more historically, with Moltmann looking to the future (the *parousia* and coming of the Kingdom) and van Buren to the past (Jesus' part in the history of the covenant) for evidence of this historical continuity. Second, while Barth approached the "Jewish question" in the

30s and after in a narrowly theological manner, Moltmann and van Buren have allowed the historical relationship between Christians and Jews and its culmination in the Holocaust to add a new dimension to their theological interpretations of Israel.

Van Buren and Moltmann each look to the "Lord's Prayer" as evidence of Jesus' Jewish understanding of God and Jewish hope for the world, and as a point of contact for contemporary Christian-Jewish relations. Both perceive the Gentiles as encountering Israel and Israel's history through the opening up of Israel to the nations which occurs in Jesus. In both Moltmann and van Buren the church "rises to life," in Israel through Jesus, in a reversal of Barthian thinking. Both theologians stress that Jews reject primarily the claims of traditional Christianity, not Jesus himself. Furthermore, both are convinced that the key to recapturing a Jesus whom Jews will recognize is a rediscovery of true Christianity, in the form of the church's "early witness" (van Buren) or "authentic" Christian faith (Moltmann).

Furthermore, both Moltmann and van Buren display what we have described as a tendency toward primitivism. Moltmann takes seriously the potential contributions of salvation-historical theology of the sixteenth to nineteenth centuries for post-Holocaust theology. In the process, however, he romanticizes these schools and is insufficiently critical of their pre-Holocaust understandings of Israel's "special calling." As we have said, we wish from Moltmann a more in-depth description of how this theology can be applied to the contemporary situation. Meanwhile, van Buren reveals too much confidence that the "early witness" to Jesus in the Apostolic Writings can be isolated, and that it affirms unequivocally his interpretation of Jesus' relationship to "Israel." Van Buren is also overconfident in the ability of scholars like himself to isolate and interpret this early witness with the help of historical criticism.

Finally, van Buren and Moltmann each are convinced that Israel has more significance for the church than vice versa, an example of how far they have departed from the thinking of Barth. But they also agree that Israel should consider more carefully the significance of the church for Jewish faith. The church can be viewed as a *preparatio messianica* (Moltmann) or a "codicil" to God's covenant with Israel (van Buren). But Israel's blindness to the church's identity as a *preparatio messianica* and to its "novelty in continuity" with Israel's covenant is explained in part by the church's anti-Judaic past. Thus Moltmann and van Buren issue sobering charges for the church to become what they believe Israel should recognize it to be.

To complete our analysis, we shall focus more carefully on the ways the vision of the church-Israel relationship differs in the work of Moltmann and van Buren. Recalling the categories of Bertold Klappert introduced in chapter one, we argued that Moltmann develops a complementarity model, while van Buren's model is one of dependence. For both Moltmann and van Buren, Jesus represents God's will for Gentiles. But Moltmann differs from van Buren in his implicit universalizing of Jesus and his message. Jesus is not only the Lord of the church, but is also Israel's Messiah, and will be eschatologically vindicated as savior of the world. As we saw in chapter three, Moltmann is careful to avoid spiritualizing or individualizing the meaning of Christ and the reconciliation inaugurated by God in him. Moltmann does believe, however, that the future will reveal the universal truth of Christ's righteousness as God's plan for all nations and peoples, including Jews.

If Moltmann's is a universalizing approach to the relationship of Jesus and the Jewish people, van Buren's is particularizing. While Moltmann's theology of Israel moves from particular to universal and historical to eschatological (thus following what he sees as the prophetic vision), van Buren maintains the scandal of particularity which is the hallmark of the Sinai and covenant traditions. This scandal of particularity is also a characteristic of Barthian Neo-Orthodoxy as well, though van Buren focuses on the particularity of Israel's divine election and not the Christ-event. By means of covenant-thinking which is "particular" and "historical," van Buren seeks to identify what is unique about Israel and about the church as ways of walking in the one Way of God. If there is a general category under which to bring Israel and the church together, according to van Buren, it is not "Jesus as Messiah of Israel and Lord of the church," but one covenant of Israel into which the church has been engrafted through the faithful Jew Jesus.

There are other differences in vision: Van Buren sees in the service owed to "Israel" by the church concrete protection and support for Jews and the state of Israel. Moltmann believes this "service" consists primarily in the church's emphasis on its own messianic hope. Moltmann argues Christians may not become champions of the fulfillment of the land promise in present-day Palestine. Van Buren, on the other hand, claims Christians are obliged to become champions of such a fulfillment. While van Buren believes the church's message for Jews is "be Israel," Moltmann summons the church to testify to God's reconciliation with (not redemption of) the world attested to by the Christian gospel. Another important difference is the starting point of the two theologians. While Moltmann apparently believes he must demonstrate the theological connections between Judaism and Christianity, van Buren assumes these connections and makes them his point of origin. For example, on the question of Jewish monotheism versus Christian trinitarianism, van Buren begins by stressing the simple affirmation that the church worships Israel's Lord, while Moltmann takes pains to argue that Jewish monotheism and Christian trinitarianism are not ultimately contradictory. This difference is due in part to the fact that in post-war Germany, the social context for Moltmann's work, the Christian theologian often feels burdened to demonstrate that Jews and Christians have anything in common at all.

B. The Post-Holocaust Significance of Barth

The creative and often original approaches to the problem of Israel in the work of Moltmann and van Buren implicitly demonstrate the limits of Barth's understanding of Israel for contemporary Jewish-Christian relations. We have seen that while Moltmann and van Buren both remain indebted to Barth, neither adopts in detail Barth's understanding of the relationship between Israel and the church. They build on the foundations laid by Barth when these foundations are solid, and they look elsewhere when it is apparent the edifice of Barth's theology has been erected upon the sands of Christian anti-Judaism. What may we conclude from this situation about possible points of continuity between "pre-" and "post-Holocaust" understandings of Israel?

The significant points of continuity uncovered by this study are 1. Barth's demand that Judaism be considered a unique manifestation of God's will for humanity and not a "non-Christian religion" 2. his emphasis on the intimate theological connection between the church and Israel 3. his concerns with the Jewishness of Jesus and the anti-Christian nature of anti-Semitism 4. his decision to abandon traditional talk of "mission" to the Jews 5. his willingness to risk radical interpretations of

Scripture in an attempt to understand the mystery of Israel 6. his affirmation of Israel's continuing role in salvation history, and 7. his emphasis on Israel's eternal election. As we have seen, each of these aspects of Barth's theology have served as foundations for the work of Moltmann and/or van Buren.

Barth's legacy for post-Holocaust theology, then, is a dual one. On the one hand, Barth articulated some radical positions on the church's relationship with Israel, positions which continue to hold a place in contemporary theological reflection. On the other hand, Barth demonstrates the fact that when the church has possessed a developed theologies of Israel, these have often had a destructive effect on Jewish existence and on Jewish-Christian relations. Barth's systematic Israel-doctrine reveals that the church's traditional silence concerning the significance of Israel is not the only problem it must overcome. Just as important is the fact that when the church does recognize "Israel," it tends to transmit Christian anti-Jewish biases. These biases cannot be overcome unless the church undertakes a thoroughgoing critique of its traditions, and listens carefully to what Jews have to say about themselves.

As we have argued, there are ways in which Barth's theology of Israel is original and progressive. Both Moltmann and van Buren respond favorably to the aspects of Barth's theology of Israel which we have described as "radical," and van Buren in particular gives Barth credit for a vision which may in some ways serve as a basis for post-Holocaust thinking. But at many other points, where Barth essentially systematizes the anti-Jewish attitudes implicit in church teaching for centuries, his theology of Israel is in need of a thoroughgoing post-Holocaust critique.

C. Radical Theology or Messianic Theology: Which Way Forward?

A question which remains to be answered is whether the work of Moltmann or van Buren represents the proper direction for this post-Holocaust theological critique of Protestant theology. We have shown that these thinkers differ considerably in their approach to helping the church confront the reality of Israel. Van Buren assumes a "radical" approach indebted to the work of Franz Rosenzweig, "Holocaust theology," the American radical theology of the 60s, and revisionist readings of the New Testament. Moltmann develops a "messianic" approach to post-Holocaust theology that combines the eschatological orientation of a theology of hope, the emphasis on historical suffering manifest in his theology of the cross, and the praxis-orientation of political theology.

Three of the issues on which it is important to judge these theologies are their understanding of Judaism, their approach to the state of Israel, and their revisions of the church's Christology. As we have said, both theologians reveal an interest in and willingness to dialogue with Jewish thought and tradition that is uncommon among Christian theologians. But this observation can obscure the fact that both Moltmann and van Buren dialogue with a limited spectrum of Jewish thought and belief--and one which suits their own distinct purposes. Moltmann engages the messianic and prophetic traditions of Judaism and van Buren the legal, covenantal and mystical. But can post-Holocaust Christian theology afford to limit its understanding of "Israel" by focusing on one such group of traditions and ignoring another?

It is certainly to the detriment of Moltmann's theology that he ignores the ritual, legal and ethical Jewish traditions which are non-prophetic; not least because his casting of Judaism as messianic/prophetic religion perpetuates traditional Protestant interpretations of what is important and unimportant in Judaism. More unfortunate, however, is van Buren's tendency to ignore Israel's prophetic traditions altogether. This is partly because these traditions transmit of a kind of universalism--based in visions of God's just future for all nations--which complement nicely van Buren's emphasis on historical particularism. But it is also because these traditions contain a non-idealized view of the Jewish people and of Jewish history which van Buren claims is necessary in the church, but which he does not possess himself.

Van Buren views Israel as a community grounded in election,and extends this definition to include the state of Israel as well. This issues in idealized conceptions of what the Jewish state is and should be--and one which many, if not most Jews, simply do not share. Van Buren claims that dissenters from his perceptions of what "Israel" means are out of touch with their own tradition. But we must reply by asking how this attitude is any different from traditional Christian attempts to define the essence and meaning of their faith for Jews? Throughout his theology, van Buren claims to know what it means to "be Israel" (acceptance of divine election, Torah-faithfulness) in a manner which simply excludes many Jews, and which for those who are excluded must seem no less imperialistic than Karl Barth's.

In the end, whether one shares Moltmann's or van Buren's interpretation of Jewish tradition depends on whether one is focused primarily on Jewish liberation or human liberation (or, to use biblical terms, whether God's voice is mediated primarily through kings or prophets). Van Buren stresses that the election of Israel is expressed primarily in its Torah-life after Sinai, not in its salvation in the Exodus. A corollary to this perspective is his observation that revelation finds its primary form in commandment, not liberation.

Moltmann, in nearly precise opposition to van Buren, begins from the perspective of a liberationist or "political" hermeneutic. Moltmann believes Christians and Jews must be liberated from a destructive past, a past which climaxed in Germany earlier in this century. But he reminds us that those liberated from the bondage of hatred and powerlessness must beware of new forms of oppression with which liberation tempts us. A Christian post-Holocaust theology, Moltmann's theology argues, must focus not on a fulfilled present (whether this takes the form of a triumphal church or a reborn Israel) but on a redemptive future in which the Kingdom of justice becomes manifest. The theological notion of the "restoration of Israel" remains spiritual this side of the eschaton. It can be a sign of the Kingdom--but it is also a sign of what remains to be accomplished in the liberation and redemption of all people.

This brings us to the issue of the understanding of the state of Israel in the theologies of Moltmann and van Buren. These thinkers react very differently to claims that support for the state of Israel is a non-negotiable prerequisite for Jewish-Christian dialogue. This fact is especially evident when Moltmann and van Buren speak about the church's response to the political empowerment of the Jewish people. Moltmann affirms that Jewish-Christian dialogue takes on a political dimension as a result of the existence of the state of Israel, but claims this does not mean Christians must support the aims of this state. Moltmann describes Israel as a sign (and only a sign) of the consummation of God's promises to his people in history, warning that

Christians cannot interpret this sign as an unambiguous manifestation of God's Kingdom. Although Moltmann does not say it, he suggests that Christians are precluded from adopting a Zionist stance, since this would mean theological support for a secular political entity, and one that may threaten the rights and the well-being of oppressed people in the region. Van Buren, on the other hand, reveals none of Moltmann's ambivalence about the state of Israel. Since, in van Buren's view, to be anti-Zionist is to be anti-Semitic, and to be anti-Semitic is to be anti-Christian, then to be a post-Holocaust Christian means to be a Christian Zionist. Van Buren's brand of Zionism includes care and protection for the Jewish people, but it does not stop there. It also entails support for the state of Israel and a pro-Israel orientation in the Middle East, and leads to problematical theological claims, such as the statement that Christology must take the state of Israel into account.

The salient question with regard to the "Zionism issue" is whether the approach of Moltmann or van Buren is more appropriate for Christians in the post-Holocaust environment. Ultimately, neither van Buren's argument for the necessity of Christian Zionism nor Moltmann's virtual silence about Zionism's relationship to Christian faith provide a sufficient basis for the church's theological reflection. The vagueness of Moltmann's position (related, no doubt, to his critical stance toward all political ideologies) opens it to abuse by the kinds of vehement anti-Zionism which *are* anti-Semitic. Van Buren's position, on the other hand, relies on a perspective on Israel that is insufficiently critical, and which simplistically identifies Arab hatred of Jews as the root of all problems in the Middle East. Van Buren also seems caught in a contradiction with regard to his view of the state of Israel and the expectations he places upon it. Van Buren emphasizes that this state, no less than the Jewish people themselves, exists on the basis of divine election. This view is unacceptable to many so-called secular Jews, but more seriously, it lends support to the notion that Israel is to be held to a higher standard than other nations in its treatment of neighbors and internal aliens, a view most Israelis suspect is born of anti-Semitism. Very simply, van Buren uses a double standard when speaking of Israel and every other political entity, and this double standard can perpetuate the very hostility to Israel among non-Jews which van Buren is trying to combat.

Ultimately, Moltmann's position on the Jewish state is more useful, because it is less rigid. In a time when many Jews consider a Zionist outlook as a non-negotiable item among Christians wishing to dialogue with the Jewish community, it is tempting to embrace van Buren's position that Zionism is part of what Christians owe the Jewish people. But current events in the Middle East continue to impress upon thoughtful Christians that Zionism can become an oppressive ideology when it is placed by well-meaning outsiders in the service of a state held to be beyond serious criticism.

Christology is the third area in which the approaches of Moltmann and van Buren differ significantly. It is especially their revisions of traditional Christology in response to the Jewish "No" to Jesus which merit our attention. Moltmann accepts the Jewish insight that because the world remains in an unredeemed state, redemption cannot have occurred, and argues that while *reconciliation* with God was achieved through Jesus Christ, *redemption* will not be experienced until Christ's return. This position, which he believes is actually a restatement of an early Christian view of the matter, leads Moltmann to elaborate an unfulfilled messianism based on a Christ who is "on the way." Moltmann's vision of a "convergence" of Jewish and Christian hope arises from his confidence that Jesus will be revealed as Messiah of Israel and savior of the world when he returns. While this view may be triumphalist in a delayed sense, it affirms the church's historic christological confessions while creating room for the coexistence of Christian and Jewish hopes. Since Christians and Jews share such deep theological and spiritual roots, an eschatological convergence of these hopes is not impossible. While Moltmann's Christology may be affected by a theological imperialism rooted in the eschatological vindication of Christian claims, Moltmann's theology is aimed at eschewing triumphalism by announcing a provisional Christian "Yes" that affirms a Christ who is "becoming." It is not supersessionist in any meaningful sense, and Jews who have responded formally to Moltmann's theology have accepted it as advanced in good faith and have not described it as triumphalist or imperialist.

Van Buren's christological revision is aimed at maintaining the intimate connection between Jews and Christians by understanding Jesus as a faithful Jew called by the God of Israel who responded in a way which this God used to bring Gentiles into the history of the covenant.

In order to maintain Jesus' connection with the covenant, the law and the God of Israel, van Buren interprets the absolute claims of the church in functional or phenomenological terms. The affirmation "God is triune" means that the church encounters God in a trinitarian manner--not that God is "Trinity" in an essentialist sense. "Jesus is Lord" means that Jesus is the church's Lord, not the Lord of all creation whose identity was subsequently revealed only to the church. Van Buren is actually to be applauded for salvaging what he does of Christian belief. He is able to unconditionally affirm the Jewish people and their God while at the same time maintaining most Christian dogmas in some form or another. This is no mean feat. Van Buren does this, very simply, by affirming the uniqueness of Christianity--as an extension of God's unique covenant with Israel to the Gentiles--while discarding traditional concepts of its absoluteness.

The crucial question with regard to Christology is whether van Buren sacrifices too much of Christian *identity* in order to achieve *relevance* to the post-Holocaust Jewish-Christian encounter. Van Buren has made a career of relating Christian faith to the challenges represented by its dialogue partners. In *The Secular Meaning of the Gospel*, van Buren explores the emerging secular paradigm and its implications for theology. In *A Theology of the Jewish-Christian Reality*, he focuses on another religious tradition and the church's historical failures *vis-'a-vis* that tradition. However, many Christians have concluded, in the 1960s and in the 1980s, that van Buren's attempts to make Christian faith relevant have resulted in a theology they can no longer identify as Christian. We are left wondering, then, how efficacious a *Christian* post-Holocaust theology will be which fails to speak to the church. This failure is particularly troubling given that van Buren adopts the Barthian view that theology is a function of the church, while Moltmann qualifies this view in response to his understanding of the provisional nature of the church relative to the coming Kingdom.

Furthermore, post-Holocaust theology, while taking both the Holocaust and the Jewish state with the utmost seriousness, may not allow its focus on either to replace or obscure its vision of the Jewish people themselves, or the universal hope in the Kingdom characterized by justice and peace. Van Buren recognizes this necessity in relation to the Holocaust, but often loses sight of it when discussing the state of

Israel. Moltmann, despite the weaknesses of his theology of "Israel," is closer to keeping sight of this principle in relation to both the Holocaust and the Jewish state. Does Moltmann, then, represent the way into the future for post-Holocaust theology done in the Reformed tradition and in the shadow of Barth?

We should recall that some critics have concluded Moltmann is at times so anxious to affirm Christian *identity* that he sacrifices *relevance* before an epoch-making event like the Holocaust. This concern does not arise in van Buren's theology of Israel, since it is clear throughout that for van Buren the Holocaust is the event which reveals the rupture in traditional Christian theology, as well as a new stage in God's dealings with humanity. Van Buren even argues, carefully and at length, that the Holocaust may yet qualify as a revelatory event for the church. In the unique way it treats the Holocaust, then, van Buren's theology would seem more genuinely post-Holocaust then Moltmann's.

Van Buren's theology of Israel seems superior to Moltmann's on another front as well. While van Buren shares with Moltmann (and Barth) an affirmation of Israel's irrevocable election, he removes from his theology every tinge of triumphalism or supersessionism by explicitly denying that Israel's future is in the church or that Israel's promises can be fulfilled within the context of Christology or messianic hope. While Moltmann has eschatologized Christian redemption and Christian hope in a way that radically qualifies Barth's integrationist view of Israel, critics from the tradition of Holocaust theology still perceive in his work a triumphalism in the guise of anti-triumphalism.

Another basis for the superiority of van Buren's theology lies in his emphasis on covenant--rather than promise--for understanding Israel's relationship to God. The notion of promise, it would seem, necessarily implies fulfillment, and is thus perpetually open to being understood triumphalistically. While Moltmann is especially critical of Christian theology that denies the promises of Israel, he is less sensitive to theology which undermines the uniqueness of Israel's covenant. Moltmann denies that his Christian universalism--rooted as it is in the messianic fulfillment of Israel's promises--abolishes the special character of Israel. But here Moltmann is susceptible to the criticism van Buren directs at Barth--that while he clearly affirms Israel's continuing election, he fails to recognize the continuing relevance of the Sinai covenant. Van Buren's theological focus on this covenant leads him to the view that Jesus calls Israel to Torah-life, not into the church or even toward an eschatological fusion with the church rooted in hope for the Kingdom.

When the relative merits of these theologies are considered, we are left with a troubling doubt as to whether a Christian theology can qualify as authentically post-Holocaust as long as it is *open to a triumphalist interpretation*--even though it decries Christian anti-Judaism and disavows supersessionism and the so-called "teaching of contempt." If the answer is "no," then van Buren's is the only contemporary theology in the Barthian tradition worthy of the title "post-Holocaust." As we suggested in chapter one, it is not an emphasis on the Holocaust alone which makes Christian theology post-Holocaust. Part of what is promising about van Buren's theology of Israel is that he moves beyond the bounds of early Holocaust theology. Van Buren's claim to have transcended Holocaust theology is vindicated in his response to Roy Eckardt's denial of the resurrection of Jesus, his careful theological approach to establishing the revelatory nature of the Holocaust, and the relatively limited role which "dead Jews" play in his theology.

Given what has been said in the preceding paragraphs, we conclude that the work of both Moltmann and van Buren is necessary to the church's task of constructing a post-Holocaust Christian theology. Moltmann's theology speaks to the church in a commanding way, and is inspired by his own experiences of war and reconstruction in Germany. Van Buren's work offers creative and often original reflection on the theological issues involved in a post-Holocaust reconstruction of the church's understanding of Israel. While the church requires what both theologians offer, Moltmann promises to be more influential than van Buren among non-theologians and in grass-roots Christian communities.[61] Yet only if a new generation of theologians can combine Moltmann's ability to envision a common hope and articulate this hope with Jewish dialogue partners in ways which speak to the church with van Buren's penchant for careful theological reflection and systematic thought will the church realize the kind of relationship between Christians and Jews that animates the work of both thinkers.

Notes

1. See Willis, "Bonhoeffer and Barth on Jewish Suffering," where the author compares Barth's "systematic" accomplishment with the "doctrinal" achievement of "Nostra aetate."

2. See Peter Gorday, *Principles of Patristic Exegesis: Romans 9-11 in Origen, John Chrysostom, and Augustine* Studies in the Bible and Early Christianity, vol. 4 (New York: Edwin Mellen Press, 1983). Gorday points out that Augustine's understanding of Romans 9-11, characterized by its emphasis on election, predestination and grace as the the keys to Paul's epistle, and by its tendency to ignore Paul's expressions of passion for his Jewish kinsmen, became the dominant approach to these chapters in the patristic age and the ages which followed. Origen's sympathy for the Judaism of his time and his reading of Romans 9-11 as an attempt by Paul to mediate between Jewish and Gentile Christians was lost until the twentieth century "Scandinavian school" reclaimed these themes.

3. Ibid., 171.

4. See Klappert, 38.

5. Cf. Sulzbach: "Barth is a Protestant and as such he goes back to the Bible. What the Church Fathers taught and what subsequent popes have decreed has no significance for him" ("Karl Barth and the Jews," 590). Again, Sulzbach overstates her case, but the point that Barth is a child of the Reformation is beyond dispute.

6. See *CD* II:2, 263; and "The Jewish Problem...," 201.

7. Barth actually displays many of the important elements of the anti-Jewish tradition in Christian theology and exegesis, as described, for example, by Charlotte Klein, *Anti-Judaism in Christian Theology.*

8. I use the term "supersessionistic" here to describe the kind of theology which Klappert demonstrates with his negative models. Klappert sees the "integration" model as Barth's main point of contact with the "negative" tradition.

9. That references to contemporary Judaism as "the Synagogue" generally have a negative and polemic function in Christian theology and confession, one can observe from the way this term is used in the confessions of Barth's Reformed tradition. See *The Book of Confessions of the Presbyterian Church (U.S.A.),* especially chaps., 1-5. See also my "Presbyterians and Jews: A Theological Exploration of the Book of Confessions."

10. Klappert understands "the dialectic of law and gospel" as Barth's major systematic premise in *CD* II:2, paragraph 34. It is in terms of this dialectic, Klappert argues, that one must understand Barth's discussions of crucifixion and resurrection and their relation to God's judgment and mercy, the promise of God heard and

believed, the passing and coming man, and Israel as a witness to judgment and the church as a witness to mercy (43ff.).

11. See, e.g., T. F. Torrance, "Karl Barth and Patristic Theology," in Thompson, ed., *Theology Beyond Christendom*, 215-240.

12. This discussion of the patristic witness-people theory is dependent on Edward Flannery, *The Anguish of the Jews*, 52-53. See also Sulzbach, "Karl Barth and the Jews," where the author gives an excellent description of the witness people doctrine in Christian history (without using this term), including quotes form medieval sources. Ironically, however, she does so only in introduction to her discussion of Barth, and not in direct relation to his theology (587-89).

13. According to Flannery, the theory actually began with Lactantius (d. 330). See 309 n80.

14. Ibid., 53. This passage includes references to Augustine's "The Creed" and "Tractate Against the Jews."

15. Augustine, "Tractate Against the Jews," in Flannery, 53. For an English translation and commentary on this work, see A. Lukyn Williams, *Adversus Judaeos* (Cambridge: Cambridge University Press, 1935), 312-317.

16. See *CD* II:2, 209; IV:I, 2, 877; *Ad Limina Apostolorum*, 36.

17. Barth does not say that the Jews are Christ-killers, *per se*, only that they "delivered Jesus up" to be crucified. Still, the connection here with what has come to be called the deicide charge is evident. Jules Isaac defines the three main components of the teaching of contempt as the dispersion of the Jews as a providential punishment, the degenerate state of Judaism at the time of Jesus, and the Jews as "the killers of Christ." There are at the very least echoes of each of these components in Barth's theology. [See *The Teaching of Contempt* (New York: Holt, Rhinehart and Winston, N. D.), 29ff.]

18. 196-98, passim.

19. See, e.g., Flannery, 53.

20. See Eliezer Berkovits, *Faith After the Holocaust*, 19.

21. *Community, State and Church*, 57. Intensifying the irony of Barth's lack of contact with living Judaism is the influence his own thought has had on Jewish theology, especially in the United States. See, especially Robert G. Goldy, *The Emergence of Jewish Theology in America* (Bloomington: Indiana University Press, 1990, where Barth's influence on men like Heschel, Herberg and Soloveitchik is discussed.

22. Klappert, 43, trans. mine.

23. Since the meaning of the term Zionism is disputed, concepts like "Christian Zionism" are bound to be somewhat unclear. Zionism has been labelled a form of "racism" by some (United Nations General Assembly Resolution, 1975). Some view Zionism as a political nationalism focused on aspirations for and independent Jewish homeland. Others expand the definition to include not only the political but also the social and spiritual aspirations of Jews. With the term Christian Zionism I am attempting to describe Christian support for the return of the Jewish people to their "homeland" and for the state of Israel and its policies. "Christian Zionism" can be motivated by philosemitism, anti-semitism, or a selfish indifference to Jews (see chapter six). I am using the term here to refer primarily to a political ideology, and not to the more broad Zionist movement for the social, cultural and moral renaissance of the Jew. On the history of non-Jewish Zionism, see Regina S. Sharif, *Non-Jewish Zionism: Its Roots in Western History,* (London: Zed Press, 1980), especially chapter two.

24. See, e. g., Walter Laqueur, *A History of Zionism* (New York: Holt, Rhinehart, and Winston, 1972), especially the first of the author's concluding "theses." See also Arnold Toynbee, *The Study of History,* where the author makes a psychological connection between anti-Semitism and Zionism (cited in Sharif, *Non-Jewish Zionism,* 121).

25. See, e. g., Leonhard Goppelt, "Israel and the Church in Today's Discussion and in Paul," where the author shows how it is possible for Christians to affirm Israel's unique relationship to the church, and its continuing special election, "even though the promise given to Abraham is exclusively fulfilled in Jesus, and therefore in his church."

26. See "Church and Israel: A Common Way of Hope?," 211; and *Jewish Monotheism,* 42.

27. "Church and Israel: A Common Way of Hope?," 215.

28. See "Jewish and Christian Messianism," 68 n9, where Moltmann quotes Scholem's statement that "the messianic idea is the real anti-existentialist idea."

29. For the influence of Dutch Apostolate theology on Moltmann, see Meeks, *Origins,* 24-30.

30. See "Theology in Germany Today," 198ff.

31. See *Christology,* 32; *The Church in the Power of the Spirit,* 136; and "Forgiveness and Politics," 46-50.

32. See *The Church in the Power of the Spirit,* 147; and "Who Is Jesus Christ For Us Today?"

33. *Christology,* 10.

34. For expressions of this openness to Judaism in works not discussed in this chapter, see *Theology Today*, 45-6; "Theology in Germany Today," 203-4; and *Experiences of God*, 16.

35. *Kirche und Israel: Ein Gemeinsamer Weg?*, 88.

36. Cf. Eckardts, *Long Night's Journey*, 107.

37. Cf. *Theology Today*, 10-38; and *The Crucified God*, ch. 1.

38. See Rebecca S. Chopp, *The Praxis of Suffering: An Interpretation of Liberation and Political Theologies* (Maryknoll, NY: Orbis, 1986), 116.

39. Cf. Eckardts, *Long Night's Journey*, 107.

40. See, e.g., Uriel Tal, "Law, the Authority of the State, and the Freedom of the Individual," *Christian-Jewish Relations* 14:1 (1981), 28-42; and Marc H. Ellis, *Toward a Jewish Theology of Liberation* (Maryknoll, NY: Orbis, 1987).

41. Cf. Karlsberg, "Israel as Light to the Nations," 210.

42. Cf. the review by Alan Davies, 281.

43. Cf. the review by David Novak, 117.

44. John K. Roth, in "The Silence of God," *Faith and Philosophy* 1:4 (October, 1984), 407-420, elaborates this "philosophical objection" to van Buren's theology, and adds that, according to Brenner's study of Holocaust survivors, only a very small percentage of those who experienced the Holocaust agree with van Buren's claim that God was unable to prevent it.

45. Cf. Rosemary Radford Ruether, "Speaking of Israel II," *Christianity and Crisis* (October 12, 1987), 343: "he [van Buren] is quite ready to declare that what's good for the Jews is good for the world. Palestinians, Central Americans, or black South Africans might feel that what seems good for the Jews is in fact very bad for them..." In the same article Ruether observes that while van Buren's work is taken quite seriously by Israelis and Israeli leaders, Palestinian Christians perceive it as having abandoned them (340).

46. In *Long Night's Journey Into Day*, the Eckardts criticize van Buren's *The Burden of Freedom* because they believe it requires special behavior from the Jewish people, and therefore reflects a Christian "ideology" which imposes abnormal obligations on the Jews (121).

47. Ruether observes that in addition to ignoring Palestinian Christians and other Arabs, van Buren's work fails to speak to "progressive Jews" as well ("Speaking of Israel II," 342).

48. "Israel as Light to the Nations...," 208.

49. "Speaking of Israel II," 343.

50. "After the Holocaust...," 639.

51. Surprisingly, van Buren's work is not referred to in the recent statement by the Presbyterian Church (U.S.A.) entitled *A Theological Understanding of the Relationship Between Christians and Jews.* Nor is van Buren's work mentioned in the bibliography which follows the published version of the statement.

52. Macquarrie, *New Directions,* 23.

53. As we observed in chapter two (n105), Klappert responds to Barth's concept of a Christian"placeholding for Israel" with the comment that after Auschwitz we must ask "whether the Gentile Christian placeholding for Israel expressed by Barth has reversed itself through suffering and martyrdom into Judaism as an Israel placeholding for the church" (32). It might be possible to interpret van Buren's inclusion model as a reversal of the "placeholding" scheme of traditional theology as envisioned here by Klappert. For van Buren, however, it is the Apostolic Writings and not Auschwitz which leads us to think in terms of the inclusion of the Gentiles into Israel.

54. *The Olive Tree Connection: Sharing Messiah With Israel* (Downer's Grove, MO: Inter-Varsity Press, 1983). See also, Hal Lindsey, *The Road to Holocaust* (New York: Bantam, 1989); and Marvin R. Wilson, *Our Father Abraham: Jewish Roots of the Christian Faith* (Grand Rapids: Eerdmans, 1989). In the materials produced by The Center for Judaic-Christian Studies in Dayton, OH (formerly Austin, TX) we see another example within the evangelical tradition of a radical rediscovery of the church's Hebrew heritage.

55. See Amos Elon, "Letter from Israel," *The New Yorker* February 13, 1989.

56. Van Buren writes in *A Christian Theology of the People Israel* that "as the event of Jesus began "from above," so should the church's reflection upon that event" (241). Christology which is carried out "from above" traditionally begins with the question, "how did the second person of the Trinity become a human being?" Christology which proceeds "from below" begins with the question of the relation between Jesus of Nazareth and God. This distinction has been popularized by Karl Rahner. It is perhaps surprising that van Buren follows Barth's approach to Christology "from above," given the metaphysical and mythological overtones of this starting point. Van Buren's anthropocentric emphasis would seem to predispose him (as it does Rahner) toward a saving history type of Christology that begins "from below." Yet, as van Buren makes clear in *Christ in Context,* Christology must keep before it the task of establishing the continuity between Jesus and the God of Israel.

57. Van Buren's uneasiness with the term "Messiah" is perhaps the place where his thought is most incompatible with that of Moltmann. Van Buren supports "leaving out the ambiguous term 'Messiah,' focusing instead on the solidarity of Jesus with his people as reflected in his concern for the lost sheep of the house of Israel and his longing to draw Jerusalem into a movement of renewal" (*A Christian Theology of the People Israel*, 264).

58. *Discerning the Way*, 53. Cf. *CD* IV:3, 2, 877. Barth's alternative to Jewish mission, the church's attempt to make the synagogue jealous, is unacceptable to van Buren, of course.

59. Van Buren, II:248.

60. For this insight concerning van Buren, I am indebted to Ruether and Ruether, *The Wrath of Jonah*, 211.

61. One example of this fact, and its frustrating implications for Holocaust theology may be seen in A. Roy Eckardt's response to the publication of a section of chapter one of Moltmann's recent book on Christology in *The Christian Century*. Eckardt describes Moltmann's neo-Pauline position as "old hat," since, he claims, it is anticipated in his own theology, and concludes: "An unselfconfident presumption seems to be still prevalent within American theology: until a German theologian says something, it has not really been said" ["Moltmann on the Jews," (letter to the editor) *The Christian Century*, January 2-9, 1991, 28-29].

CHAPTER SIX

OBSTACLES

I. CHRISTIAN TALK ABOUT ISRAEL: ELECTION AND OTHER PROBLEMS

At this point we shall continue the critique of the work of the theologians we have been considering by bringing to bear some general objections levelled against Christian theological talk about Israel in the post-Holocaust era. In doing so we will be focusing on some of the problems facing those who will try to utilize the prospects for post-Holocaust theology in the work of Barth, Moltmann and van Buren.

1. The theologians we have examined are all white, male, and mainline Protestant. These personal factors alone do not disqualify their work, but they do serve to contextualize it. Surely the perspectives of Christian theologians who are female, non-white, non-Western, or non-Protestant will illuminate aspects of the Israel-church relationship which Barth, Moltmann and van Buren have ignored. Especially instructive would be a comparison of the views of Israel we have considered with those of Christians representing oppressed groups or classes. In the critique of Paul van Buren's theology of Israel developed by the Palestinian Christian theologian Naim Stifan Ateek, we see an example of first world and third world perceptions of Israel in conflict.[1]

2. There is a natural tendency for Christian theologians to engage in dialogue with those Jews most open to such encounters. This tendency is quite understandable, but it is possible that unrepresentative pictures of Judaism and Jewish views of Christianity arise among Jews eager to make theological peace with Christian dialogue partners. For example, some Jews worry that Pinchas Lapide goes too far in affirming Christian beliefs and accepting Christian characterizations of Judaism. These tendencies are apparent in Lapide's dialogues with Jürgen Moltmann and call into question the universal acceptability of Moltmann's overtures to Judaism. For example, while it may not trouble Lapide to call Jesus as the *possible* Messiah of Israel, most Jews do not share such an openness to the claims of Christianity.

3. Christians who wish to dialogue with Judaism, personally or theologically, are tempted to present this religion in monolithic terms. In fact, Judaism is probably no more monolithic than Christianity, and when Christians attempt to present "the Jewish view" of a particular issue they risk over-simplification and distortion. The realization that there are a variety of Jewish perspectives on most issues has taken root in van Buren and in Moltmann's more recent work. But although van Buren seems to recognize the diversity in Jewish thought and belief in a way uncharacteristic of Christian theology as a whole, he understands certain Jewish perspectives as more essentially "Jewish." Taking seriously the diversity and nuance in Jewish thought is a task with which post-Holocaust Christian theology has only begun to deal.

4. The gap which persists between official ecclesiastical statements on "Israel" and general Christian attitudes toward Jews and Judaism is disturbing, and is often not addressed or overcome in the work of academic theologians. This gap between theological proclamation and grass-roots opinion exists in many areas, but is most troublesome when it involves issues of such importance for the church's credibility as its relationship to Israel. Works written by academic theologians and read by others in the academy can, of course, be of only limited help in bridging the gap between the church's theology and its practice. Barth, Moltmann and van Buren each are explicit about their intentions to write theology for "the church," and in Barth's case, one can see the influence which his work has had on various ecclesiastical documents. But this influence has taken decades to reveal itself in many cases, and it is often unclear the extent to which these

statements affect the views of grassroots Christian communities. Ultimately, the effect of academic theology on popular Christian opinion is probably minimal, and in any case it is quite slow to reveal itself. This problem has to be kept in clear view by post-Holocaust Christian theology.

5. A question which remains unanswered for many is what place to assign in Jewish-Christian dialogue the voices of Jewish converts to Christianity and Gentile converts to Judaism. Do members of groups like "Jews for Jesus" possess a unique and important perspective on the church-Israel relationship, or should their confusing (and confused?) identity exclude them from Jewish-Christian dialogue? Van Buren takes this question seriously, but it must receive more attention, especially as "Hebrew Christians" grow in number and influence within Christianity.

6. As we saw in connection with the Israel-doctrine of Karl Barth, Christian theology has long been characterized by its tendency to place special demands upon the Jewish people. Moltmann and van Buren are both sensitive to this problem, but their critics argue that it has not been overcome in their work. Alice and A. Roy Eckardt, for instance, detect requirements of special behavior from Jews in the work of both Moltmann and van Buren.[2] If van Buren's argument that Jews are not free to be other than God's elect people is construed as a Christian requirement placed on Jews, such a "requirement" must be distinguished from the kind found in the work of Barth and others. Still, as we suggested in the last chapter, it is arguable that even in van Buren's work we find remnants of a powerful Christian ideology which "fabricates abnormal obligations for Jews."[3] The Eckardts' charge represents the warnings of Holocaust theologians who believe Christians no longer possess the right to place demands of any kind on Jews. According to this perspective, Christians should allow Jews to be ordinary, secular human beings, and nothing else: "as long as the Christian community tries to make Israel something special, to trumpet forth that Israel has obligations greater than or different from those of other human beings, the burden of the Christian past will not be lifted."[4] Can or should post-Holocaust Christian theology avoid making "something special" of the Jews? This question, which faces all Christian attempts to speak of Israel, leads us to a consideration of the Christian doctrine of election and its function in the theologies we have examined.

7. Both Barth and van Buren begin their theologies of Israel with a consideration of God's election of Israel. In doing so, neither is imposing Christian categories on the Jewish people. Rather, both are attempting to remain faithful to the biblical witness and Jewish self-understanding. Since van Buren, unlike Barth, is keenly aware of the murderous implications of traditional Christian views of the Jewish people, he is determined to do all in his power to develop and communicate a Christian understanding of Israel that will reverse this tradition forever. Can it be, however, that van Buren's starting point in Israel's special election entails certain pitfalls which remain hidden? In attempting to answer this question, our response should be guided by two considerations.

First, the focus on Israel's election as God's "chosen people" found in the theologies we have considered must be placed in perspective. An emphasis on the original, continuing, and unconditional election of the Jewish people has been a common characteristic of nearly every post-Holocaust Christian statement concerning Israel. In post-Holocaust Christian theology, Israel's election has been elevated as a powerful symbol of the Jewish people's intimacy with God, and as proof of the continuing efficacy of their covenant. To give but one example, Bertold Klappert's *Israel und die Kirche* distinguishes positive from negative models for understanding the church's relationship to Israel precisely on the basis of their attitude toward Israel's continuing covenant and unconditional election. So the stress on the election of Israel found in the theologies we have considered, and especially prominent in the work of Barth and van Buren, is neither original nor unusual in the context of post-Holocaust theological revision.

Second, we should recall our analysis of Barth's Israel-doctrine. In chapter two we argued that Barth's attention to Israel's election in *Church Dogmatics* II:2 did not overcome his rather negative apprehension of Jewish existence and his fatalistic approach to anti-Semitism in *CD* III:3. In view of this unfortunate fact, we suggested that Barth's option for a theological rather than an ethical solution to the "Jewish problem" was unsatisfactory. Barth's "mythical" analysis of Jewish existence in III:3, we concluded, might actually perpetuate anti-Semitism since it is based on the notion that persecution by non-Jews is the fate of the Jewish people in salvation history. On the basis of these considerations, we suggested that an ethical-humanitarian emphasis might be required to supplement Christian approaches to the "Jewish problem" which focus on the providential persistence of the Jewish people in history.[5]

Having made these observations, we may return to a consideration of the difficulties faced by a post-Holocaust theology of Israel which makes the election of the Jewish people its starting point. Richard Rubenstein was one of the first to claim a connection between the Christian conviction that the Jews are God's chosen people and Christian acquiescence in the persecution and slaughter of Jews by the Nazis in the 1930s and 40s.[6] In *After Auschwitz*, Rubenstein observed that even in the 1960s many German Christians persisted in two interrelated beliefs: that "nowhere in the world were the fruits of God's activity in history more evident than in the life and the destiny of the Jewish people," and that the *Heilsgeschicte* of the Jewish people had continued to unfold in the Nazi era.[7] Rubenstein's critical gaze was focused on Dean Grüber, the Christian survivor of the Nazi era whose views on the Jews' fate prompt some of Rubenstein's radical conclusions in *After Auschwitz*. What is fascinating about the person of Grüber is the way in which the conviction that "for some reason, it was part of God's plan that the Jews died [in the Holocaust]"[8] exists in a man who demonstrated exemplary opposition to the mistreatment of Jews in Nazi Germany. Rubenstein discovered that most German Christians who had opposed the anti-Jewish policies of the Third Reich finally eventually jettisoned their theological conviction that God's providence was particularly evident in the history of the Jews, and concluded that God did not will the Holocaust.[9] But for "the Dean," Hitler remained a "rod of God's anger," just as Nebuchadrezzar had been in biblical times.

Rubenstein was led by his interaction with German Christians in the early 60s to ask whether "there is something in the logic of Christian theology, *when pushed to a metaphysical extreme*, which ends with the justification of, if not the incitement to, the murder of Jews."[10] Evidence of Christian complicity in and indifference toward Hitler's scheme to rid the world of Jews seems to answer this question in the affirmative. In the person of Dean Grüber, Rubenstein believes he has met face to face the theological result of a "German mentality which demands utter metaphysical consistency" combined with the extraordinary historical circumstances of the Nazi era. Rubenstein

extrapolates to Christian belief in general in words which bring to mind
the critique of Christian Holocaust theologians like the Eckardts:

> it may be impossible for Christians to remain Christians without
> regarding Jews in mythic, magic and theological categories....The
> Christian Church must insist on the separate and special character of the
> Jewish people in order that its claims concerning the significance of
> Jesus may gain credence. As long as Jews are thought of as special and
> apart from mankind in general, they are going to be the object of both
> the abnormal demands and the decisive hatreds of which the Dean
> spoke."[11]

Rubenstein's story of "the Dean," and the disturbing conclusions he
draws from it are important to recall at this point in our study because
they demonstrate that it is not only Christian anti-Judaism of which
post-Holocaust theology must beware. If indeed there is "something in
the logic of Christian theology itself," in its tendency to view Jews in
"mythic" categories (to use Rubenstein's phrases), which is a threat to
Jewish existence, then Christian theology is an activity which is to be
exercised with caution.

Rubenstein's reaction to the murderous tendencies he perceives in
Christian theology is expressed as a question aimed at Jews: "Can we
really blame the Christian community for viewing us through the prism
of a mythology of history when we were the first to assert this history
ourselves?" Does the way in which Jews regard themselves, Rubenstein
is asking, contribute to the capacity of Christians to theologically justify
the persecution and murder of Jews? Rubenstein asks Jews to consider
discarding the long-standing doctrine of Jewish election as a way of
bringing to an end this dangerous cycle. The matter which concerns us
here, of course, is the implications of Rubenstein's' arguments for post-
Holocaust *Christian* theology.

Some Christian theologians have followed Rubenstein's lead in
suggesting that the church adopt a "secular" approach to Israel.[12] Such a
secular theology of Israel, it is argued, would avoid placing demands on
the Jewish people, viewing them as normal, ordinary persons, entitled
to the same rights and subject to the same expectations as all other
persons. Not surprisingly, this secular approach has also included calls
for a "revolution in the doctrine of election."[13] The Eckardts have
suggested, in fact, that the doctrine of election be radically humanized

to ensure that "chosenness" becomes election to life rather than destruction, with Jews able to experience an "unqualifiedly normal reality."[14]

Ironically, is has become clear in our study that an "unqualifiedly normal reality" is not something Barth, Moltmann and van Buren believe can ever be experienced by the Jewish people. Each views the Jews as God's unique people, a people whom have been chosen for and called to a special task in the world. While Barth is the only one of these theologians who clearly perceives God's hand in the "judgment" of the Jewish people, Barth, Moltmann and van Buren all understand God's providential care to be evident in the history of Israel as nowhere else. Furthermore, van Buren is adamant in stressing that divine election, and nothing else, makes the Jewish people unique in the world and important for the church. He explicitly rejects a "secular" approach to the state of Israel, arguing that without election Israel can only become one nation among others--an unacceptable situation.

The questions to which this extended discussion brings us are these: is there inherent in this emphasis on the uniqueness of Israel, a uniqueness founded in its divine election, the ripple which may at some time in the future become a new wave of Christian anti-Jewishness? Does the Christian affirmation of the election of Israel constitute a "mythical" way of understanding Jews which, when incorporated into Christian theology, makes the Jewish people subject to the special demands and easy denunciations of the church? Does the belief in Israel's election imply expectations that ultimately may be transformed into justifications for Jew-hatred when Christians perceive that Jews do not live up to the requirements of their election? While it is not clear that an insistence on the centrality of Jewish election *must* lead to anti-Jewish sentiment, post-Holocaust Christian theology must reflect carefully on the possible risks of proceeding in this direction. The evidence we have considered suggests it is possible that, in its decision to base post-Holocaust Christian theological reflection on Israel's unconditional election, the church may actually be setting the stage for future outbreaks of anti-Judaism.

If we admit the possibility of this ironic situation in which the plight of the Jewish people in contemporary history can be interpreted as divine punishment for its failure to live up the obligations connected with its special election, we are confronted by a new set of questions.

How, for example, can a Christian theology of Israel avoid emphasizing the divine election of the Jewish people, while continuing to affirm its own intimate relation with the God of Israel whom it believes has elected it? As Barth and van Buren in particular try to make clear, Israel's election serves as the theological basis for the church's recognition that it has been elected by God. Even if the majority of Jews were to accept Rubenstein's call for a rejection of the "mythology of history" he perceives in traditional talk of Israel's election,[15] could the church adopt a secular theology of the Jewish people and have any basis for speaking of its own unique relationship with God? The theologians we have studied think not.

8. "Appendicism" (the view that Christianity is essentially an appendix to Judaism, or "Judaism for Gentiles"), while intended to establish the intimate connection between Judaism and Christianity, can actually become a barrier to Christian reflection on the meaning of Israel. This is because here it is possible and even tempting to establish and elaborate the common origins and common hope of Jews and Christians in a way that blurs the important distinctions between the two religions and threatens to undermine the identity of each group.

9. In addition to the problems outlined above, there are Jewish objections to Christian talk about Israel that must receive a serious hearing by post-Holocaust Christian theology. First, there is the common belief that while Christianity may need Judaism, Judaism does not need Christianity. Jews who express this sentiment sometimes tell Christians that the greatest service they can render the Jewish people is to leave them alone. Although the Christian theologians we have considered stress that church and Israel, Christians and Jews, *need each other,* post-Holocaust Christian theology will continue to encounter resistance from Jews suspicious of Christians who are not content to respect them from a distance. Second, some Jews complain that Christians are unable to understand them and refuse to let them define themselves. As we have mentioned, inattention to Jewish self-definition has been a perennial problem in the church and among Christian theologians. But this is not a problem unique to Christian understandings of Judaism,[16] and it is one which post-Holocaust Christian theology has made strides toward overcoming. Third, many Jews are wary of the threat to their identity they perceive in the inevitable subsumption of Israel into a Christian theological system,

"post-Holocaust" or otherwise. This view is common among Jews who doubt whether there can be any Christian theology which does not result in a triumphalist orientation toward Judaism.[17]

II. TOPICS FOR POST-HOLOCAUST CHRISTIAN THEOLOGY IN THE 1990S

At this point we shall try to outline the major issues with which post-Holocaust Christian theologies of Israel must grapple in the last decade of the twentieth century. These issues have been illuminated by our analysis of the theologies of Barth, Moltmann and van Buren, but remain as focal points for future post-Holocaust Christian theological reflection.

Covenant. What is the correct (biblical?) notion of covenant? Is there one covenant, or more than one? Is/are the covenant(s) conditional or unconditional, particular or universal? Overall, there is still much disagreement in contemporary Christian theology about the number and nature of the covenant(s), a fact which mitigates the influence of the positive apprehensions of Israel in the work of theologians like Moltmann and van Buren.

Jewish Monotheism vs. Christian Trinitarianism. The relationship between Jewish and Christian apprehensions of God is given serious attention in the work of Moltmann and van Buren, but careful theological reflection is still required in this area. Future work must insure that neither false oppositions nor easy parallels obscure a real dialogue on this important issue, and that Christian and Jewish believers can recognize what theologians are saying about the way they view God.

Messianism. The "messianism" is actually two related issues. The first issue is whether it is necessary or useful to refer to Jesus as the Messiah of Israel. As we have seen, van Buren answers this question differently than Barth and Moltmann, but his answer brings to light another question: "is the identity of Jesus as Israel's Messiah an essential part of Christian faith?" The second issue is how far the church can and should go in affirming an unfulfilled messianism in response to the

Jewish insight that the redemption of the world has not yet taken place. Should the church emphasize the distinction between redemption and reconciliation, should it stress that creation's redemption has been inaugurated in Jesus Christ but not completed, or should it follow some other path?

The church-Israel relationship. Here there are two important questions: first, what is the nature of this relationship and, second, how is it best expressed? As our analysis of the theologies of Barth, Moltmann and van Buren has shown, there is disagreement among Christian theologians on the very nature of the theological relationship between church and Israel. This problem is compounded by the fact that theologians who have similar views of this relationship often use different terms to describe it. This became clear in chapter one, where we outlined a number of competing typologies for expressing the relationship between church and Israel. While universal agreement on the nature of and proper means for expressing the church-Israel relationship is not likely, work in this area can continue to be helpful in identifying and describing Christian understandings of Israel and in pointing out the theological and practical implications of these understandings.

The theological significance of the Holocaust. Of the theologians whose work we have analyzed, only van Buren places this issue at the center of his work.[18] Van Buren argues that the Holocaust may qualify as revelation, not because it is inherently unique among events on the plane of history, but because as a part of Jewish history it has led to a reinterpretation of tradition, as well as to the reorientation of those persons who have tried to comprehend it. Of course, the question of the importance of the Holocaust for post-Holocaust Christian theology is made more difficult by the fact that there is serious disagreement among Jewish thinkers about the significance of the Holocaust for theology and faith.[19]

The status of Christian anti-Judaism. It remains to be seen whether the close bond and unique relationship between Israel and the church which post-Holocaust Christian theology has emphasized are enough to insure that Christian anti-Judaism will not rear its ugly head in the future; whether, that is, the relationship between Christians and Jews which has been forged in many places since the Holocaust is irreversible. If Christian theologians are concerned that a theological expression of the special bond between Jews and Christians is not a sufficient safeguard against anti-Judaism, how should they proceed? Can they simply emphasize the ethical duty which Christians have toward all peoples, or should they respond to calls for the secularization of theology by abandoning all "mythical" categories for viewing the Jewish people, including the category of election?

The place of Scriptural and theological traditions in the church's revision of its understanding of Israel. Should Scripture and the theological tradition continue to function as primary sources for Christian theology after Auschwitz? Each of the theologians whose work we have examined has answered this question differently. And yet each takes a position toward the church's theological and Scriptural traditions which is conservative, at least in relation to earlier forms of post-Holocaust theological reflection, referred to throughout this essay as Holocaust Theology. In chapter one we discussed the "return to Scripture" as an important resource for bolstering the theological basis for Christian-Jewish relations. We also noted, however, that the return to the Bible as a source for theological revision, the kind of return we see in the work of Krister Stendahl and Paul van Buren, for example, often assumes a reliance on and confidence in an historical-critical method whose usefulness has been challenged in contemporary biblical studies. The methodological question concerning how Scripture is to be used and interpreted in the service of post-Holocaust theology is an important one, but one to which many theologians (including those we have studied) are offering an implicit answer: despite the clearly anti-Jewish uses to which Scripture has been put through the centuries, it remains an irreplaceable part of the Christian tradition and should be utilized wherever it sheds light on the church's relationship to Israel.

A related issue which deserves closer attention is the extent to which the Apostolic Writings, and particularly the letters of Paul, should serve as primary sources for reconciling the church-Israel relationship. We see the importance of this concern in the fact that nearly every post-Holocaust church statement on Israel stresses Romans 9-11 as the basis for a proper Christian understanding of Israel.

Furthermore, each of the theologians we have considered in this study has looked to Romans 9-11 and other biblical passages to receive guidance for contemporary theological reflection. At the same time, however, some Christian scholars argue that the writings of the New Testament, whose effective history has been so devastatingly anti-Jewish, should not be the starting point for a Christian reconsideration of Israel. Perhaps there is a real danger that the quest to "recover the real Paul" and utilize the apostle as the original advocate of a positive Christian approach to the problem of Jewish unbelief may, ironically, obscure truly anti-Jewish elements in the New Testament. In any case, inattention to elements in the New Testament that may be incorrigibly anti-Jewish is not in the interest of insuring positive Christian attitudes toward Judaism.

The issue of the reliance of post-Holocaust Christian theology on the broader theological tradition also has tended to be addressed implicitly. In the work of Paul van Buren, and especially that of Jürgen Moltmann, we encounter attempts to recover moments when the Christian tradition saw more clearly the special relationship between the church and Israel, and the unique and irrevocable nature of Israel's covenant with God. And yet, as these thinkers' ambivalent relationship to Barth's theology of Israel shows, neither Moltmann nor van Buren is comfortable with the supersessionism in the theology of even their finest teachers. More careful study will be necessary to establish precisely which pre-Holocaust aspects of the church's theology of Israel can be successfully rehabilitated in the post-Holocaust environment.

Jewish desires to be left alone. A further topic for reflection is how seriously post-Holocaust Christian theology shall take Jewish voices which insist that Christians simply leave Jews alone? And, how seriously shall it take the voices of Christians like Roy Eckardt who insist that the church must allow Israel to become "secularized," and become a "normal" people like any other people in the world?

Christian Zionism. What is the relationship between post-Holocaust Christian theology and Zionism? Moltmann, van Buren, and most other Christian theologians concerned with the meaning of Israel agree that the church's talk of "Israel" cannot be limited to biblical Israel, but must include contemporary Jews and the state of Israel as well. But how are Christians to arbitrate the claims arising from different sides that Zionism is a form of racism and a nationalist ideology which spawns oppression, or that Zionism is the obligatory stance of Christians toward the Jewish people and toward the state of Israel?

The first step toward addressing this issue, of course, is a description of the nature of Zionism itself. Many use the term to describe the overall movement for the reformation and reaffirmation of Jewish life and Jewish personhood in the modern era. For these persons, a Zionist outlook is incumbent upon Christians who wish to establish positive relations with Jews in the post-Holocaust environment. Many other Jews and non-Jews view Zionism primarily as a movement for the political empowerment of the Jews in the land of Palestine, and thus view it as one nationalist ideology among others. Still others perceive Zionism as an expansionist movement that is a direct threat to the existence of Arabs in the occupied areas of Palestine. In Christian circles, each of these connotations, and others as well, is attached to the term "Zionism." The term "Christian Zionism"[20] is generally reserved for referring to a form of non-Jewish Zionism popular among conservative Christians who believe the land and people of Israel are to play a key role in the events associated with the return of Christ. Christian Zionism, then, places primary stress on the land of Israel and its theological and geopolitical significance, rather than on the duty of Christians to affirm and protect the Jewish people. Many have recognized an element of selfishness in such Christian Zionism, as well as an uncritical willingness to lend political support to the state of Israel and its policies.

This form of Christian Zionism has led many Christians on the left to eschew Zionist attitudes altogether. Many of these persons adopt a "liberal-universalist"[21] attitude to Zionism, an Enlightenment-inspired opposition to what they perceive as one more nationalist ideology. These Christians often set against Christian support for Zionist aims the universalist strands of biblical faith, and in particular the calls of the prophets for peace and justice. The liberal critique of Zionism is given momentum by reports of Israel's ill-treatment of Palestinians, and of its frustrating reluctance to negotiate peace with its Arab neighbors. Some Christians on the left take an avowedly anti-Zionist approach, while others, though not comfortable with Zionist aims, do not perceive themselves as anti-Zionist. In either case it is not unusual for such Christians to be suspected of harboring anti-Semitism.[22] In fact, it is assumed by many Jews and some Christians that anti-Zionism (or even non-Zionism) is only a more socially acceptable manifestation of anti-Semitism.

If post-Holocaust Christian theology should reach a consensus on what the term "Zionism" means when applied to Christian attitudes toward Jews, then the question becomes the *appropriateness* of Zionism; that is, whether Zionism is the proper Christian attitude toward the state of Israel and/or the Jewish people. Many in the church, often influenced by Palestinian Christians and their supporters, have argued that Zionism is an inappropriate Christian attitude, since it is destined to be in conflict with the biblical mandates for peace and justice which extend to all people. This perception of Zionism makes it difficult for many Christians to embrace it, even when they desire to affirm Jewish identity and personhood. Christian theologians who wish to establish positive relations with the Jewish people, but who desire to keep in view a Palestinian perspective on conflicts in the Middle East, may, tragically, find themselves cut off from dialogue with many Jews.[23] But even if Zionism is determined by theologians to be a necessary precondition for establishing positive Jewish-Christian relations, another problem presents itself. Many Christians are rightly suspicious of arguments that there is one "Christian" stance on any social or political issue. Especially in Protestant circles, Christians continue to fight to preserve the right of the individual conscience to oppose what an official body of the church might prescribe. Insofar as Christian Zionism seems to imply political support for a particular state, attempts to make such a position normative for Protestant Christians will certainly encounter opposition. In fact, a truly "Protestant" view of the matter would seem to demand that each Christian be permitted to decide, based on his or her own perceptions of the Middle Eastern political situation, whether Christian Zionism is an appropriate Christian response to the perceived need to support and affirm solidarity with Jews.[24]

A further question related to the issue of Zionism's relationship to post-Holocaust Christian theology is the *adequacy* of Zionism; that is, whether Christian Zionism is actually effective in perpetuating positive Christian attitudes toward the Jewish people. At the end of our discussion of Karl Barth in the last chapter, we asked whether Zionism qualifies as an adequate Christian response to the Holocaust. At this point, we must put the question even more forcefully: Is it possible that Christian Zionism is actually a way for Christians to put Jews and the "Jewish problem" at arm's length without really coming to terms with their historic guilt *vis-'a-vis* the Jewish people? And does Christian Zionism, even when it represents genuine support for the empowerment of Jews living in Israel and a desire that Jewish existence be liberated from dependence on charity,[25] fulfill the responsibility Christians have toward their Jewish brothers and sisters? Some scholars have argued that a collective feeling of guilt for the Holocaust, while a hopeful sign of changing attitudes, is no guarantee of improving Jewish-Christian relations.[26] Is it certain that a Christian Zionist perspective, were it adopted by post-Holocaust Christianity as a whole, would guarantee positive Christian attitudes toward the Jewish people? Do improved Jewish-Christian relations require positive Christian attitudes toward Jews, or merely a commitment to Jewish survival? These are some of the questions that will confront those who seek in the future to inform Christian attitudes toward Israel and the Jewish people.

Whose "Israel"? This issue, which is perhaps the most basic with which post-Holocaust Christian theology will have to deal, can be expressed simply: whose definition of Israel will determine the starting point for Christian reflection upon the church-Israel relationship? This question is tied up with several others: What is the relationship between biblical and post-biblical Israel? Does the term "Israel" include all Jews, or only those faithful to Torah or who otherwise "live up" to their Jewishness in some way? And what is the relationship between the people "Israel" and the Middle Eastern state of the same name? In order to answer this final question the church will have to arbitrate between many voices, including those of Zionist Christians like Paul van Buren and those of non-Zionist Jews like Marc Ellis who are critical of the political empowerment which the state of Israel represents.[27]

Secular vs. theological conceptions of Israel. We have been concerned in this essay with the work of systematic theologians. The question we have not entertained is whether this is the best place to seek resources for improving Jewish-Christian relations. There may be good reasons for moving outside the confines of theology and working toward a secular understanding of the Jewish people, one which is aimed at insuring Jewish existence in a world that remains hostile to Jews. Post-Holocaust Christian theology will continue to face the objection that the theological enterprise be abandoned since the Christian theological tradition has been implicated so deeply in the perpetuation of the kind of anti-Judaism which led to the Holocaust. In Moltmann and van Buren, we have theologians who transmit Holocaust theology's critique of the theological enterprise, and yet who move beyond Holocaust theology by attempting to purify and rehabilitate aspects of the theological tradition. To put it another way, these theologians have taken to heart--in both its parts--Emil Fackenheim's observation that "Christianity is ruptured by the Holocaust and stands in need of a *Tikkun*" (mending).[28] No Christian *Tikkun* is possible unless the rupture is recognized,[29] but this rupture cannot be comprehended fully by Christianity until attempts are made to mend it. Repentance of the supersessionism and anti-Judaism which led to this *Tikkun* is, at least in part, a theological task--a task which requires constructive as well as critical reflection.

It may ultimately become clear that the "theological trust"[30]--the tradition which links the contemporary theologian to the saints and scholars of past centuries--is indeed ruptured. Then non-theological or "secular" talk of Israel will be all that is left to the church. But until the rupture is revealed *theologically,* theology cannot be abandoned. Rather, the "trust" must be reconstructed through a "destructive recovery"[31] of the Christian tradition, the kind of destructive recovery we have encountered in the work of Moltmann and van Buren. In the meantime, theology may be forced to exist on a "wilderness ration,"[32] but exist it must. For only when *theologians* can bravely say "I" in the face of Auschwitz will *Christians* be permitted again to say "we" in good faith.[33]

III. CONCLUSIONS

In the preceding chapters we have analyzed some prospects for post-Holocaust theology in work already done, and in the preceding section we have outlined some issues which remain. Finally, we offer a few observations which might serve as guidelines for work yet to be done.

1. In the past, theology could be "wrong about the Jews" (to use van Buren's phrase) and still be "good theology." This is no longer possible for post-Holocaust theology. For the Holocaust itself teaches us that theology which is wrong about the Jews may lead to evils so great that they overwhelm any other advantages of such a theology and render it nearly useless. For this reason, the effective history of texts (both biblical and theological) becomes as crucial to their understanding and their classification as their authorial intent or their official interpretation.

2. The problems and issues we have outlined in the preceding two sections should not lead the church to silence with regard to Israel. Karl Barth once expressed the paradoxical situation of the theologian in this way: "as theologians we ought to speak of God. We are human, however, and so cannot speak of God."[34] We might well adapt his words to describe the situation of the Christian theologian after the Holocaust: as a theologian one ought to speak of Israel; as a Christian, however, one cannot speak of Israel. This version of the statement would appear to capture the dilemma of the post-Holocaust Christian theologian. This person is simultaneously aware of the duty and the problems associated with Christian reflection on Israel. Taking both aspects of this paradoxical situation to heart should not lead to silence, however, but to fresh ways of speaking which take the past and the future with equal seriousness.

3. Post-Holocaust Christian theology must not ignore the Jewish people as they exist in contemporary society. This focus on the Jewish people can be lost either in an emphasis on biblical Israel, or on a preoccupation with Jews who were lost in the Holocaust. It is true that it is only possible to go beyond Auschwitz with its victims in mind.[35] But since all Jews (and indirectly, all non-Jews) are "victims" of Auschwitz in one sense or another, the church would do well to adopt Paul van Buren's maxim that live, not dead, Jews should serve as the focus for its theological inquiries.

4. The Protestant churches need to insure perpetual recognition of two important facts. First: some Christian theologians, clergy and lay persons resisted Hitler and his anti-Jewish policies. The stories of these persons should be recounted in the community of faith, and the theological rationale for their stances of opposition studied and critiqued. Second: in most cases the resistance offered by these

theologians and other Christians was insufficient and ineffective in deterring the Nazis' slaughter of the Jews. The first of these recognitions has led many Protestant churches to celebrate the "Barmen Declaration" of 1934. The second recognition should result in the churches taking more seriously the "Stuttgart Declaration" of 1945, where leaders of the German Church confessed that, "unending suffering has been brought by us to many peoples and countries...we accuse ourselves that we did not witness more courageously, pray more faithfully, believe more joyously, love more ardently."[36]

5. Post-Holocaust Christian theology must not sacrifice either its identity (and thus, its connection with the Christian tradition) or its relevance (and thus, its ability to hear and speak to Jews). All theology which is to remain relevant after the Holocaust must either be post-Holocaust theology, or theology which is subjected to a thorough post-Holocaust critique. If it is to be theology for the church, however, it must retain its distinctive Christian identity, no matter how radically it reinterprets the church's traditions. What aspects of the church's theology are absolutely necessary to this identity is unclear, but they certainly include the life, death and resurrection of Jesus Christ as attested in Scripture.

6. The Protestant churches must encourage significant contacts with Judaism and Jews if theological visions of complementary existence are to become reality. The church must also envision new ways of overcoming the actual separation between Christians and Jews, which remains nearly as common in institutions of theological study as in places of worship and society in general.

7. A single "Christian" understanding of the significance of the Holocaust and the founding of the state of Israel is probably not possible or desirable as long as there is so much disagreement among Jews. Post-Holocaust Christian theology, however, cannot afford to ignore these matters, and must arrive at some guidelines for Christian thinking about them. In each case, Christian opinion is broad: the Holocaust is seen as "revelation" on one hand, and as one more example of humanity's inhumanity on the other. The state of Israel is perceived as a "sign,"[37] as a realization of God's Kingdom within history, or as another secular state. While arrival at a single "Christian" view of either the Holocaust or the state of Israel is not likely, post-Holocaust theology must

continue to pursue theological clarity in its understanding of these elements of what Paul van Buren calls "Jewish history."

8. Despite the difficulties outlined earlier concerning the doctrine of election and Christian-Jewish relations, post-Holocaust theology, especially in the Reformed tradition, must not abandon the notion of Israel's divine election, since it is the theological foundation of the church's calling and existence. The task of establishing Israel's unconditional election without adopting an understanding of Jewish existence which is open to "mythological" interpretation in the Christian imagination is still before Christian post-Holocaust theology, however.

9. Post-Holocaust Christian theology must find its way and establish its position between the Christian Zionism popular among premillennialists, biblical literalists and some Holocaust theologians and the forms of hostile anti-Zionism which can often influence the churches.[38] In doing so, any "Christian philosemitism" or "Christian Zionism" which it adopts must be motivated by a positive response to the church's awakening perception of its unique relationship with Israel, by the church's coming to terms with its history *vis-'a-vis* the Jewish people, and by the church's responsibility for encouraging peace and righteousness among all parties in the Middle East.

Many Jews and Christians doubt that Christian theology has come far enough to provide a basis for genuine dialogue and mutual acceptance between "average" Christians and Jews. Jürgen Moltmann and Paul van Buren would no doubt agree with such a verdict. Our analysis of Barth, Moltmann and van Buren has allowed us to observe the extent to which theologians living in the post-war era have advanced in affirming "Israel" in its many dimensions, and in overcoming traditional forms of anti-Judaism. Although it appears that the weaknesses to which Barth was blind in his own work are in the process of being corrected by followers of the second generation, much is left to be done. We have argued in this essay that the work of Moltmann and van Buren contains a variety of prospects for post-Holocaust theology, not that the church has succeeded in creating such a theology, and certainly not that all or even most Christians perceive the need for it. If such prospects for post-Holocaust theology are to become an effective part of the history of the church-Israel relationship which has been so poisoned in the past, courage and imagination will be required in the future, as well as the grace of the God whom Jews and Christians serve.

Notes

1. *Justice, and Only Justice: A Palestinian Theology of Liberation* (Maryknoll, NY: Orbis, 1989). See especially 63-65, where Ateek is critical of the disregard for injustice and oppression he perceives in van Buren's work.

2. See Eckardt, *Long Night's Journey Into Day,* 87ff. (on Moltmann), and 121 (on van Buren's *The Burden of Freedom).*

3. Ibid., 121. Ruether and Ruether make a similar claim in *The Wrath of Jonah,* where they argue that van Buren refuses to allow Jews to be ordinary human beings (215).

4. Ibid., 106.

5. This realization that the doctrine of Israel's election carries potential dangers was arrived at in dialogue with Richard Rubenstein's observations in *After Auschwitz.* Rubenstein argued there that a Christian understanding of the Jews which combines a belief in Israel's election with the conviction that God punishes the disobedience of Jews in history leads inexorably to the conclusion that God willed the Holocaust.

6. Ibid., chapter two, "The Dean and the Chosen People."

7. Ibid., 52.

8. Ibid., 54.

9. Rubenstein cites one German Christian he interviewed as saying "theologically this [God willing the Holocaust] may be true, but humanly speaking and in any terms that I can understand, I cannot believe that God wanted the Nazis to destroy the Jews" (53).

10. Ibid., 48, emphasis in the text.

11. Ibid., 56.

12. In applying Rubenstein's approach to a critique of left- and right-wing Christian approaches to Israel, A. Roy Eckardt ["Toward a Secular Theology of Israel," *Religion in Life* 48:4 (Winter, 1979), 462-73] has insisted that Christian attempts to view in history God's mercy toward or God's judgment on the Jewish people lead to an atmosphere in which "Israel's physical destruction tomorrow would have to be treated as a sign of God's returning wrath" (466). Therefore, Eckardt argues, the legitimation of the State of Israel should be based on the historic rights of the Jewish people within Palestine. This does not mean that the church ignores the

special divine relationship with Israel, but that it eschews both "liberal" universalism and Christian Zionism and respects the mutual autonomy of the religious and political realms.

13. Eckardts, *Long Night's Journey Into Day,* 123. Rosemary R. Ruether argues that "Christians cannot accept a monopolar doctrine of the election of Israel as God's one exemplary people," and that the claim of special election needs to be "contextualized, rather than absolutized" ("Speaking of Israel II, 343).

14. Eckardts, *Long Night's Journey Into Day,* 123.

15. Such a Jewish forsaking of the concept of election appears no more likely now than when Rubenstein wrote in the 1960s. The images associated with the corporate election of the Jewish people are very much alive in recent Jewish literature. See, e. g., Michael Wyschogrod, *The Body of Faith: Judaism as Corporeal Election* (Minneapolis: Seabury, 1983).

16. For an example of distortion on the part of a Jewish commentator on Christian theology, see David Novak, "A Jewish Response to a New Christian Theology," where the author claims that "there are, no doubt, Christian theologians who see the Holocaust as a confirmation of Christian triumphalism, namely, once again the Jews have been punished for their rejection of the Christhood of Jesus of Nazareth" (113). This is a serious claim, and if by "theologians," Novak means serious interpreters of Christian faith, it appears to be a misrepresentation.

17. See, e. g., Jacob Neusner, "The Absoluteness of Christianity and the Uniqueness of Judaism: Why Salvation is Not of the Jews," *Interpretation* 49: 3 (1988), 18-31.

18. Barth, of course, did not consider the nature of the Holocaust *per se* in his work at all. But given Barth's attitude toward the work of Tillich and other thinkers who wished to use the term "revelation" to refer to extra-biblical events (see, e.g., *Church Dogmatics* I:1), it is probably safe to assume that Barth would not have been able to see revelation in the Holocaust, no matter how long he had lived.

19. See especially, Steven T. Katz, *Post-Holocaust Dialogues: Critical Studies in Modern Jewish Thought* (New York: New York University Press, 1985); and Alan L. Berger, "Holocaust and History: A Theological Reflection," *Journal of Ecumenical Studies* 25:2 (Spring, 1988), 194-224. See also "The Jews in Britian," *The Sunday Times Magazine,* April 16, 1989, 66-74.

20. A. Roy Eckardt distinguishes two types of Christian Zionism found among "evangelical" Christians, one political (in which "God's will is insinuated unqualifiedly into the political process"), the other christological (in which "the return of the Jews to their land is construed instrumentally, in accordance with certain alleged timetables of heaven"). See "Toward a Secular Theology of Israel," 465.

21. Ibid., 462-3. Eckardt refers to this position as "liberal"-universalism to distinguish it from what he views as more genuine forms of liberalism.

22. The judgment that "anti-Zionism" is only a more acceptable, or more subtle form of "anti-Semitism" is not universal among Zionists, whether Christian or Jewish, but it is often expressed. This view illuminates the fact that Zionism arose and is in some measure sustained as a direct response to the persistence of anti-Semitism in the West. When this connection leads to the "anti-Zionism=anti-Semitism" equation, however, problems arise. First, the label "anti-Zionist" is often applied to anyone not explicitly supportive of Israel and its policies; and second, even in the case where one is explicitly "anti-Zionist," it is unclear that there is any necessary connection between opposition to Israel and its policies and hostility toward Jews as such.

This does not mean that anti-Zionism is never anti-Semitic [see, e.g., Bernard Lewis, *Semites and Anti-Semites* (New York: Norton and Co., 1986)], but that the two are not synonymous. Statements like "the United Nations has become a center of antisemitism under the cloak of anti-Zionism and anti-Israelism" (Eckardts, *Long Night's Journey*, 50) must be examined more critically than is often the case.

23. A Christian theologian who has found himself in just this situation is Markus Barth. In an interview, Barth recalled that the Jewish community in the United States was very receptive to his early attempts at interpreting "Israel" for the church. After the appearance of an essay entitled "Israel and the Palestinians," however, Barth's dialogue with American Jews came to an abrupt end. ["Israel and the Palestinians"--originally a lecture delivered in 1974--was published in *Jesus the Jew* (Atlanta: John Knox Press, 1978), 41-95]. Marc Ellis has referred to this Christian dilemma in terms of an "ecumenical deal." See "The Ecumenical Deal and the Bishops' Middle East Statement," *Ecumenical Trends* 19:3 (March, 1990), 33-36.

24. It may be possible to argue, on grounds more amenable to Protestant Christianity, that Christians should be "philosemitic," rather than Zionist. Philosemitism is a troublesome, term, however, since it carries racial overtones which Jews and Christians alike have tried to deny are part of a Zionist outlook.

25. Liberation of Jewish existence from dependence on charity is the rationale given by Emil Fackenheim for Christian Zionism. Zionism, which Fackenheim defines as "the commitment to the safety and genuine sovereignty of the State of Israel," is not negotiable: "Without Zionism--Christian as well as Jewish--the Holy Spirit cannot dwell between Jews and Christians in dialogue" (*To Mend the World*, 284-5).

26. See, e.g., the statement of Krister Stendahl, quoted in Ateek, *Justice, and Only Justice,* 66.

27. See Marc H. Ellis, *Toward A Jewish Theology of Liberation* (Maryknoll, NY: Orbis, 1987).

28. *To Mend the World,* 278ff.

29. Ibid., 280.

30. Ibid., 284.

31. Ibid., 283. Fackenheim borrows this term from Martin Heidegger.

32. See Clark M. Williamson, *Has God Rejected His People?*, 159ff.

33. Metz, "Facing the Jews: Christian Theology After Auschwitz," in *The Holocaust as Interruption*, 27.

34. The quote is from "The Word of God and the Task of Ministry" (1922), in Eberhard Jüngel, *Karl Barth: A Theological Legacy*, 69.

35. See Johann B. Metz, "Christians and Jews After Auschwitz."

36. From "The Stuttgart Declaration," a document of the Evangelical Church in Germany (October 18-19, 1945), in Moltmann, "Forty Years After the Stuttgart Confession," 53. See Moltmann's article for references to other statements which confess the church's failure to effectively resist Nazism.

37. Christian theologians seem to have a penchant for describing the state of Israel as a "sign." This ambiguous terminology, found in Barth and in the Barthian Hendrikus Berkhof, really cuts in two directions. It can be used to argue for Israel's unique relation to God's Kingdom, or to remind us that "Israel" is a mirror of human selfishness and evil. See Berkhof, "Israel as a Theological Problem in the Christian Church"; and Wesley H. Brown, "Christian Understandings of Biblical Prophecy, Israel and the Land, and the Christian-Jewish Encounter," *Immanuel* 18 (Fall, 1984), 79-95. For a Christian argument that the land cannot be ignored in Christian-Jewish encounter, see Walter Brueggemann, *The Land: Place as Gift, Promise, and Challenge in Biblical Faith* (Philadelphia: Fortress, 1977).

38. For an example of how susceptible church bodies are to anti-Zionist influences, see Wesley Brown, "Christian Understandings of Biblical Prophecy...," 93-4.

WORKS CITED

Ateek, Naim S. *Justice and Only Justice: A Palestinian Theology of Liberation.* Maryknoll, NY: Orbis, 1989.

Attfield, D. G. "Can God Be Crucified? A Discussion with J. Moltmann." *Scottish Journal of Theology* 30:1 (1977): 47-57.

Augus, Jacob B. "The Covenant Concept: Particularistic, Pluralistic or Futuristic?"*Christian-Jewish Relations* 14:1 (March, 1982): 4-18.

Badenas, Robert. *Christ the End of the Law: Romans 10:4 in Pauline Perspective.* Journal for the Study of the New Testament Supplement Series, 10. Sheffield: JSOT Press, 1985.

Barth, Karl. *Ad Limina Apostolorum.* Translated by Keith R. Crim. Edinburgh: St. Andrews Press, 1969.

_____. "The Jewish Problem and the Christian Answer." In *Against the Stream: Shorter Post-War Writings, 1946-52.* Edited by Ronald Gregor Smith. London: SCM, 1954, 195-201.

_____. *Church Dogmatics.* Four Volumes. G. W. Bromiley and T. F. Torrance, eds. Edinburgh: T & T Clark, 1936-1969.

_____. *Community, State and Church.* Garden City, NY: Doubleday, 1960.

_____. *The Epistle to the Romans,* Sixth Edition. Translated by Edwyn C. Hoskyns. Oxford: Oxford University Press, 1968.

_____ and Eduard Thurneysen. *Revolutionary Theology in the Making: The Barth-Thurneysen Correspondence 1914-1925.* Translated by James D. Smart. Richmond: John Knox, 1964.

_____ and Jacob Petuchowski. "Fragen von Rabbi Petuchowski, Antworten von Karl Barth." *Criterion: A Publication of the Divinity School of the University of Chicago* 2:1 (1963): 18-24.

Barth, Markus. *The Broken Wall.* Chicago: The Judson Press, 1959.

_____. *Jesus the Jew.* Atlanta: John Knox Press, 1978.

_____. *The People of God.* Journal for the Study of the New Testament Supplement Series, 5. Sheffield: JSOT Press, 1983.

_____. Interview by Author. January 10, 1989, Riehen, Switzerland.

Bauckham, Richard J. "Bibliography: Jürgen Moltmann." *The Modern Churchman* 28:2 (1986): 55-60.

_____. *Moltmann: Messianic Theology in the Making.* Basingstoke: Marshall Pickering, 1987.

Baum, Gregory. *Theology After Auschwitz.* London: Council of Christians and Jews, 1976.

_____. Review of Paul van Buren's *Discerning the Way. Commonweal* (October 24, 1980): 598-601.

_____. *The Social Imperative: Essays on the Critical Issues That Confront the Christian Churches.* New York: Paulist, 1979.

Bea, Augustin. *The Church and the Jewish People.* London, 1966.

Beck, N. A. *Mature Christianity: The Recognition and Repudiation of the Anti-Jewish Polemic of the New Testament.* (Cranbury, NJ: Susquehanna University Press, 1986.

Berger, Alan L. "Holocaust and History: A Theological Reflection." *Journal of Ecumenical Studies* 25:2 (Spring, 1988): 194-224.

Berkhof, Hendrikus. *Christian Faith.* Translated by Sierd Woudstra. Grand Rapids: Eerdmans, 1979.

_____. "Israel as a Theological Problem." *Journal of Ecumenical Studies* 6:34 (Summer, 1969): 329-347.

Berkouwer, G. C. *The Triumph of Grace in Karl Barth's Doctrine of Election.* Grand Rapids: Eerdmans, 1956.

Berkovits, Eliezer. *Faith After the Holocaust.* New York: Ktav, 1973.

Bonhoeffer, Dietrich. "The Church and the Jewish Question." In *No Rusty Swords: Letters, Lectures and Notes, 1928-1936*. The *Collected Works of Dietrich Bonhoeffer*, Vol. 1. Edited by Edwin H. Robinson and John Bowden. New York: Harper and Row, 1965.

The Book of Confessions. Part One of The Constitution of the Presbyterian Church (U.S.A.). New York: Office of the General Assembly, 1983.

Borowitz, Eugene B. *Contemporary Christologies: A Jewish Response*. New York: Paulist, 1980.

Braaten, Carl. "A Trinitarian Theology of the Cross." *Journal of Religion* 56 (1976), 113-121.

Brockway, Allan R. "Implications of Interfaith Dialogue for Christian Theology." *International Review of Mission* 74 (October, 1985): 518-523.

Brown, Wesley H. "Christian Understandings of Biblical Prophecy, Israel and the Land, and the Christian-Jewish Encounter." *Immanuel* 18 (Fall, 1984): 49-95.

Brueggemann, Walter. *The Land: Place as Gift, Promise and Challenge in Biblical Faith*. Philadelphia: Fortress, 1977.

Bultmann, Rudolf. "The Task of Theology in the Present Situation." In *Existence and Faith*. Edited by Shubert M. Ogden. London: Hodder and Stoughton, 1961, 158-165.

Busch, Eberhard. *Glaubensheiterkeit Karl Barth: Erfahrungen und Begegnungen*. Vluyn: Neukirchner, 1986.

_____. *Karl Barth: His Life From Letters and Autobiographical Texts*. Philadelphia: Fortress, 1976.

Calvin, John. *Institutes of the Christian Religion*. Two Volumes. Library of Christian Classics, Volume XX. Edited by John T. McNeill. Translated by Ford Lewis Battles. London: SCM Press, 1960.

Campbell, W. S. "Christianity and Judaism: Continuity and Discontinuity." *Christian-Jewish Relations* 18:1 (1985): 3-15.

Capps, Walter H. *Hope Against Hope: Moltmann to Merton in One Decade*. Philadelphia: Fortress, 1976.

Charlesworth, James H., ed. *Jews and Christians: Exploring the Past, Present and Future*. New York: Crossway, 1990.

Chopp, Rebecca S. *The Praxis of Suffering: An Interpretation of Liberation and Political Theologies*. Maryknoll, NY: Orbis, 1986.

"The Churches and the Jewish People: Toward a New Understanding." World Council of Churches, Sigtuna, Sweden, November 4, 1988.

Cobb, John B., Jr. "Barth and the Barthians: A Critical Appraisal." In Donald McKim, *How Karl Barth Changed My Mind*, 172-177 (see entry).

Cobb, John B. and Christopher Ives, eds. *The Emptying God: A Buddhist-Jewish-Christian Conversation*. Maryknoll, NY: Orbis, 1990.

Cohen, Arthur A. *The Tremendum: A Theological Interpretation of the Holocaust*. New York: Crossroad, 1981.

Cohen, Martin, and Helga Croner, eds. *Christian Mission-Jewish Mission*. New York: Paulist/Stimulus, 1982.

The Confessional Nature of the Church. Advisory Council on Discipleship and Worship of the Presbyterian Church U.S.A., 1986.

Cook, James I. "The Christian Witness to the Jews: A Biblical Perspective." *Scottish Journal of Theology* 36:2 (1983): 145-161.

Cott, Jeremy. "The Biblical Problem of Election." *Journal of Ecumenical Studies* 21:2 (1984): 199-228.

Cranfield, C. E. B., and J. A. Emerton, eds. *The International Critical Commentary: The Epistle to the Romans, Volume Two*. Edinburgh: T & T Clark, 1978.

_____. "Light From St. Paul on Christian-Jewish Relations." In David W. Torrance, ed. *The Witness of the Jews to God*. Edinburgh: The Handsel Press, 1982.

Croner, Helga, ed. *More Stepping Stones to Jewish-Christian Relations: An Unabridged Collection of Christian Documents 1975-1983*. New York: Paulist/Stimulus, 1985.

_____, ed. *Stepping Stones to Further Jewish-Christian Relations: An Unabridged Collection of Christian Documents*. New York: Paulist/Stimulus, 1977.

Danielou, Jacques. *Dialogue With Israel*. Baltimore, 1966.

Davies, Alan T. *Anti-Semitism and the Christian Mind*. New York: Herder and Herder, 1969.

_____. "Review of Paul van Buren's Discerning the Way." *New Catholic World* (November/December, 1981): 280-281.

Davies, Alan T., ed. *Anti-Semitism and the Foundations of Christianity*. New York: Paulist, 1979.

Davies, W. D. *Paul and Rabbinic Judaism*. London: SCM Press, 1970.

Dunn, J. D. G. "The New Perspective on Paul." *Bulletin of the John Rylands Library of Manchester* 65:2 (1980): 95-122.

Early, Glenn D. "The Radical Hermeneutical Shift in Post-Holocaust Christian Thought." *Journal of Ecumenical Studies* 18:1 (Winter, 1981): 16-32

Eckardt, A. Roy. *Black-Woman-Jew: Three Wars for Human Liberation*.Bloomington: Indiana University Press, 1989.

_____. "Burned Children" (a review of Paul van Buren's *Discerning the Way*).*The Christian Century* (October 1, 1980): 922-924.

_____. *Christianity and the Children of Israel*. New York: King's Crown Press, 1948.

_____. "Jürgen Moltmann, The Jewish People and the Holocaust." *JAAR* 44:4 (December, 1976): 675-691.

_____, and Alice Eckardt. *Long Night's Journey Into Day: Life and Faith After the Holocaust*. Detroit: Wayne State University Press, 1982.

_____. "Moltmann on Jews" (letter to the editor). *The Christian Century*, January 2-9, 1991, 28-29.

_____. "Recent Literature on Christian-Jewish Relations. *JAAR* 49:1 (1981): 99-111.

_____. "Toward a Secular Theology of Israel." *Religion in Life* 48:4 (Winter, 1979): 462-473.

_____. *Your People, My People*. New York: Quadrangle, 1974.

Ellis, Marc H. *Beyond Innocence and Redemption: Confronting the Holocaust and Israeli Power*. San Francisco: Harper and Row, 1990.

_____. *Toward a Jewish Theology of Liberation*. Maryknoll, NY: Orbis, 1987.

Elon, Amos. "Letter From Israel." *The New Yorker* (February 13, 1989).

Erickson, Robert. *Theologians Under Hitler*. New Haven: Yale University Press, 1985.

Fackenheim, Emil. *To Mend the World: Foundations of Future Jewish Thought.* New York: Schocken Books, 1982.

_____. *God's Presence in History: Jewish Affirmations and Philosophical Reflections.* New York: Harper and Row, 1972.

Fangmeier, Jürgen and Hinrich Stoevesandt, eds. *Karl Barth, Letters 1961-68.* Translated by Geoffrey W. Bromiley. Edinburgh: T & T Clark,1981.

Feuer, Lewis. "The Reasoning of Holocaust Theology." *Judaism* 35:2 (Spring, 1986): 198-210.

Fiorenza, Elizabeth Schüssler, and David Tracy, eds. *The Holocaust as Interruption.* Concilium, Volume 175. Edinburgh: T & T Clark, 1984.

Fischer, John. *The Olive Tree Connection: Sharing Messiah With Israel.* Downer's Grove, MO: Inter-Varsity, 1983.

_____. "Paul in His Jewish Context." *Evangelical Quarterly* 57:3 (1985): 211-36.

Flannery, Edward H. *The Anguish of the Jews: Twenty-three Centuries of Anti-Semitism.* New York: Paulist/Stimulus, 1985.

Fleischner, Eva. *Judaism in German Christian Theology Since 1945: Christianity and Israel in Terms of Mission.* ATLA Monograph Series, 8. Metuchen, NJ: The Scarecrow Press and the American Theological Library Association, 1975.

_____, ed. *Auschwitz: Beginning of a New Era?: Reflections on the Holocaust.* New York: Ktav, 1977.

Fritz, Maureena. "Nostra Aetate: A Turning Point in History." *Religious Education* 81 (Winter, 1986): 67-78.

Gibellini, R. *La Teologie di Jürgen Moltmann.* Brescia: Queriniana, 1975.

Gilkey, Langdon. *Naming the Whirlwind: The Renewal of God-Language.* Indianapolis: Bobbs-Merrill, 1969.

Glasser, Arthur F. "Christian Ministry to the Jews." *The Presbyterian Communique* 11:2 (1988): 6-7.

Goldy, Robert G. *The Emergence of Jewish Theology in America.* Bloomington: Indiana University Press, 1990.

Goppelt, Leonhard. "Israel and the Church in Today's Discussion and in Paul." *Lutheran World* 10:4 (October, 1963): 352-72.

Gorday, Peter. *Principles of Patristic Exegesis: Romans 9-11 in Origen, John Chrysostom, and Augustine.* Studies in the Bible and Early Christianity, Volume 4. New York: Edwin Mellen Press, 1983.

Greenberg, Irving. "Cloud of Smoke, Pillar of Fire: Judaism, Christianity and Modernity After the Holocaust." In Eva Fleischner, ed. *Auschwitz: Beginning of a New Era?,* 7-55 (see entry).

_____. "The Third Great Cycle of Jewish History." In *Perspectives.* New York: CLAL, The National Jewish Center for Learning and Leadership, n. d., 1-26

Gutteridge, Richard. *Open Thy Mouth For the Dumb: The German Evangelical Church and the Jews 1879-1950.* Oxford: Basil Blackwell,1976.

Hall, Douglas J. "Rethinking Christ." In Alan Davies, ed. *Antisemitism and the Foundations of Christianity,* 167-187. (see entry)

Hanson, Paul D. *The People Called: The Growth of Community in the Bible.* San Francisco: Harper and Row, 1986.

Hartman, David. *A Living Covenant: The Innovative Spirit in Traditional Judaism.* New York and London: Macmillan/Free Press, 1985.

Haynes, Stephen, R. "Presbyterians and Jews: A Theological Exploration of the Book of Confessions." *Perspectives in Religious Studies* 15:3 (September, 1988): 249-267.

_____. "'Recovering the Real Paul': Theology and Exegesis in Romans 9-11." *Ex Auditu: An International Journal of Theological Interpretation of Scripture* 4 (1988): 70-84.

Heppe, Heinrich. *Reformed Dogmatics.* Edited by Ernst Bizer. Translated by G. T. Thomson. Grand Rapids: Baker, 1950.

Herzog, F., ed. *The Future of Hope: Theology as Eschatology.* New York: Herder and Herder, 1970.

Hilberg, Raul. *The Destruction of European Jewry.* Chicago: Quadrangle, 1961.

Hofius, O. "Das Evangelium und Israel: Erwagungen zu Römer 9-11." *Zeitschrift für Theologie und Kirche* 83:3 (1986): 297-324.

Hooker, M. D. *Continuity and Discontinuity: Early Christianity in its Jewish Setting.* London: Epworth, 1986.

Hunsinger, George. "Barth, Barmen and the Confessing Church Today: Summary of the Original Text." *Katallegete* (Fall, 1987): 11.

_____., ed. *Karl Barth and Radical Politics.* Philadelphia: Fortress, 1976.

Isaac, Jules. *Jesus and Israel.* Translated by Sally Gran. New York: Holt, Rinehart and Winston, 1971.

_____. *The Teaching of Contempt.* Translated by Helen Weaver. New York: Holt, Rinehart and Winston, 1964.

Ising, Dieter, et. al., eds. *Bibloiographie Jürgen Moltmann.* München: Christian Kaiser, 1987.

Jansen, J. "Parners op Weg naar het ene Rijk van God? Kerk en Israel in de Theologie van Jürgen Moltmann." Ph. D. Dissertation, Tilburg, Netherlands, 1984.

Jaspert, Berndt. "Karl Barths Theologie am Ende 20 Jahrhunderts." *Theologische Literatturzeitung* 112 (October, 1987): 707-730.

"The Jews in Britian." *The Sunday Times Magazine* (April 16, 1989): 66-74.

Jüngel, Eberhard. *Karl Barth: A Theological Legacy.* Translated by Garrett E. Paul. Philadelphia: Westminster, 1986.

Karlsberg, Mark W. "Israel as Light to the Nations: a Review Article." *Journal of the Evangelical Theology Society* 28:2 (June, 1985): 205-211.

_____. "Legitimate Discontinuities Between the Testaments." *Journal of the Evangelical Theology Society* 28:1 (1985): 9-20.

Käsemann, Ernst. "Justification and Salvation History in the Epistle to the Romans." In *Perspectives on Paul.* London: SCM Press, 1971, 60-78.

Katz, Steven T. *Post-Holocaust Dialogues: Critical Studies in Modern Jewish Thought.* New York: New York University Press, 1985.

Keegan, Terrence J. *Interpreting the Bible: A Popular Guide to Biblical Hermeneutics.* New York: Paulist, 1985.

Kelsey, David H. *The Uses of Scripture in Recent Theology.* Philadelphia: Fortress, 1975.

Klappert, Bertold. *Israel und die Kirche: Erwagungen Zur Israellehre Karl Barths.* Theologische Existenz Heute, 207. München: Christian Kaiser, 1980.

Klein, Charlotte. *Anti-Judaism in Christian Theology.* Translated by Edward Quinn. Philadelphia: Fortress, 1977.

Klein, R. W. "Anti-Semitism as Christian Legacy: The Origin and Nature of Our Estrangement From the Jews." *Currents in Theology and Mission* 11:5 (1984): 285-301.

Kliever, Lonnie D. *The Shattered Spectrum: A Survey of Contemporary Theology.* Atlanta: John Knox, 1981.

Kraft, Dieter. "Israel in der Theologie Karl Barths." *Communio Viatorum* 27:1 (1984): 59-72.

Küng, Hans. "Karl Barth and the Post-Modern Paradigm." *Princeton Seminary Bulletin* 9:1 (1988): 8-31.

Langer, Lawrence L. *The Holocaust and the Literary Imagination.* New Haven: Yale University Press, 1975.

Laqueur, Walter. *A History of Zionism.* New York: Holt, Rinehart and Winston, 1972.

Leggett, Paul. "Against the Swastika: The Challenge of the Anti-Nazi Film to Political Theology." Ph. D. Diss., Union Theological Seminary in New York, 1982.

Leith, John. *Assembly at Westminster: Reformed Theology in the Making.* Richmond: John Knox, 1973.

Lewis, Bernard. *Semites and Antisemites.* New York: Norton and Co., 1986.

Lindbeck, George A. *The Nature of Doctrine: Religion and Theology in a Post-Liberal Age.* Philadelphia: Westminster, 1984.

Lindsey, Hal. *The Road to Holocaust.* New York: Bantam, 1990.

Littell, Franklin. *The Crucifixion of the Jews.* New York: Harper and Row, 1975.

Marquardt, Friedrich-Wilhelm. *Die Entdeckung des Judentums für die Christliche Theologie: Israel im Denkens Karl Barths.* Abhandlung zum Christlich-Judischen Dialog, Volume One. Edited by Helumt Gollwitzer. München: Christian Kaiser, 1967.

_____. "Theologische und Politische Motivationen Karl Barths im Kirchenkampf." *Jungekirche* (May, 1973): 283-303.

Marsch, W.-D., ed. *Diskussion über die 'Theologie der Hoffnung' von Jürgen Moltmann.* München: Christian Kaiser, 1967.

Macquarrie, John. *God and Secularity.* New Directions in Theology, Volume Four. Philadelphia: Westminster, 1976.

McGarry, Michael. *Christology After Auschwitz*. New York: Paulist, 1977.

McKim, Donald, ed. *How Karl Barth Changed My Mind*. Grand Rapids: Eerdmans, 1987.

McKnight, Edgar A. *The Bible and the Reader*. Philadelphia: Fortress, 1985.

Meeks, M. Douglas. *Origins of the Theology of Hope*. Philadelphia: Fortress, 1974.

Metz, J. B. "Facing the Jews: Christian Theology After Auschwitz." In Fiorenza and Tracy, eds., *The Holocaust as Interruption*, 26-33 (see entry).

Minear, Paul S. "Barth's Commentary on Romans, 1922-1972; or Karl Barth vs. the Exegetes." In Martin Rumscheidt, ed. *Footnotes to a Theology: the Karl Barth Colloquium of 1972*. The Corporation for the Publication of Academic Studies in Religion in Canada, 1974.

Miskotte, Kornelius. *When the Gods Are Silent*. Translated by John W. Doberstein. London: Collins, 1967.

_____. *Das Judentum als Frage an die Kirche*. Wuppertal: Brockhaus,1970.

Moltmann, Jürgen. "The Challenge of Religion in the 80s." *The Christian Century* (April 23, 1980): 405-408.

_____. "Christian Hope: Messianic or Transcendent?: A Theological Discussion With Joachim of Fiore and Thomas Aquinas." *Horizons* 12:2 (1985): 328-348.

_____. "Church and Israel: A Common Way of Hope?" In *On Human Dignity: Political Theology and Ethics*. Translated by M. Douglas Meeks. Philadelphia: Fortress, 1984.

_____. *The Church in the Power of the Spirit: A Contribution to Messianic Ecclesiology*. Translated by Margaret Kohl. London: SCM, 1977.

_____. "Jewish and Christian Messianism." In *The Experiment Hope*. Translated by M. Douglas Meeks. Philadelphia: Fortress, 1975, 60-68.

_____. *Experiences of God*. Translated by Margaret Kohl. Philadelphia: Fortress, 1980.

_____. *Following Jesus Christ in the World Today: Responsibility for the World and Christian Discipleship*. Elkhart, IN/Winnipeg: Institute of Mennonite Studies, CMBC Publications, 1983.

_____. "Forgiveness and Politics: Forty Years After the Stuttgart Confession." In *Case Study 2*. New World Publications, 1987, 40-52.

_____. "God Is Unselfish Love." In *The Emptying God: A Buddhist-Jewish-Christian Conversation*, 116-124 (see entry).

_____. Interview by Author. January 8, 1989, Tübingen, West Germany.

_____. *The Future of Creation*. Translated by Margaret Kohl. London: SCM Press, 1979.

_____. *Im Gespräch mit Ernst Bloch: Eine Theologische Wegbegleitung*. München: Christian Kaiser, 1976.

_____. "Messianic Hope in Christianity." In *Christians and Jews*. Concilium 93. Edited by Walter Kasper and Hans Küng. New York: Seabury, 1974, 61-67

_____. "Theology in Germany Today." In Jürgen Habermas, ed. *Observations on the "Spiritual Situation of the Age": Contemporary German Perspectives*. Translated by Andrew Buchwalter. London and Cambridge, MA: MIT Press, 1984.

_____. *Theology of Hope: On the Ground and Implications of a Christian Eschatology*. Translated by James W. Leitch. New York: Harper and Row, 1967.

_____. *Theology Today: Two Contributions Towards Making Theology Present*. Translated by John Bowden. London: SCM Press, 1988.

_____. *The Way of Jesus Christ*. Translated by Margaret Kohl. San Francisco: Harper and Row, 1990 (references are to proofs supplied by author, translations are my own).

_____. "Who Is Jesus Christ For Us Today?: Christology Between Christians and Jews." The 1989 Samuel Ferguson Lectures, Number One. Manchester University, February 20, 1989.

_____ and Pinchas Lapide. *Israel und Kirche: Ein Gemeinsamer Weg?: Ein Gespräch*. München: Christian Kaiser, 1980.

_____. *Jewish Monotheism and Christian Trinitarian Doctrine*. Translated by Leonard Swidler. Philadelphia: Fortress, 1981.

Moore, George F. "Christian Writers on Judaism." *Harvard Theological Review* 14 (1921): 197-254.

Moore, James F. "A Spectrum of Views: Traditional Christian Responses to the Holocaust." *Journal of Ecumenical Studies* 25:2 (Spring, 1988): 212-224.

Morse, C. *The Logic of Promise in Moltmann's Theology*. Philadelphia: Fortress, 1979.

Munck, Johannes. *Christ and Israel: An Interpretation of Romans 9-11*. Translated by Ingeborg Nixon. Philadelphia: Fortress, 1967.

Mussner, Franz. *Tractate on the Jews*. Translated by Leonard Swidler. Philadelphia: Fortress, 1984.

Neusner, Jacob. "The Absoluteness of Christianity and the Uniqueness of Judaism: Why Salvation is Not of the Jews." *Interpretation* 43:1 (January, 1989): 18-31.

Niebuhr, Reinhold. *Essays in Applied Christianity*. Edited by D. B. Robertson. New York: Meridian, 1959.

Novak, David. "A Jewish Response to a New Christian Theology." *Judaism* 31 Winter, 1982): 112-120.

Pawlikowski, John T. "The Holocaust and Contemporary Christology." In Fiorenza and Tracy, *The Holocaust as Interruption*, 43-49 (see entry).

Polish, David. "Covenant: Jewish Universalism and Particularism." *Judaism* 34 (Summer, 1985): 284-300.

Prolingheuer, Hans. *Der Fall Karl Barth: Chronographie Einer Betreibung 1934-1935*. Vluyn: Neukirchner, 1977.

Raschke, Carl A. *Theological Thinking*. Atlanta: Scholars Press, 1988.

Reformed Dogmatics. Edited and Translated by John W. Beardslee II. New York: Oxford University Press, 1965.

Rentdorff, R., and E. Stegemann, eds. *Auschwitz--Krise der Christlichen Theologie*. München: Christian Kaiser, 1980.

Ricoeur, Paul. *Freud and Philosophy: An Essay in Interpretation*. Translated by Denis Savage. New Haven and London: Yale University Press, 1970.

Roberts, Richard H. "The Reception of the Theology of Karl Barth in the Anglo-Saxon World: History, Typology and Prospect." In *On Being the Church*. Edited by C. G. Gunton and D. W. Hardy. Edinburgh: T & T Clark, 1989.

Rogers, Jack. *Presbyterian Creeds: A Guide to the Book of Confessions*. Philadelphia: Westminster, 1985.

Röhkramer, Martin. "Karl Barth in Herbstkrise 1938." *Evangelische Theologie* 48:6 1988): 521-45.

Rolston, Holmes III. *John Calvin Vs. the Westminster Confession*. Richmond: John Knox, 1972.

Rosato, Philip J. "The Influence of Karl Barth on Catholic Theology." *Gregorianum* 67:4 (1986): 659-678.

Rosenzweig, Franz. *The Star of Redemption*. Translated by William W. Hallo. London: Routledge and Kegan Paul, 1970.

Roth, John K. "The Silence of God." *Faith and Philosophy* 1:4 (October, 1984): 407-420.

Rottenberg, Isaac C. "Fulfillment Theology and the Future of Christian-Jewish Relations." *The Christian Century* 97:3 (January 23, 1980): 66-69.

_____. "The Glory of God and the People of Israel." *Reformed World* 34: 5 (1977): 215-221.

_____. "Witness in Christian-Jewish Relations: Some Observations." *Reformed World* 35:2 (1978): 58-65.

Rubenstein, Richard L. *After Auschwitz*. Indianapolis: Bobbs-Merrill, 1966.

_____ and John K. Roth. *Approaches to Auschwitz: The Holocaust and Its Legacy*. Atlanta: John Knox, 1987.

Ruether, Rosemary R. *Faith and Fratricide: The Theological Roots of Anti-Semitism*. Minneapolis: Seabury, 1974.

_____. "Speaking of Israel II." *Christianity and Crisis* (October 12, 1987): 340-343.

_____, and Herman J. Ruether. *The Wrath of Jonah: The Crisis of Religious Nationalism in the Israeli-Palestinian Conflict*. San Francisco: Harper and Row, 1989.

Sanders, E. P. *Paul and Palestinian Judaism*. London: SCM Press, 1977.

Schaefer, Francis A. *The God Who is There*. Downer's Grove, IL: Inter-Varsity Press, 1969.

Scholder, Klaus. *The Churches and the Third Reich, Volume Two, The Year of Disillusionment: 1934: Barmen and Rome*. Philadelphia: Fortress, 1989.

Schwarz, R. "Israel und die Nichtjudische Christen im Römerbrief (Kapitel 9-11)." *Bibel und Liturgie* 59:3 (1986): 161-64.

Sell, Alan P. F., ed. *Reformed Theology and the Jewish People*. Geneva: World Alliance of Reformed Churches, 1986.

Sharif, Regina S. *Non-Jewish Zionism: Its Roots in Western History*. London: Zed Press, 1983.

Sherman, Franklin. "Speaking of God After Auschwitz." *Worldview* 17:9 (September, 1974): 26-30.

Sigal, Philip. "Aspects of Dual Covenant Theology: Salvation." *Horizons in Biblical Theology* 5:2 (1980): 1-48.

Simon, Ulrich. *A Theology of Auschwitz*. London SPCK, 1978.

Sloyan, Gerard S. "Some Theological Implications of the Holocaust." *Interpretation* 39:4 (1985): 402-413.

Snider, T. M. *The Continuity of Salvation: A Study of Paul's Letter to the Romans*. London and Jefferson, NC: McFarland and Co., 1984.

Steiger, Lothar. "Die Theologie Vor der 'Judenfrage'--Karl Barth als Beispiel." In *Auschwitz--Krise der Christliche Theologie*, Edited by E. Stegemann and R. Rentdorff.

Stendahl, Krister. *Paul Among Jews and Gentiles and Other Essays*. Philadelphia: Fortress, 1976.

Stroup, George M. *The Promise of Narrative Theology: Recovering the Gospel in the Church*. Atlanta: John Knox, 1981.

Sulzbach, Maria. "Karl Barth and the Jews." *Religion in Life* 21:4 (1952): 585-593.

Tal, Uriel. "Law, the Authority of the State, and the Freedom of the Individual." *Christian-Jewish Relations* 14:1 (1981):28-42.

Talmage, Frank. *Disputation and Dialogue*. New York: Ktav, 1975.

Theobald, M. "Kirche und Israel nach Rom 9-11." *Kairos* 29:1-2 (1987): 1-22.

A Theological Understanding of the Relationship Between Christians and Jews. New York and Atlanta: General Assembly of the Presbyterian Church U.S.A., 1987.

Thoma, Clemens. *A Christian Theology of Judaism*. Translated and Edited by Helga Croner. New York: Paulist/ Stimulus, 1980.

Thompson, John, ed. *Theology Beyond Christendom: Essays on the Centenary of the Birth of Karl Barth*. Allison Park, PA: Pickwick Press, 1986.

Thompson, Norma H. "The Covenant Concept in Judaism and Christianity." *Anglican Theological Review* 64 (October, 1982): 502-24.

Tillich, Paul. "What Is Wrong With the 'Dialectic' Theology?" *The Journal of Religion* 15:2 (April, 1935): 127-135.

Torjesen, Leif. "Resurrection and Ideology: The Theological Origins and Political Setting of Karl Barth's Attack on Natural Theology." Ph. D. Diss., Claremont Graduate School, 1986.

Torrance, Thomas F. "Karl Barth and Patristic Theology." In Thompson, ed., *Theology Beyond Christendom,* 215-240 (see entry).

_____. *The Mediation of Christ.* Exeter: Paternoster, 1983.

Tracy, David. *Blessed Rage For Order: The New Pluralism in Theology.* Minneapolis: Winston-Seabury, 1975.

Van Buren, Paul. *The Burden of Freedom: Americans and the God of Israel.* New York: Crossroad/Seabury, 1976.

_____. "Christian Theology and Jewish Reality: An Essay-Review." *JAAR* 45:4 (1977): 491-495.

_____. "Comments on Tillich." *NICM Journal* 7 (Spring, 1982): 15-20.

_____. "Discerning the Way to the Incarnation." *Anglican Theological Review* 63:3 (July, 1981): 291-301.

_____. *The Edges of Language.* New York: Macmillan, 1972.

_____. "How shall We Now Exegete the Apostolic Writings?" *American Journal of Theology and Philosophy* 3 (1981): 97-109.

_____. "Karl Barth as Teacher." *Religion and Intellectual Life* 2:2 (Winter, 1985): 84-85.

_____. "Probing the Jewish-Christian Reality: How My Mind Has Changed" (Twenty-First in a Series). *The Christian Century* 98 (June 17-24, 1981): 665-668.

_____. *The Secular Meaning of the Gospel.* New York: Macmillan, 1963.

_____. "Theology Now." *The Christian Century* 91 (May 29, 1974): 585-589.

_____. "Theological Education for the Church's Relationship With the Jewish People." *Journal of Ecumenical Studies* 21 (Summer, 1984): 489-505.

_____. *Theological Investigations.* New York: Macmillan, 1968.

_____. *A Theology of the Jewish Christian Reality. Three Parts. Part One: Discerning the Way. Part Two: A Christian Theology of the People Israel. Part Three: Christ in Context.* San Francisco: Harper and Row, 1980-88.

_____. Interview by Author. July 16-17, 1988, Boston.

Van Ruler, Arnold. *Die Christliche Kirche und das Alte Testament.* München: Christian Kaiser, 1955.

Van Til, Cornelius. *The New Modernism: An Appraisal of the Theology of Barth and Brunner.* London: James Clarke, 1946.

Von Balthasar, Hans Urs. "Towards a Christian Theology of Hope." *Münchener Theologische Zeitschrift* 23:2 (1981): 81-102.

Vernoff, Charles E. "After the Holocaust: History and Being as Sources of Method Within the Emerging Interreligious Hermeneutic." *Journal of Ecumenical Studies* 21:4 (Fall, 1984): 639-663.

Villa-Vicencio, Charles, ed. *On Reading Karl Barth in South Africa.* Grand Rapids: Eerdmans, 1988.

Von der Osten-Sacken, Peter. *Christian-Jewish Dialogue: Theological Foundations.* Translated by Margaret Kohl. Philadelphia: Fortress, 1986.

Voskuil, Dennis. "Neoorthodoxy." In *Reformed Theology in America: A History of Its Development,* ed. David F. Wells. Grand Rapids: Eerdmans, 1985.

Walter, N. "Zur Interpretation von Römer 9-11." *Zeitschrift für Theologie und Kirche* 81:2 (1984): 172-95.

Wiesel, Elie. "Art and Culture After the Holocaust." In Fleischner, ed. *Auschwitz: Beginning of a New Era?* (see entry).

Williams, A. Lukyn. *Adversus Judaeos.* Cambridge: Cambridge University Press, 1935.

Williamson, Clark W. "The New Testament Reconsidered: Recent Post-Holocaust Scholarship." *Quarterly Review* 4:4 (1984): 37-51.

_____. *Has God Rejected His People?: Anti-Judaism in the Christian Church.* Nashville: Abingdon, 1982.

Willis, Robert E. "Bonhoeffer and Barth on Jewish Suffering: Reflections on the Relationship Between Theology and Moral Sensibility." *Journal of Ecumenical Studies* 24:4 (Fall, 1987): 598-615.

Wilson, Marvin R. *Our Father Abraham: Jewish Roots of the Christian Faith.* Grand Rapids: Eerdmans, 1989.

Wyschogrod, Michael. *The Body of Faith: Judaism as Corporeal Election.* Minneapolis: Seabury, 1983.

_____. "Faith and the Holocaust." *Judaism* 20:3 (Summer, 1971): 268-294.

_____. "Why Was and Is the Theology of Karl Barth of Interest to a Jewish Theologian?" In Martin Rumscheidt, ed. *Footnotes to A Theology,* 95-111.

_____. "A Jewish Perspective on Karl Barth." In Donald McKim, ed. *How Karl Barth Changed My Mind,* 156-161 (see entry).

Yerushalmi, Yosef H. "Response to Rosemary Ruether." In Eva Fleischner, ed. *Auschwitz: Beginning of a New Era?,* 97-108 (see entry).

"Zehn Punkte zur Selbstkontrolle Christlichen Redens mit und über Juden: Eine Einladung zum Umdenken." *Evangelische Theologie* 48:6 (1988): 565-69.

Ziesler, J. A. "Some Recent Work on the Letter to the Romans." *Epworth Review* 12:2 (1985): 96-101.